The Foreign Policy of Iran, 1500-1941

A Developing Nation in World Affairs

This publication is a volume in the American Association for Middle East Studies series.

The Foreign Policy of Iran

A Developing Nation in World Affairs

1500 – 1941

Rouhollah K. Ramazani

University of Virginia
Woodrow Wilson Department of Government
and Foreign Affairs

University Press of Virginia / Charlottesville

The University Press of Virginia
First published 1966

Library of Congress Catalog Card Number: 66-12469
Printed in the United States of America

TO THE
UNIVERSITY OF VIRGINIA
IN WHOSE SERVICE FOR A DECADE
I HAVE FOUND
FREEDOM AND HAPPINESS

Foreword

Western writers on international politics have dealt with Iran as a pawn in the game of power politics among the great powers, and Iranian writers have dealt with it to illustrate the immorality of those powers. Dr. Ramazani, born in Iran but educated in the West and now an American citizen, has traced the history of Iranian foreign policy from 1500 to 1941 as a matter of interest in itself, and has done it with great objectivity but due appreciation that the perceptions of both Iranians and Westerners must be considered in deciding what is important. He narrates the decisions and actions of the Iranian government and the motivations and conditions accounting for them. The " dynamic triangular interaction " of foreign policy, internal conditions, and external environment is emphasized throughout the book, providing a basis for a theory of international politics and particularly of the foreign policy of small states, a matter of increasing importance as empires disintegrate and the small states which emerge exert influence in the United Nations.

Although in the modern world Iran has been a small state, its long history includes periods when it was a great, if not the greatest, power, and this fact has been of continuing influence. Iran has sought to reacquire territories which were once its own and has often failed to appreciate the gap between these objectives and the means available for their realization.

Dr. Ramazani finds that the traditional policy of Iran has been dominated by absolute monarchy, usually more intent on personal pleasure than on national interests; maintenance of independence, often precarious; irredentism seeking impossible expansions; and unrealism, losing wars in pursuit of hopeless objectives. With a few exceptions the Shahs did not modify these traditions until the twentieth century, when the transitional policy of Riẕā Shah (1925-41) developed a concept of national interest; established central government, controlling military, religious, parliamentary, and provincial institutions; gave meaning to independence by establishing firm national boundaries; and utilized effective diplomacy rather than inadequate armed forces to carry out reasonable foreign policies. He utilized the balancing influence of third powers, usually the United States or Germany, to withstand encroachments by Great Britain or the Soviet Union and to modify earlier impositions. He pursued a policy of the good neighbor toward Turkey, Afghanistan, and Iraq by settling a number of boundary and other disputes. He utilized the League of Nations for security against aggression. His policy failed, however, in World War II, when neutrality with a leaning toward Germany led to joint Anglo-Soviet invasion and the end of Riẕā Shah's reign. Failure to realize the power position and the vital national interest in preventing German control of Iran after Hitler's invasion of Russia led Riẕā Shah to procrastination, which was fatal. The gap between means and ends was evident as it has been on some subsequent occasions such as the muddle resulting from Mussadiq's oil nationalization policy.

The internal situation of Iran – without national unity; divided among tribes, religions, and social classes; accustomed to absolutism; lacking in skilled diplomats; and obsessed by a history of past greatness – has only in recent times been moderated by the influence of technology, communications, and education of a small elite, introducing sentiments of nationalism, modern political institutions, an interest in economic development, an appreciation of the importance of resources such as oil, and an understanding of the objectives and capabilities of Iran and other powers.

The external conditions faced by Iran were, in the sixteenth and seventeenth centuries, the pressure of Turkey, then a great power, and in the nineteenth and twentieth centuries, the pressures of Russia, whether intent on territorial expansion, economic control, or Communist propaganda, and of Britain, generally intent on defending India from Napoleon or the Tsar, but allied with Russia against Germany, from 1907 to 1917 and in World War II. These periods of alliance presented Iran with its greatest danger of dismemberment, as indicated by Morgan Shuster, the American adviser, in his book *The Strangling of Persia* (1912) and by the joint Anglo-Soviet invasion of August 1941, ousting Riẓā Shah.

Generally foreign policy has been more influenced by the necessities of the external situation than by the principles and practices of the domestic constitution, but Dr. Ramazani's study suggests that in Iran the opposite was true: traditional policy was generally followed and was usually inadequate to meet the situation.

The study is a fascinating one, and Dr. Ramazani's readable style and full documentation from both Western and Persian sources will please both the general reader and the specialist. In addition, theorists of international politics will find here a wealth of empirical material with which to test their theories.

Charlottesville, Virginia
September 1, 1965

QUINCY WRIGHT

Preface

This study is the first attempt to describe systematically and analyze critically Iranian foreign policy from 1500 to 1941. The sixteenth, seventeenth, and eighteenth centuries are dealt with in broad terms and only to identify some of the basic characteristics of the political system and foreign policy of Iran at that time. The century and a half since 1800 are treated in greater detail as befits a study by a political scientist rather than a historian. Furthermore, only in this later period was Iran drawn into the scheme of European power politics.

So far as my analysis is concerned, I have not let the desideratum of scholarly objectivity keep me from expressing critical judgment. I do not believe that objectivity consists in withholding judgment, because such withholding would be a value judgment insofar as it might imply satisfaction with a state of affairs, past or present. My concept of objectivity demands that my judgments be supported by the available evidence and be tentative until more complete and reliable data become accessible. All the judgments in this book are of this nature. My analytic scheme includes the normative element of the school of political realism; that is, I consider a rational foreign policy directed toward good ends to be good foreign policy, and this is the fundamental assumption underlying my systematic critique of Iranian foreign policy.

This study draws on Persian and Western sources, both primary and secondary. The utilization of the Persian sources has presented special problems, which I have tried to overcome. Apart from the inconvenience caused by the general lack of indexes, Persian works frequently suffer from gross inaccuracies in the reporting of facts, figures, and dates. Furthermore, the interpretations advanced by many Iranian authors and editors are often not supported by evidence. Nevertheless, careful use of Persian materials is indispensable because they are the main sources for the Iranian viewpoint. Moreover, the habit of Iranian writers of reprinting the text of scarce documents renders their works valuable in this respect as well.

Citations serve several purposes. The most obvious one is to document assertions in the text or to amplify or supplement what is stated therein. Many citations are included in the hope of assisting others in doing research on Iranian politics and foreign policy in greater detail on specific problems or periods. Wherever discrepancies between Persian and Western sources have appeared, I have pointed them out in the notes. As a rule I have avoided referring the reader to a document in Persian if it was possible to cite an English source; unfortunately, a great many documents are available only in Persian.

In transliterating Persian words, I have tried to follow the form approved by the American Library Association and the Library of Congress. In some instances it seemed best not to conform too rigidly to the prescribed rules. For example, I have generally avoided transliterating Anglicized Persian words, geographic names, and the names of Persian authors of English books. It may be that a thoroughly satisfactory transliteration system is yet to be worked out, but it has seemed advisable to use some form of transliteration rather than none at all.

Permission to quote short passages from the following books has kindly been granted: by Cambridge University Press, for Edward G. Browne's *The Persian Revolution, 1905-1909*; by Houghton Mifflin Company, for Winston Churchill's *The Second World War*, Vol. III, *The Grand Alliance*; by John Murray (Publishers) Ltd., for Sir Valentine Chirol's *The Middle Eastern Question or Some Political*

Problems of Indian Defence; by J. C. Hurewitz, for his *Diplomacy in the Near and Middle East*; by the Royal Central Asian Society, for Sir Reader Bullard's "Persia in the Two World Wars," *Royal Central Asian Journal*, January 1963; and by Stanford University Press, for Zenia Joukoff Eudin and Robert C. North, *Soviet Russia and the East: 1920-1927*.

I can hardly begin to acknowledge my indebtedness in the limited space of a preface. In the course of seven years of intermittent research and writing I have received moral and intellectual support from many in the United States and abroad. Among those who should be mentioned are Professor T. Cuyler Young, chairman of the Department of Oriental Studies at Princeton University, for his solid encouragement from the inception of this study and for his critical and helpful comments on the manuscript; Professor C. Ernest Dawn, of the University of Illinois, and Professor George Hourani, of the University of Michigan, for reading the manuscript and making helpful suggestions; Dr. Donald Wilber for his moral support; and Professors Percy Corbett, formerly of Princeton University, Paul T. David, chairman of the Woodrow Wilson Department of Government and Foreign Affairs, University of Virginia, Rowland Egger, of Princeton University, John J. Kennedy, of the University of Notre Dame, Majid Khadduri, of the School of Advanced International Studies of The Johns Hopkins University, and Charles A. Micaud, of the University of Denver, for their continuing interest. Aid during my search for materials was given by Messrs. Robert Ogden, Ibrahim Pourhadi, and Zuhair E. Jwaideh of the Library of Congress, also by Dr. Taylor Parks, of the Department of State, and Mrs. Patricia G. Dowling, of the National Archives. The invaluable editorial aid of Miss Catherine Sturtevant of the University Press of Virginia is acknowledged with gratitude. My indebtedness to my friend and colleague, Professor Quincy Wright, for writing the Foreword is obvious.

Had it not been for the financial assistance of several foundations this work would not have been completed. A grant by Richmond Area University Center, Inc., made possible the purchase of materials from Iran in 1958. A grant by the Old Dominion Foundation provided free time for research in the summer of 1961. The Wilson Gee Institute for Research in the Social Sciences at the University of Virginia has been most helpful through its continuing support. The staff of the

Alderman Library, particularly Mr. John Cook Wyllie, the librarian, and Miss Helena Coiner, deserve heartfelt thanks for their unreserved assistance to me over the years. Sincere thanks are also due Miss Ruth Ritchie, the secretary of the Wilson Gee Institute, for her typing of several drafts of the manuscript.

To my wife and children I offer my apologies as well as thanks for their understanding, patience, and love on the many weekends in the past seven years when I was preoccupied with this study. To my wife, in particular, I owe an immeasurable debt for her unremitting encouragement and assistance in every step that I have taken in the preparation of this volume. For her sake especially, I am happy to report that the American Association for Middle East Studies has honored the manuscript of this book with the award of its 1964 prize.

Charlottesville, Virginia R. K. R.
September 1965

Contents

PART TWO

Prelude to Transition in Foreign Policy, 1905-1920

PART THREE

Transitional Foreign Policy, 1921-1941

Introduction

A Theoretical Approach

In an age of superpowers and intercontinental ballistic missiles there would seem to be little future for small states. Their capacity to defend themselves against nuclear giants is nil. The technical revolution in modern warfare promises an increasing gap between the military capabilities of small and those of big and superpowers. If it was likely in 1946 that small states would lose "the right to an independent foreign policy," [1] it is all the more true today.

Yet the past two decades have witnessed a paradoxical increase in the influence of small states in world affairs within and without the United Nations. In a thermonuclear holocaust the helplessness of small states may be granted, but they play an increasingly significant part in the Cold War. In 1944 Arnold Wolfers said that only agreement and cooperation among the great powers could provide a framework within which all nations could hope to live in peace, but the existence of small states imposed self-restraint and patience on the mightier countries.[2] In the past two decades the role of small countries

[1] See Martin Wight, *Power Politics* (London, 1946), pp. 28-32.

[2] Arnold Wolfers, "In Defense of the Small Countries," *Yale Review*, Winter 1944, pp. 201-20.

has extended to maintenance of the framework of cooperation that the great powers constructed. The unremitting support of the United Nations by small states has helped the organization survive as the major arena within which superpowers as well as diminutive nations can strive to live in peace.

The foreign policies of small states are not expressed in the United Nations only. Outside the United Nations their policies are frequently of particular concern to the superpowers and the international community as a whole. Yet their significance has been overlooked because, as Annette Baker Fox has stated, a "traditional great-power stereotype of the small state was that of a helpless pawn in world politics." From the small-power point of view, "the great states were perceived as cynical manipulators of power and the small states as virtuous and law-abiding countries." [3]

These stereotypes adversely affected the development of theories of international relations and comparative foreign policy. Many scholars in the West concerned themselves with the foreign policy of great powers in, rather than that of, small states. On the other hand, many writers in small states failed to examine the foreign policy of their countries partly because of preoccupation with the "immoral " behavior of great powers. As a result, the foreign policy of small states received little attention from the students of international relations and foreign policy.

This inattention persists today, particularly among the developing nations. In most of these countries the "injured sense of morality" of the intellectuals is compounded with nationalistic sentiments. The obsession with blaming the ills of society on the "imperialistic" manipulations and intrigues of great powers is often responsible for failure to undertake and complete serious and constructively critical studies about their countries. The paucity of reliable data tends to aggravate the problem. But this is a problem only for those few writers who are committed to scholarly investigation guided by an overriding sense of integrity. Most do not care about the canons of scholarship, and the unavailability of reliable data does not seem to pose a critical problem. As the result in part of this attitude toward scholarly research, many fields of study, including foreign policy, remain largely unworked.

[3] *The Power of Small States: Diplomacy in World War II* (Chicago, 1959), pp. 1-2.

The emerging interest in non-Western studies among Western social scientists in recent years is encouraging.[4] Political scientists have begun to devote much research and writing to non-Western political systems.[5] So far these efforts have been concerned only incidentally with the foreign policy of developing nations. Lucian W. Pye's "outline of some of the dominant and distinctive characteristics of the non-Western political process" contains significant implications for the foreign policies of developing nations,[6] but little systematic research in these policies has been undertaken. One of the fruitful ways of doing this research is to concentrate on the foreign policy of a single country as an example of the foreign policy of developing nations.

This emphasis avoids the traditional concern with the unique features of the foreign policies of individual countries. Study of the foreign policy of Iran, for example, provides some basis for generalization because of important similarities between its experience in international politics and those of other developing nations. The fundamental problems facing most of these states today are essentially of the same nature as those encountered by Iran before World War II. Anglo-Russian rivalry was the dominant external factor influencing Iranian foreign policy for nearly one and a half centuries just as the East-West struggle influences the foreign policy of many newly independent states today. Furthermore, Iran began to experience modernization and its impact on the substance and process of foreign policy nearly a century ago; most developing nations have begun to feel it only in the past decade or two.

This study of Iran's foreign policy from the country's rise to power

[4] On this movement, see, for example, David Easton, *The Political System: An Inquiry into the State of Political Science* (New York, 1953); James C. Charlesworth (ed.), *The Limits of Behavioralism in Political Science* (A symposium sponsored by the American Academy of Political and Social Science; Philadelphia, October 1962); Quincy Wright, *The Study of International Relations* (New York, 1955); Klaus Knorr and Sidney Verba (eds.), *The International System: Theoretical Essays* (Princeton, N. J., 1961); and Richard N. Rosecrance, *Action and Reaction in World Politics: International System in Perspective* (Boston, 1963).

[5] See, for example, Gabriel A. Almond and James S. Coleman (eds.), *The Politics of the Developing Areas* (Princeton, N. J., 1960). On the political system of Iran, see Leonard Binder, *Iran, Political Development in a Changing Society* (Berkeley, Calif., 1960).

[6] "The Non-Western Political Process," *Journal of Politics*, XX (1958), 468-86.

in modern times to the abdication of Riẕā Shah in 1941 was prompted by the fact that a comprehensive history of Iranian foreign policy is not available. The reasons for this lack are in part the same as those indicated earlier for other developing countries. Iranian authors have often been largely concerned with ascribing the ills of their society to the manipulations and intrigues of foreign powers, particularly the British.[7] Western scholars, on the other hand, have concentrated on the rivalry of great powers in Iran. Their studies shed some incidental light on the foreign policy of Iran, but, of course, these studies are not intended to be substitutes for detailed and systematic research on Iranian foreign policy.[8]

The analytic concern of this writer derives from a general interest in comparative foreign policy. More particularly, it stems from specific interest in the foreign policy of developing nations. This interest demands that the history of the foreign policy of Iran be combined with analysis of it as an example of the foreign policy of developing nations. This is a difficult task and requires the use of some ordering concepts that take account of this twofold interest in the foreign policy of Iran.

Before discussing these basic concepts, the writer must disclaim any authority as a political theorist, although he cannot help being concerned with the theoretical problems inherent in any attempt to do systematic research. The notions and concepts discussed here have undoubtedly been influenced by existing theoretical literature in the social sciences. The writer's intellectual indebtedness will become evident whether or not specific sources of inspiration are given. It has not been possible to adopt any one of the existing approaches to the foreign policy of states in this study of the foreign policy of a developing nation. The major concepts and categories utilized in this

[7] See, for example, Maḥmūd Maḥmūd, *Tārīkh-i Ravābiṭ-i Sīyāsī-i Īran va Inglīs dar Qarn-i Nūzdahum-i Mīlādī* (8 vols.; Tehran, 1331–1336 [1952/53–1957/58]). For my criticism of the state of research in social sciences in Iran, see "Modernization and Social Research in Iran," *American Behavioral Scientist*, March 1962, pp. 17-20.

[8] See George Lenczowski, *Russia and the West in Iran, 1918-1948: A Study in Big-Power Rivalry* (New York, 1949). As the subtitle indicates, this is mainly concerned with big-power rivalry in Iran. Nevertheless, the author's incidental treatment of the foreign policy of Iran during 1918-48 in this study and in the period of 1948-52 in a supplement is most valuable.

work are discussed below in the hope that they will prove suggestive for the study of the foreign policy of other developing states.

Foreign Policy: The concept of "foreign policy" as it is utilized here is composed of two major elements – objectives and actions. In addition, the techniques and consequences of action are of concern. "Foreign policy" is thus the sum total of all the objectives and actions of a developing nation vis-à-vis all other states. As we shall see, however, "all other states" may often be reduced to a dozen or less. This is true in part because developing nations possess rather limited objectives and commitments. They usually have more local than global interests. Their limited power often impels them to seek to protect and promote their interests by friendship with neighbors and nonalignment with superpowers. Even in instances where they are formally allies of such powers or are in conflict with neighbors, they do not necessarily acquire global commitments. The task of selecting the relations with certain states for examination rests upon the shoulders of the investigator, who chooses states whose relations are of particular relevance to the totality of the foreign policy of the developing state.

Mere description of the objectives, actions, and techniques of diplomacy of a developing nation is not sufficient. Critical analysis of the relationship of these, particularly the relationship of objectives and means, is involved; this brings in the concept of rationality. The decision-making approach does not seem to subscribe to the concept of rationality; that is, it does not regard the policy of a state as irrational if the state selects objectives beyond its means.[9] Conversely, the approach used here accepts the concept of rationality; that is, it holds "a rational foreign policy to be good foreign policy."[10] More importantly, this approach utilizes the concept of rationality because this concept alerts the researcher to the impact of modernization processes on the foreign policy of a developing state and such processes seem to be gradually accompanied by the selection of objectives commensurate with the means of achievement. This point will be elaborated below, but first one other aspect of the concept of foreign policy as used in this study should be discussed.

[9] Richard C. Snyder, H. W. Bruch, and Burton Sapin (eds.), *Foreign Policy Decision-Making* (New York, 1962), p. 101.

[10] Hans J. Morgenthau, *Politics among Nations: The Struggle for Power and Peace* (New York, 1960), pp. 3-15.

The researcher is not merely interested in systematic description and critical analysis of foreign policy of a developing state. He also seeks to show continuities and changes in foreign policy in order to ascertain the major characteristics of foreign policy and its direction. This means that objectives, actions, techniques of diplomacy, and consequences of action should be studied over a long span of time.

Situation: The second basic concept of this study, "situation," refers to the major factors and forces which, in the eyes of the observer, have repeatedly influenced the foreign policy of a developing state. There are two kinds of situations, the internal and the external. The internal situation comprises the factors and forces that fall within the territory of a developing state. These factors and forces include the human as well as the nonhuman and the governmental as well as the nongovernmental elements. Hence, the political system, *including the foreign-policy maker*, is a component of the internal situation.[11]

In highly developed societies where the decision-making process occupies a prominent place, where institutional as well as individual roles are complex, and where decision makers truly *mediate* between the internal and external "setting," stress on the decision-making process and decision makers is important. In the developing societies where the ends and means of the state are usually those of an individual or a clique of some kind, such an emphasis does not seem to be warranted. In characterizing non-Western political processes in general, Pye states:

> In most non-Western societies, just as in traditional societies, the pattern of political relationships is largely determined by the pattern of social and personal relations. Power, prestige and influence are based largely on social status. The political struggle tends to revolve around issues of prestige, influence, and even of personalities, and not primarily around questions of alternative course of policy action.[12]

As these social and personal relations as well as other aspects of life in developing nations are changing and as these changes are reflected in the objectives and means of foreign policy, it is essential to utilize the concepts of "traditional foreign policy" and "transitional foreign policy," and consequently the related concepts of "traditional

[11] Cf. Snyder *et al., op. cit.*, pp. 66-67.

[12] In James N. Rosenau (ed.), *International Politics and Foreign Policy* (New York, 1961), p. 286.

policy makers," "transitional policy makers," "traditional objectives," "transitional objectives," and "traditional techniques of diplomacy" and "transitional techniques of diplomacy." A researcher can detect the continuity of traditional cultural, social, and psychological elements and the emergence of new values and attitudes in the foreign policy of developing countries by isolating, describing, analyzing, and relating the objectives and means of policy over a long span of time.

Identification, description, and analysis of the old as well as the new characteristics of the foreign policy of developing nations must not disregard the processes of modernization. The essence of modernization is change, and a focus of change is essential for the study of the foreign policy of developing states, just as it is important for the study of international relations in general. Quincy Wright attributes general changes in the character of international relations to "(a) general changes in the field, (b) to interaction between the capability and the value fields, and (c) to interaction between the geographic and analytical fields." He then states: "The most important general factors which influence both the geographical and the analytical fields appear to have been the accelerating progress of science and technology."[13] It is evident that modernization processes are bringing this progress to the developing societies at a rapid pace.

Modernization as the basic factor in the internal situation in developing states will, in the long run, involve a quantitative as well as a qualitative estimate of the impact of science and technology on the entire life and hence the character of the policies of new countries. At the present time the student of the foreign policy of developing societies will have to confine himself largely to broad characterizations of that policy. Developing societies are, as is well known, low-information societies. Even some of the most elementary data are lacking. Hence, at this stage of our knowledge the student will have to content himself with demonstrating the changes in the character of foreign policy by comparing the transitional objectives and means with the traditional ones and by analyzing in particular the relationship between the objectives and the means. Traditional foreign policy is heavily marked by frequent discrepancies between objectives and means, whereas transitional foreign policy shows a degree of rational relationship between the two.

[13] For details, see Wright, *op. cit.*, pp. 560-67.

The external situation refers to the factors and forces operating outside national boundaries which in the eyes of the researcher have repeatedly influenced the foreign policy of developing states. The researcher generally selects those items which he has reason to believe are of particular relevance to the foreign policy of the developing nation under study. However, the most important factors and forces in the external situation of developing nations are the policies of great powers and neighboring states. It is not necessary to assume a constant state of bipolarity or continuing conflict in order to justify the inclusion of this category. Depolarization and cooperation involving great powers would be of no less relevance to the foreign policy of developing countries.

To apply these general concepts and categories systematically and simultaneously to the foreign policy of Iran as a developing state, the concept of "interaction," has been adopted: interaction between external situation and foreign policy, internal situation and foreign policy, and internal-external situation and foreign policy. These sets of interaction are riveted systematically to historical empirical data within a chronological framework. This application of concept to data is called "dynamic triangular interaction."

Once again the writer wishes to disclaim any intention of building theories. These introductory pages reveal the nature of the basic assumptions and concepts. However simplified, crude, and general, these ideas have assisted the research and have been modified during the process. For this reason the study presented here is not merely a story of the foreign policy of Iran. And for this reason, also, it is hoped that these concepts will be suggestive to others studying the foreign policy of developing nations.

Part One

The Traditional Foreign Policy, 1500-1905

Chapter I

Interaction between Internal Situation, External Setting, and Foreign Policy, 1500-1801

Early in the sixteenth century an Iranian foreign policy began to develop concomitant with Iran's rise to power. Only at the beginning of the nineteenth century, however, was Iran drawn into European power politics. The intervening three centuries were marked by Iran's overriding concern, first, with Turkey and, subsequently for a comparatively short time, with Russia also. The foreign policy of Iran during these centuries was far less significant in itself than in its interaction with the rise of the state at the turn of the sixteenth century, with the revival of the state after a dramatic collapse in the eighteenth century, and with the progressive weakness of the state in the last years of the eighteenth century.

EMERGENCE OF THE STATE

The fundamental factor contributing to the rise of Iran in modern times was the adoption of the Shī'ī creed as the official religion of the state by Shah Ismā'īl (1499-1524), the founder of the Ṣafavī dynasty. He set himself the task of clearing "the flower-garden of religion of the chaff and rubbish of insubordination."[1] He regarded himself as "the Absolute Agent of God" and demanded *sijdah* – that is, prostration before God – from his newly converted subjects, the great majority of whom had been forcibly converted from Sunnī to Shī'ī Islam.[2] This conversion of the population and the formation of an army were followed by a *jihād* against the Georgian "infidels." Some of the Shah's partisans were aroused by his dynamic religious ideology to the point of regarding him as a "god," a belief which he shared, as is evident from some of his Turkish poems. One of the war cries of his soldiers was, "My spiritual lord and master, I am thy sacrifice and alms!"[3]

His campaign of conquest and conversion gave him vast territories in Iran, which at the time was under the control of many "petty rulers." These victories almost restored the ancient Iranian frontiers of Sassanian times.[4] Shah Ismā'īl probably aspired to extend the Shī'ī creed beyond these frontiers, but his defeat at Chaldiran (1514) checked his ambition.[5] Toynbee states that the Shah had wished to establish a "world empire."[6]

Shah Ismā'īl's attempts to restore the Persian Empire were continued by his son, Shah Ṭahmāsb (1524-76). The Shah matched, if he did not surpass, his father in his commitment to the Shī'ī ideology. In his memoirs he shows his intense devotion to 'Alī, the leading Shī'ī *imām*: "Were the ocean ink, the trees of the forest pens, the seven heavens folios, and all the Jinns and all mankind to keep on writing till the resurrection day, they could not record a thousandth part of Ali's merits."[7] Shah Ṭahmāsb's religious zeal was as much a unifying factor among the Iranian people as his father's. One observer stated that "the reverence and love of the people for the King are incredible, as they worship him not as a king but as a god."[8]

[1] E. D. Ross, "The Early Years of Shah Ismail, Founder of the Safavi Dynasty," *Journal of the Royal Asiatic Society*, 1896, p. 326.

[2] V. Minorsky, "The Middle East in Western Politics in the 13th, 14th and 15th Centuries," *Journal of the Royal Asian Society*, 1940, pp. 450-52.

[3] L. Lockhart, *The Fall of the Safavi Dynasty and the Afghan Occupation of Persia* (Cambridge, 1958), p. 20.

[4] Edward G. Browne, *A Literary History of Persia* (Cambridge, 1953), IV, 60.

[5] Lockhart, *op. cit.*, pp. 20-21.

[6] Arnold J. Toynbee, *A Study of History* (Oxford, 1939), I, 392.

[7] H. Beveridge, "The Memoirs of Shah Tahmasp, King of Persia from 1524 to 1576," *Asiatic Review*, n.s., IV (1914), 461.

[8] Cited in Browne, *op. cit.*, p. 86.

A second factor that contributed to the consolidation of the Iranian state was hostility toward the Ottoman Empire. The early conflicts with the empire assisted the process of differentiation and consolidation of the nascent Iranian state. It is interesting to note that a prolonged absence of conflict with the Turks at a later date was regarded by at least one historian as a cause of general internal decay in Iran:

> Persia never enjoyed a more perfect tranquility than in the beginning of the present [the eighteenth] century. The treaties she had concluded with her neighbors were perfectly observed and secured her against any foreign invasions; whilst the effeminacy and luxury of her inhabitants, the ordinary consequence of a long peace, left no room to apprehend any danger from the ambition of her own subjects. This monarchy, which had suffered so many revolutions in past ages, seemed to be settled on a solid foundation when the news of its subversion surprised the world.[9]

The most important and lasting peace contributing to Iranian complacency was concluded with the Ottoman Empire in 1639. The treaty of that year provided for "a perpetual peace" for the first time. It ended more than a century-old state of war between Iran and the empire. Doubtless the inconclusive hostilities were a severe drain on Iran's human and material resources, but at the same time these early wars assisted in unifying Iran.[10]

CONFLICT WITH TURKEY

The early conflicts and wars with the Ottoman Empire were in principle the result of Shī'ī and Sunnī sectarian antagonism. The Shī'ī doctrine was feared in Turkey before Shah Ismā'īl took power. In the fifteenth century after Ismā'īl's father had been killed, two of his adherents entered Turkey and for a time stayed as hermits in the wild mountainous region of the south. These two, Hasan Khalifah and Karabiik, were not the only Shī'ī partisans who entered the

[9] Jonas Hanway, *Revolutions of Persia* (London, 1754), I, 22.

[10] Philip K. Hitti states, with respect to the early Ṣafavī wars with Turkey, that "far from weakening Shah Ismail's position the episode [the battle of Chaldiran] served to rally his people around his new throne with intensified loyalty. Nor did the repeated occupation of Tabriz and other Persian towns by Salim's successor Sulayman undermine the power of Ismail's son" (*The Near East in History* [Princeton, N. J., 1961), p. 378).

Ottoman Empire; many others were scattered throughout the country. But these two figures were considered "pious" leaders. In 1502 it was rumored in Istanbul that five hundred Shī'ī partisans were in the city, and for five days all gates were closed to prevent their escape and to facilitate their capture. Of the two leaders, Karabiik, or Shah Qulī, was particularly active in the province of Tekke and in the city of Antalya. From there and from the whole of Anatolia, groups of Shī'ī partisans were deported to Greece and Albania in keeping with a program of persecution that had already begun.[11]

Turkish rulers feared not only the Shī'ī adherents actually in their territory but also the religious appeal of Shah Ismā'īl to residents of Turkey. Shah Ismā'īl belonged to the Baktashi order of dervishes, to which the janissaries also belonged.[12] Because he feared the ideological appeal of the Shah in Turkey, Bayezid, the Turkish Sultan, in 1501 issued an edict "falsely stating" that Shah Ismā'īl was dead. This "rather nonsensical bit of psychological diplomacy" having produced no result, the Turkish Sultan made friendly gestures toward the Shah.[13] In 1504, for example, Sultan Bayezid dispatched an ambassador to congratulate the Shah on the conquest of Fars and Iraq. Subsequently the Shah assured the Sultan that Ottoman lands and troops would be respected, but mutual suspicion did not subside as the result of these reassurances.

The growing strife between the two Muslim states finally led to the first major armed conflict between Turkey and Iran, in 1514. This war was preceded by two massacres of the Shī'ī inhabitants in Turkey. The first massacre followed a Shī'ī rebellion under the leadership of Shah Qulī, mentioned earlier. Having escaped years of persecution, he gathered his forces to ravage the Ottoman Empire in 1511, clashed with Turkish troops, and made several serious assaults on his adversaries. On one occasion his Shī'ī partisans took a number of sanjakbeys. "The news of their success almost paralyzed Istanbul, but the Porte rose to the occasion and set the crack troops in motion to rout the heretics."[14] Shah Qulī himself was killed in battle, the rebellion subsided, and Ottoman soldiers then began to pillage in Anatolia, "robbing

[11] Sydney Nettleton Fisher, *The Foreign Relations of Turkey: 1481-1512* (Urbana, Ill., 1948), p. 92.

[12] *Ibid.*, pp. 91-92.

[13] *Ibid.*

[14] For details, see *ibid.*, pp. 97-99.

and taking many of the inhabitants as slaves, saying that they were of the *Sofi* sect. The extent of the ravaging by soldiers is uncertain but undoubtedly it was not so great a vengeance as that wrought on the *Sofis* by Selim I several years later." [15]

Selim's massacre occurred in 1514. Its "unparalleled cruelty" is universally acknowledged. During his reign the wish, "Mayst thou be the vizir of Sultan Selim," became a common cursing formula among Ottomans.[16]

Selim distributed troops throughout the empire, and stationed them in each city and district, in strength proportioned to the number of the Schiis that it contained. He then suddenly sent forth the messengers of death, and the whole of those unhappy beings were arrested. 40,000 of them were slain; the rest were condemned to perpetual imprisonment.[17]

The first insolent letter from Sultan Selim to Shah Ismā'īl in 1514, written in Persian, was a declaration of war on Iran. It reveals the prominent role of sectarian differences in the outbreak of the war, stating in part:

The Ulema and our teachers of the law have pronounced death upon thee [Shah Ismā'īl], perjurer and blasphemer as thou art, and have laid upon every good Mussulman the sacred duty of taking arms for the defence of religion, and for the destruction of heresy and impiety in thy person and the persons of those who follow thee.[18]

The armed conflict thus begun continued intermittently until 1590. During the reign of Shah Ismā'īl wars were fought between 1514 and 1520; during the reign of Shah Ṭahmāsb (1524-76) they were fought in 1533-35, 1548, 1553, and 1555. They were continued during the reigns of Ismā'īl II (1576-77), Muḥammad Khudābandah (1577-87), and Shah 'Abbās the Great (1587-1629).[19]

By 1601 when Shah 'Abbās resumed the war with the Ottoman Empire a significant change had occurred in the character of the Iranian state. The state had been unified in part by the Shī'ī creed,

[15] *Ibid.*, pp. 98-99.

[16] Sir Edward S. Creasy, *History of the Ottoman Turks: From the Beginning of Their Empire to the Present Time* (London, 1877), p. 127.

[17] *Ibid.*, p. 132. See also Lord Eversley, *The Turkish Empire: Its Growth and Decay* (London, 1917), p. 105.

[18] For the text of the letter, see Creasy, *op. cit.*, pp. 133-36.

[19] *Ibid.*, pp. 140-72.

which was relentlessly espoused by Shah Ismā'īl and his successors. This fact had made Iran a basically theocratic state. But by the time of Shah 'Abbās this characteristic had undergone a significant change. Secular monarchical absolutism rather than Shī'ism was the dominant feature of the state. The Shī'ī creed was still the official religion, but it was overshadowed by the secular absolutism of the monarch. Allegiance of subjects to monarch no longer derived primarily from the latter's religious standing. The Shah was feared and the millennial institution of the monarchy respected. One historian affirms that, as the result of Shah 'Abbās' management, the state had "become despotic and absolute to such a Degree, that it may be said, that there is not, perhaps, in the Universe, a King that is more Master of the Life and Fortunes of his subjects, than was Shah Abbas and his Successors." [20]

This change in the internal setting influenced the foreign policy of Iran. In the long era of intermittent and inconclusive wars with Turkey the predecessors of Shah 'Abbās had lost vast territories. This had occurred particularly since the death of the founder of the Ṣafavī dynasty in 1524. By the time Shah 'Abbās took power Turkey had conquered from Iran at least "one hundred and fifty leagues in length from South to North, reckoning from Tauris to the extremities of the Kingdom of Caket, and as much more in breadth, from the Western Coast of the Caspian to the Black Sea." [21] Upon his accession to the throne, the Shah made the restoration of these territories the fundamental objective of his policy toward Turkey.[22] Something similar to the principle of territorial sovereignty thus overshadowed sectarian animosity. In fact, the Shah concluded a significant "peace" with Turkey in 1590, in which he pledged that Iran would abandon the cursing of "the first three Caliphs," a practice that had come to symbolize Shī'ī antagonism toward the Sunnī Ottoman Empire. This concession to Turkey as well as the surrender of vast territories to the Porte was a tactical device designed to buy temporary peace with Turkey in the west in order to check the encroachments of the Uzbeks in the east. When the Shah resumed war with Turkey in 1601, restoration of Iranian territories was his principal objective.[23]

[20] Father Krusinski, *The History of the Revolution of Persia* (London, 1729), p. 28.

[21] *Ibid.*, p. 26.

[22] *Ibid.*, p. 25.

[23] See Browne, *op. cit.*, p. 106, and Krusinski, *op. cit.*, pp. 26-27.

Subordination of sectarian considerations to territorial ambitions was not a foreign policy adopted only by Shah 'Abbās the Great. His successor, Shah Ṣafī (1629-42), followed suit. In 1639 he concluded a peace treaty with Turkey that was to last "till the day of resurrection." Although this was prompted by his defeat in the war of 1630-38, the "Treaty of Peace and Frontiers" of 1639 no less than the 1590 "treaty" of Shah 'Abbās embodied something like the principle of *cuius regio eius religio,* although this Western concept was probably alien to the Muslims.

To appreciate the significance of this doctrine in Iran's foreign policy it must be recalled that ever since the first major war with Turkey Shī'ī antagonism toward the Sunnī sect had often influenced Iran's policy toward the Ottoman Empire. The treaty of 1639 reflected a significant change in Iran's policy. The two Muslim states invoked the Islamic precept, "Fear God and reconcile yourselves," while they were actually for the first time basing their relations on territorial considerations and establishing boundaries between themselves.[24] The peace thus confirmed lasted more than eighty years, and the boundaries set endured for more than two hundred years.

SURVIVAL OF THE STATE

The struggle to ensure the survival of the Iranian state in the eighteenth century conditioned foreign policy. Before discussing the interaction of events and policy we must first note the collapse of the state in 1722, when Iran's independence was destroyed. The ignominious downfall of the Ṣafavī dynasty during that year marked the culmination of a long era of decline. It was no coincidence that the end of the dynasty came after the reign of Shah Sultān Ḥusayn (1694-1722), the most inept policy maker Iran had ever known. His ill-advised policies precipitated the disaster of 1722. The Ghalzai tribe, the most powerful tribe of Qandahar, had been subjected to the repressive measures of the Shah's agents for several years. Mīr Ways, a leading chief of the tribe, decided in 1711 to defy the Shah and to protest his

[24] For the text, see J. C. Hurewitz, *Diplomacy in the Near and Middle East* (Princeton, N. J., 1956), I, 21-23.

"intolerable" measures. His son, Maḥmūd, went so far as to march the Afghan troops toward Isfahan, the capital of Iran. The struggle between Qandahar and Isfahan finally resulted in the occupation of the latter by Afghan forces in 1722. The collapse of the government and the confusion that ensued presented Turkey, the traditional foe, and Russia, a new enemy, with a most propitious opportunity for aggrandizement.

The Turkish invasion of Iran was in part motivated by the desire to compensate for territorial losses in the west by gaining new dominions in the east. Shortly before the invasion of Iran, Turkey had suffered enormous territorial losses at the hands of European powers. Turkish losses in 1699 and again in 1718 were reflected in the historic treaties of Carlowitz and Passarowitz. The memories of territorial conquests at the expense of Iran as well as of Egypt and Syria in the sixteenth century were encouraging. In eight years Turkey had gained as much territory in the Middle East as it had conquered elsewhere within the two preceding centuries.[25] This had taken place when a relatively powerful Iran had just been established. The prospects for territorial expansion were still more inviting in the 1720's, when Iran was torn by internal dissensions and paralyzed by the Afghan occupation.

The Turkish invasion was also prompted by the Russian advance into Iran. Russia's expansionist objective in the Middle East in 1722 was concentrated on the vast plain between the Black and the Caspian seas. Domination of this area would enable Russia to establish a commercial highway over the Caspian Sea and to control the Black Sea. Russia regarded freedom of navigation on the Black Sea and free egress from its waters into the Mediterranean as essential to its achievement of great-power status.

In 1722, however, the Black Sea was a Turkish lake, and the Porte was determined to retain it at almost any cost. It had, in fact, demonstrated this determination in 1695 and again in 1696, when Turkish forces had blocked Russian encroachments. But Peter the Great proved much bolder in 1722. He descended the Volga and captured Derbend. The Tsar tried to justify his action on the ground that Maḥmūd, the Afghan ruler of Isfahan, had denied responsibility for

[25] *Cambridge Modern History*, III, 12-13.

the plunder of the property of Russian subjects by the Uzbeks and Lesgians.[26]

The bold advance of Russia in Transcaucasia brought the problem to a head. Russia and Turkey talked about settling their differences peacefully but prepared for war. While engaged in dispatching military forces to Georgia, Turkey received an offer of mediation from France. The French attempt was doomed from the outset because the rival powers were not ready to compromise on a single point. The Porte indignantly demanded the abandonment of Derbend, noninterference in the affairs of Iran, and denial of arms to the Georgians. The Tsar retorted that Russia would not abandon Derbend or "a palm of the new acquisitions." [27]

Under the circumstances Turkey decided that it would be easier to prevent further advance by Russia into Iran by invading that country itself, forestalling its rival in Iran rather than invading Russia. Furthermore, the Porte was displeased with both factions in Iran. As a Sunnī Muslim, Maḥmūd, the Afghan ruler of Isfahan, acknowledged the Sultan as Caliph, but he adamantly refused to recognize the suzerainty of the Sultan. The Porte apparently disliked Ṭahmāsb Mīrzā, the son of the dethroned Shah Sultān Ḥusayn, because he was a Shīʿī Muslim, a "heretic Persian!" [28]

The Porte declared war on Ṭahmāsb Mīrzā. Faced with Turkish hostility and eager to restore the throne to the Ṣafavī dynasty, he sought the assistance of Russia. That country responded with enthusiasm and signed an agreement with him in September 1723. Russia promised to supply Ṭahmāsb Mīrzā with arms for suppressing the Afghans and recovering the throne of Iran. In return for this assistance, Ṭahmāsb Mīrzā agreed to cede to Russia the towns of Derbend and Baku and the provinces of Gilan, Mazandaran, and Astarabad.[29]

Upon hearing of this agreement the Porte complained about "the

[26] Sir Percy Sykes, *A History of Persia* (London, 1930), II, 232-33. The invasion of Iran had been urged on Peter the Great as early as 1715 by Artemii Volynski, the Russian Minister at Isfahan. See Stanley Lane-Poole and others, *Turkey* (New York, 1899), p. 217.

[27] Mary Lucille Shay, *The Ottoman Empire from 1720 to 1734 As Revealed in Dispatches of the Venetian Baili* (Urbana, Ill., 1944), pp. 105-6.

[28] *Ibid.*

[29] Mohammad Ali Hekmat, *Essai sur l'histoire des relations politiques irano-ottomanes* (Paris, 1937), pp. 100-103. See also, for the text of the treaty, Saʿīd Nafīsī, *Tārīkh-i Ijtimāʿī va Sīyāsī-i Īrān* (Tehran, 1335 [1956/57]), pp. 292-93.

insidious, secret and illusory" action of Russia at a time when the Iranian problem still was the subject of negotiation with Turkey at Constantinople.[30] The Russo-Turkish tension reached a new height and threatened war. Motivated by its desire to keep Turkey strong against Austria, France mediated for the second time and succeeded in averting a war. More important, the French conciliatory efforts produced an agreement between St. Petersburg and Constantinople in regard to their conflicting interests in Iran.

By this agreement (signed in 1724), Russia and Turkey decided to partition Iran. Turkey was to obtain, in addition to the territories already conquered, Erivan, Ganja, and Nakhichevan plus large areas in Azerbaijan such as Tabriz, Marand, and Urumiyah. In return for these territorial gains Turkey withdrew its previous objection to the cession of Gilan, Mazandaran, and Astarabad to Russia as contemplated by Russia's agreement with Ṭahmāsb Mīrzā. Russia also promised Turkey to persuade Ṭahmāsb Mīrzā, or compel him if necessary, to surrender all the provinces that were allotted to the Porte under the partition treaty of 1724.[31]

The death of Peter the Great in 1725 brought Russia's bold advance in Iran to a halt, but Turkey lost no time in taking possession of the Iranian territories allotted to it under the agreement with Russia. By 1727, despite the stiff opposition of Ashraf, the Afghan ruler of Isfahan, Turkey had conquered all the western provinces of Iran. This dramatic advance brought Turkey closer to subjugating Iran than at any other time in the long era of Irano-Turkish hostility. Ashraf felt compelled to acknowledge, as the head of the government of Isfahan, that his state was a "tributary state" depending upon the Porte.[32] As the result of the Afghan, Turkish, and Russian occupations Iran was stripped of its territorial sovereignty and political independence.

[30] Shay, *op. cit.*, p. 113.

[31] For the text of the treaty, see Hurewitz, *op. cit.*, I, 42-45. For details of the circumstances surrounding the treaty, see Shay, *op. cit.*, pp. 115-22.

[32] Shay, *op. cit.*, p. 125.

INDEPENDENCE FROM TURKEY AND RUSSIA

The situation was soon, however, dramatically reversed. The Iranian state was revived, and its dramatic internal consolidation interacted dynamically with its foreign policy.

This revival was signaled by the rise of Nādir Qulī to power in 1727. His military ability proved exceedingly important in forging a united country out of a fragmented land occupied by the Afghan, Turkish, and Russian forces. By 1730 he had expelled the Afghans from Isfahan and recovered the province of Kerman and the cities of Kashan, Qazvin, and Tehran. Nevertheless, Iran was still far from being an independent country capable of conducting its domestic or foreign affairs. Turkey held sway over all of Georgia, Armenia, Azerbaijan, Kurdistan, Hamadan, and Kermanshah and part of Daghistan and Shiravan. Russia was in possession of the rest of Daghistan and Shiravan as well as Baku, Derbend, and the provinces of Astarabad, Gilan, and Mazandaran.

The task before Nādir was colossal. Having expelled the Afghans from Isfahan, he made the restitution of Iranian provinces the primary objective of his foreign policy. This aimed at both Turkey and Russia. He turned first to Turkey. At the outset both Nādir and the Porte claimed that they wished to settle their differences by peaceful means. But as time went by it became evident that neither was ready to make any substantial concession toward a negotiated settlement. Nādir began his military campaign against the Turks in 1730 with the objective of recovering Iranian territories. This decision was made after he learned from Riẕā Qulī Khān Shāmlū, the Iranian envoy who had been dispatched to Constantinople, that the Porte was not ready to evacuate the Iranian provinces.

Nādir had made some headway against the Turkish forces when he was abruptly called away from the battlefield and forced to march hundreds of miles in order to quell a rebellion in Khorasan. Ṭahmāsb Shah II, whom Nādir was serving at this time, decided to pursue his general's campaign against the Turks, but his attempt miscarried and in a decisive battle he was utterly defeated. Under a treaty dictated by Turkey in 1732, the humiliated Shah ceded all the territories that

Nādir had recovered.[33] The news of this treaty infuriated the ambitious general, who renounced it at once and utilized it masterfully in deposing the Shah four years later.

Even before ridding himself of the nominal lordship of Ṭahmāsb Shah, Nādir resumed his Turkish campaign with renewed vigor and fresh assaults. His adversary, Topal Osman, proved indomitable in the first round, but suffered a crushing defeat in a second round in 1733. The Turks then sued for peace, but only as a means for gaining time. They signed a treaty, but later refused to ratify it because it was "dishonorable." War flared up once again in 1734 and was not concluded until 1736. Nādir's initial strategy was a move against Russia as well as Turkey. His attack on Shiravan recovered it from the Turks while it simultaneously forced Russia to relinquish Derbend and Baku. The campaign of 1735 produced further territorial gains, and Ganja, Tiflis, and Erivan were brought under Iranian control. The truce of 1736, not a treaty, finally marked the end of Nādir's successful campaigns against the Turkish occupation forces.[34]

Nādir's policy toward Russia was executed with relative ease. This was to a significant degree because of the ever-present Turko-Russian tension, which he exploited skillfully. The tense relations between Turkey and Russia were in part due to the Iranian problem. All during the Irano-Turkish wars the Porte suspected Russia of secretly providing Nādir with assistance. As a matter of fact there were definite grounds for suspicion. Russia on at least one occasion assisted Nādir in strengthening his military forces. General Levashev, on the authorization of St. Petersburg, sent several Russian artillery and engineer officers disguised as Iranians to help Nādir.[35]

Russia watched the Irano-Turkish wars with some anxiety. The more its relations with Turkey deteriorated, the more it favored Iran. Russia relished Nādir's victorious campaigns against the Turks, and when the latter dealt the Iranian forces under Ṭahmāsb Shah a humiliating defeat Russia came to the assistance of Iran. Russia hurriedly concluded a most favorable treaty with the Shah in 1732, promising withdrawal of its own forces from Iranian provinces, including Gilan, and pledging "perpetual friendship." The news of this

[33] For the full text, see Nafīsī, *op. cit.*, pp. 299-304. See also Hurewitz, *op. cit.*, I, 45-47.

[34] For details, see L. Lockhart, *Nadir Shah* (London, 1938).

[35] *Ibid.*, p. 50.

treaty increased Turkish suspicion, while Russia tried to justify its action by claiming that it had signed the treaty because Gilan was "a thorn not a profit." [36]

Russia's interest in keeping Nādir at war with Turkey was augmented by the outbreak of the so-called War of the Polish Succession in 1733. Involvement in this war made it mandatory for Russia to induce Nādir to end a truce with Turkey so that the Porte would be compelled to keep the peace with Russia. But Nādir was not too happy with Russia because it was still holding Derbend and Baku. Although Russia was entitled to control them under the Treaty of Rasht (1732) so long as the Turks remained in possession of Azerbaijan, Armenia, and Georgia, Nādir insisted on their evacuation. This was finally forced on Russia when Nādir attacked Shiravan in 1734. The relinquishment of those towns by Russia was provided for in the Treaty of Ganja, signed in 1735.[37] This marked the end of Nādir's successes vis-à-vis Russia.

This treaty with Russia together with the treaty of 1736 with Turkey, mentioned previously, heralded the complete restoration of the Iranian territories and the nearly miraculous survival of the Iranian state. In the same year that the recovery of the Iranian provinces from Turkey was militarily finalized (1736) Nādir was proclaimed the Shah of Iran.

WEAKNESS OF THE STATE

Although Iran had survived the internal convulsions and external occupations of the turbulent period of 1722-27, it was basically a much weaker state by the time it was sucked into the whirlwind of European power politics at the beginning of the nineteenth century. The factor that contributed most to this weakness was the lack of social cohesion. The divisive forces in Iranian society can be traced back to ancient times. The earliest available records of the Iranian people before their migration into eastern Iran reveal the dichotomy between the settled and semisettled elements.[38] In the ancient structure of family, clan,

[36] For details, see Shay, *op. cit.*, pp. 135-46.
[37] For the text of this treaty, see Nafīsī, *op. cit.*, pp. 305-11.
[38] Ann K. S. Lambton, *Landlord and Peasant in Persia* (Oxford, 1953), p. 10.

tribe, and country the society was ideally divided into classes of priests, warriors, farmers, and traders; and Zoroastrianism, the official creed of the Sassanians, gave these divisions the sanctity of religion. The Arab conquest of Iran in the seventh century A.D. made Iranian society part of the "greater society" of Islam. But this did not create major alterations in the characteristic grades of Iranian society. The ideal society, as described by the philosophers in medieval Islamic times, was a hierarchic society, with mankind graded into various classes.[39]

Nor did the Muslim conquest of Iran bring about any significant degree of unification of "races" or cohesion among various linguistic, tribal, religious, or other groups. The *'umma,* the "community," merely integrated the existing particularisms without destroying them. It unified but did not transcend the tribal, ethnic, and other groups. In fact, the Arab conquest introduced new divisions into Iranian society. Not only did the Arabs bring with them into the conquered territories "their tribal loyalties and also their feuds," but as the result of their conquest of Iran there soon arose a dichotomy between Arab and 'Ajam, or non-Arab, which cut across the division between the Muslim and non-Muslim.[40] Later invasions of Iran by the Seljuk Turks and the Mongols added even more divisions: those between the Turks and Tājīk, or non-Turk, and between the conquered and the conqueror. Although the forcible conversion of the inhabitants of Iran to the Shī'ī creed by Shah Ismā'īl was the fundamental basis of the new Iranian political system, it simultaneously introduced a new dichotomy into Iranian society. The bulk of the population became Shī'ī, but the Kurds, the Afghans (except for the Hazaras), a majority of the Arabs, and the non-Christian elements in Caucasia and Transcaucasia were Sunnīs.[41]

The mosaic character of Iranian society had been a source of Ṣafavī weakness. Each ethnic, tribal, linguistic, or religious community owed primary allegiance to its own authority. But the Shī'ī creed acted as a countervailing influence. It assisted the process of consolidation. However, as the dynamism of Shī'īsm wore off, the divisive forces predominated. Nevertheless, a degree of conformity, rather than unity,

[39] Ann K. S. Lambton, *Islamic Society in Persia* (London, 1954), p. 3.
[40] *Ibid.*, pp. 5-6.
[41] Lockhart, *Safavi Dynasty*, p. 11.

was attained as the result of the "patrimonial absolutism" of Shah ʿAbbās the Great.[42] The monarchy held the Iranian polity together so long as the reigning monarch was capable of conducting the affairs of the state. But few, if any, successors of Shah ʿAbbās the Great were capable policy makers. In fact, as we shall see later, the Shah himself was in part responsible for the lack of ability of his successors.

But he did much to strengthen Iran at the beginning of his reign. As a realistic policy maker, he recognized the necessity of military preparedness before undertaking a war with Turkey for the restitution of the Iranian provinces. The military force of Shah Ismāʿīl had been organized "on purely tribal principles." As this condition had endangered the existence of the state, Shah Ṭahmāsb had begun to disband and disperse the "unruly" tribes, but the fundamental reform was accomplished only under ʿAbbās I, who reduced the number of tribal forces and side by side with them created new troops armed with up-to-date weapons and fully dependent on the central government. Like the Ottoman janissaries, the Shah's new regiments were recruited chiefly from the converts to Islam (Georgians, Armenians, and others), who were free from the drawback of tribal allegiance.[43]

In contrast to the Shah's successful efforts to strengthen Iran was his practice of taking the life or weakening the character of possible successors. This was a second factor underlying the weakness of Iran. Shah ʿAbbās the Great not only murdered one of his sons and blinded two others but introduced the pernicious practice of immuring the claimants of the throne in the harem. As a result, the policy makers of the country, whose character and experience were of the utmost importance in an absolute monarchy such as Iran, ascended the throne one after another with little or no experience in affairs of state. Shah Ṣafī (1629-42), who was either "chilled with opium" or drunk with wine, "meddled very little with affairs of the Government, passing his whole life with his bottle, his wives or in hunting."[44] Sulaymān (1666-94), one of the cruelest kings Iran has known, was utterly indifferent to affairs of state. When he was told of the menace of the Turks to Iran and its finest provinces, "he answered very indifferently, that he did not care provided they left him Isfahan."[45]

[42] V. Minorsky, *Tadhkirat Al-Muluk: A Manual of Safavi Administration* (London, 1943), p. 14.
[43] *Ibid.*, pp. 30-31.
[44] Krusinski, *op. cit.*, pp. 32-33.
[45] *Ibid.*, p. 40.

A third factor that contributed to the weakness of Iran was Shī'ī fanaticism. The dynamic force of the Shī'ī ideology assisted the consolidation of the state, but blind adherence to Shī'ī dogma narrowed the intellectual horizon of the people. Shī'ī fanaticism mentally isolated Iranian rulers and their subjects alike. Isolation from Europe proved prejudicial to the interests of Iran. At a time when European intellectuals were beginning to see how dogma had been overturned by scientific research and how the same method could be applied to politics and religion, the unquestioning acceptance of Shī'ī dogma left little room for receptivity to new ideas in Iran. Of all the Ṣafavī policy makers only Shah 'Abbās the Great made any significant effort to broaden the contacts of Iran with Europe. Even this did not produce any lasting or significant ties with Europe. In a *farmān* (royal decree) issued in 1600 and addressed to the Christian powers, the Shah assured them of generous capitulatory privileges in Iran.[46] But he was not motivated by any great desire to broaden the cultural horizon of Iran. His fundamental motive was to find European allies in "the common struggle" against the Ottoman Empire.[47] This coincided with an age-old objective of Europe in Iran. Throughout the sixteenth century there had been European statesmen

> whose intrigues were directed towards the maintenance of Turko-Persian hostility which would deter the Sultan from aggressive operations in Europe. In particular, for more than twenty years after 1525 the Emperor Charles V had been in communication with Persia, and there is ground to believe that the Persian effort of 1551 to recover the territories lost to Solayman the Magnificent in 1534-6 was due in part to the Emperor's instigation.[48]

It is also believed that Shah 'Abbās' renewal of war with Turkey in 1601 was prompted by Sherley's "solicitation."[49]

[46] For the text of the *farmān*, see Hurewitz, *op. cit.*, pp. 15-16.

[47] The Shah was "moreover desirous of opening up direct communication with the European markets for the raw silk of Persia, which was largely a royal monopoly. The passage of this product through the Turkish dominions yielded a valuable revenue to the Sultan, to deprive him of which would be a good stroke of policy." See Sir William Foster, *England's Quest of Eastern Trade* (London, 1933), p. 297. On the Shah's primary motive in approaching the European powers, see also K. Bayani, *Les relations de l'Iran avec l'Europe occidental à l'époque safavide* (Paris, 1937), pp. 10-14, 57-58.

[48] Samuel C. Chew, *The Crescent and the Rose: Islam and England during the Renaissance* (New York, 1937), p. 250.

[49] *Ibid.*, p. 260.

A fourth factor weakening Iran was the superstitious nature of Iranian rulers. While Shīʿī dogma inhibited contact with the outside world, Shīʿī superstition paralyzed the policy-making process. Shah Ṭahmāsb based many of his domestic and foreign policy decisions on dreams in which he invariably saw ʿAlī. In one dream, for example, ʿAlī promised him victory over the Uzbeks about 1528, and at Herat a year or two later ʿAlī advised him in another dream how to wage a campaign.[50] Probably no Ṣafavī policy maker was so much a victim of superstition and excessive "religious" devotion as Shah Sultān Ḥusayn (1694-1722). He turned his attention away from the mundane concerns of the state and immersed himself in eschatology. He surrounded himself with such dubious characters as the *Shaykh al-ajinnah* ("Master of the Jinns"),[51] the court astrologers, and the eunuchs of the harem and left affairs of state in their hands. Even when, purely as a matter of form, a proposal was submitted to him for approval, hc would invariably say: *Yakhshidir* ("It is good"); for this reason he was nicknamed "Yakhshidir." [52] During the reign of this monarch ignorant eunuchs became the "Arbiters of Affairs," and crucial decisions of state such as making peace or war and concluding treaties with foreign powers were all referred to

> the Sovereign Senate of the Eunuchs, who while the King was buried up in the delights of his harem, and not so much taken up with the Government of his Dominions as the least of his subjects, disposed of all the chief places of his kingdom, and of the fortunes of all the grandees they pleased, in his name.[53]

It is no surprise, in the perspective of history, that the Ṣafavī dynasty ended with him.

Another weakening factor before Iran's full-fledged involvement in European power politics at the turn of the nineteenth century was the expansionist wars of Nādir Shah. Nādir's relentless military efforts from his rise to power in 1727 to his ascent of the throne in 1736 had aimed, as we have seen, at the fundamental objective of restoring Iran's territorial sovereignty and political independence. But after becoming the Shah, he began wars of expansionism which weakened

[50] Browne, *op. cit.*, pp. 86-87.

[51] See the historical novel of Ṣanʿatīzādah Kirmānī, *Nādir Fātaḥ-i Dihlī* (Tehran, 1957), pp. 72-73.

[52] See Lockhart, *Safavi Dynasty*, pp. 41-42.

[53] Krusinski, *op. cit.*, p. 62.

the Iranian political system. Nādir Shah, like Shah 'Abbās the Great, did much for Iran, but he, also like Shah 'Abbās, dealt its power position some severe blows.

As an irredentist monarch, Nādir Shah dragged Iran into war with Turkey in 1743. There was no question, at this time, of driving Turkish occupation forces out of Iran, as had been the case during the wars of 1730-36. Nādir's fundamental objective now was to reestablish Iranian control over Baghdad. He attempted to cloak his irredentist claims by demanding that the Sultan recognize an artificially created sect, the Ja'farīyah, under the threat of war.[54] The war of 1743 produced no gains. He captured Kirkuk and Mosul but could not hold them. Having concluded peace with Russia in 1739, Turkey stiffly resisted Nādir's "World-Conquering" army. The result was that he was forced not only to abandon his campaign but also to relinquish his demand that the Sultan recognize the Ja'farīyah sect.[55] He then signed a treaty of peace with Turkey at Kurdan in 1746, although he was assassinated by his own oppressed subjects before its ratification.

Nādir's insatiable territorial greed and military adventures were not confined to the "former territories" of Iran. In 1738 Nādir invaded India and in 1740 Turkistan and Daghistan. At the same time he planned to gain a foothold in Musqat and Oman in order to establish naval supremacy in the Persian Gulf and the Gulf of Oman.

In comparing Nādir with Alexander, an eighteenth-century writer said:

> It evidently appears, that in these ravages of the eastern world, Alexander and Nadir were actuated by the same predominant passion; an unbounded desire of conquest. Alexander indeed had the strongest desire of fame and glory; Nadir added to his delight in military achievements an insatiable thirst of accumulating riches. . . . Alexander was most beloved; Nadir most feared. The one affected to a love to mankind; the other did not so much as pretend to act upon principles of humanity.[56]

It was not, however, Nādir's irredentist and expansionist wars as such that weakened Iran. No doubt they were a severe drain on

[54] See Lockhart, *Nadir Shah*, p. 226.
[55] *Ibid.*, p. 250.
[56] Hanway, *op. cit.*, II, 353.

Iranian material and human resources. But still worse was his unrealism. Whether he fought "wars of liberation" or of imperialist expansion, the welfare of his country, the relationship between his military capabilities and territorial objectives, the relationship between military means and political ends, and the coordination of military and nonmilitary forms of power never received any serious consideration. For these reasons it is perhaps unfortunate that some historians have spoken of him as a "military genius." Nādir was a military adventurer. His boldness and courage were eclipsed by the way he sacrificed Iran's human and material resources for the satisfaction of his insatiable passions.

Finally, a sixth factor that contributed to the weakness of Iran was fratricide and murder of rivals generally. In the absence of accepted principles governing succession to the throne, Iranian monarchs and royal families engaged in this practice from the reign of Shah Ṭahmāsb (1524-76) to the establishment of the Qājār dynasty in 1794. To list a few examples, Ismā'īl II put to death his two brothers for fear of their rivalry for the Crown. He then killed in one day six other princes. Shah 'Abbās the Great killed his eldest son and blinded two others. Nādir was succeeded by his nephew, who was murdered by his brother, who was in turn killed by the partisans of Nādir's grandson. The fratricidal activities of the Ṣafavī monarchs were matched by similar practices among various tribal groups and dynastic factions claiming the Crown of Iran after the death of Nādir Shah and during the ensuing chaos. Nādir's grandson, Shāhrukh Mīrzā, who was twice deposed and restored to the throne and blinded in the process, ruled only over Khorasan, while in Isfahan and Shiraz the struggle for the throne occupied some tribal groups. From these Karīm Khān of the Zand clan first emerged as the *de facto* ruler of southern Iran, and by 1779 he practically ruled over all of the country except Khorasan. His short rule was followed by another series of fratricidal wars which destroyed the strength of his dynasty, while his former prisoner, Āghā Muḥammad, of the Qājār tribe, was consolidating his control over Iran. He was the actual founder of the Qājār dynasty, which was the ruling dynasty at the time when Iran was drawn into European power politics.

THE LEGACY OF THE EARLY CENTURIES

In the foregoing discussion of the emergence, survival, and weakness of Iran we have seen the triangular interaction between internal conditions, external affairs, and the foreign policy of Iran in the sixteenth, seventeenth, and eighteenth centuries. This interaction bequeathed a composite legacy to Iran's policy makers in the nineteenth century. The legacy of the early centuries may be summarized to show the main characteristics of Iran's political system and foreign policy.

The most outstanding characteristic of the political system was the monarchy. The basically theocratic state which had emerged at the turn of the sixteenth century was marked by secular absolutism about a century later. Absolute monarchy was the most important unifying factor so long as the monarch in power possessed the will and the means necessary to maintain order. In the absence of such a ruler, the lack of social cohesion and political consensus compounded by the decline of the Shīʿī ideology was an important source of weakness in Iran. This weakness was aggravated by Iranian isolationism, which was in part a product of fanatic adherence to Shīʿī dogma. It was also accentuated by irredentist and expansionist wars.

Iranian foreign policy in the early centuries was generally marked by two basic characteristics. One characteristic concerned the foreign-policy process. The monarchy was the most structured unit of foreign-policy making. The nature of the foreign-policy decisions was significantly influenced by the character of the individual monarch. An incompetent ruler would be incapable of maintaining political order, and his failure to do so would invite foreign intervention and occcupation. A strong ruler, on the other hand, would be able to revive the state after its collapse and reestablish its former political boundaries and independence.

The other outstanding characteristic of Iran's foreign policy was the tendency of its policy makers to adopt objectives beyond their means. The objectives and means of the state were those of the monarch. The means most often preferred was war, whether it was motivated by religious dogmatism, by irredentism and expansionism, or by the desire to restore or defend the independence of the state with which the monarch and his dynasty were closely identified.

Chapter II

The Internal and External Situation, the Alliances, and the Wars, 1801-1857

IN THE nineteenth century, as earlier, the foreign policy of Iran interacted with the internal and external situation. But conditions were not quite the same. The external environment in the nineteenth century in particular was vastly different from that of the sixteenth to eighteenth centuries. On the other hand, there were striking resemblances in the internal conditions of Iran during the two periods.

THE INTERNAL SITUATION

The basic features of Iran's internal setting in the sixteenth to the eighteenth centuries continued into the nineteenth century. The outstanding feature of the political system was the monarchy. This institution remained as the most structured unit of decision making. It also continued as the all-important unifying factor, although the lack of social cohesion, the divided loyalties, and the problem of succession to the throne continued to haunt the Iranian polity. Monarchical absolutism in the nineteenth century was almost identical with that in the times of Shah 'Abbās the Great and Nādir Shah. J. B. Fraser's remarks about the absolute nature of the monarchy in the early nineteenth century bring to mind the comments of Father Krusinski about the despotism of Shah 'Abbās the Great. Said Fraser:

The nobles and superior officers of the court subjected absolutely to the caprice of a tyrant who can neither endure opposition nor disappointment, though they may continue cringing and abject to him, become in their turn, cruel, haughty and imperious to their inferiors; and these again are delighted, when they can exercise the same petty tyranny upon such as may be unhappily subjected to their power.[1]

The monarch's absolutism at the end of the nineteenth century was as unbridled as it had been before. Lord Curzon aptly summarized the Iranian government:

In a country so backward in constitutional progress, so destitute of forms and statutes and characters, and so firmly stereotyped in the immemorial traditions of the East, the personal element, as might be expected, is largely in the ascendant; and the government of Persia is little else than the arbitrary exercise of authority by a series of units in a descending scale from the sovereign to the headman of a petty village.[2]

As a consequence of the introduction of the electric telegraph into Iran in the latter part of the nineteenth century, Nāṣir al-Dīn Shah became "the most powerful monarch of Persia since Nadir Shah."[3] He had absolute command over the life and property of every one of his subjects. His sons had no independent power and could be reduced to impotence or beggary in the twinkling of an eye. The ministers were elevated and degraded at the royal pleasure. The sovereign was the sole executive, and all officials were his deputies.[4]

In the nineteenth century, as in the previous centuries, the character of the monarch was of crucial significance for the state. The Shah's decisions were final. If he was unwise and capricious, the country suffered with – and from – him. If he was prudent and realistic, the country profited accordingly. But the latter was seldom the case in the nineteenth century, in part because, side by side with absolutism, the

[1] Quoted in Ann K. S. Lambton, *Landlord and Peasant in Persia* (London, 1953), p. 136.

[2] George N. Curzon, *Persia and the Persian Question* (London, 1892), I, 391.

[3] *Ibid.*, II, 615.

[4] *Ibid.*, I, 392.

Qājār monarchs inherited the injurious practices and superstitions of their predecessors. One of the most harmful practices had been, it may be recalled, that of confining heirs to the throne to the harem, with the result that rulers ascended the throne with little or no experience in affairs of state. The Qājār dynasty continued this practice after a fashion. The reigning monarch would appoint the future Shah to the governorship of Azerbaijan, a province that he could not leave; and exiled there, he remained "in total ignorance of the politics and statecraft of Tehran, of the ministers whom he might have to depend upon, the system which he might have to dispense, the people whom he might have to rule." [5] Furthermore, some of the Qājār rulers were swayed as much by Shī'ī superstitions as had been the Ṣafavī rulers generations before them. Fatḥ 'Alī Shah, in particular, resembled Shah Ṭahmāsb and Shah Sultān Ḥusayn in this respect.[6]

In the nineteenth century, as previously, the death of the ruling monarch would plunge the country into chaos and disorder, partly because the problem of succession had not been resolved. For example, various claimants to the throne rose up in arms after the deaths of Āghā Muḥammad Shah in 1797 and Fatḥ 'Alī Shah in 1834. The death of Muḥammad Shah in 1848 was followed by a general outbreak of rebellion in the country.[7] In both 1834 and 1848 foreign intervention – British and subsequently Anglo-Russian [8] – was needed to settle the problem of succession and to maintain the appearance of unity.

The age-old problem of lack of social cohesion also continued into the nineteenth century. This problem, it may be recalled, had been aggravated as the result of the Turkish and Mongol invasions, which had introduced additional divisions between Turks and Tājīk and conqueror and the conquered into Iranian society. The former division had far-reaching political consequences in the nineteenth century. The Turks and Persians for all practical purposes "divided the kingdom," to borrow the words of Sir Henry Rawlinson. By the mid-nineteenth century it was feared that an internecine struggle between the two factions would lead to the "dismemberment of the empire." [9]

[5] *Ibid.*, p. 413.

[6] Sa'īd Nafīsī, *Tārīkh-i Ijtimā'ī va Sīyāsī-i Īrān* (Tehran, 1335 [1956/57]), I, 76.

[7] *Ibid.*, pp. 74-75.

[8] Curzon, *op. cit.*, I, 406.

[9] *England and Russia in the East* (London, 1875), pp. 74-76.

Finally, in the nineteenth century as in previous centuries the fortunes of the state were closely tied to the strength of the monarch. In the absence of a ruler who had the will and the means to keep the country united, disintegrative tendencies would well up and threaten the political stability and independence of the state. Traditionally the rulers subdued divisive forces by force of arms, but in the nineteenth century it was more often the British commitment to the *status quo* in Iran that discouraged internal disruption. Such disruption, the British feared, would play into the hands of Russia, their most persistent rival.

THE EXTERNAL SITUATION

Although Iran's internal affairs had many of the same characteristics as those of the earlier era, its external affairs were significantly different. For over two centuries Iran had been primarily concerned with Turkey. During much of that time the two Muslim states had been engaged in inconclusive wars. This bilateral antagonism had been replaced for a short time by a triangular struggle between Iran, Turkey, and Russia in the eighteenth century. By the end of that century Iran was no longer preoccupied with Turkey. And soon thereafter it became an object of Anglo-Russian rivalry. This rivalry characterized the external background of Iranian foreign policy during most of the nineteenth century and, as we shall see, continued on into the twentieth century.

The rivalry was a product of the conflicting interests of Great Britain and Russia in Iran. Great Britain's interests in Iran were inextricably bound up with British imperial interests in India.[10] Whether it was the Persian, the Central Asian, or the Persian Gulf Question that occupied the minds of British policy makers, the paramount consideration was the maintenance of British imperial interests in India. Because of this preeminent objective, the British government was basically committed to a policy of the *status quo* in Iran.[11] Pursuance of this policy often required advancing British influence,

[10] See *ibid.* and Rose Louise Greaves, *Persia and the Defence of India, 1884-1892* (London, 1959).

[11] T. E. Gordon, "The Problem of the Middle East," *Nineteenth Century*, XLVII (1900), 413-24.

but on the whole this influence was sought primarily in order to counter the Russian threat to the independence of Iran. Great Britain needed Iran as a buffer state, and perhaps the stronger the buffer the better.[12]

It is oversimplification, however, to ascribe a single definite characteristic to British policy in Iran throughout the nineteenth century. Even opposition to Russia was not always uniform. Some of the severest criticisms of British policy in Iran were based on occasional British failures to oppose the expansion of Russia. One critic went so far as to call the sometime British lethargy "criminal." [13] But a more sophisticated critic, Lord Curzon, stated that British policy had always been "characterized by a note of exaggeration." [14] A similar characterization had been given earlier by Rawlinson. His treatment of British policy from 1800 to 1875 revealed British vacillation in Iran with its extremes of lethargy and zeal.[15]

It is possible, however, to generalize about Anglo-Russian influence in Iran during the nineteenth century. By the latter part of the century British influence had diminished as compared with earlier years. At the same time the influence of Russia had escalated until it was dominant in Iran in 1900.[16] The feverish activities of the British toward the end of the nineteenth century did not put their influence on a par with that of the Russians even though Britain was paramount in the south as was Russia in the north.

The center of the Anglo-Russian rivalry was not constant throughout the century. In the early years Azerbaijan was the main focus of pressure because of the direction of Russian expansion – into the Caucasus. By the latter quarter of the century the center of rivalry was Khorasan in the east, again because of the direction of the Russian expansion, which was then into Central Asia. By the end of

[12] Most Iranian writers take the view that Great Britain, being "afraid" of the cultural influence of Iran in India, strove to weaken Iran! See, for example, such Iranian sources as Nafīsī, *op. cit.*, and Maḥmūd Maḥmūd, *Tārīkh-i Ravābiṭ-i Sīyāsī-i Īrān va Inglīs dar Qarn-i Nūzdahum-i Mīladī* (Tehran, 1336 [1957/58]).

[13] See Armenius Vambery, *The Coming Struggle for India* (London, 1885).

[14] *Op. cit.*, II, 606.

[15] *Op. cit.*, pp. 1-135.

[16] Russia believed, at this time, that its position in northern Iran was "unassailable." See William L. Langer, *The Diplomacy of Imperialism, 1890-1902* (New York, 1935), p. 666. See also Arminius Vambery, *Western Culture in Eastern Lands: A Comparison of the Methods Adopted by England and Russia in the Middle East* (New York, 1906), pp. 367-69.

the century the Persian Gulf was also a center of Anglo-Russian rival ambitions because of Russian attempts to obtain a foothold in the Gulf.

The foregoing general discussion of the basic characteristics of the internal and external settings provides an over-all context for the analysis of Iran's foreign policy during the nineteenth century. This discussion has given us a general view of those internal and external patterns which interacted with foreign policy. The rest of this chapter and the next two chapters will examine the major aspects of Iran's foreign policy in the nineteenth century. An attempt will be made to show systematically the constancy of interaction between specific foreign-policy decisions of Iran and concrete internal and external factors. The remaining pages of this chapter will be devoted to an examination of Iranian wars and alliances of the nineteenth century. These developments signaled Iran's increasing involvement in European power politics.

THE FIRST ALLIANCE WITH GREAT BRITAIN

Iran's first alliance with a European power was made with Great Britain in 1801. The initiative came from Great Britain, which believed that its interests in India were threatened and that an alliance with Iran might mitigate the danger. The threat emanated from two different sources, Afghanistan and France. Afghan designs on India dated back to the establishment of Afghanistan by Aḥmad Khān (1743-73), but the Afghan threat increased during the reign of Zamān Shah (1793-1800). Following his grandfather's policy toward India, Zamān Shah invaded the Punjab in 1797, reached Lahore, and prepared to march on Delhi.[17]

A simultaneous threat to India was posed by Napoleon. He landed troops in Egypt in 1798, took Alexandria and Cairo, and subsequently planned an invasion of India. Napoleon conceived the plan in collaboration with Paul I of Russia. According to the plan, a large force of Cossacks and Russian irregulars would march by way of Turkistan, Khiva, and Bokhara to the Upper Indus Valley. At the same time French troops would descend the Danube and, going by way of the

[17] For details, see Sir Percy Sykes, *A History of Afghanistan* (London, 1940), I, 370-73.

Black and the Caspian seas, would attack Iran and unite with the Russians near the Indus.[18]

Fatḥ ʿAlī Shah and his courtiers favored the British-Indian move for an alliance with Iran. The Shah was influenced by two major considerations. First, the British proposals for an offensive alliance against Afghanistan were in full accord with his irredentist expeditions against that country. The Shah had personally led the army against Afghanistan in 1799 before the British proposals reached the Court.[19] Second, the Shah and his Vizier, Hājī Ibrāhīm, found it difficult to turn down the British proposals, which were accompanied by lavish expenditures, generous gifts, and bribes on the part of Captain Malcolm, the British agent.[20]

The major provisions of this treaty of alliance follow:

1) *Afghanistan*: Iran would attack Afghanistan if it invaded India. Iran would also obtain an Afghan promise to abandon aggressive designs on India in any peace treaty that it might sign with Afghanistan.

2) *France*: Iran and Great Britain would take joint action against any attempt by France at gaining a foothold in Iran.

3) *Military Aid*: Great Britain would assist Iran with military equipment and technicians in case Iran was attacked by Afghanistan or France.[21]

The course of events soon scrapped the alliance. Great Britain lost interest because it recognized that the threat to India had passed away. The Afghan menace disappeared with the death of Zamān Shah, and French designs on India were overshadowed, at the time, by the Peace of Amiens (1802).

Conversely, the alliance took on added significance for Iran. The Shah was at war with Russia. He claimed British military assistance

[18] J. A. R. Marriott, *The Eastern Question: An Historical Study in European Diplomacy* (4th ed., repr. Oxford, 1951), p. 171.

[19] Rawlinson, *op. cit.*, pp. 6-7.

[20] J. W. Kaye, *The Life and Correspondence of Sir John Malcolm* (London, 1856), I, 133, 138.

[21] This instrument was ratified by a *farmān* on the part of Iran because the Shah could not sign a treaty made with an envoy coming from a ruler of a lower rank, that is, the Governor-General of India. See *ibid.*, p. 143. The text of the treaty is in J. C. Hurewitz, *Diplomacy in the Near and Middle East* (Princeton, N.J., 1956), I, 68-70.

under the treaty, but Great Britain was reluctant to aid Iran. This reluctance was due mainly to improved relations with Russia in 1804. The early signs of Anglo-Russian *rapprochement* were emerging "owing to their alarm at the intrigues of Napoleon in Albania and Morea." At the same time the Shah was finding it increasingly difficult to resist the expansion of Russia. The Tsar's forward thrust in western Georgia, Armenia, and Azerbaijan, and particularly the Russian conquest of Erivan, alarmed the Shah.

THE ALLIANCE WITH FRANCE

Iran's second alliance with a European power was with France. Resistance to Russian expansion influenced Fatḥ 'Alī Shah's decision to ally himself with France, but the alliance was influenced by other considerations as well. One of the most important was irredentism. The alliance with Great Britain had been aimed principally at the recovery of the Afghan territories, and the one with France was to aid the regaining of Georgia from Russia. Aware of the Shah's territorial ambitions, Napoleon flattered the Shah with the memory of the extensive empire of Nādir Shah [22] and promised to compel Russia to return Georgia to Iran.

The fundamental objective of France in Iran was to gain a stepping stone to India. Toward this end France sought to ally itself with Iran in 1802, 1804, and 1805 without success. The main reason for the failure of France was the paramount British influence at the Iranian Court. This influence began to diminish, however, as the war with Russia progressed and as Great Britain proved reluctant to aid Iran militarily. The way for an alliance between France and Iran was thus opened. The Shah dispatched Mīrzā Muḥammad Riẕā Khān, the governor of Qazvin, to Europe to sign an alliance with Napoleon.[23] This was done in Finkenstein in 1807. The major provisions of the treaty may be summarized as follows:

[22] Napoleon sent two letters to Fatḥ 'Alī Shah, one in 1805 and the other in the following year. He wrote the Shah that in an alliance with "the most powerful state in the West" (namely, France) the Iranian ruler would be able to expand his territory beyond the former boundaries of Nādir Shah. For the text of these letters, see Maḥmūd, *op. cit.*, I, 39-44.

[23] *Ibid.*

1) *France*: France recognized that Georgia "legitimately" belonged to Iran and promised to do everything in its power "to compel Russia to relinquish Georgia." France also pledged to supply Iran with military equipment, to train the Iranian forces, and to assist the construction of military facilities.

2) *Iran*: Iran promised to break diplomatic and commercial ties with and to declare war on Great Britain at once, to incite the Afghans to attack India, and to grant France a right of way over Iranian territory if France decided to invade India.[24]

Napoleon regarded his alliance with the Shah quite seriously at first. He sent Lucien Bonaparte, the most able of his brothers, to fill the post of Ambassador at Tehran and dispatched a military mission to Tehran under General Gardane. The mission began reorganizing and modernizing the Iranian army, but Iranian officials proved apathetic and interested primarily in personal gains.[25] Other compelling reasons, however, halted the activities of the mission. First, France became friendly with Russia. In 1807, the year of the signing of the Franco-Iranian alliance, Napoleon and Alexander met at Tilsit to end their war and form an alliance. Second, Great Britain seriously opposed the activities of the French mission. Napoleon had instructed General Gardane "to institute inquiries, reconnaissance operations and reports which might conduce to discerning the obstacles that an expedition would encounter in passing through Persia, a route that ought to be followed into India, whether the point of departure is Aleppo or one of the ports of the Persian Gulf." [26] Britain might well have been expected to object.

The weakening of the French alliance did not change Fatḥ 'Alī Shah's determination to recover Georgia. He refused General Gardane's offer of mediation between Iran and Russia,[27] continued the war, and cast about for a new ally.

[24] The text is in Hurewitz, *op. cit.*, I, 77-78.

[25] For detailed information on the Gardane mission and its activities, see Nafīsī, *op. cit.*, pp. 100-21.

[26] For the text of these instructions, see Hurewitz, *op. cit.*, I, 78-81.

[27] See Nafīsī, *op. cit.*, p. 121.

OTHER ALLIANCES WITH GREAT BRITAIN

Great Britain had its own reasons for concluding several new alliances with Iran. Alarmed by the French activities and the increasing French influence at the Iranian Court, Great Britain sought to undermine the Shah's friendship with France.[28] This was easy to accomplish after Iran's alliance with France lapsed and Russia's alliance with Napoleon began. As a result, Great Britain and Iran signed a new treaty in 1809.[29] Between this year and 1814 the two countries concluded three treaties. Their major provisions were as follows:

1) Iran's alliance with Napoleon was nullified, and the Shah's government undertook to prevent the French army from proceeding to India through Iranian territory.

2) Great Britain would refrain from interfering in any war between Iran and Afghanistan, and Iran would send an army against the Afghans if they entered into war with Great Britain.[30]

3) Great Britain would assist Iran financially and militarily if it was attacked by any European power. However, the financial aid would not be given "in case the war with such European nation shall have been produced by an aggression on the part of Persia."

The last provision gave rise to differences between Iran and Great Britain in 1826 when war broke out between Iran and Russia after Russia occupied Gokchah, a disputed territory, in 1825. The Shah demanded British assistance, under the terms of his alliance with Great Britain. Great Britain refused to consider the demand and contended that "the occupation by Russian troops of a portion of uninhabited ground, which by right belonged to Persia, even if admitted to have been the proximate cause of hostilities, did not constitute the cause of aggression contemplated in the treaty of Tehran (1814)." [31]

Ultimately the British did give the Shah financial assistance –

[28] Rawlinson, *op. cit.*, pp. 18-20. See also Kaye, *op. cit.*, pp. 418-19.
[29] This preliminary agreement was signed by Sir Harford Jones, the London representative, while Sir John Malcolm was also in Iran representing the British India government. See Kaye, *op. cit.*, p. 439.
[30] The text of the definitive treaty is in Hurewitz, *op. cit.*, I, 86-88.
[31] Rawlinson, *op. cit.*, pp. 33-38.

200,000 tomans – to pay the indemnity demanded by the Russians in the Treaty of Turkumanchai (1828) which ended the war (see below). But the Shah had to consent to British cancellation of the aid provisions of the alliance of 1814 in return for the money. For Great Britain this cancellation was a diplomatic triumph inasmuch as it wished "to disencumber" itself "of a falling ally." Great Britain "had awoke to a sense of the worthlessness of Persia." British efforts "to make her strong had but contributed to her weakness. We had been building on a quicksand. The country existed only by the sufferance of her northern neighbour; and it was useless therefore to undergo further expense, or to encounter further risk on her behalf." [32]

AN IRANIAN IRREDENTA

Fatḥ ʻAlī Shah's determination to recover Georgia motivated in part his wars with Russia as it did his alliance with Great Britain and France. Iran lost Georgia in the eighteenth century. This loss was consequent to the assassination of Nādir Shah and the subsequent internal chaos. In the absence of a strong ruler Iran's control over Georgia became untenable. Prolonged economic oppression and maltreatment had caused much discontent among the Georgian people. These and other factors prompted Heraclius, the ruler of Georgia, to free his land upon Nādir's death. In order to avoid reannexation by Iran, he threw in his lot with Russia in 1783, signing a treaty by which all his ties with Iran were renounced and Russia was declared an ally.[33]

In 1795 Āghā Muḥammad, the founder of the Qājār dynasty, claimed Georgia on the ground that it had "belonged" to Iran.[34] Heraclius refused to do homage to him, and Āghā Muḥammad overran Erivan, Shisha, and Ganja, captured Tiflis, and massacred Georgian men, women, and children of all ages. In 1796 Catherine attempted to avenge Āghā Muḥammad's "encroachments" and extend

[32] *Ibid.*

[33] Detailed information may be derived from David Marshall Lang, *The Last Years of the Georgian Monarchy, 1658-1832* (New York, 1957), and from W. E. D. Allen, *A History of the Georgian People: From the Beginning down to the Russian Conquest in the Nineteenth Century* (London, 1932).

[34] Nafīsī, *op. cit.*, pp. 230-36.

Russia's control over Georgia, but the news of her death caused the withdrawal of the Russian army. Āghā Muḥammad attacked Georgia again and captured the stronghold of Shisha. A rising tide of discontent, however, led to his assassination in 1797.[35]

Fatḥ 'Alī Shah (1797-1834), Āghā Muḥammad's nephew and successor, continued his predecessor's irredentist policy. He aimed at Georgia's complete and unconditional surrender to Iran.[36] George XII, the Georgian ruler, wished to keep his land out of the control of both Iran and Russia, but the Shah's demand for total control forced him to turn to Russia.

This fitted in most advantageously with Russia's desire to control all of Transcaucasia. In 1800 George offered his Crown to Paul. A year later Russia officially annexed Georgia. In a manifesto Alexander claimed that the object of Russia's annexation was not aggrandizement because the annexation was in the interest of "humanity and justice."[37]

THE FIRST WAR WITH RUSSIA

Fatḥ 'Alī Shah fought two wars with Russia over Georgia. The first war broke out in 1804. The Shah's irredentism was matched by the expansionist zeal of Alexander, "the Tsar of Peace." He suddenly turned his attention from Russia's internal problems to the field of foreign relations. Russia was already in possession of eastern Georgia. Alexander now embarked upon the conquest of western Georgia, which was regarded by Russia as the strategic key to all the northern provinces of Iran. The Russian forces overran the Sultanate of Shurgel, a part of the Khanate of Erivan. The Iranian army took the field under the command of 'Abbās Mīrzā, the heir apparent. The war dragged on until 1813.

Iran's objective was the recovery of Georgia. The fact that the Georgians had thrown in their lot with Russia and the latter had officially annexed Georgia did not deter Fatḥ 'Alī Shah. Nor did he take cognizance of the fact that his own policy and that of Āghā

[35] Allen, *op. cit.*, pp. 213-14.
[36] *Ibid.*, pp. 215-17.
[37] For detailed information, see Nafīsī, *op. cit.*, pp. 237-42, and Lang, *op. cit.*, pp. 245-66.

Muḥammad Shah before him had created much dissatisfaction among the Georgian people.[38] Yet, it was not the Shah's objective as such that proved harmful to Iran. The fundamental harm came from the disparity between objective and capability. The Shah attempted to recover Georgia from Russia with an unprepared army. A close observer of the Iranian forces described them harshly:

> The disciplined forces of Persia, considered as an army – were from the epoch of their first creation contemptible. Beyond drill and exercise, they never had anything in common with the regular armies of Europe and India. System was entirely wanted, whether in regard to pay, clothing, food, carriage, equipage, commissariat, promotion or command; and under a lath-and-plaster Government like that of Persia, such must have inevitably been the case.[39]

Fatḥ 'Alī Shah not only fought an unprepared war but also refused to conclude a favorable peace when it was possible. After France made peace with Russia at Tilsit, it strove to mediate between Iran and Russia. Russia was willing to negotiate a peaceful settlement at the time, but Fatḥ 'Alī Shah insisted intransigently that peace would be made only if Russia relinquished Georgia.[40] The loss of this opportunity in 1807 prolonged the war. Finally, in 1812 the Iranian forces were annihilated in a battle at Aslandoz. In 1813 Iran signed the unfavorable Treaty of Gulistan with Russia as a result of British mediation.

The main provisions of the treaty may be summarized as follows:

1) *Territorial*: Iran acknowledged the sovereignty of Russia over Karabagh, Georgia, Shaki, Shiravan, Derbend, Kobeh, Daghistan, Abtichar, a part of Talish, and "all the territory between the Caucasus and the Caspian Sea."

2) *Maritime*: Iran conceded to Russia the exclusive right to sail ships of war on the Caspian Sea.[41]

[38] Nafīsī, *op. cit.*, p. 75.
[39] Rawlinson, *op. cit.*, p. 31.
[40] Nafīsī, *op. cit.*, pp. 139-51.
[41] The text is in Hurewitz, *op. cit.*, I, 84-86.

THE SECOND WAR WITH RUSSIA

The disastrous defeat of the Iranian army and Iran's acknowledgment of the loss of Georgia did not deter Fatḥ 'Alī Shah from pressing for the recovery of Georgia. A pretext was soon found. The vagueness of the Treaty of Gulistan gave rise to a dispute between Iran and Russia over three districts in Transcaucasia, including Gokchah. Hasty negotiations having failed, Russia promptly occupied it in 1825. Iran regarded this as a *casus belli.* The Shī'ī clergy, aroused by Russia's mistreatment of the Muslims of Ganja and Karabagh, issued a *fatwā* (a religious decree) for holy war against Russia.[42]

Once again the Shah went to war without being prepared for it. The war broke out in 1826. The Iranian army was no better equipped in 1826 than in 1813. In fact, it was worse off. "When Persia again came into collision with Russia," Rawlinson testifies, "Her means and power as a military nation were positively inferior to those which she had possessed at the close of her former struggle." The war continued until 1828 and was a disaster for Iran. Its cavalry was demoralized by Russian artillery fire at the battle of Shamkar, and the Russian forces overran Erivan, Nakhichevan, and Abbasabad. The arsenal at Tabriz was captured, in part because the Shah refused to supply the necessary funds for its defense.[43]

Having occupied Tabriz, Russia dictated the peace. The Treaty of Turkumanchai, which was concluded in 1828, was not so unfavorable to Iran in terms of territorial losses as had been the Treaty of Gulistan. Nevertheless, it has gone down in Iran's diplomatic history as the most humiliating treaty Iran ever signed with a foreign power. It provided the basis for the establishment of a capitulatory regime in Iran. Its main provisions were:

1) *Territorial*: Russia annexed Erivan and Nakhichevan. The former involved the territory on both sides of the Aras River.

2) *Capitulatory*: No Iranian official was allowed to enter the

[42] Robert Grant Watson states that the contemptuous treatment of Muslims by Russia in the area under its sway prior to the occupation of Gokchah had increased the pressure of the clergy on the Shah so greatly that after the seizure of the area he had to go to war. See his *A History of Persia* (London, 1866), ch. viii.

[43] Nafīsī, *op. cit.*, pp. 76-77.

premises owned by Russian subjects residing in Iran without prior authorization by Russia. All litigations involving the subjects of Russia came under the exclusive jurisdiction of Russian authorities in Iran.

3) *Pecuniary*: Iran was to pay twenty thousand silver rubles as indemnity for "the considerable sacrifices that the war had occasioned to Russia." [44]

THE WAR WITH GREAT BRITAIN OVER HERAT

Iran fought its last irredentist war of the despotic period in 1856-57. This war, which was with Great Britain over Herat, was similar to the ones with Russia over Georgia.

Iran had lost Herat, like Georgia, in the eighteenth century after the assassination of Nādir Shah and amid the ensuing internal disorder. Aḥmad Khān, the commander of the Abdālī contingent, broke away from the Iranian army, occupied Herat, and set the foundation of the independent kingdom of Afghanistan.

The Qājār rulers claimed Herat as they had claimed Georgia. Fatḥ 'Alī Shah led two expeditions for the recovery of Herat – in 1799 and 1800. The outbreak of his first war with Russia (1804) left the question of Herat in abeyance. Once the protracted hostilities with Russia were finally terminated, the problem of Herat was revived. 'Abbās Mīrzā, the heir apparent, marched on Herat. His purpose was twofold: he wished to return Herat to the control of Iran; he also sought to repair his prestige, which had suffered grievously in the war with Russia.[45]

Iran's decision to recover Herat brought it into conflict with Great Britain. The British interests in Herat were linked to Great Britain's imperial interests in India. Herat was regarded as the starting point of routes to Kabul and Qandahar from which ran natural lines of invasion into India. For this reason Great Britain opposed Fatḥ 'Alī Shah's plan to capture Herat. British opposition stiffened when Muḥammad Shah (1834-48) ascended the throne of Iran. He, in contrast to Fatḥ 'Alī Shah, favored Russia over Great Britain. His

[44] The text of this treaty and an important commercial treaty signed on the same date are in Hurewitz, *op. cit.*, I, 96-102.

[45] Rawlinson, *op. cit.*, p. 49.

control of Herat, then, might well bring Russian influence to the gates of India.[46]

In spite of British opposition the Shah attempted to seize Herat in 1836-38. The Iranian army, however, failed here as it had failed in the wars with Russia. And this defeat was even more humiliating. The Shah's army proved unequal to an undisciplined eastern army without the benefit of any modern weapons of warfare. The Afghan swordsmen drove the Iranian besiegers back. The Shah attempted to cover up the ensuing disgrace by blaming the defeat of his army on Perovski, a Russian general who had planned the attack. In the meantime Great Britain began a show of force in the Persian Gulf. The Shah utilized the British maneuver as a face-saving device. He pretended that only the action of a great power like Great Britain could force him to terminate the seizure of Herat, and he proclaimed officially that Herat belonged to Iran and that its capture was still an important objective of his policy.[47]

This objective was inherited by his successor, who clashed with Great Britain in 1856. Nāṣir al-Dīn Shah (1848-96) was no less an irredentist monarch than his predecessors. The real instigator in this second attempt against Herat was probably Mīrzā Āqā Khān Nūrī, the Shah's Grand Vizier, rather than Russia, but Great Britain still suspected Iran's attitude toward Russia.[48] In anticipation of the Crimean War (1854-56) Russia had secretly obtained an agreement from the Shah in 1853 to take military action, at Tabriz and Kermanshah, against the enemies of Russia. Great Britain regarded this undertaking as a committal on the part of Iran to a course of quasi-hostility. The deteriorating relations between Great Britain and Iran took a turn for the worse in 1856, when Iran marched on Herat and occupied it without resistance.

Reluctantly Great Britain declared war on Iran. Strategically it was easier to attack Iran from the Persian Gulf than overland. The island of Khark was occupied, and the British forces overwhelmed the Iranian army, which twice fled panic-stricken, leaving munitions behind. The government of the Shah then sued for peace, and a

[46] Philip E. Mosely, *Russian Diplomacy and the Opening of the Eastern Question in 1838 and 1839* (Cambridge, 1934), pp. 3-4.

[47] The text of this proclamation is in Maḥmūd, *op. cit.*, pp. 275-76.

[48] A. P. Thornton, "British Policy in Persia, 1858-1890," *English Historical Review*, LXIX (1954), 554-79.

treaty was signed in Paris in 1857. By this agreement Iran relinquished all its territorial claims to Afghanistan, recognized the latter's independence, and pledged not to interfere in its internal affairs.

LACK OF A SENSE OF REALITY

The sovereign being "the sole executive" who could, to recall Lord Curzon's words, reduce his ministers or others "to impotence and beggary in the twinkling of an eye," the Qājār Shahs were the true makers of these alliances and the real instigators of these wars. They, like the Iranian monarchs of previous centuries, were identified with the state itself, and their means and ends were those of Iran. Before Iran was drawn into the scheme of European power politics, the process of weakening had already set in. Nevertheless, at the turn of the nineteenth century Iran enjoyed not only vast possessions but, more importantly, freedom from foreign domination. This was still the case when Fatḥ 'Alī Shah ascended the throne of Iran.

The policies of Fatḥ 'Alī Shah and his successors reduced Iran's power swiftly. In slightly over a decade the Shah lost enormous territories to Russia, losses which made the Caspian Sea a Russian lake. In the second war with Russia he lost more territory and opened the country to foreign domination through the grant of capitulatory privileges, first to Russia and subsequently to other European powers. Later the various campaigns against Afghanistan by Muḥammad Shah and Nāṣir al-Dīn Shah further dissipated Iran's human and material resources. These campaigns also led to the war with Great Britain, as the result of which Iran acknowledged the loss of Afghanistan. All these unprepared wars within a few decades resulted in Iran's becoming a weak state, inexorably caught between two rival powers pursuing opposing aims.

In all these wars, as well as alliances, Iran's fundamental objective was the recovery of former territories. The irredentist tendencies of the Qājār rulers surpassed those of Shah Ismā'īl, Shah Ṭahmāsb, Shah 'Abbās, Nādir Shah, and other Iranian monarchs of the sixteenth to the eighteenth centuries. Acquisition of the ancient frontiers of Iran, and even areas beyond, had been the goal of the foreign policy of many pre-nineteenth-century rulers. They had sought to maximize their personal and dynastic power by recovering former territories, by utilizing the Shīʿī ideology, or by recalling the greatness of the ancient past. The nineteenth-century monarchs aspired to reach the limits of the empire of Nādir Shah, if not of Cyrus the Great.

Monarchial irredentism was accompanied by a persistent disparity between the means and ends in the nineteenth-century wars. Fatḥ ʿAlī Shah went into unprepared wars with Russia, Muḥammad Shah with the Afghans, and Nāṣir al-Dīn Shah with Great Britain. They all insisted on the same goal of recovering Iran's former territories without recognizing the limitations of their power. As a result, to paraphrase Walter Lippmann's remarkably applicable words, preventable wars were not prevented, unavoidable wars were fought without being adequately prepared for, and settlements were made which were the prelude to a new cycle of unprepared wars and unavoidable settlements.

Chapter III

Boundary Problems, 1821-1905

IF ALLIANCES and wars dominated Iran's foreign policy in the first half of the nineteenth century, boundary problems and economic activities received major emphasis later. Not, of course, that boundary problems, with which this chapter will be concerned, did not exist earlier. But the Anglo-Russian rivalry, which continued to be such an important factor in Iranian foreign policy, reached a peak after Russian advances into Central Asia, and this intensified Iran's own boundary difficulties with Russia.

Anglo-Russian rivalry continued to be the most important factor with which Iran had to contend in foreign affairs. This rivalry intensified in the second half of the nineteenth century and reached a new peak after the spectacular Russian expansion in Central Asia. Iran's boundary problems with Russia and Afghanistan were intimately interwoven with the whole Central Asian Question.

Russia's advance into Central Asia has been attributed to a wide variety of considerations, different observers emphasizing different motives. Some have mentioned economic advantages, while others have remarked that "civilized Russians" had to advance against the "half-savages." Still others have characterized Russia's expansion in Central Asia as a way to solve the Eastern Question, a "detour on the royal road to Constantinople and the Straits." The road to the Straits had been barred by Great Britain; hence Russia had to strike at the enemy's heart – India. It has also been stated that Central Asia proved so attractive that Russia could not resist the temptation of conquest. The attraction of the area, it is argued, lay in the fact that a vast power vacuum stretched all the way from the Caspian Sea to the borders of China, from Afghanistan to the edge of the Siberian plain.[1] Another view stresses that the object of Russian policy in Central Asia was the attainment of an outlet to the ocean both in the Near and Middle East. This view linked the Central Asian Question to the Persian Gulf, where Russia wished to get a foothold.[2]

Whichever one of these interpretations is favored, the fact is that the Russian thrust in Central Asia posed a serious challenge to Great Britain. The Russian movement into Central Asia in the nineteenth century was a late phase in an expansion that had been in progress over several centuries.[3] But that expansion had never taken the form or reached the intensity of the momentous nineteenth-century forward advance. This conquest, which gained momentum in the 1860's, gave rise to grave concern on the part of the English public,[4] as well as to the British government. One of the earliest signs of apprehension may be found in Sir Henry Rawlinson's "Memorandum on the Central Asian Question" for government guidance. This memorandum had immediate effects in India.[5] It urged that action and zeal must replace the existing official apathy toward the Russian expansion. Rawlinson insisted that the easiest route for Russia to take toward India was not through the heart of Afghanistan by way of the difficult mountain passes to Kabul and the Khyber, but via the country's western flank, from the Caspian littoral down to Merv, Herat, and Qandahar. This

[1] See Firuz Kazemzadeh, "Russia and the Middle East," in Ivo J. Lederer (ed.), *Russian Foreign Policy: Essays in Historical Perspective* (New Haven, Conn., 1962), pp. 492-96. Information was also derived from Richard A. Pierce, *Russian Central Asia, 1867-1917: A Study in Colonial Rule* (Berkeley, Calif., 1960), pp. 17-18.

[2] See Geoffrey Drage, *Russian Affairs* (London, 1904), p. 564.

[3] Pierce, *op. cit.*, p. 17.

[4] See Charles Marvin, *Reconnoitring Central Asia* (London, 1886), p. 2.

[5] A. P. Thornton, "British Policy in Persia, 1858-1890," *English Historical Review,* LXIX (1954), 558.

flank was commanded, or at any rate presided over, by Iran. Iran's existence had always been a political necessity for the Indian Empire; now Iran's strength had become "a military requisite." [6]

The Central Asian problem affected Iran in two different but related ways. First, the Russian conquests east of the Caspian Sea made Russia the immediate neighbor of Iran along the borders of Khorasan. No definite frontiers had previously existed between Iran and its nomadic neighbors, and Russia's move into the area faced Iran with the question: Where would Russia stop? Second, Iran was affected by the strategic significance that the Russian advance in Central Asia added to the areas coveted by Iran. Sistan was one of these areas. Its geographic position and other features made it "an object of much interest both to Russia and Great Britain. Situated at the point of junction of the frontiers of Persia, Afghanistan, and Baluchistan, its future affects the destinies of all the three countries." [7] Great Britain, therefore, became directly involved in Iran's frontier problem with Afghanistan.

Before we discuss Iranian boundary problems with Russia and Afghanistan let us consider Iran's frontier problems with Turkey. As will be seen, this problem also became an object of interest to the rival powers.

BOUNDARY PROBLEMS WITH TURKEY

Iran's boundary dispute with Turkey in the nineteenth century was a legacy from an earlier era. The inconclusive wars of the Ṣafavīs had been concluded by a treaty in 1639. The ambiguous boundary provisions of this treaty had done little to help the relations of Iran and Turkey. The same vague provisions had been confirmed in the peace treaty of 1746 that terminated Nādir Shah's war with Turkey.[8]

The problem of the controversial boundaries continued into the

[6] *England and Russia in the East* (London, 1875), pp. 263-92. See also Thornton, *op. cit.*

[7] Rose Louise Greaves, *Persia and the Defence of India, 1884-1892* (London, 1959), p. 18.

[8] See Chapter I. The text of the treaties of 1639 and 1746 are in J. C. Hurewitz, *Diplomacy in the Near and Middle East* (Princeton, N. J., 1956), I, 21-23, 51-52.

nineteenth century.[9] Whether the war between Iran and Turkey which started in 1821 was instigated by Russia,[10] or by Great Britain,[11] the ambiguous terms of the old boundary treaties did not help the situation. The immediate cause of the war was, however, a dispute over wandering tribes. In 1821 the seraskier of Erzerum (in Turkey) and the governor of Tabriz (in Iran) wrangled over two wandering tribes which Iran claimed as its subjects and to which Turkey offered protection. The Turkish seraskier imprisoned an Iranian agent who was dispatched to him to present Iranian grievances. Fatḥ 'Alī Shah regarded the event as an insult and ordered the Iranian forces to attack the Turkish territory.[12]

The armed clash dragged on until 1823, when, as the result of British mediation, a new peace treaty was signed at Erzerum. The Treaty of Erzerum, like its predecessors signed in 1639 and 1746, failed to come to grips with the boundary dispute and the related problem of the tribes. Instead, it confirmed the terms of the previous treaty (signed in 1746) and confined itself to the two tribes, Hydranlo and Sibiker, over which had arisen the dispute that precipitated the war.[13]

The failure to demarcate the boundary definitively led to further tense relations between the two countries. Soon after the Treaty of Erzerum was signed, claims and counterclaims began to mount. Iran complained that some of its Kurdish tribes had been "unfairly" abstracted from its territory and demanded pecuniary compensation for having allowed the Turkish tribes of Sulaymaniyah to pasture their flocks on Iranian soil during the summer months. Turkey protested Iran's retention of the district of the bridge of Zohab on the frontier of Kermanshah.[14] From 1834 to 1840 tensions increased dangerously. The districts of Kotur and Khoi were ravaged, the district of Margavar was plundered, and Turkish troops attacked and demolished the commercial town of Mohammarah. Iran demanded immediate satisfaction. The Porte retorted that Mohammarah, like Basra and

[9] Sir A. W. Ward and G. P. Gooch, *The Cambridge History of British Foreign Policy* (New York, 1923), II, 204.

[10] Sir Percy Sykes, *A History of Persia* (London, 1930), II, 316.

[11] Maḥmūd Farhād Mu'tamid, *Tārikh-i Ravābiṭ-i Sīyāsī-i Īrān va Us̱mānī* (Tehran, 1326 [1947/48]), p. 29.

[12] Robert Grant Watson, *A History of Persia* (London, 1866), pp. 197-202.

[13] The text of the Treaty of Erzerum is in Hurewitz, *op. cit.*, I, 90-92.

[14] Watson, *op. cit.*, pp. 336-37.

Baghdad, belonged to Turkey, and no compensation was due. In the meantime a number of the Shī'ī inhabitants of Kerbela were murdered.[15]

War between Iran and Turkey threatened, but British mediation averted it. Great Britain's active conciliatory efforts, beginning in 1842, added an international dimension to the boundary dispute. British interest in the boundary settlement was both political and commercial. The Foreign Office feared that more armed clashes between the two Muslim states would further weaken them. This was contrary to the British policy for the Middle East, as these states separated the possessions of Russia from those of Great Britain in India.[16] Great Britain was also interested in opening new channels of commercial intercourse with the East through the Irano-Turkish domains. It was hoped that the activities of British agents in the border areas in connection with boundary demarcation endeavors would produce useful knowledge in regard to "these little known areas." [17]

Consistent British efforts resulted in the creation of a boundary commission, composed of Iranian, Turkish, British, and Russian commissioners – Russia participated at the invitation of Great Britain. The commission's work between 1843 and 1847 produced a new agreement between Iran and Turkey (1847), which confirmed some of the provisions of the previous treaties but also contained a few new boundaries. Iran undertook to relinquish the extensive province of Zohab, i. e., its western territory. In return, Turkey recognized the sovereignty of Iran over the town and port of Mohammarah, the island of Al Khizr, and the lands on the left side (the eastern bank) of the Shatt al-Arab, which were admittedly in the possession of Iranian tribes.[18]

The boundary having been defined in general terms, another commission, composed like the first one, covered the frontier zone (1848-52). Its surveys were discontinued during the Crimean War but were resumed in 1857. The British and Russian surveyors labored for eight years in St. Petersburg and in 1865 produced two separate maps "in the eight first sheets of which were four thousand dis-

[15] Mu'tamid, *op. cit.*, p. 36.

[16] Rawlinson, *op. cit.*, p. 66.

[17] See "Correspondence respecting the Demarcation of the Frontier between Turkey and Persia, 1847-1865," Great Britain, *British and Foreign State Papers* (1865-66), LVI, 648-67.

[18] For the text of the 1847 agreement, see Mu'tamid, *op. cit.*, pp. 44-48.

crepancies."[19] The task was continued until 1869, when the *Carte identique* was completed. During the same year Iran and Turkey agreed to preserve the *status quo* and respect the disputed lands until the boundary lines were settled as the result of the efforts of the four-power commission.[20]

Despite the conclusion of this agreement no conclusive settlement was reached. The anomalous composition of the commission was in part responsible for this failure. Apart from the opposing purposes of the great rival powers, the intransigency of Iran and Turkey did not help the situation. At one point, in 1851, Palmerston was tempted to take the matter completely out of the hands of the disputants. Great Britain was "confirmed in the opinion," he stated, "that the boundary between Turkey and Persia can never be finally settled except by an arbitrary decision on the part of Great Britain and Russia."[21]

In one instance it appeared for a time that a "settlement" was reached. Differences over Khoi and Kotur flared up after the 1847 agreement. Iran charged that contrary to the spirit of the agreement Turkish troops had occupied both areas. The bitter controversy was aggravated by the divergent positions of Russia and Great Britain on the matter. The former stood by Iran and the latter favored Turkey. The controversy dragged on for years; finally a basis for settlement was arrived at in 1878. Article 60 of the Treaty of Berlin provided that Turkey would "cede to Persia the town and territory of Khotour, as fixed by the mixed Anglo-Russian Commission." Apparently the Turks first refused to comply with this provision, but they later yielded Kotur to Iran.[22] However, the Kotur as well as other boundary disputes between Iran and Turkey remained largely unsettled until the twentieth century.[23]

[19] See S. Whittemore Boggs, *International Boundaries–A Study of Boundary Functions and Problems* (New York, 1940), p. 147.

[20] The text of the temporary boundary agreement of 1869 is in Sir Edward Hertslet, *Treaties etc. Concluded between Great Britain and Persia and between Persia and Other Foreign Powers, Wholly or Partially in Force on the 1st April, 1891* (London, 1891), pp. 176-78.

[21] This statement is in Viscount Palmerston's letter of October 11, 1851, to Sir G. H. Seymour. The text is in *Brit. & Foreign S. P.*, LVI, 663-64.

[22] For the text of the protocol respecting the delimitation of the territory of Kotur in conformity with the Treaty of Berlin, see Hertslet, *op. cit.*, pp. 219-20. See also Mu'tamid, *op. cit.*, pp. 49-50.

[23] See the excellent study by Maurice Harari, *The Turco-Persian Boundary*

THE BOUNDARIES WITH RUSSIA

Iran's boundary problems with Russia involved both sides of the Caspian Sea. The boundaries west of the Caspian were established in the first half of the nineteenth century. Russian conquests were confirmed by the treaties of Gulistan (1813) and of Turkumanchai (1828). The Irano-Russian boundary as set by the second of these treaties was to run from the Turkish frontier to the summit of the Little Ararat and then descend to the Lower Karassou River (Article 4). Thence it was to follow the Aras and the Astara rivers to the point of the latter's discharge into the Caspian Sea.

East of the Caspian, Iran's boundary problem was the result of the Russian conquests in Central Asia. Russia occupied Krasnovodsk in 1869. Iran regarded this Russian advance as a threat to its claims to Merv and Akhal. These areas were inhabited by the Turkumans, who did not owe allegiance to Iran. Twice between 1857 and 1861 the Governor-General of Khorasan had attacked and occupied Merv, but he had failed to establish Iran's control over it.[24]

During the Russian advance in Turkumania, Iran had mixed feelings. It was alarmed because one of the nine tribes dwelling along the Iranian border and on the shores of the Caspian Sea for the most part owed allegiance to Iran.[25] On the other hand, although Iran had watched the Russian subjugation of the tribes with considerable alarm, it could hardly protest the result. Iran, like Russia, nursed many grievances against the ruthless Tekeh Turkumans who had plundered Khorasan, Iran's northeastern province, for many generations.[26] It is believed that in 1873 Iran had been so aggrieved by the Tekeh border raids that the Shah promised Russia cooperation in punishing the tribes in Merv and Akhal.[27]

Iran finally signed a treaty regarding its eastern boundary with Russia in 1881. By the Treaty of Akhal-Khorasan, Iran and Russia agreed not to allow the Turkumans arms or ammunition. Iran also relinquished its claims to Merv. The frontier was drawn along the lower Atrek, beginning at the Hasan Quli Gulf on the Caspian Sea,

Question; A Case Study in the Politics of Boundary-Making in the Near and Middle East (Ph. D. dissertation, Columbia University, 1958).

[24] Sykes, *op. cit.*, pp. 358-60.

[25] Rawlinson, *op. cit.*, p. 328.

[26] *Ibid.*

[27] *Ibid.*

following the Atrek and thence along the outer flanks of the Kopeh Dagh to the Tejen River.[28] Iran also undertook to evacuate the forts of Gimab and Gulgulab.

Although the treaties of Turkumanchai and Akhal-Khorasan defined the frontiers of Iran with Russia to the west and to the east of the Caspian Sea, frontier controversies between the two countries continued. On the eastern side, for example, Russia pressured Iran into signing a new agreement in 1893 by which the frontier village of Firuzah was taken from Iran in return for a piece of land on the west side of the Caspian.[29] Boundary problems with Russia as with Turkey continued to plague twentieth-century policy makers.

IRANO–AFGHAN BOUNDARY DISPUTES

Iran's third major boundary quarrel during the second half of the nineteenth century was with Afghanistan. As mentioned earlier, Great Britain became involved in the boundary problem between Iran and Afghanistan because of its strategic interests in the latter country. A dispute flared up in 1870 over sovereignty in Sistan. This problem can be traced back at least to the time of Nādir Shah. After Nādir's assassination in 1747 and the breakup of his empire, Sistan had formed a part of the new Afghan Empire. Afghan control over the area continued for over a century, and Yār Muḥammad Khān, the ruler of Herat, held it as a tributary until his death in 1851.[30]

From 1851 on the situation at Herat and Sistan favored Iran. Yār Muḥammad's immediate successors pursued pro-Iranian policies. Nāṣir al-Dīn Shah's decision in 1856 to recover Herat by force of arms was influenced by favorable conditions at Herat. In fact, the ruler of Herat welcomed the army of the Shah, although subsequent developments in the city, and also Great Britain's reluctant war with Iran, forced him to abandon his plans.[31]

The Treaty of Paris (1857), which terminated that war and by which Iran recognized the independence of Afghanistan, made no pro-

[28] The text of the Akhal-Khorasan treaty is in Hertslet, *op. cit.*, pp. 136-40.

[29] For details, see Sipahbud Amānullāh Jahānbānī, *Marz'hā-yi Īrān va Shawravī* (Tehran, 1336) [1957/58]), pp. 25-26.

[30] Sykes, *op. cit.*, pp. 326-66.

[31] *Ibid.*

vision for Sistan. The Shah complained to the British of Afghan aggression against Sistan and repeatedly requested the British government, during 1861-63, to intervene under the terms of the Treaty of Paris. Great Britain, however, was pursuing a policy of "masterly inactivity" and did not recognize the sovereignty of Iran over Sistan in any case. When Great Britain was pressed for a definite answer by the Shah, the Foreign Office stated that "Her Majesty's Government, being informed that the title to the territory of Sistan is disputed between Persia and Afghanistan, must decline in the matter, and must leave it to both parties to make good their possession by force of arms." [32]

This statement marked the peak of the British laissez-faire policy, which was soon abandoned. In 1870, when Shīr ʿAlī Khān, the ruler of Kabul, threatened war with Iran over Sistan, the British decided to intervene. British political interests in 1870 were, in essence, the same as in the 1840's. In the Irano-Turkish dispute they had intervened to avert a war because it would have further weakened the two Muslim states separating the vast possessions of Great Britain in India from those of Russia. In the Irano-Afghan boundary dispute the same considerations predominated and Sistan's strategic significance for Great Britain increased as the result of the Russian advance in Central Asia.[33]

Great Britain complied with Iran's request for an arbitrator in 1872. Sir Frederic Goldsmid was appointed for the task. He proceeded to Sistan and examined the claims and counterclaims of the disputants. In general, the Iranian claim to Sistan rested upon two major grounds: ancient rights and present possession. The Afghan claim, on the other hand, rested primarily on its recent exercise of sovereignty over Sistan, i. e., from 1747, when the province formed a part of the Afghan Empire, until 1855, when Iran began to exercise considerable, if not complete, control over it.

In the arbitral award Sir Frederic first disposed of the Iranian claims based on ancient rights. He found them to be uncertain and not clearly supported by historical evidence. Conversely, he found more than a century of Afghan control over Sistan to be cogent evidence in favor of Afghanistan. The second question, i. e., "present possession," was more difficult. Although it was clear that since 1855

[32] Rawlinson, *op. cit.*, p. 103.

[33] See Greaves, *op. cit.*

Iran had exercised considerable authority over Sistan, it was problematic what the term "Sistan" included at the time of arbitration. It was "very vague," the award said, "for ancient limits have long become obsolete." [34]

The arbitration award distinguished between "Sistan Proper" and "Outer Sistan." The former was "compact and concentrated" and the latter was "detached and irregular." These two Sistans were separated by the Helmand River. The award gave Sistan Proper to Iran, on the grounds of geographical and political requirements, and Outer Sistan to Afghanistan, which was also given both banks of the Helmand above the Kobah Band. Furthermore, the award emphatically stated that "no works are to be carried out on either side calculated to interfere with the requisite supply of water for irrigation on the banks of the Helmand." [35]

In spite of the award the problem continued. "The lasting disadvantages of a boundary which cuts an irrigation system into two" were prophetically foreseen by an astute student of British policy at the time. In commenting on the award, Rawlinson stated,

> Indeed it would seem that tied as he [Goldsmid] was by definitive conditions of procedure, no other course was open to him than that which he adopted; but at the same time it is impossible to avoid seeing that there is not one element of permanence in the recorded terms of settlement. . . It must occur to every student of political geography that the refilling of the old or western bed of the Helmand, which the river left only forty years ago, and to which it may at any moment return, would alter the whole hydrography of the province, and annihilate those distinctive physical features on which the recent arbitration was based.[36]

This was almost exactly what happened in 1891. The Helmand began to change its course. By 1896 the main channel of the river flowed considerably west of the channel which Goldsmid had designated as the boundary in 1872. The local governors of Iran and Afghanistan managed to compose their differences over utilization of the water for a number of years, but in 1902 Iran felt that the problem should again be referred to the British for arbitration because the local officials were no longer able to handle the matter. In requesting the appointment of a new arbitrator, however, Iran made it absolutely

[34] The arbitration award is in *The Sistan Arbitration,* I, 395-414.
[35] *Ibid.*
[36] *Op. cit.,* p. 116.

clear that any award that might be given "must completely comply" with Goldsmid's award of 1872.[37]

Great Britain complied with the request and dispatched Henry McMahon to head an arbitration commission to Sistan. Having completed its exhaustive studies, the commission gave an award in 1905. Its fundamental point was that Sistan had often suffered, not so much because of a shortage of water but because of flood. On the basis of this observation, the award provided that Iran should have one-third of the water of the Helmand River from the Kamal Khan Dam down. It also repeated the earlier injunction that no works were to be carried out by either Iran or Afghanistan that would interfere with the requisite amount of water needed for irrigation on both sides of the banks of the Helmand. Subject to this important provision, however, both countries were allowed to cut new canals or reactivate old ones on either side of the river.

Iran vigorously protested the award, objecting in particular to its small share of the water. Iran believed that the award was incompatible with Goldsmid's ruling in 1872 and that it could therefore be rejected. The Foreign Office retorted that Iran could not reject it; the Iranian government might only appeal to the British government if it had any reasonable grounds for complaint. It also warned that should Iran fail to file an appeal within a reasonable period of time, the award would be regarded as final and binding.[38] The Helmand River problem had not been settled.

THE NEW FRONTIERS: MYTH AND REALITY

The boundary problems of Iran in the nineteenth century were the consequence of a long period of diminishing power as an empire. This weakening had set in, as we have seen, long before the nineteenth century. The fall of the Ṣafavī empire marked Iran's lowest point in the eighteenth century, but the meteoric rise of Nādir arrested the decay. The former territories were recovered, and Iran even launched

[37] For a detailed account of these developments and the text of some of the letters exchanged between Great Britain and Iran, see Maḥmūd Maḥmūd, *Tārīkh-i Ravābiṭ-i Sīyāsī-i Īrān va Inglīs dar Qarn-i Nūzdahum-i Mīlādī* (Tehran, 1332 [1953/54]), VII, 2010-33.

[38] *Ibid.*, p. 2018.

its own imperialist campaigns. Then the assassination of Nādir Shah was followed by the loss of Afghanistan and Georgia. The Qājār monarchs including Āghā Muḥammad Shah, Fatḥ 'Alī Shah, Muḥammad Shah, and Nāṣir al-Dīn Shah all resorted to force of arms in an attempt to recover the lost territories.

Their irredentist wars, however, did not regain what had been lost; instead their failures forced them to acknowledge and confirm their losses. Fatḥ 'Alī Shah acknowledged the loss of Georgia in the Treaty of Gulistan (1813), and Nāṣir al-Dīn Shah affirmed that of Afghanistan in the Treaty of Paris (1857). The outbreak of war with Turkey in 1821 was probably least influenced by irredentist considerations, but even in this conflict Iran's determination to regain its former terirtories in the west played a part.

Iran's acknowledgments of its losses and its acceptance of its diminished frontiers did not necessarily mean recognition of its position as a weak state. The Shahs were still *Shāhinshāh,* King of Kings, and Iran continued as an "Empire." The empire had died, but the myth survived. The ever-present past with its real as well as its mythological glories lived on. The lure of this past was a powerful influence in Iran's foreign policy whether it led to the imperialist expansion of Nādir Shah, the irredentism of Fatḥ 'Alī Shah, or the boundary hagglings of Nāṣir al-Dīn Shah.

Chapter IV

Foreign Economic Policy, 1863-1904

ECONOMIC as well as boundary problems demanded the attention of Iranian rulers in the second half of the nineteenth century. This preoccupation marked a significant change in Iran's foreign policy and was caused mainly by a transformation in the basic external factor conditioning Iran's foreign affairs, namely, the Anglo-Russian rivalry. In the second half of the nineteenth century this rivalry became a furious economic competition between Great Britain and Russia in Iran.

Great Britain's economic interests had increased in India as well as in Iran. By the latter part of the century the Industrial Revolution had stocked British warehouses with a surplus of manfactured goods. Sale abroad was possible, but competition with industrial states, especially those with high tariffs like the United States and Germany, was stiff. It was easier in British colonies, including India, where Great Britain could manipulate the tariff and control the currency.[1] This additional imperial interest in India increased the value of Iran to Great Britain. Iran also became more important economically in

[1] Mary Evelyn Townsend, *European Colonial Expansion since 1871* (New York, 1941), p. 4.

British policy because "indifference to Persia might mean the sacrifice of a trade that already feeds hundreds of thousands of our [British] citizens in this country and in India. A friendly attention to Persia will mean so much more employment for British ships, for British labour, and for British spindles." [2]

By the latter part of the nineteenth century Russia's economic interest in Iran had also increased. Russia, unlike Great Britain, was not bursting with surplus capital and manfactured goods, but its meager development put it far ahead of Iran, which still had a medieval economy. Russia's search for markets led it to Iran:

> The impetus which he [M. Witte, Russia's Minister of Finance] had given to the development of Russian industry by intensified methods of protection made it absolutely necessary for him to find new markets for the products of Russian industry. The severe crisis through which Russia was passing as a consequence of overproduction under artificial conditions only served to stimulate his activity. In Persia he discovered a market in which the advantage of geographical proximity goes far to counterbalance the disadvantage at which such a hothouse growth as Russian industry is apt to find itself placed when in competition with the industry of other countries, and especially with British industry. If to geographical proximity he could superadd other advantages, he might well hope to turn the scales so completely in favor of Russian industry as to drive its competitors altogether out of the field. That its chief competitor happens here to be British industry, and that commercial rivalry therefore runs on the same lines as political rivalry, is merely an incident which no doubt adds zest to the game.[3]

Iran's economic foreign policy was mainly an answer to the significant change of emphasis in the Anglo-Russian rivalry. The frantic economic activities of Nāṣir al-Dīn Shah and his son could only in part be attributed to their interest in remedying the over-all economic backwardness of the country. Their overriding objective was to find access to new sources of funds for dynastic survival as well as royal pleasure and comfort.

A new internal development significantly influenced the new economic policy. This development owed its origin to the appearance of an unexpected personality on the Iranian political scene. During the

[2] George N. Curzon, *Persia and the Persian Question* (London, 1892), II, 604.

[3] Valentine Chirol, *The Middle Eastern Question or Some Political Problems of Indian Defence* (London, 1903), p. 56.

early rule of Nāṣir al-Dīn Shah when "ruin and revolution appeared to be imminent," Mīrzā Taqī Khān, the Amīr Niẓām, or Amīr Kabīr as he is generally known in Iran, held the post of Prime Minister for a short time. Apart from the internal reforms that this "really extraordinary person, who was far in advance of his age and country," [4] introduced into the Iranian administration, army, and education, he was the originator of the policy of "equilibrium." Since 1800 the Shahs had thrown their lot first with one power and then another by making alliances and waging wars, but the Amīr Niẓām introduced the concept of equilibrium in combating Anglo-Russian rivalry. He consistently opposed European pressures.

> If he pertinaciously withstood, for instance, the efforts of Russia to replace Bahman Mirza in Azerbaijan, he was equally obstinate in refusing to admit the intercession of England in favour of the Assef ed-Douleh and his family in Khorasan; and so thoroughly, indeed, did he observe this impartiality of political conduct, that when obliged by circumstances to yield in one direction, he at once sought to redress the balance by a corresponding concession in the other.[5]

The significant and lasting impact of "equilibrium" on the foreign policy of Iran will be discussed in later chapters. At first, however, the policy, which was formulated initially to protect the interests of Iran, in the hands of the inexperienced Shahs actually militated against those interests. The weak country found it nearly impossible to implement the policy of equilibrium in a positive manner, that is, in such a way as to deny the rival powers or their subjects their demands for economic concessions or excessive commercial and other privileges. Instead, the application of the concept of equilibrium to the economic sphere resulted in the granting of all sorts of economic concessions to both rival powers.

FOREIGN CONCESSIONS

The grant of economic concessions was one of the three major components of Iran's foreign economic policy in the nineteenth century. Nāṣir al-Dīn Shah (1848-96) and subsequently his son, Muẓaffar

[4] Sir Henry Rawlinson, *England and Russia in the East* (London, 1875), pp. 83-84.
[5] *Ibid.*, p. 82.

al-Dīn Shah (1896-1907), granted a wide variety of economic concessions to European powers. The most important of these were obtained by British or Russian interests.

The first major concession was granted to Great Britain in 1863. This was a concession for the establishment of an overland telegraph line through Iran. Great Britain wanted it as an alternative line to India. Earlier in the year Great Britain had concluded a convention with Turkey enabling it to lay down wire from Constantinople, through Asia Minor and Mesopotamia, to Baghdad. For fear that the direct line of communication between Baghdad and the head of the Persian Gulf might suddenly break down, perhaps because of hostility on the part of the Arab tribes living in the area, Great Britain sought and obtained the convention with Iran in the same year. By the end of 1864 this alternative line was completed from Khanaqin via Kermanshah and Hamadan to Tehran, and from there via Isfahan and Shiraz to Bushire, where it joined the marine cable to the telegraph terminus at Karachi. According to the terms of the convention, the line was to be constructed by England at Iran's expense. Iran was to be paid a maximum of 30,000 tomans a year for English messages.[6] In contrast with other concessions the telegraph concessions of 1863 and 1865[7] – the latter providing for a free wire for Iranian use – proved not only economically advantageous but also culturally significant in bringing Iran into close contact with Europe.[8]

Immediately after the construction of the telegraph line, Iran studied various plans for inviting in European capital and skill as set forth by a number of private investors. Having concluded that the greater part of these plans were put forward by "adventurers and speculators," the Shah decided to put into the hands of a single man the entire responsibility for Iran's economic and industrial development! To this end the Shah in 1872 granted to Baron Julius Reuter,[9] a naturalized British subject, an all-encompassing economic concession for a period of seventy years. This concession was, in Lord Curzon's words, "the most extraordinary surrender of the entire industrial

[6] For details, see Curzon, *op. cit.*, p. 609.

[7] The texts of these concessions are in Maḥmūd Maḥmūd, *Tārīkh-i Ravābiṭ-i Sīyāsī-i Īrān va Inglīs dar Qarn-i Nūzdahum-i Mīlādī* (Tehran, 1335 [1956/57]), III, 605-6.

[8] Rawlinson, *op. cit.*, p. 107.

[9] Maḥmūd asserts that Great Britain "forced" Iran to grant this concession. He does not substantiate his statement (*op. cit.*, p. 773).

resources" of the country.[10] The concessionaire was given the exclusive right (1) to construct, among other things, all railways, dams, and canals throughout Iran; (2) to regulate rivers; (3) and to exploit all mines, except those of gold and silver. He was also promised priority over any person or corporation that might in the future seek concessions for the establishment of banks and industrial plants or for any other purpose.[11]

The grant of such a gigantic monopoly to a British national aroused severe Russian opposition. Russia claimed that the grant had completely repudiated Iran's claim to adhere to the principle of equilibrium between the great powers.[12] Russian opposition was voiced on two major grounds. It was claimed that under the Reuter concession Great Britain would have the right to evaluate Russian goods for the payment of duty. Since there was no ground for such a supposition, it seems evident that this argument was used to camouflage the interest of Russian merchants in preventing any proper exaction of customs duties, which they had previously avoided paying and which they would probably have to pay in the event of improvement in the administration of customs. The second ground for opposition related to the exploitation of mines, including those of the Elburz range, which were coveted by Russia.[13]

The cancellation of the Reuter concession in 1873 was not due only to the resolute opposition of Russia. Two other factors were involved. First, the fulfillment of the concession required enormous capital. The concessionaire could have raised the money with the assistance of the British government, but the government's reluctance to give him a guarantee or protection for forming a company in England rendered implementation of the concession impossible.[14] Second, the concession aroused Iranian "popular" opposition. This opposition was stirred up and intensified by some members of the elite (i. e., those who get the most of the best) during the Shah's absence in Europe.[15]

[10] *Op. cit.*, I, 480.

[11] The text of the concession is in Maḥmūd, *op. cit.*, pp. 774-79. An abstract of the concession may be found in Rawlinson, *op. cit.*, pp. 373-76.

[12] For details on Russian opposition and other related matters, see Ibrāhīm Taymūrī, *'Aṣr-i Bīkhabarī yā Tārīkh-i Imtīyāzāt dar Īrān* (Tehran, 1332 [1953/54]), pp. 130-50.

[13] Rawlinson, *op. cit.*, p. 125.

[14] *Ibid.*, p. 126.

[15] Ibrāhīm Taymūrī states that the opposition was instigated by a few mullahs with Russia's support (*op. cit.*, p. 123).

These malcontents argued that the concession spelled the surrender of his royal powers to foreigners. In comparison with the opposition of Russia and the indifference of Great Britain, the popular resentment played a minor role in forcing the Shah to abrogate the concession, but the opposition is significant as perhaps the earliest manifestation of the Iranian national awakening.

After the cancellation of the Reuter concession Iran granted a wide variety of concessions to Great Britain and Russia. In 1888 Great Britain obtained a concession for the establishment of regular commercial navigation on the Karun River.[16] Russia feared British penetration and commercial competition in northern Iran. This apprehension was intensified when Great Britain attempted to acquire a concession for the construction of a railway from the upper Karun to Tehran. Russia therefore decided to prevent the construction of this or any other railway in Iran. This marked the beginning of Russia's obstructive railway policy, which was continuously successful until the First World War.[17] In 1889 Russia was satisfied when Nāṣir al-Dīn Shah promised that Iran would not grant railway concessions to any power except Russia. (This promise was renewed in 1899 to last until 1910.[18])

In that same year Iran granted to Reuter a new concession, for the establishment of the Imperial Bank of Persia.[19] This concession was demanded by the British government as compensation for the cancellation of Reuter's earlier concession. There was, however, more than compensation involved. Iran had retained his caution money because of delay in performance. Upon the establishment of the bank, Reuter recovered that money. The bank began transactions with a capital of £1,000,000. It was given the exclusive right to issue bank notes in Iran for a period of sixty years and to exploit the mineral resources of the country, with the exception of precious stones. The latter right was sold to the Persian Bank Mining Rights Corporation.

In 1890 Nāṣir al-Dīn Shah granted another sweeping concession

[16] On this concession, see A. P. Thornton, "British Policy in Persia, 1858-1890," *English Historical Review*, LXX (1955), 61; Taymūrī, *op. cit.*, pp. 151-78; and J. D. Rees, "The Persia of the Shah," *Nineteenth Century*, XXVI (1889), 170.

[17] Firuz Kazemzadeh, in *Harvard Slavic Studies*, IV (1957), 355-73.

[18] B. H. Sumner, "Tsardom and Imperialism in the Far East and Middle East," *Proceedings of the British Academy* (London, 1941), p. 54.

[19] Taymūrī, *op. cit.*, pp. 178-210.

to a British subject, Major G. Talbot, for a period of fifty years. The prospective company was granted the exclusive right to sell in Iran and to export tobacco, cigars, cigarettes, and snuff. Iranian producers and owners of such products would be compelled by the government to sell their products to the company immediately upon its formation. The company was exempted from all customs duties and taxes on all the materials necessary for its work. In return for all these privileges, the Shah would receive a fixed amount, £15,000 annually, and would also receive one-quarter of the company's annual profit after the deduction of all business expenses and after the payment of dividends of 5 per cent on its capital.[20]

The overly generous terms of this concession aroused the opposition of Russia, but more important was the resistance of the Iranians themselves. Both Western and Iranian writers regard the opposition to this concession as the first major milestone in the history of the national awakening in Iran. The people would not submit to being obliged to buy from a foreign corporation the tobacco which they themselves grew and gathered in.[21] The Shah had, "for a comparatively insignificant personal profit, needlessly and recklessly saddled his long-suffering subjects with an intolerable burden." [22] The popular dissatisfaction first appeared among the people of Tabriz; it soon spread to Isfahan and Tehran. When the news of popular discontent reached Ḥāj Mīrzā Muḥammad Ḥasan-i Shīrāzī, a Mujtahid, he wrote to the Shah that the concession was contrary to the Koran. The Shah then considered modifying the terms of the concession by confining to the company only the sale of tobacco abroad.[23]

This device failed to placate the demand of Ḥāj Mīrzā Javād of Tabriz, Āqā Najafy of Isfahan, and Ḥāj Mīrzā Muḥammad Ḥasan-i Shīrāzī for the abrogation of the concession. Faced with the Shah's stubborn resistance, Mīrzā Muḥammad Ḥasan issued a *fatwā* enjoining the people to abandon smoking completely until the concession was cancelled. The response was overwhelming, and as a result the Shah had no alternative but to comply with the popular demand.

[20] The text is in J. C. Hurewitz, *Diplomacy in the Near and Middle East* (Princeton, N. J., 1956), I, 205-6.

[21] Edward G. Browne, *The Persian Revolution, 1905-1909* (Cambridge, 1910), p. 50.

[22] *Ibid.*, p. 57.

[23] Aḥmad Kasravī, *Tārīkh-i Mashrūṭah-'i Īrān* (4th ed.; Tehran, 1316 [1937/38]), I, 16.

As it turned out, however, the annulment of the concession led to even greater immediate economic and political difficulties for the country. The company demanded £650,000 as indemnity for its concession; it finally obtained £500,000. The depleted Iranian treasury could not pay such a sum. The Shah had to borrow the compensation money from the British bank at 6 per cent interest.

While engaged in feeding and exploiting popular discontent over the tobacco concession, Russia acquired the railway concession mentioned earlier and also the consent of the Shah to establish the Banque d'Escompte de Perse (1891), a branch of the Russian Ministry of Finance and a part of the Central Bank of Russia.[24] The bank was consciously used as a powerful instrument of Russian policy in Iran. In advancing loans the British bank had to consult the interests of its shareholders as it could not afford losses, but the Russian bank consulted "only the requirement of the policy it [had] been created to carry out, and was quite prepared to incur losses in promoting it." In the years immediately after its establishment the bank began to wield increasing control over a number of princes, a few influential clergymen, and some merchants by providing them with loans on easy terms. Through such methods Russia by 1900 had nearly bought off the ruling elite in Iran.[25]

In the same year Kitābchī Khān, an Iranian customs official of Armenian origin, asked the former British Minister in Tehran, Sir Henry Drummond Wolff, who was then in Paris, to find someone in London who would be willing to invest in Iranian oil. Kitābchī Khān's attention had just been called to the findings of a French archaeologist which had been published in *Les annales des mines* (1892) claiming that oil existed in the Qasir-i Shirin region near the Irano-Turkish border in Mesopotamia. Some time later Wolff, who had known Kitābchī Khān in Iran during his mission at Tehran, summoned him to London. There Kitābchī Khān explained his plan to William Knox D'Arcy, an adventurous British millionaire who had made his fortune as a shareholder in the mine of Mount Morgan in Australia.

After the completion of an investigation into the possibilities of the Iranian fields by a geologist, H. T. Burls, D'Arcy dispatched his

[24] For details, see Taymūrī, *op. cit.*, pp. 336-49.

[25] Mahdī Malikzādah, *Tārīkh-i Inqilāb-i Mashrūṭīyat-i Īrān* (Tehran, 1328 [1949/50]), I, 164-65.

representative, Alfred Marriott, together with Kitābchī Khān to acquire an oil concession from Muẓaffar al-Dīn Shah. Knowing of the firm grip of Russia over the ruling elite in Iran, Wolff was convinced that without the support of the British government the efforts of a private investor would fail. He therefore asked his successor as Minister in Tehran, Sir Arthur Hardinge, to intervene in D'Arcy's behalf.

Hardinge resorted to the old British practice of bribery.[26] The Iranian Prime Minister, Atābak, fell in line and proposed a scheme to Hardinge by means of which they bypassed Russian opposition. The oft-quoted ruse need not be repeated here.[27] Suffice it to say it worked; it circumvented the Russian opposition. However, in drawing up the terms of the concession (signed in 1901), Hardinge saw to it that the traditional preserve of Russian influence, i.e., the five northern provinces of Iran, were excluded from the British concession in compliance with his instructions from London.[28]

The major provisions of the concession were as follows:

1) *Area of Concession*: The concessionaire acquired a special and exclusive privilege in natural gas, petroleum, asphalt, and ozocerite "throughout the whole extent of the Persian Empire," except the five northern provinces, for a period of sixty years.

2) *Financial*: The first exploitation company was to pay the Iranian government, within a month of its formation, £20,000 in cash and the equivalent of this sum in paid-up shares. It was also to pay the government annually a sum equal to 16 per cent of the annual net profits of any company or companies that were formed. If the concessionaire failed to establish the first of these companies within two years, the concession would become null and void.[29]

The First Exploitation Company was organized in 1903, within the period specified by the concession. Publicly the Iranian government received the sum of £20,000 and also the equivalent of that amount in paid-up shares. Privately another £25,000 in shares was paid to Atābak, Mushīr al-Dawlah, and Muhandis al-Mamālik. This,

[26] This practice may be dated from 1801 when Sir John Malcolm bribed some Iranian courtiers. See Chapter II of this study and note 20 therein.

[27] For Sir Arthur Hardinge's own account of this ruse, see his *A Diplomatist in the East* (London, 1928), pp. 278-79.

[28] Muṣṭafā Fātaḥ, *Panjāh Sāl Naft-i Īrān* (Tehran, 1335 [1956/57]), p. 212

[29] For the text, see Hurewitz, *op. cit.*, I, 249-52.

according to an Iranian account, was the bribe that Sir Henry Wolff had advised Hardinge to promise the high Iranian officials, particularly the Prime Minister, when he first intervened on behalf of D'Arcy.[30]

FOREIGN LOANS

Iran's foreign economic policy involved also the procurement of loans. Nāṣir al-Dīn Shah's grants and cancellations of concessions led to popular discontent, which, in part, led to his assassination in 1896. Upon accession to the throne, his son, Muẓaffar al-Dīn Shah, was confronted by numerous claims for arrears of salary on the part of a huge and corrupt bureaucracy. He felt the need for a new fiscal policy because he wanted money for his medical and pleasure trips to Europe.[31]

In 1900 the Shah borrowed £2,400,000 from Russia. Iran had first approached Great Britain, which had "hesitated and procrastinated," insisting on immediate control of the Iranian customs as security for a British loan.[32] Russia profited by British slowness and made the loan through the convenient medium of its bank in Iran. The loan was guaranteed by the Russian government and carried 5 per cent interest. The security was the Iranian customs revenues except those of Persian Gulf ports. The loan agreement had a number of important conditions to which the government of the Shah agreed. These were aimed at economic and political subjugation of Iran. The Shah and Atābak A'ẓam, the Prime Minister, agreed that the proceeds of the new loan should be devoted to repayment of the balance of the British loan which had been contracted to provide compensation for the withdrawal of the tobacco concession.

Having fulfilled all the conditions attached to the loan, the Shah and his entourage drew upon what money was left to pay the expenses of their longed-for trip to Europe.[33] Upon his return the Shah found the Treasury empty. In 1901 he borrowed from Russia again, this time an amount equivalent to about £1,500,000. To obtain the loan, the Shah agreed to extend to 1912 the period during which he would

[30] See Fātaḥ, *op. cit.*, p. 252.
[31] See Taymūrī, *op. cit.*, p. 91.
[32] For criticism of British procrastination, see Chirol, *op. cit.*, p. 52.
[33] See Kasravī, *op. cit.*, p. 25.

contract no loans from any power except Russia. The Shah also agreed to revise Iran's tariffs, with the consent of Russia, as soon as possible.

Thus within three years the Shah had contracted two Russian loans amounting to a total of approximately £4,000,00. This sum equaled the whole of Iran's revenues for the same period. There is no evidence that any of this money was used for productive purposes.[34] It is well known, however, that once again the Shah and his entourage drew upon the public loan to pay the expenses of another lush and leisurely trip to Europe.

Muẓaffar al-Dīn Shah's fiscal policy produced popular opposition just as had his father's concessionary policy. It was during the years when the Russian loans were being negotiated that the earliest secret society was formed in Iran. No free press was allowed in Iran, and no newspaper published in Persian abroad could enter the country.[35] The secret society, which was composed of some of the influential personalities who later led the Constitutional Movement, mimeographed and circulated an "evening newspaper" (*Shabnāmah*), vigorously protesting the negotiations for acquiring loans from Russia.

Nevertheless, the decision to borrow was not abandoned. The failure of the opposition may be attributed to two major factors. First, by means of advancing loans and credits on easy terms the Russian bank had gained too firm a grip upon a number of merchants and some of the influential clergy. Second, the opposition was not broadly based; only a few educated individuals could see the injurious economic and political consequences of Iran's heavy indebtedness to Russia.

FOREIGN TRADE

A third component of Iran's foreign economic policy was foreign trade. The foundation for an expansion of trade with Russia had been set by the commercial instrument appended to the Treaty of Turkumanchai, which assured Russian subjects extraterritorial privileges and established the pattern of capitulatory terms for Europeans under the Qājār dynasty. It also provided that Iranian customs duties, both

[34] Chirol, *op. cit.*, p. 54.

[35] One such newspaper was the well-known *Hablul Matin.* See Malikzādah, *op. cit.*, p. 161.

import and export, should be 5 per cent *ad valorem*. This simple formula also governed Iran's trade relations, through the operation of most-favored-nation clauses, with other European powers, the most important of which was Great Britain.

Although Russo-Iranian trade increased subsequent to the signing of the 1828 treaty, at first the competition of European goods in Iranian markets was too stiff for Russia. To overcome this competition, Russia abolished the free-transit zone through Transcaucasia in 1883. This compelled European exporters to carry their goods for Iran by the expensive Trebizond-Erzerum-Tabriz caravan route. It also assisted Russian exports to northern Iran.[36]

By 1890 Russian exports to Iran, consisting principally of sugar, petroleum, and cotton fabrics, were valued at over 10,000,00 rubles. By the time Iran consented to the revision of its tariff rates in 1901 (see below), they reached the value of nearly 21,000,000 rubles. This phenomenal increase in Russian exports was matched by an equally significant rise in Iranian exports to Russia, consisting primarily of dried fruits, raw cotton, and nuts. These exports, valued at nearly 11,000,000 rubles in 1890, were worth over 20,000,000 by 1901.[37]

Iran's foreign trade became closely tied to its loans from Russia. In the second loan agreement (1901) the Shah had promised a revision of Iranian tariffs subject to the approval of Russia. This was effected the same year by means of a new commercial treaty with Russia, which successfully, and secretly, dictated the terms with the assistance of a Belgian official. This official, a Monsieur Naus, had been put in charge of the customs houses of Kermanshah and Tabriz in 1898 and had later been made the Minister of Customs in recognition of his "effective improvement of the administration of customs."

The Shah had naïvely entrusted the destiny of Iran's most important source of revenue to the hands of this "protégé and agent of the Russian Government." [38] He had also ingenuously signed the new agreement primarily serving Russia in disregard of the interests of Iran and those of its other important trade partner, Great Britain. The Russian gains were threefold: the new tariff rates (1) improved the security of Russian loans to Iran, (2) discriminated against British commercial interests, and (3) increased Russia's control over Iran's fiscal policy.

[36] See Sumner, *op. cit.*, p. 47.
[37] Chirol, *op. cit.*, p. 445.
[38] W. Morgan Shuster, *The Strangling of Persia* (New York, 1912), p. 313.

The new tariff formula was directed mainly against Great Britain. The principal imports and exports of Russia were treated with relative lenience under the new system, but those of Great Britain and India were "severely penalized." [39] Faced with this *fait accompli*, the British government rushed through a new commercial convention with Iran just four days before the Russo-Iranian agreement went into effect.[40] At the time this seemed to be the most desirable course of action. The new Anglo-Iranian convention merely gave a British imprimatur to the far-reaching changes in the commercial regime of Iran already effected by the Russo-Iranian convention. It was an attempt to make the best of a bad situation.[41]

As a consequence of the new tariffs, Iran suffered in three important and related ways. The new rates (1) linked Iran's trade to Russia so closely that Iran's international trade was hampered, (2) increased Russia's grip over Iranian fiscal policy, and (3) discouraged the development of local manufacturing and handicraft by throwing Iranian markets wide open to Russian goods. A most important item of local manufacture was cotton fabrics. The removal of tariff protection forced many Iranian manufacturers to close their shops. This, in turn, produced further unemployment, which increased the emigration of the country's small number of skilled workers to Transcaucasia.[42]

The vigorous and "arbitrary" implementation of the new tariffs by Naus and his entourage soon gave rise to local opposition. The first cry against it was voiced by the clergy,[43] who pinned the blame on Naus. Some of the *'ulamā'* went so far as to demand his dismissal. They charged that he had ridiculed the religion of Islam and insulted the clergy. The main opposition, however, came from the merchants, who had found their interest directly threatened. Their goods had been burdened with heavy duties, and they had suffered arbitrary treatment at the hands of the customs officials. They also demanded the dismissal of Naus.

These demands fell on deaf ears. The Shah did not see how the new tariffs could be disadvantageous. They had increased customs

[39] Chirol, *op. cit.*, p. 78.

[40] Sir Edward Hertslet's *Commercial Treaties* (London, 1905), XXXIII, 1213-16.

[41] For details, see Chirol, *op. cit.*, pp. 76-88.

[42] Kasravī, *op. cit.*, p. 25.

revenues, which gave him more security on which he could borrow still more from Russia. The merchants, however, continued to add to their list of grievances and clamored for an opportunity to present them to Naus in person. This opportunity was finally accorded to them, but produced no satisfactory results so far as the merchants were concerned. They saw no alternative but to close down their stores in protest and take sanctuary (*bast*) in the shrine of Shāh 'Abd al-'Aẓīm.

THE TRIANGUAR INTERACTION

Similar patterns were present in other areas of Qājār foreign policy. Ignorance, unrealism, caprice, and avarice were evident in alliances and wars as much as in foreign economic policy. In granting concessions and contracting loans, Nāṣir al-Dīn Shah and his son paid as little attention to the consequences of their actions as did Fatḥ 'Alī Shah in committing the country to capricious alliances and unprepared wars. Not that such wars were new to the nineteenth century; Fatḥ 'Alī Shah favored resort to arms no more than did Nādir Shah long before him.

Nineteenth-century foreign policy was influenced by the internal situation just as was that of the earlier centuries. In the nineteenth century the most important decisional unit was still the monarchy. The monarch's absolute control over affairs of state made his character and military support of crucial importance not only for foreign policy but also for Iran's existence as a state. The military strength of the Shah was often decisive in maintaining stability at home and success abroad, but mere support by the army was not sufficient. Shah 'Abbās the Great created a strong army, but his success lay in his wise choice of strategies and a degree of political realism. Unfortunately Iran did not have many prudent policy makers like Shah 'Abbās, and even he did not realize how he injured the country by keeping possible successors from gaining experience.

In the nineteenth century, as in previous centuries, other harmful internal factors also influenced Iranian foreign policy. Fatḥ 'Alī Shah's policy decisions were at times as much swayed by Shī'ī

[43] For the names of some of these early clerical opponents of the Shah, see *ibid.*, pp. 37-38.

fanaticism as were those of Shah Ṭahmāsb. The early Qājār policy makers listened to astrologers and soothsayers as had Shah Sultān Ḥusayn and other Ṣafavī monarchs generations before. Whatever salutary effects the European trips of Nāṣir al-Dīn Shah and Muẓaffar al-Dīn Shah might have had on these monarchs, their foreign policy showed few signs of improvement. Instead of becoming alert to the intellectual, socioeconomic, and technological underpinnings of the power and prestige of European states, these monarchs became disillusioned and despondent as the result of their trips. The ignorance, lust for pleasure, and extravagance of the Shahs were thus compounded by a sense of inferiority not without effects on their policies.

While these basic characteristics of the internal situation significantly conditioned the making of foreign policy, the implementation of foreign-policy decisions in turn produced changes in internal affairs. Alliances, wars, and economic policies all produced changes, but economic policies were the most important initiators of change. The economic activities of foreigners in the establishment of telegraph lines, the construction of new and better roads, or the development of other concessions and the expansion of trade made a significant break in the centuries-old crust of traditional Iranian isolationism. These activities brought a small but growing number of Iranians into contact with foreign experts, officials, and skilled workers. They also furthered those social, economic, and intellectual conditions associated with the rise of an intelligentsia, a commercial middle class, and labor. The stage was thus set for a national awakening, the earliest signs of which were the popular opposition to the tobacco monopoly, the Russian loans, and the Russian-inspired tariffs.

The triangular interaction between external factors, foreign policy, and internal conditions which was pointed out at the outset of this study persisted dynamically from 1500 to 1905. This interaction produced two major developments which have already been discussed but must be recalled here because of their significance for an understanding of the foreign policy of Iran in the twentieth century. One was the appearance of popular unrest and dissatisfaction with the traditional political system, which led to the Constitutional Revolution. The other was the fact that at the turn of the twentieth century Iran was a backward and weak state, whose independence was largely in name only.

Part Two

Prelude to Transition in Foreign Policy, 1905-1920

Chapter V

The Constitutional Revolution, Foreign Intervention, and Foreign Policy, 1905-1913

THE years between the Constitutional Revolution in Iran (1905-6) and the *coup d'état* of 1921 were a prelude to a transition in foreign policy. Although this period witnessed the intensification of Iranian nationalism, it was not until after the First World War that the early signs of a departure from traditional foreign-policy making became discernible. However, this does not necessarily mean that all the elements of traditional foreign policy continued as before. The impact of the national awakening on the policy-making process was significant in two principal ways. One was the nationalization of the objectives of foreign policy. The other was the emergence of new policy makers. The continuation of traditionalism in foreign policy was apparent particularly in the persistent disparity between the means and ends of Iranian foreign policy. But interestingly enough, even this pattern of political unrealism was no longer so much influenced by traditional factors such as Shī'ī fanaticism, ignorance, and forcible seclusion. Rather, it was profoundly conditioned by a growing nationalism.

THE INTERNAL SITUATION: THE CONSTITUTIONAL MOVEMENT

The adjective "Constitutional" by which the movement is commonly designated does not reveal the true nature of the stirrings that occurred in the turbulent years under discussion. It might convey the impression that establishment of democratic institutions was the primary object of the movement. Such an impression may even be reinforced by the statements of some of the leaders of the movement. Malik al-Mutikallimīn, a leading Constitutionalist orator, went so far as to state that liberty was "the highest goal" of the movement, and that all other goals such as justice and independence from foreign control were of secondary significance.[1] There is little doubt that a few of the Constitutionalists shared this view, but the movement was primarily born out of opposition to foreign domination as exemplified by the tobacco monopoly uprising and the "popular" opposition to the Russian loans and, finally, to the Russian tariffs.[2]

Constitutionalism (*Mashrūṭīyat*) was little understood, misunderstood, or, at best, confused with parliamentarism. As such, it could not have become the rallying point of the movement. In fact, some of the supporters of the movement confused constitutionalism with the reestablishment of Islamic law (*Mashrū'īyat*) as the foundation of the "new" order. Once they discovered the discrepancy between their conception of constitutionalism and that of some of the Western-educated leaders of the movement, they withdrew their support and joined the ranks of the opposition.[3]

Constitutionalism became the symbol around which various groups gathered because it meant to most of its supporters a movement for

[1] He stated this in one of his well-known speeches. The full text is in Mahdī Malikzādah, *Tārīkh-i Inqilāb-i Mashrūṭīyat-i Īrān* (Tehran, 1328 [1949/50]), I, 187.

[2] See Chapter IV.

[3] In describing the popular support of the Constitutional Movement Aḥmad Kasravī identifies four major groups: the Western-educated intellectuals, patriotic mullahs, unpatriotic mullahs, and the masses. The first and second, he states, supported the Constitutional Movement, though for different reasons; the third group opposed it, and the fourth, without understanding constitutionalism, followed the Constitutionalist leaders. See his *Tārīkh-i Mashrūṭah-i Īrān* (4th ed.; Tehran, 1316 [1937/38]), I, 259-60.

the "true independence" of Iran. The bazaar merchants, the clergy, the Western-educated intellectuals, and some members of the newly emerging groups in Iranian society all were agreed, at least in principle, that independence was a worthy cause. Nationalism cloaked in constitutionalism was the predominant feature of the movement. Said E. G. Browne:

> My own conviction is that the mere tyranny of an autocrat would hardly have driven the patient and tractable people of Persia into revolt had tyranny at home been combined with any maintenance of prestige abroad or only moderately effective guardianship of Persian independence. It was the combination of inefficiency, extravagance and lack of patriotic feeling with tyranny which proved insupportable; and a constitutional form of government was sought not so much for its own sake as for the urgent necessity of creating more honest, efficient, and patriotic government than the existing one.[4]

In other words, the movement was, as Browne characterized it, more *nationalistic* than *democratic*. Given the nature of the Constitutional Movement and the status of Iran as a country virtually controlled by Great Britain and particularly Russia, it is evident that the movement contained far-reaching implications for the foreign relations of Iran. This must be borne in mind in the discussion of the development of the Constitutional Movement below.

The Nationalist Uprising

The accumulation of grievances nursed by several groups against Nāṣir al-Dīn Shah and Muẓaffar al-Dīn Shah over a period of fifteen years reached its peak in December 1905. The growing discontent at the latter's ever-increasing extravagance and love of foreign travel, at the new tariffs and the arrogance of the Belgian official, and at the exploitation of the country by foreign concessionaires was focused, not unustifiably on 'Aīn al-Dawlah, the Prime Minister. A large number of merchants took sanctuary (*bast*) in the Masjid-i Shah ("Royal Mosque"), where they were joined by many leading mullahs. Thc Primc Minister ordered his paid supporters to beat the refugees, who, however, did not disperse but went to the holy shrine of Shah 'Abd al-'Aẓīm, a few miles from the city. The threats and promises of

[4] "The Persian Constitutional Movement," in *Proceedings of the British Academy* (London, 1917-18), pp. 323-24.

the Shah and his unpopular Prime Minister did not break up the gathering or prevent new sympathizers, including theological students (*ṭullāb*) and artisans, from joining it.

The scandal finally became so grave and intolerable that the Shah sent an autograph letter (*dast-i khaṭ*) in which he promised the crowd to dismiss the Prime Minister, to convene the ʿAdālatkhānah ("House of Justice"), to abolish favoritism, and to make all Persians equal in the eyes of the law. A few months elapsed before the mullahs of Tehran realized that these were but empty promises. In April 1906 they presented to the Shah a petition reminding him of the disturbances of December 1905 and praying His Majesty to fulfill his promised reforms. This petition produced no effect. Instead, it prompted the Shah and his Prime Minister to resort to every possible means to ensure that such demands were not pressed further. Their repressive measures, however, backfired. Many outstanding mullahs and *vuʿāẓ* ("preachers") began to denounce tyranny from the pulpit. This prompted the Prime Minister to take more severe measures. He first ordered the expulsion of two mullahs from the city. The seizure by the soldiers of one of them aroused great opposition. In the course of the upheaval the soldiers fired on a crowd and killed a number of innocent people. The bloodshed stirred up further turmoil in the now-garrisoned city of Tehran.

These events led to another important *bast*. The mullahs, joined by artisans and tradesmen, took refuge in the "Congregational Mosque" in the center of the city, but on being besieged by soldiers they retired to Qum, eighty miles south of Tehran. In the meantime the Prime Minister ordered the merchants to open their shops, which had been closed as a gesture of protest, or else have their merchandise looted by his soldiers. Upon this threat some bankers and merchants approached the officials of the British Legation inquiring if they could seek protection on legation premises. This led to the last and most important *bast*. By the first of August 1906 about 14,000 Iranians had taken refuge in the British Legation demanding, as the condition of their return to their homes and businesses, the dismissal of the Prime Minister, the recall of the religious leaders from Qum, the grant of a constitution, and the establishment of a national assembly.

The mounting discontent and the increasing popular pressure for reforms and a constitutional regime compelled the Shah "to bend his proud neck before his humble subjects," and he issued a *farmān* for the formation of an assembly. On September 8, 1906, the regulations for an assembly, as drafted and embodied in an electoral law, were submitted to the Shah and ratified by him on the following day. Nevertheless, the nationalists were apprehensive. They feared that the Shah and his supporters might have new tricks up their sleeves and might, under favorable circumstances, revoke the new instrument of government. Furthermore, because of poor roads and inadequate transportation facilities it would probably be a long time before the provinces could complete their elections and send their representatives to the capital.

The National Assembly or Majlis, composed only of representatives of Tehran, met for the first time on October 7, 1906, amid great popular enthusiasm and in the presence of many Iranian and foreign dignitaries. The new Prime Minister, Mushīr al-Dawlah, in addressing the Majlis, assured the deputies of the Shah's support. He also declared that His Majesty was conscious of the need for reforms and hoped that with the cooperation of the Majlis any steps necessary for "the welfare of the nation" and the country would be taken with due speed.

The Shah's assurances were not matched by action. The most pressing task before the Majlis was the drafting of the Fundamental Law of the Constitution. By the end of the month this law had been written by a committee of the Majlis, but the Shah put off ratifying it. The pressure of public opinion finally forced the Shah to give his approval on December 30, 1906, shortly before his death.[5]

The Constitution, in fifty-one articles,[6] provided for the Majlis, set forth its duties, limitations, and rights, detailed how laws were to be drafted, and regulated the formation of the Senate. In the light of the capricious nature of the traditional foreign policy and more particularly in view of the ruinous foreign economic policy of Mu-

[5] Fuller details about these events can be found in Edward G. Browne, *The Persian Revolution, 1905-1909* (Cambridge, 1910), pp. 98-132. See also Kasravī, *op. cit.*, pp. 1-188, and Malikzādah, *op. cit.*, II, 1-234.

[6] The English text of the Fundamental Law of the Constitution is in Browne, *Persian Revolution*, pp. 384-400. The English text as amended and supplemented on May 7 and 8, 1949, is in Helen Miller Davis, *Constitutions, Electoral Laws, Treaties of States in the Middle and Near East* (rev. ed.; Durham, N. C., 1953), pp. 106-16. For an excellent exposition of the origin and development of the constitutional laws of Iran up to 1959, see Laurence Lockhart, "The Constitutional Laws of Persia," *Middle East Journal*, XIII (1959), 372-88.

ẓaffar al-Dīn Shah, the framers of the Constitution took pains to reserve for the Majlis the power to regulate important economic matters, particularly those involving foreign interests.

The regulation of financial matters and the preparation and management of the Budget – all changes in fiscal arrangements – were made subject to the approval of the Majlis. More importantly, any proposal to transfer or sell a portion of the national resources or any change in the boundaries of the country was to be approved by the Majlis. Without its approval no concession for the formation of any public company of any sort was to be granted by the state. The power to conclude treaties and convenants and to grant commercial, industrial, agricultural, and other concessions to Iranian or foreign nationals was also given to the Majlis. State loans, under whatever title, whether internal or external, were to be contracted only by the Majlis, whose approval was also made necessary for the construction of railroads and roads by the government or by any company of Iranian or foreign nationality.[7]

From its inception the Majlis was beset by opposition. This opposition was both domestic and foreign, as the interests of Muḥammad 'Alī Shah, who was crowned on January 19, 1907, and those of Russia coincided. The new Shah was perhaps

> the most perverted, cowardly, and vice-sodden monster that had disgraced the throne of Persia in many generations. He hated and despised his subjects from the beginning of his career, and from having a notorious scoundrel for his Russian tutor, he easily became the avowed tool and satrap of the Russian Government and its agents in Persia for stamping out the rights of the people.[8]

Russia's opposition to the Majlis stemmed from its interest in keeping Iran under its politico-economic bondage, a bondage which had been achieved through the media of its bank, its loans, and its trade.[9]

As we shall see later, the Majlis was destroyed with the support of Russia and by the hands of Russian agents. This destruction served to enhance the concept of constitutionalism. The nationalists were determined to reestablish the Majlis, at whatever cost. They believed that the independence of their country could not be preserved by a ruler who did not care in the least for it or for the welfare of

[7] For these provisions see Articles 19 and 22-26.

[8] W. Morgan Shuster, *The Strangling of Persia* (New York, 1912), p. 21.

[9] See Chapter IV.

his subjects.[10] The destruction of the Majlis and the reestablishment of autocracy, or the "lesser autocracy," were momentous setbacks for the nationalists, but on the very day that the Majlis was destroyed they began the struggle against the Royalist forces in Tabriz.[11]

The nationalist struggle to reestablish "the new order," to promote domestic reforms, and to conduct an independent foreign policy proved far more severe than the initial conflict which led to the founding of the Constitutional regime. The severity of the struggle derived in part from the fact that Russia was giving both moral and material support to the Royalists. Nevertheless, under the leadership of Bāqir Khān and Sattār Khān, the nationalist leaders of Tabriz, the struggle that began with little hope and few prospects soon gained considerable momentum. The nationalist success at Tabriz despite incredible odds alarmed the Shah. On October 11, 1908, he decided to send a force composed of 400 Cossacks, accompanied by some Russian officers, from Tehran to Tabriz to overthrow the nationalists, who were in undisputed possession of the city by October 12. The Shah's troops marched toward Tabriz, surrounded the city, and prevented its inhabitants from getting provisions from the outside. By January 1909 many were starving or barely subsisting on grass. The desperate food situation, the Shah hoped, would force the nationalists to abandon their struggle. Despite the remarkable degree of order maintained by a local Constitutional government, the situation in Tabriz provided Russia with an excuse to meddle, and on April 20 it decided to send four squadrons of Cossacks, three battalions of infantry, two batteries of artillery, and a company of sappers to that city even though it had been posing as a mediator between the Royalists and the nationalists and in a recent convention with Great Britain had undertaken not to intervene in Iran.

In the meantime other groups had begun to fight for the reestablishment of the Constitutional government. The flame that the nationalists of Tabriz had so successfully kept alive ever since the destruction of the Majlis spread to other cities and provinces of Iran. The revolt broke out at Isfahan on January 2, 1909, at Rasht on February 8, at the ports of Bandar Abbas and Bushire on March 17, at Hamadan and Shiraz on March 25, and at Mashhad on April 6.

[10] Browne, *Persian Revolution*, p. 160.

[11] A detailed account of the nationalist struggle at Tabriz can be found in Kasravī, *op. cit.*, pp. 676-906. See also Browne, *Persian Revolution*, pp. 249-91.

The nationalist forces at Isfahan and Rasht soon began to move toward the capital. Having occupied the city of Isfahan, the chief of the Bakhtyārī tribesmen, Ṣamṣām al-Saltanah, was joined by his brother educated in Europe, Sardār Asad. The latter was "a more dedicated nationalist," who had worked for the cause of constitutionalism while still in Europe. The nationalist army of Rasht was commanded by Sipahdār A'ẓam, who was blessed by the active cooperation of a skillful Armenian named Ephraim Khān. On May 5, 1909, Sipahdār's forces took Qazvin, some ninety miles north of Tehran. A day later a force of Iranian Cossacks, commanded by the Russian Captain Zapolski, was dispatched from Tehran to guard the pass and bridge at Karaj, thirty miles northwest of the capital.

On June 16 the Bakhtyārī forces actually started for Tehran, and shortly thereafter they were in communication with the nationalists at Qazvin. Thus the two forces could coordinate their strategy from the north and south in moving toward Tehran, which had been prepared for defense by the Royalists. On July 13 the nationalists slipped through the Royalist lines "with remarkable skill" and entered the capital, where street fighting took place throughout the day. By July 15 the nationalist forces, "received with great enthusiasm by the people," were in full possession of Tehran. A day later the Shah took refuge in the Russian Legation and thereby abdicated the throne. On November 15, 1909, the Second Majlis began its term.

EXTERNAL DEVELOPMENTS: THE ANGLO-RUSSIAN *RAPPROCHEMENT*

Anglo-Russian rivalry was still the dominant external factor in Iranian foreign policy when the Constitutional Revolution broke out. Russia's influence was far greater than Great Britain's in Tehran. Inasmuch as the early stirrings of nationalism had been a protest against the unbridled economic activities of Russia, Great Britain watched the development with particular interest. In July 1906 when Grant Duff, the British chargé d'affaires at Qulhak, was asked by representatives of the discontented merchants and bankers whether they would be protected by the British Legation if they took refuge there, the answer was emphatically in the affirmative. At this time the interests of the nationalists and Great Britain coincided.

But circumstances soon began to change dramatically when, for the first time in their age-old rivalry, Great Britain and Russia decided to cooperate for the sake of their "greater interests." This *rapprochement*, which was crystalized in the Anglo-Russian Convention of 1907, produced an entirely new set of conditions with which Iran had to contend until the Bolshevik Revolution. For about a century the British counterweight had kept Russia from unilaterally absorbing Iran. The *rapprochement* gave Russia an unprecedented opportunity to intervene in Iran.

Partition of the Country into Spheres of Influence

Many considerations underlay the Anglo-Russian Convention of 1907. One was Germany. Germany was determined to challenge Great Britain's rule of the seas. In 1898 and 1900 Berlin launched its program of naval rearmament. The "big navy" policy was the pet child of Admiral von Tirpitz, Secretary of the Navy from 1897 to 1916, who was supported by Kaiser Wilhelm. Germany was also bent on penetration of the Middle East, a policy that alarmed both Great Britain and Russia. The ambitious Baghdad railway plan was designed to link the Persian Gulf with Konia, the terminal point of the German-controlled Anatolian railway. The concession for the railway was secured by Germany from Turkey in 1902, and in spite of British and Russian opposition the 200-kilometer stretch from Konia to Eregli was completed by the autumn of 1904.

Great Britain's traditional interests in India and the Persian Gulf played an important part in the conclusion of the convention. For more than thirty years the government of India had feared that Russian influence might penetrate to the province of Sistan, the eastern province of Iran contiguous to the Indian frontier. Lord Curzon, in his famous dispatch of September 21, 1899, accorded Sistan great significance. By reason of its geographical position in relation both to northern Khorasan, to western Afghanistan, to British Baluchistan, and to the Persian Gulf, Sistan, he said, is of no small strategical importance. It "is the present meeting point of the advanced pioneers of British and Russian influence." "The Government of India could not contemplate without dismay the prospect of Russian neighbourhood in Eastern and Southern Persia."[12] Sir Arthur Nicolson, afterward Lord Carnock, who began the official negotiations for the 1907 convention with Alexander Izvolsky, the Russian Foreign Minister, therefore approached "the Persian problem solely from the point of view of the defense of India."[13]

Great Britain's interests in the Persian Gulf were numerous. For example, British trade acquired almost a monopoly of the foreign commerce of the Gulf ports. Indians had settled in considerable numbers at Lengah, Bandar Abbas, Bushire, and Bahrein. Foregn imports and exports passed through the hands of these settlers. The many Anglo-Indian companies maintained a merchant steamer service between Karachi and Basra. British communication interests in the Gulf were equally significant. Great Britain maintained the submarine cables of the Indo-European Telegraph Company from Fao to Jask and of the land lines from Jask to Karachi. Furthermore, Great Britain had important political agreements with the Gulf states. The Sheikh of Kuwait, for example, had agreed not to receive the representatives of any other power. Great Britain also controlled Musqat, whose trade was in Anglo-Indian hands.

Maintenance of the British position in the Persian Gulf was regarded as "vital to the safety of India." As early as February 1900 Russia had attempted to gain a foothold in the Gulf, but had failed. In the following years Russian warships toured the Gulf, but no further attempts were made to acquire a footing. Consulates, however, were established at Basra, Bushire, and Bandar Abbas. Russia's ambitions and its concerted efforts to gain influence in the Gulf alarmed the British, but it was not until the termination of the Boer War that Great Britain made the most important declaration of British policy in relation to the Gulf since Sir Edward Grey's pronouncement in 1895. Lord Lansdowne declared:

> Firstly, we should protect and promote British trade in the Gulf. Secondly, we should not exclude the legitimate trade of others. Thirdly, we should regard the establishment of a naval base or a fortified port in the Gulf by any other Power as a very grave menace

[12] For the text, see J. C. Hurewitz, *Diplomacy in the Near and Middle East* (Princeton, N. J., 1956), I, 219-49.

[13] Harold Nicolson, *Portrait of a Diplomatist, Being the Life of Sir Arthur Nicolson First Lord Carnock, and a Study of the Origins of the Great War* (Boston, 1930), pp. 176-77.

to British interests, and we should certainly resist it by all the means at our disposal.[14]

In view of the significance attached to the Gulf, Great Britain was "anxious that in the Convention an article should be inserted by which Russia would recognize [British] special interests in the maintenance of the status quo in the Persian Gulf" [15] but because of Russia's apprehensions the Gulf question was settled later by a letter from Grey to Nicolson which was appended to the convention and published with it.[16] Grey's letter states: "For the Russian Government have, in the course of the negotiations leading up to the conclusion of this agreement, explicitly stated that they do not deny the special interests of Great Britain in the Persian Gulf – a statement of which His Majesty have formally taken note." [17]

Russia's interests in reaching an agreement with its traditional rival were also manifold. Anglo-Russian hostility, which had reached its zenith during the Dogger Bank incident, subsided after the Russo-Japanese War. Izvolsky, who had opposed the policy that had led to the conflict with Japan, believed in the need for friendship with Great Britain.[18] He realized that Russia was greatly weakened by its war with Japan and that the Franco-Russian Alliance had consequently lost weight as compared with the Triple Alliance. Both Russia and the Franco-Russian combination needed the strengthening which could come from closer relations with the greatest sea power in the world. Izvolsky's belief in the need for strengthening Russia was reinforced by his suspicion that Japan was preparing for a new struggle in the Far East.[19] The natural bridge between Russia and Japan seemed to be Great Britain, Japan's ally since 1902. Furthermore, the fact that both Russia and Great Britain were linked to France – the former by an alliance of 1897 and the latter by the Entente Cordiale of 1904 – seemed to favor friendly cooperation between St. Petersburg

[14] Sir A. W. Ward and G. P. Gooch, *The Cambridge History of British Foreign Policy* (New York, 1923), III, 320-21.
[15] Nicolson, *op. cit.*, p. 184.
[16] For these Russian "apprehensions," see *ibid.*, pp. 184-85.
[17] The text of this letter is in Ward and Gooch, *op. cit.*, p. 359.
[18] On Russia's motives, see Michael T. Florinsky, *Russia: A History and An Intepretation* (New York, 1953), II, 1286-87.
[19] Sidney Bradshaw Fay, *The Origins of the World War* (New York, 1956), p. 215.

and London.[20] Nevertheless, Russia could hardly hope to enhance its international posture through friendship with Great Britain so long as the long-standing conflict of interests in the Near and Middle East remained unresolved.

Reconciliation of such conflicting interests could pay off for Russia in two important ways. First, it would remove a dangerous source of trouble with Great Britain at a time when Russia needed long years of peace to recover from the effects of its war with Japan. The Crimean War and the Penjdeh incident which nearly led to war between Russia and Great Britain in 1885 were still fresh memories. Second, an understanding with Great Britain might allow Russia to adopt an even more expansionist policy in the Middle East after having been checkmated in the Far East.

Official negotiations began in June 1906 and lasted for fifteen months, leading to the signing of the convention on August 31, 1907. "While the Anglo-French Treaty of 1904 included the world in its embrace, the Anglo-Russian Treaty was confined to Persia, Afghanistan and Tibet, for it was in the Middle East alone that friction remained." "Thus the Pact of 1907, though more limited in scope than that of 1904, achieved a similar result by cleaning off the slate the causes of antagonism between the two historic rivals." [21]

The provisions of the convention in regard to Iran amounted to *de facto* partition of the country, although the preamble contained the customary sanctimonious reference to the preservation of Iran's integrity and independence. After stating that Great Britain and Russia had mutually engaged to respect the integrity and independence of Iran, the convention went on to divide the country into spheres of influence. Because Anglo-Russian penetration of Iran had been accomplished chiefly by means of concessions, spheres of influence were allotted by reference to the concessions that the two powers allowed each other to obtain in certain areas. The major provisions of the convention were as follows:

1) *British Sphere*: Great Britain would not seek for itself, or support in favor of British or third-power subjects, any commercial or political concessions beyond a line from Qasir-i Shirin, passing through Isfahan, Yazd, Kakhk, and ending at a point on the Iranian

[20] Florinsky, *op. cit.*, p. 1287.
[21] Ward and Gooch, *op. cit.*, p. 358.

frontier at the intersection of the Russian and Afghan frontiers. The places mentioned were excluded from the British sphere.

2) *Russian Sphere*: Similarly Russia undertook not to seek commercial or political concessions beyond a line going from the Afghan frontier by way of Gazik, Birjand, Kerman, and ending at Bandar Abbas. The places mentioned were excluded from the Russian sphere.

3) *Neutral Zone*: Great Britain and Russia undertook reciprocally not to seek any kind of concessions in the zone situated between their spheres.[22]

The Russian zone was far larger and richer than the British and included Tehran, the capital city. This was a consequence of the fact that Russia, by the time of the convention, possessed far superior influence in Iran. Russia had already penetrated all the sphere allotted to it and was rapidly expanding into the regions beyond. Its political influence at Tehran was proverbial. The commercial value of the British zone was not its main attraction in 1907, although it was known to be a region of oil fields, the full richness of which became apparent only subsequently. Many Englishmen, although recognizing their inferior influence in Iran at the time, criticized the convention, particularly its clauses on Iran. Lord Curzon, for example, launched a full-dress attack upon it in the House of Lords. After calling it "the most far-reaching and the most important treaty which had been concluded by the British government during the past fifty years," he charged that "we had thrown away the efforts of our diplomacy and our trade for more than a century, and had handed over to Russia not only the trade route from Baghdad but also the important marts of Isfahan and Yazd." [23]

The convention was favorably received in Russia. The Russian Duma welcomed Izvolsky's speech and his mention of the convention amid applause and shouts of "bravo." [24] Judging from what had been demanded by some "Russian imperialists" during the course of negotiations, it may be safely assumed that even in Russia the convention met with some criticism, although by no means so severe as in Great Britain and western Europe. "Russian imperialists" had demanded

[22] The text is in Hurewitz, *op. cit.*, I, 265-67.

[23] Nicolson, *op. cit.*, p. 187. For further criticisms and their rebuttal, see Ward and Gooch, *op. cit.*, pp. 361-66.

[24] For further information see Rogers Platt Churchill *Anglo-Russian Convention of 1907* (Cedar Rapids, Iowa, 1939), pp. 332-33.

that Iran come entirely under Russian influence and that Russia build a trans-Iranian railway and press on to the Persian Gulf.[25] Both British and Russian critics argued for a larger share for their respective countries rather than against the partition of Iran.

Destruction of the First and Second Majlis

One consequence of the new Anglo-Russian friendship was the destruction of the new Iranian parliament. Foreign hostility, with domestic aid, destroyed the foundations of the Constitutional government twice in about four years. Prior to the 1907 convention Great Britain had acted as a midwife of the new order, but subsequently, in spite of Grey's good intentions, British performance generally favored Russia at the expense of Iran. Grey's policy toward Iran from beginning to end was nonintervention and friendship with Russia, and, if the two objects clashed, the former had to yield. "If the Persian question was mismanaged," he argued, "the Persian question might disappear, and bigger issues would arise." It was this conviction which governed his actions, resulting in the subordination of purely Iranian interests to the demands of the European situation.[26] Russia was quite aware of British thinking and took advantage of it. S. D. Sazonov[27] aptly described the situation in a significant letter to the Russian Minister at Tehran: "The English, engaged in the pursuit of political aims of vital importance in Europe, may, in case of necessity, be prepared to sacrifice certain interests in Asia in order to keep a Convention alive which is of such importance to them. This is a circumstance which we can, of course, exploit for ourselves, as for instance, in Persian affairs."[28]

Russian opposition to the Constitutional government was welcomed by Muḥammad 'Alī Shah from the beginning of his reign on January 19, 1907. His acts defying the Majlis are too numerous to mention here,[29] but the nature of his fight against it is well summarized by E. G. Browne:

[25] Fay, *op. cit.*, p. 217.
[26] Ward and Gooch, *op. cit.*, p. 423.
[27] Sazonov was the Russian Foreign Minister from 1910 to 1916.
[28] Fay, *op. cit.*, p. 222.
[29] For details, see Browne, *Persian Revolution*, pp. 133-71.

On the one hand we see a King, selfish, obstinate, headstrong, who having looked forward to enjoying one day the unrestricted power of his predecessors and indulging in his turn in their lavish extravagance, suddenly finds himself checked and thwarted in his aims by a young but sturdy Parliament, for the destruction of which he is willing to pay any price, even the price of Persia's freedom and independence. On the other hand we see an ancient and talented people, long oppressed and downtrodden, long schooled to servitude and silence, but now suddenly awakened to new hopes and conscious of new powers, and resolute not to suffer the cup of Freedom, as yet hardly tasted, to be dashed from their lips.[30]

The storm broke on December 15, 1907, when the Shah summoned the Cabinet to the palace and had Nāṣir al-Mulk, the Prime Minister, imprisoned with a chain around his neck. He also hired ruffians, mostly muleteers and grooms, who, under the protection of the Shah's Cossacks, agitated against the Majlis. The Russian bank provided the Shah with the money, which he raised on the security of jewels and other valuables, for paying his hired agitators.[31] People from all walks of life took up arms and protected the Majlis building while the deputies were in session. On December 18, 1907, after receiving visits from the French and the Turkish Ambassadors, the Shah gave in, promising to punish the rioters whom he had incited.

This abortive *coup d'état* intensified the enmity between the Shah, still supported by Russia, and the Majlis in spite of the latter's conciliatory efforts, between December 1907 and May 1908, to improve relations with the Shah. The Majlis continued to demand the dismissal from their posts of six of the most stubborn anti-Constitutionalists while the Shah was pressing for restrictions on the freedom of the press and speech. The most obnoxious of the six were Amīr Bahādur Jang and Shapshāl Khān, the Shah's Russian ex-tutor. Having obtained some concessions from the Majlis, the Shah consented to their dismissal, but they did not go far away. Amīr Bahādur Jang took refuge in the Russian Legation, and Shapshāl Khān, with Colonel Liakhoff, the Russian commander of the Persian Cossacks, secretly plotted against the deputies. In the meantime De Hartwig, the Russian Minister, accompanied by the British chargé d'affaires, visited the Iranian Minister of Foreign Affairs and said to him:

[30] *Ibid.*, pp. 159-60.
[31] *Ibid.*, p. 170.

> The life of the Shah is in jeopardy. What business have these Nationalists to interfere with His Majesty's personal servants, especially the old Amir Bahadur Jang who watches over his master's safety like a faithful watch-dog? The *anjumans* and Nationalists have transgressed all bounds, and wish now to depose the Shah. This we can not tolerate, and should it happen, Russia will be compelled to interfere and will do so with the approval and sanction of England.[32]

Russia's intervention in favor of the Shah and his Russian agents stiffened the opposition to the Constitutional regime. The Shah, with the aid of Liakhoff and Shapshāl Khān, embarked upon a plan for the destruction of the Bahāristān, the Majlis building, and the dispersal of the deputies. Ostensibly for rest and fresh air, but in reality in order to prepare for waging war against the Majlis, he left the city and resided in Bāgh-i Shah ("King's Garden"), to which he moved arms and ammunition. He collected troops, seized all the telegraph offices, cut off the Majlis from communication with the provinces, established martial law, and filled the town with Cossack patrols under the command of Liakhoff. He then demanded the expulsion from the capital of eight of the great nationalist leaders and the suppression of the press. The nationalists and their sympathizers reacted with vigor and speed. Nationalist volunteers took up arms and gathered in the precincts of the Bahāristān. Riots broke out in the provinces, and the city of Tabriz dispatched 300 horsemen for "the defense of the Constitution."

On June 23, 1908, Russia achieved its goal. Colonel Liakhoff, accompanied by six other Russian officers and their men, drove up to the parliament building, divided his troops, and placed his guns in positions facing the nationalists guarding the building. The Russian officers gave the order to fire on the building. Many nationalists were killed. Ḥāj Mīrzā Ibrāhīm, one of the eight nationalist leaders whom the Shah wished to expel from Tehran, was killed resisting capture. Malik al-Mutikkalimīn, the nationalist orator, and Mīrzā Jahāngīr Khān, the editor of the newspaper *Ṣūr-i Isrāfīl,* were strangled. For several days the homes of nationalists and their sympathizers were bombarded and looted. The parliament building was reduced to ruins, and the records of the Majlis were destroyed. In recognition of all these accomplishments Liakhoff was appointed the military governor

[32] *Ibid.,* p. 201.

of Tehran. He practically ruled the capital until the "Nationalist Victory" of July 16, 1909.

Russia's enmity toward the Constitutional regime was evidenced not only in assisting the destruction of the First Majlis[33] but also in causing the overthrow of the Second Majlis. For the betterment of the financial administration of Iran the Second Majlis, on June 13, 1911, passed a law favored by Morgan Shuster, the American financial adviser, to establish a central organization to be known as the Office of the Treasurer-General of Iran. This office was to be responsible for the collection and disbursement of all revenues and government receipts, from whatever source. The very day that the law was passed

the Russian Legation openly declared war upon it and the Russian Minister announced that the Belgian Customs employees should not be subjected to the control or supervision of the American Treasurer-General, and even went so far as to threaten to have Russian troops seize the customs houses in the north and put Russian officials in charge.[34]

Russia's opposition stemmed from the fact that the law signaled the determination of the Majlis to effect financial reforms and emancipation. Financial independence could not be tolerated by Russia, which had managed to attain political ascendancy in Tehran through the control of Iranian finances, a control which Russia had maintained ever since it gave Muẓaffar al-Dīn Shah the first loan in 1900.[35] By enacting the law of June 13, 1911, the Majlis was granting Shuster "full Powers" over finances. For this reason the Russian war with the Majlis took "the form of a cantankerously vindictive opposition" to Shuster.

Russia's next strike at the Second Majlis was not long delayed. In order to collect the revenue a Treasury Gendarmerie was required. Major Stokes, then near the end of his four years' service as military attaché at the British Legation, seemed to Shuster "the ideal man" for the task of organizing the Gendarmerie. Shuster took up the matter with the British Legation by letter and on July 22, 1911, was

[33] Russia denied responsibility for Colonel Liakhoff's bombing of the Majlis building, contending that he served the Iranian government, but there is plenty of documentary and circumstantial evidence to show that he was consciously serving the interests of Russia. See, for example, Browne, *Persian Revolution*, pp. 210-32, and Kasravī, *op. cit.*, pp. 589-93.

[34] Shuster, *op. cit.*, p. 53.

[35] For details, see Chapter IV.

informed by the British Minister that the major would have to resign his commission in the Indian army before accepting the command of the Gendarmerie. The major immediately cabled his resignation, and Shuster regarded the matter as practically settled. But in the meantime Russia learned of the project and began to protest. Sir Edward Grey referred the matter to St. Petersburg and then "informed Tehran that Major Stokes had been appointed without consulting Great Britain; that his employment in the North might involve political difficulties and that he could not deprecate Russian objections to it."[36] In order to placate Russia, Grey told the Iranian government that Great Britain could not accept Stokes's resignation from the Indian army.

In the meantime Russia had intervened directly in the matter. On August 19, 1911, the Russian Legation addressed a memorandum to the Iranian Foreign Office stating,

> The Imperial Government of Russia, for reasons explained at the time to the Persian Government, considers the engagement by the latter of Major Stokes as chief of the armed forces – called gendarmerie – for the collection of taxes as incompatible with its interests, and I am charged to protest against the appointment. Failing satisfaction, the Imperial Government would reserve to itself the right to take such measures as it might judge to be necessary for the safeguarding of its interests in the North of Persia.[37]

Russia's third blow to the Second Majlis was even more severe. After the "Nationalist Victory" and the restoration of the Constitutional government in 1909 Muḥammad 'Alī Shah had taken refuge in the Russian Legation and later escaped to Odessa. The Russian government, acting for itself and Great Britain, then assumed the responsibility of keeping the ex-Shah to his agreement not to indulge in any political agitation against the Constitutional regime in Iran. When, however, it seemed that the Second Majlis was determined to cast off Russian financial and political controls, Russia decided to fight the Constitutional government on all fronts. The ex-Shah had long been subservient to Russia, whose interests he had served in the Russian-financed *coup d'état* of December 1907 and in the Russian-supported destruction of the First Majlis in June 1908. He could now be unleashed to destroy the Second Majlis.

[36] Ward and Gooch, *op. cit.*, p. 420.
[37] The text of the memorandum is in Shuster, *op. cit.*, p. 75.

On July 18, 1911, the ex-Shah embarked, with a group of supporters and munitions of war, on the Russian steamer *Christoforos* at a Russian port just north of Baku and, crossing the Caspian Sea, landed at Gumesh-Tappeh. His "filibustering expedition to regain the throne of Persia was not only known in the highest circles of the Russian government but also it was well known throughout the entire bureaucracy of that country." [38] Sir Edward Grey at first was "thoroughly roused," stating, "I do not see how we or Russia can acquiesce in his [the ex-Shah's] return." [39] But in this instance, as in the Stokes crisis, its interest in keeping the Convention of 1907 alive restrained Great Britain from raising serious objections to the ex-Shah's return. In a "colorless communication" Great Britain, joined by Russia, declared that since the ex-Shah was in Iranian territory they could not interfere.[40]

The ex-Shah and his brothers, Shu'ā al-Saltanah and Sālār al-Dawlah, launched attacks on government forces with the object of capturing Tehran. Arshad al-Dawlah, "the bravest general" of the ex-Shah, defeated government troops at Damghan northeast of Tehran, on August 8, 1911, but soon the latter won a significant victory at Firuzkuh, in the mountains northeast of Tehran. By August 28 the general had advanced along the road to Tehran as far as Ayvan Kayf, where he defeated the government forces for the second time. However, when he and his men were about forty miles from the capital, the nationalist forces, under the command of Ephraim Khān, attacked and defeated them, subsequently capturing Arshad al-Dawlah, who later faced the firing squad in punishment for his rebellion. By the early part of October 1911 the ex-Shah and his brothers were in flight and their forces completely shattered.

Soon a new crisis developed. This provided Russia with a propitious opportunity to deal its fourth and fatal blow to the Constitutional regime. In October 1911 the government decided to confiscate and seize the estates and property of the rebellious brothers of the ex-Shah. Shuster was ordered to carry out the decision and take over the properties in the name of the Treasury. The principal estate was the park and palace of Prince Shu'ā al-Saltanah. While attempting to seize this palace in Tehran, Shuster's agents were driven off by

[38] *Ibid.*, p. 108.
[39] Ward and Gooch, *op. cit.*, p. 420.
[40] *Ibid.* The text of this communication is in Shuster, *op. cit.*, p. 110.

officers of the Russian Consulate and armed Cossacks, who threatened to fire on them if they did not leave the estate. "I feel sure," wrote Shuster to S. Poklewski-Koziell, the Russian Minister, "that your Excellency will recognize that this action by your consular officers is wholly unwarranted and unlawful." [41]

Nevertheless, on November 2, 1911, the Russian Minister called at the Iranian Foreign Office and demanded that the Treasury gendarmes be immediately withdrawn from the park of Shu'ā al-Saltanah. The Russian demands were reiterated on November 11, 1911, when the Iranian government was told that if they were not complied with within forty-eight hours, diplomatic relations between Russia and Iran would be broken off. Seven days later the Russian Legation informed the Iranian government that inasmuch as the ultimatum had not been accepted diplomatic relations were thereby broken off. In the meantime the news reached Tehran that 4,000 Russian troops were en route from the Caucasus to Iran.

On November 29 the Russian government presented to Iran its second ultimatum, asking that it be accepted within forty-eight hours. This remarkable ultimatum demanded (1) the dismissal of Shuster; (2) an undertaking by the Iranian government not to engage foreign subjects in the service of Iran without first obtaining the consent of the Russian and British Legations, and (3) the payment of an indemnity to defray the expenses of the troops then on their way to Iran.[42]

In this crisis, as in the previous ones, Great Britain went along with the Russians. The British argument was the same as before. In defense of his Iranian policy the Foreign Secretary invoked the 1907 convention and stated in part:

The independence of Persia must take account of the interests of her neighbours, and her hostility to Russia is unjustified by facts. If the Russian officers in Tehran had intervened on behalf of the ex-Shah, he would never have been turned out. But the Persian Government, having got rid of the Shah, determined to get rid of Russian influence in Persia. That was a perfectly hopeless policy.[43]

[41] For the complete text of the letters exchanged, see Shuster, *op. cit.*, pp. 139-42.

[42] For the complete text, see *ibid.*, pp. 166-67.

[43] Ward and Gooch, *op. cit.*, p. 422. Grey did not object to the demand for the dismissal of Shuster. Nor did he object to the demand that the British and

The drama in Tehran was, however, witnessed with indignation "by the British friends of Persian reform." "It had been the policy of Russia," cried a member of the House of Commons, "to make the government of Persia impossible, so as to have an excuse to come in; and Great Britain had condoned every step she had taken." [44]

In the crisis that now confronted the Iranian government the administration split into two factions. The Cabinet under Ṣamṣām al-Saltanah took the view that the Russian ultimatum should be accepted, while the Majlis opposed it vehemently. In the face of Russia's menacing position disunity could spell nothing but disaster. On December 1, 1911, the Cabinet proposed to the Majlis a resolution authorizing it to accept Russia's demands within forty-eight hours. The vote had to be taken before the time expired and there was little opportunity for long speeches. "It may be the will of Allah," one of the deputies stated briefly but firmly, "that our liberty and our sovereignty shall be taken away from us by force, but let us not sign them away with our own hands." [45] Other deputies followed with similarly brief appeals, and then the vote was taken.

And when the roll call was ended, every man, priest or layman, youth or octogenarian, had cast his own die of fate, had staked the safety

---

Russian Legations should be consulted in the appointment of foreign advisers. But the demand for indemnity, he believed, would doubtless be withdrawn (*ibid.*, p. 423). This single objection to the Russian demands was influenced by British commercial interests in Iran. The payment of such an indemnity would, it was feared, cripple Iran's security forces policing the southern trade route and thus prejudice British commerce (Shuster, *op. cit.*, p. 169).

In order to preserve British commercial interests, the British government at one time resorted to the threat of force. Even with the termination of the nationalist-Royalist fighting in late 1909 and the abdication of the Shah, order and security did not immediately return to the provinces and anarchy threatened British commerce. In March 1910 gunboats were sent to Bushire and Bandar Abbas, and on October 14, 1910, Grey sent an ultimatum to Tehran on the state of the southern roads. Unless order was restored on the road from Bushire to Isfahan within three months, Great Britain would police it. Iran's strong reply of October 21, 1910, put the blame squarely on the British and Russians but gave assurances that order would be restored as soon as possible. The British threat was never carried out, and the task of restoring order was left in the hands of the Swedish Gendarmerie serving the Iranian government. For details, see Aḥmad Kasravī, *Tārīkh-i Hījdah Sālah-'i Āẕarbāijān* (Tehran, 1333 [1954/55]), pp. 145-56.

[44] Ward and Gooch, *op. cit.*, p. 421.

[45] Shuster, *op. cit.*, p. 182.

of himself and family, and hurled back into the teeth of the great Bear from the North the unanimous answer of a desperate and down-trodden people who preferred a future of unknown terror to the voluntary sacrifice of their national dignity and of their recently earned right to work out their own salvation.[46]

By this vote the Cabinet fell, according to the Constitution, and the Majlis was left alone to face the grim prospects that lay ahead. Meanwhile thousands of Russian troops, with Cossacks and artillery, were pouring into northern Iran from Tiflis and Julfa by land and from Baku across the Caspian Sea, to the Iranian port of Enzeli, whence they took up their 220-mile march over the Elburz Mountains toward Qazvin and Tehran. By December 15, 1911, about 4,000 Russian troops had reached Qazvin. On that day the Russian Legation informed the Iranian government that if the conditions of the ultimatum were not complied with within six days, the Russian troops would start for Tehran.[47]

Russia, however, did not have to capture Tehran in order to destroy what was left of the Constitutional government – the Majlis. By this time 12,000 Russian troops were occupying the entire northern part of Iran, the country was once again plunged into confusion and disorder, and the members of the deposed Cabinet were still striving to persuade the Majlis – perhaps by the same means that Russia had used to persuade them [48] to accept the Russian demands. Russia had been assisted by the ex-Shah in destroying the First Majlis. The ex-Cabinet served a similar purpose this time. On December 24 the ex-Cabinet executed a *coup d'état* against the Majlis; the deputies were expelled from the parliament building and were told that their lives would be in danger should they return. Thus, to quote from Shuster's *The Strangling of Persia,* "they abolished the last vestige of Constitutional rule in Persia, and left their country at the mercy of seven oriental statesmen who had already sold out to the Russian Government. It was a sordid ending to a gallant struggle for liberty and enlightenment." [49]

[46] *Ibid.*
[47] *Ibid.*, p. 187.
[48] Shuster indicates that some members of the Cabinet had been bribed (*op. cit.*, p. 199).
[49] *Ibid.*, p. 200.

Outright Intervention

Besides partitioning Iran into spheres of influence and destroying the Majlis, the Anglo-Russian friendship induced an unprecedented degree of outright intervention in the affairs of the country. This intervention reached its peak in the period between the end of the Constitutional government (December 24, 1911) and the outbreak of the First World War. During these years foreign and domestic problems became almost indistinguishable. With the destruction of the Majlis, Nāṣir al-Mulk, the Regent,[50] became the principal political figure at a time when no substance remained to Iran's "independence and integrity." The Regent did not help the extremely difficult situation; his love of European travel kept him away from the country far too much.

Actually, however, control of the Regent was not enough to satisfy the intervening powers. Because the Cabinet was in charge of affairs of state, Great Britain and Russia became deeply involved in the rise and fall of various Cabinets. Political instability was thus compounded by foreign intervention. To preserve their commercial and political interests the powers demanded, through the medium of their legations, that the Iranian government conform its policy with the principles of the Anglo-Russian Convention of 1907. They made every effort to see that no Prime Minister took office unless he was either their man or would not stand in their way.

Sa'd al-Dawlah was the Anglo-Russian candidate for the post of Prime Minister. In November 1912 the powers outwitted Prime Minister Ṣamṣām al-Saltanah into requesting Sa'd's return from Europe.[51] In London Sazonov and Grey even discussed the conditions

[50] Nāṣir al-Mulk succeeded the aged 'Aẕud al-Mulk, who had been elected Regent after the formal deposition of Muḥammad 'Alī Shah and the succession of his twelve- or thirteen-year-old son Sultān Aḥmad Mīrzā. Nāṣir al-Mulk's election as the Regent in September 1911 was not uncontested. As early as 1908 two political "parties" had emerged on the scene in Iran. These were the Revolutionary (*Inqilābī*) and the Moderate (*I'tidālī*) parties, the members of which later became known as Democrats and Moderates, respectively. Nāṣir al-Mulk was favored by the Moderates and opposed by the Democrats, who desired the election of Mustawfī al-Mamālik. The controversial Regent dominated the scene from the time of the destruction of the Constitutional regime in December 1911 until after the outbreak of the First World War, when Sultān Aḥmad Mīrzā was crowned and the Third Majlis was opened.

[51] Muvarrikh al-Dawlah Sipahr, *Īrān dar Jang-i Buzurg* (Tehran, 1336 [1957/58]), p. 15.

of his taking office. These included his acceptance of the financial and other terms that the powers proposed.[52] Because of personal animosity between him and the Regent, as well as for other reasons, the powers failed to install him in office in spite of his return to Tehran on November 9, 1912. It was not easy for the powers to find another man whom they both trusted. Furthermore, their experience in the Sa'd al-Dawlah case made them realize that their choice should not offend certain factions and individuals active and influential in Iranian politics. The British and Russian Ministers at Tehran were asked to find out who would be reasonably acceptable as Prime Minister. The British Minister informed Grey that 'Alā' al-Saltanah might be the man, and the latter took office. On January 11, 1913, the Minister further informed his government that 'Alā' al-Saltanah's Cabinet was the most stable one that could be formed at the time. The Russians were not so enthusiastic as the British. Sazonov wrote the British Ambassador on January 13, 1913, that the Russian attitude toward the new Cabinet would depend entirely on its attitude toward Russia.[53] To be acceptable to Russia, the 'Alā' al-Saltanah Cabinet soon felt compelled to yield to Russian pressure for a concession for a railway from Julfa to Tabriz.

Russia meanwhile was acting like a predatory power in Iran. On March 29, 1912, Russian troops bombarded the holy shrine of Imām Riẕā at Mashhad because Yūsuf-i Harātī, a notorious *agent provocateur* to borrow the words of Sir Percy Sykes, who witnessed the incident, had taken refuge there. Harātī had served the Russians previously but was now disenchanted with them (apparently because his services had been rewarded inadequately). The wanton bombardment was accompanied by looting. The treasury containing the rich gifts of monarchs and other pilgrims was removed to the Russian bank. Later it was restored with some of its contents missing. "The Official Custodian of the Shrine," wrote Sykes, "was forced, under threat of death, to seal a document to the effect that he had received it back intact." [54]

Russia did not treat all its agents so ungratefully. The ex-Shah

[52] Kasravī, *Tārīkh-i Hījdah Sālah,* p. 545.
[53] Sipahr, *op. cit.,* p. 17.
[54] *A History of Persia* (London, 1930), p. 427.

had served Russia's interests most consistently, though not always successfully. In a note dated March 18, 1912, Russia, with Great Britain, demanded that the government of Iran "come to an agreement with Muhammad Ali Shah on the subject of his departure from Persia, of his pension, and of a general amnesty of his followers." [55] Russia was determined to reward the ex-Shah in spite of the fact that on July 31, 1911, when he had returned to Iran to regain the throne, it had declared that he had forfeited his right to the pension fixed by the Protocol signed with the Constitutional regime by the two powers in September 1909.

Russia found a better agent in the person of the ex-Shah's brother, the notorious Sālār al-Dawlah. After the destruction of the Constitutional regime the new government decided to appoint a governor at Kermanshah, 'Abdul Ḥusayn Mīrzā. This was opposed by the ambitious, obstinate, and corrupt Sālār al-Dawlah, who enjoyed Russia's support. His armed rebellion, accompanied by plunder, threatened the central government, which found itself incapable of dispatching any effective troops to quell it. The only significant military operation against him was undertaken by Ephraim Khān, who was killed in the course of battle after having made a brilliant record in the early stages of the Constitutional Movement.[56] Sālār al-Dawlah, who claimed the throne of Iran for himself, annoyed the British, who wished to have a stable government at Tehran. Perhaps because of British irritation Russia finally agreed that Sālār al-Dawlah should leave Iran, but the Russian Minister made certain that he, like the ex-Shah, was handsomely rewarded from the Iranian Treasury: he received a pension of 8,000 tomans a year and the village of Moradabad as the price for his departure from Iran.[57]

Russian depredation was not confined to the bombing of the holy shrine of Imām Riẓā and the looting of its treasury, the rewarding

[55] The English text is in Shuster, *op. cit.*, p. 330.

[56] At the time of the Cabinet *coup d'état* this "brave Armenian," who was then heading the gendarmes of Tehran, had apparently lost heart and fallen in with the plans of the Cabinet. This changing of sides had marred, in the eyes of the Constitutionalists, the brilliant record of gallantry that he had made in the early stages of the Constitutional Movement. His gallant fighting against the notorious Sālār al-Dawlah, in the course of which he was killed, seems to have rekindled the admiration of most Iranians for him.

[57] Kasravī, *Tārīkh-i Hījdah Sālah,* p. 573. For detailed information on Sālār al-Dawlah and his Russian connections, see *ibid.*, pp. 510-75.

of Russian agents, and the incitement of Sālār al-Dawlah. While the Majlis was being destroyed and shortly thereafter, Russian troops in Iran began unrestrained shootings, hangings, and tortures. Men were blown from cannons, and women and children were butchered in the streets. The Russians were determined to kill off the Constitutionalists, whom they called "the revolutionary dregs."

The city of Tabriz bore the brunt of Russian atrocities.[58] The Russians massacred the inhabitants of the city in late December 1911 after a fight between them and the Iranian police had developed. About 4,000 Russian troops and two batteries of artillery surrounded the city, which contained only 1,000 poorly armed Constitutionalists. After shattering the resistance of the Constitutionalists, the Russian military governor hoisted Russian flags over the government buildings at Tabriz. Here again Russia was assisted by "one of the most cruel and treacherous individuals that Iran has ever known." Ṣamad Khān, also known as Shujā' al-Dawlah, acted as a Russian instrument in the period of terrorism that followed the bombing of the Constitutionalist headquarters in Tabriz by Russian troops. In the course of mass arrests and imprisonment some of the leading Constitutionalists were hanged. On 'Āshūrā', the 10th of Muḥarram, a day of religious mourning among Shī'ī Muslims, S̲aqat al-Islām was hanged. On the same day (January 1, 1912) seven other supporters of the Constitutional regime were put to death.[59]

On the diplomatic level Russia acted in concert with Great Britain as far as possible. After the dismissal of Shuster the British and Russian Legations threatened the government with severe measures if it allowed anyone but M. Mornard, the Belgian Administrator of Customs, to succeed Shuster. With Iran's finances in the hands of their protégé, the two powers attempted to establish complete financial control over the country. On March 18, 1912, the two legations proposed to pay a sum of £200,000 to the government of Iran at the interest rate of 7 per cent a year. The advance on this loan was to be expended under the control of the Treasurer-General (Mornard), who would prepare a program of expenditures in consultation with the Cabinet and subject to the approval of the two legations. The

[58] The inhabitants of Rasht and Enzeli experienced almost simultaneously mass arrest, suppression of the press, plunder, and murder at the hands of the Russians. For detailed information, see Malikzādah, *op. cit.*, VII, 140-51.

[59] For their names and biographies, see *ibid.*, pp. 188-89.

puppet government had no choice but to accept the offer on March 20, 1912, in spite of its ominous political conditions.[60]

There were, however, areas in which traditional Anglo-Russian rivalry reappeared. At times the Anglo-Russian friendship was considerably ruffled. This was due in no small degree to the Russian understanding with Germany in regard to the Tehran-Khanaqin railway, which constituted the heart of the Potsdam Agreement, signed on August 19, 1911. By this agreement Russia formally bound itself not to obstruct the Baghdad railway, while Germany admitted Russia's special interests in Iran. Russia was to obtain the concession for the Tehran-Khanaqin line from the Iranian government. Then it was to begin work on the line within two years and to complete it within four years of the opening of the branch planned to join Khanaqin with Baghdad. While the negotiations for the agreement were progressing, Sir Edward Grey expressed his disappointment by saying that Great Britain had no legal title to protest against German control of the proposed line but that such control would give Germany financial and political influence in Iran.

> Germany is strengthened, England weakened. But I make no reproaches. I only ask Russia to keep exclusive control of the line in Persia. A Turkish army under German officers with the use of a railway to Tehran would be a danger. Germany must not have privileges in the Russian sphere which England did not get in 1907.[61]

Russia, however, was undisturbed. Sazonov took the view that the project would probably take ten to fifteen years to complete and he therefore could not see the danger of German influence in the immediate future: "Thus we have still plenty of time to take measures for our definitive control of the Persian markets." [62] To this end Russia pressed for a concession for a railway to link Tabriz with Russia via Julfa. By 1907 the latter town had been joined to Erivan and Tiflis. On February 6, 1913, the concession was granted, and

[60] According to these conditions, Iran was to conform its policy to the principles of the Anglo-Russian Convention, to dismiss the *fadā'ī* ("devotee") and irregular forces (namely, the forces supporting the Constitutional regime) in the service of the Iranian government, and to come to an agreement with Muḥammad 'Alī Shah on the subject of his pension and departure from Iran. For the text of these proposals, see Shuster, *op. cit.*, 329-30.

[61] Ward and Gooch, *op. cit.*, p. 478.

[62] B. H. Sumner, "Tsardom and Imperialism in the Far East and Middle East, 1880-1914," in *Proceedings of the British Academy* (London, 1941), XXVII, 57.

Russia advanced £200,000 to Iran. Faced with Sir Edward Grey's complaint that the government of 'Alā' al-Saltanah had favored Russia over Great Britain, Iran three days later granted to a British syndicate a concession for a railway from Mohammarah to Khoramabad. The increasing rivalry and friction between Britain and Russia suggested that there might be a revival of the antagonism that had characterized their relations prior to the 1907 convention. But this was not to be. The outbreak of the First World War found them fighting on the same side.

FOREIGN POLICY

During its interrupted and short existence, the Constitutional regime, while besieged by internal dissensions and foreign intervention, made three major decisions concerning foreign relations. One concerned a foreign loan. Muẓaffar al-Dīn Shah, who had twice borrowed from Russia under conditions injurious to Iran, nevertheless negotiated a third loan with Great Britain and Russia. Under the Constitution the proposal was submitted to the newly opened Majlis on November 23, 1906. The plan was to obtain a loan of £400,000 in equal moieties from Russia and Great Britain in return for which these countries would control the customs houses of the north and telegraph and post offices of Iran, respectively.[63]

The Majlis was urged by the ministers to act promptly because the fund was to be used to pay diplomatic and consular officers abroad and government personnel at home. The deputies proved impervious to government pressure; they believed that the loan provisions were in contravention of the country's independence.[64] As the debate proceeded it became clear that, as the new wielders of power, the deputies were trying to strike at the cabinet. Ḥāj Mu'īn al-Tujjār, for example, stated that the nation would no longer allow the country to be mortgaged to foreign powers "in the interests of a few selfish Ministers." [65] As an alternative, he proposed to raise a "national loan." This was overwhelmingly approved by the Majlis, but, though "women and children" offered their small savings, the wealthy hung

[63] Browne, *Persian Revolution,* p. 134.
[64] *Ibid.*
[65] Kasravī, *Tārīkh-i Mashrūṭah-i Īrān,* pp. 177-78.

back.[66] The Tabriz merchants endorsed the proposal in principle, but made financial reform the prerequisite.[67] The failure of the scheme prompted the Cabinet, particularly Amīn al-Sultān, the Prime Minister, to seek to persuade the Majlis to approve a Russian loan, but on August 31, 1907, he was murdered by ʿAbbās Āqā, a member of one of the *anjumans* ("political societies").[68]

The Second Majlis did, however, consider obtaining a loan from Russia and Great Britain in December 1909. The loan was for about $2,500,000 and contained a number of conditions that were regarded as "so dangerous to, and destructive of Persia's independence that the Majlis was compelled to reject it." Shortly thereafter the government entered into negotiations with a private bank in London for a loan, and they were almost complete when, as the result of action by the British government, they were broken off.[69] Finally, the Majlis approved a loan of £1,250,000 from the Imperial Bank of Persia in May 1911.

Another development in the field of foreign relations was the government's decision to protest the conclusion of the Anglo-Russian Agreement of 1907. In June of that year the Iranian Minister in London told Grey of Iranian anxiety over a division of the country into spheres of influence. Grey told the Iranian Minister that his impression was "incorrect"; instead, the agreement with Russia would include a British obligation not to push its influence in those parts of Iran which bordered on the frontiers of Russia.[70] Grey later instructed Cecil Spring-Rice, the British Minister at Tehran, to propose to his Russian colleague an identical communication in which it would be stated that both Great Britain and Russia would "absolutely" respect the independence and integrity of Iran, that the specific regions mentioned in the convention were clearly defined in order that future misunderstanding between Great Britain and Russia, which might embarrass the Iranian government, might be avoided, and that "the sole object of the arrangement is the avoidance of any cause of misunderstanding between the contracting Powers. The

[66] Browne, *Persian Revolution*, p. 137.
[67] Kasravī, *Tārīkh-i Mashrūṭah-i Īrān*, pp. 183-85.
[68] Cf. Browne, *Persian Revolution*, p. 150, and Kasravī, *Tārīkh-i Mashrūṭah-i Īrān*, pp. 1445-50.
[69] Shuster, *op. cit.*, p. 53 (in the introduction).
[70] Churchill, *op. cit.*, p. 265.

Shah's Government will be convinced that the Agreement can not fail to promote the prosperity, security and ulterior development of Persia in the most efficacious manner."[71]

Prior to the presentation of this memorandum on September 11, 1907, Spring-Rice wrote a reassuring letter to the Iranian Foreign Minister (September 5, 1907) in which he stated that Great Britain and Russia "have no sort of intention of attacking Persia's independence." "Not only do they not seek a pretext for intervention; but their aim in these friendly negotiations is not to permit one another to intervene in Persia on the pretext of safeguarding their own interest."[72] On September 24 the Iranian Foreign Ministry finally received the text of the convention insofar as it related to Iran. On November 3, 1907, the Minister of Foreign Affairs read the text of Iran's reply to the British government in the Majlis. The convention, which had been concluded between the British and Russian governments, the Iranian note stated, could only affect the contracting parties. As a sovereign and independent state, Iran had certain rights and privileges which were and would be immune from the adverse effects of any agreement which might be reached between two or more foreign states.[73]

A third foreign-policy decision during the early sessions of the Majlis concerned the employment of foreign advisers. In establishing its control over the financial affairs of Iran, Russia had seen to it that the post of Treasurer-General was filled by Mornard, a protégé of Naus, Russia's most devoted agent. As early as December 1910 the deputies of the Majlis had played with the idea of securing finance administrators from a "disinterested and distant" power. Later, in the early 1920's, this idea was raised to the level of what we have called the "third-power policy," and even after the rise of Riẕā Shah it continued as the cornerstone of Iranian foreign policy. The chosen third country in 1910 was the United States. The Cabinet, through

[71] For the text, see Ward and Gooch, *op. cit.*, pp. 413-14.

[72] The full text is translated in Browne, *Persian Revolution*, pp. 190-92. The abridged form of the letter, which was originally published in Persian in *Hablul Matin*, is in Ward and Gooch, *op. cit.*, p. 414. This source states that the letter does not appear in the Blue-Books and remained unknown to Sir Edward Grey until 1911.

[73] The text in Persian is in Maḥmūd Maḥmūd, *Tārīkh-i Ravābiṭ-i Sīyāsī-i Īrān va Inglīs dar Qarn-i Nūzdahum-i Mīlādī* (Tehran, 1333 [1954/55]), VIII, 2244.

the Minister of Foreign Affairs, Ḥusayn Qulī Khān, instructed the Iranian Legation in Washington to request the Secretary of State to put him in touch with possible American financial advisers. The Legation was also authorized to arrange preliminary employment for three years "subject to ratification by parliament of a disinterested American expert as Treasurer-General." [74]

As a result of negotiations with the Department of State, Morgan Shuster was tendered a contract to serve as Treasurer-General of Iran for three years. On February 2, 1911, the Majlis approved the terms of the contracts of Shuster and his four assistants "by a large majority and amid great enthusiasm." [75] It was well understood that Shuster was not going to Iran "in any manner as the representative of the American Government." [76] The fate of the American mission has already been related. The memory of the experiment, in spite of, or maybe because of, its dramatic failure, continued to exert a powerful influence on the foreign policy of Iran in the decades to come.

NATIONALIST UNREALISM

The Constitutional Revolution had a far-reaching impact on the foreign policy of Iran both positively and negatively. First let us consider its positive effects.

The Constitutional Movement was basically a nationalist movement, and, as such, it signaled the beginnings of a nationalization of Iranian foreign policy. Traditionally the Shah had been identified with the state, his ends and means had been those of the state, and he had dealt with foreign powers in the name of "state interests" (*maṣālah-i mamlikat*). As "the sole executive," he had made alliances, waged wars, received and dispatched envoys, granted concessions involving all the resources of the country, contracted loans, and conducted Iran's commerce with other states just about as he pleased as far as Iran was concerned. The Constitution gave the Majlis many important powers concerning foreign affairs. Financial matters, transfers or sales of any portion of the national resources, changes in the

[74] The text of the telegram is in Shuster, *op. cit.*, p. 3.
[75] *Ibid.*, p. 6.
[76] *Ibid.*, p. 4.

boundaries of the nation, concessions, and treaties and covenants were all made subject to the approval of the Majlis.

The Majlis was not remiss in using the powers granted by the Constitution. For the first time in the history of Iran "the representatives of the people" (*namāyandahgān-i mardum*) spoke and acted in "the interests of the people" (*maṣālah-i millat*). In the course of the First and Second Majlis the deputies consulted Iran's national interests, as we have seen, in the case of foreign loans, the 1907 convention, and the employment of Shuster, the American adviser. Many sympathetic observers have testified to the genuineness of the national sentiments of the deputies, a majority of whom in the First Majlis, according to E. G. Browne, "were animated by a patriotism and public spirit which would have been creditable in the members of any Parliament, whether in Europe or America." No less can be said about the deputies of the Second Majlis, who, when faced with the overwhelmingly superior force of Russia and its intrigues, bribes, and threats, refused to sign away "the honor and sovereignty of their nation." [77]

Unfortunately the Constitutional Movement also had a negative impact on foreign policy. Noble sentiments and good intentions are not sufficient in matters of foreign policy. The traditional policy makers had suffered consistently from chronic unrealism, rooted in ignorance, superstition, lack of experience, and other factors. The emerging policy makers were neither so ignorant nor so superstitious. In fact, a few were the graduates of some of the finest European universities. Yet they proved as unrealistic as the traditional policy makers. They, too, chose objectives beyond their means. They aimed uncompromisingly at "complete independence" in disregard of both the external and the internal situation.

Externally the situation was utterly hopeless. Forces beyond the control of Iran had brought the traditional rivals together. Great Britain, which had hitherto acted as a counterweight to Russian influence and intervention in Iran found it difficult to oppose Russia after the 1907 agreement. Moral or immoral, legal or illegal, the agreement was a fact. Disregard of this by the deputies closed off avenues of maneuver that could have counterbalanced to some extent Iran's want of power. It also helped provoke Russia into committing

[77] *Ibid.*, p. 203.

atrocities on Iranian soil and destroying the new parliament which some of the Constitutionalists had paid with their lives to establish.

Internal factors were also ignored by the new policy makers. They mistakenly took nationalism for national unity. They failed to recognize the divisive forces militating against the new political order. The Constitutional Movement split the society between the Royalists and the Nationalists. This division proved to be Russia's best ally in Iran as evidenced by Russian manipulation of not only such notorious characters as Sālār al-Dawlah, Shujā' al-Dawlah, Shapshāl Khān, and Amīr Bahādur Jang but also the Shah himself. Traditional factionalism persisted, although it now appeared in the form, or within the framework of, the new political institutions borrowed from the West.

The choice of "complete independence" as the objective of the new policy makers in disregard of the external and internal limitations imposed on Iran reveals the continuation of unrealism in Iran's foreign policy. The fountainhead of this neo-unrealism differed from that of the traditional one. Now its source was principally the new dogma of nationalism. Nationalism did not bestow a rational foreign policy on Iran overnight. The policy of strict neutrality during the First World War, as will be seen in the following chapter, was an important manifestation of the continuing political unrealism in Iran's foreign policy.

Chapter VI

Foreign Occupation, National Disunity, and the Policy of Neutrality, 1914-1918

World War I came in time to perpetuate and aggravate the forces of disruption that the Constitutional Revolution had added to the age-old divisions of the Iranian society. The revolution having been aborted, it is difficult to say whether the new ideas that it embraced could have worked in the milieu of the traditional society. But the tortured and interrupted existence of the Constitutional regime had lasted long enough to introduce new problems. The monarchy, which in the past had most often helped to hold the government together, had been somewhat discredited. Yet nationalism had also failed to act as a unifying force. In fact, it had introduced a new division along politico-ideological lines, between the Royalists and the Constitutionalists. Many members of the new elite came from the latter group, and when the war broke out some of them were active on the Iranian scene. The fact that Aḥmad Shah was young and ineffective [1] gave the emergent nationalist policy makers the opportunity to wield power, but whether their political ideology made it possible for them to govern remained to be seen.

[1] Shah Sultān Aḥmad was crowned July 21, 1914, in the presence of many national and international dignitaries.

Iran's international posture was no better when the war broke out than it had been earlier. Foreign intervention during the Constitutional period had been followed by Anglo-Russian manipulation of the Regent and the Cabinet after the destruction of the Second Majlis and during the postponement of the opening of the Third Majlis. In spite of the fact that Anglo-Russian friendship had cooled somewhat after the Russian understanding with Germany in regard to the Tehran-Khanaqin railway in 1911, the Anglo-Russian Agreement of 1907 was still the basis of their position in Iran when the war broke out. Furthermore, the Russian troops that had entered Iran in 1909 had remained there. In spite of this, soon after the outbreak of the war Iran announced a policy of strict neutrality in the *farmān* of November 1, 1914.[2]

The Shah, however, had little if anything, to do with the formulation of this policy. The real makers of the policy were some of the former Constitutional leaders: Mustawfī al-Mamālik, the Prime Minister, assisted by Mushīr al-Dawlah and Mu'tamin al-Mulk. Prior to the adoption of this policy, which was declared before the outbreak of Russo-Turkish hostilities on Iranian soil, the Prime Minister first approached the Turkish Minister at Tehran inquiring whether his government would respect Iran's policy of neutrality if it were officially declared. The answer was disappointing. The Minister stated that his government would like to do so, but that as Russian troops were stationed in Azerbaijan he could not see how Turkey could undertake and successfully implement an obligation to that effect. The Iranian government then approached the British and Russian Ministers, informing them that it intended to declare strict neutrality and implement it fully but that the presence of Russian forces in Azerbaijan might provide the Turks with a pretext for invading Iran. Hence Mustawfī al-Mamālik asked Russia to withdraw its troops from Iran. The British and Russian Ministers "appreciated" the Iranian views but inquired what guarantees could be given that after the withdrawal of Russian forces the Turks would not bring in theirs.[3] Later, the Russian Minister wrote the Iranian Foreign Minister that, inasmuch as only the Russian troops could maintain

[2] The text of this decree is in Muvarrikh al-Dawlah Sipahr, *Īrān dar Jang-i Buzurg* (Tehran, 1336 [1957/58]), p. 89.
[3] For more details, see *ibid.*, pp. 89-91.

security for Russian and other foreign subjects, evacuation was "impossible at the time." [4]

Thus, despite the fact that prospects for the implementation of a policy of neutrality were bleak, the Iranian government decided to announce it to the world. Adoption of this policy and failure to execute it constitute the story of Iran's foreign policy during World War I.

RUSSO-TURKISH HOSTILITIES

On October 29, 1914, the *Breslau,* a German ship then nominally under the Turkish flag, bombarded the Russian Black Sea port of Theodosia. Redress being refused, Russia declared war on the Porte. The Russo-Turkish hostilities thus touched off were bound to affect Iran, because the strategic aims and positions of the two belligerent powers clashed on Iranian soil. By the time Iran declared its policy of neutrality, Russia had brought in fresh forces and equipment to supplement those that had been in Azerbaijan since 1909 and had taken positions in Tabriz, Khoi, Daylaman, and Urumiyah [5] in order to outflank Turkey in case of war.

Turkey had acquired strategical points to the west of Lake Urumiyah, but had withdrawn its forces in 1912 when the first Balkan War broke out.[6] When Kurdish tribesmen crossed the Iranian border pushing toward Urumiyah in September 1914, Turkish soldiers reappeared on Iranian soil.[7] Then when Turkey entered the war on the side of the Central Powers, Turkish troops poured in from the Bazargan frontier advancing toward Urumiyah, and from the Baneh frontier advancing toward Sauj Bulagh. This Turkish advance created a new front for Russia and was favored by Germany, because

[4] The real reason for Russia's refusal to evacuate its forces was the fear that the Turkish troops would move in as soon as the Russians were withdrawn. The Russian Minister said this to the Prime Minister a few days before the official reason was given in a letter to the Iranian Foreign Minister.

[5] Aḥmad Kasravī, *Tārīkh-i Hījdah Sālah-'i Āẕarbāijān* (Tehran, 1333 [1954/55]), p. 600.

[6] From Sir Percy Sykes's account it would appear that the Turkish forces were already on Iranian soil when the war broke out. See his *A History of Persia* (London, 1930), p. 436.

[7] This acount is given by Kasravī, *op. cit.,* pp. 599-600. It seems to differ from Sykes's description (*op. cit.,* p. 436).

it would divert Russian energies from the main theater of war in Europe.

Both Germany and Turkey hoped to achieve political objectives also. The Turkish advance in the east was to pave the way for the extension of German influence to the Middle East and finally to India. Turkey, on the other hand, launched its advance in the east in the hope of achieving Pan-Islamic and Pan-Turanian objectives. The former aimed at the revival of the authority of the Caliphate over all Muslims; the latter aimed at the liberation and absorption of the Turkish-inhabited areas, such as Azerbaijan. The Turkish advance toward Tabriz turned Azerbaijan into a Russo-Turkish theater of war. This province suffered from all the vicissitudes of the war on the eastern Anatolian front and was gravely affected after the Russian Revolution.[8]

GERMAN AIMS AND ACTIVITIES

The other major foreign conflict that turned Iranian soil into a battlefield was that between Germany and Great Britain. In most of the last quarter of the nineteenth century German policy in Iran could be characterized as one of noninvolvement, but this was certainly not true between 1898 and 1911, when German imperialist activities in Iran began in earnest. Some of these activities are outlined here briefly.[9]

Germany made persistent efforts to acquire a "place in the sun" in the Persian Gulf. Its ambition to link the Gulf with Konia, the terminal point of the Anatolian railway, and the completion of the section from Konia to Eregli in 1904 was mentioned in Chapter V.

Germany's activities were not limited to the Gulf area, where the Wönckhaus Company established branches in Bandar Abbas, Bushire, and other cities. In 1906 Iran asked for the establishment of a German bank at Tehran, hoping for support against Russian encroachments. Desiring not to antagonize Russia, Germany hestitated to heed the Iranian request at this time and informed Russia that

[8] For details, see *ibid.*, pp. 599-622.

[9] See Chapter V; also Bradford G. Martin, *German-Persian Diplomatic Relations* (The Hague, 1959), particularly pp. 50-97.

"Germany had no political aims or interests in Persia." [10] But the Deutsche Orient Bank continued negotiations with the Iranian government and obtained a concession to establish branches in Iran. British and Russian opposition killed this concession in 1907, and the conclusion of the Anglo-Russian Convention in the same year rendered German penetration into Iran even more difficult.

The Anglo-Russian *rapprochement* of 1907 was not foolproof. Germany succeeded in causing trouble between Great Britain and Russia by concluding with the latter the Potsdam Agreement (August 19, 1911), the very heart of which involved German penetration into the Middle East by way of the Tehran-Khanaqin railway.

When the war broke out, German activities in the Middle East were intensified to an unprecedented extent. Of the two Muslim states dominating the area, the Ottoman Empire soon cast its lot with the Central Powers, but Iran declared itself neutral. The German short-run aim in Iran was twofold: first, to impel Iran to follow the lead of Berlin and Vienna and, second, to divert the British and Russian energies from the main theater of war in Europe by creating or intensifying anti-Entente sentiments and activities in Iran, Afghanistan, and India. The fact that the Iranian mood was favorable to German designs will be discussed later. Here German activities working against Iranian neutrality will be outlined.

Germany worked, in the main, through diplomatic and military channels, sparing few areas of Iranian life. The staff of the German Embassy at Tehran consisted of Prince Henry XXXI de Reuss, the Minister, and Otto von Hentig, Franz Litten, Dr. Ilberg, and R. von Kardorff. The first and the last established the closest contact with the members of the Cabinet of Mustawfī al-Mamālik and some of the members of the Democratic party of Iran. The activities of Von Reuss and Von Kardorff were greatly facilitated by an Iranian nationalist from an influential family by the name of Muvarrikh al-Dawlah Sipahr, who started his services at the German Embassy in June 1914.[11] Von Kardorff, under the sponsorship of Sipahr, visited many Iranian statesmen regularly at the home of Sālār al-Sultān. The pretext for these visits was to attend the Shī'ī passion shows at a

[10] Cited in Sidney Bradshaw Fay, *The Origins of the World War* (New York, 1956), p. 250.

[11] The book by Muvarrikh al-Dawlah Sipahr is full of his own and German activities in Iran during the war.

session of which Von Kardorff, pretending to be a newly converted Muslim, wept for the Shī'ī martyrs! The news of this event ran throughout the city, and soon thereafter the mullahs began to pray for the victory of the Germans from the pulpit.[12]

Conscious of the pro-German feelings among the prospective deputies of the Third Majlis, the British and Russian Ministers intrigued against the opening of the Majlis, while Von Kardorff worked for it. In the end the Third Majlis opened on January 4, 1915, and the major target of German diplomatic activities shifted from Qasr-i Gulistān, the Palace, to Bahāristān, the parliament building, with significant results for the Germans.[13] Von Kardorff secretly met some of the Democrats including Riẕā Musāvāt and Jalīl Ardabīlī in the house of Vaḥīd al-Mulk-i Shaybānī. At this meeting it was resolved that the Democrats and the Moderates would put aside their differences and form a coalition, under the leadership of Mīrza Muḥammad Ṣādiq-i Ṭabāṭabā'ī, with the ultimate aim of winning the Cabinet to the cause of the Central Powers and the abandonment of neutrality.[14]

A number of military missions were dispatched to Iran after the German military attaché in Tehran, Count Kanitz, had done much spadework during extensive travels in the provinces. The Zugmeyer mission operated in southern Iran, extending its activities to Kerman and Isfahan. The Klein mission was active in Kermanshah and the surrounding areas. The most important and successful German agent, however, was Wassmuss. He fomented an anti-British uprising among the Qashqā'ī and Bakhtyārī tribes in southwestern Iran. Wassmuss' success was due to his shrewd exploitation of the feud between Ṣulat al-Dawlah and his brother, Sardār Iḥtishām. Ṣulat's anti-British sentiments prompted him to heed Wassmuss' plan for tribal uprisings because he had been deposed as chief of the Qashqā'ī tribe by his brother with the assistance of the pro-British Qavām al-Mulk, the chief of the Khamsah tribe and the governor of Shiraz.[15] German military activities in Iran were masterminded in Berlin, where Niedermayer, the leader of the mission to Iran and Afghanistan, consulted

[12] *Ibid.*, p. 45.
[13] *Ibid.*, pp. 16-47.
[14] *Ibid.*, pp. 47-48.
[15] For details, see *ibid.*, pp. 73-88. On Wassmuss, see Christopher Sykes, *Wassmuss, "The German Lawrence"* (London, 1936).

some of the Iranian nationalists who had formed the Iranian Committee for Cooperation with Germany.

The German aims and activities were, in the main, directed against British interests in Iran, Afghanistan, and India. To protect their interests, the British government decided to dispatch troops to Iran, and thus three more sections of the country, the southwest, the southeast, and the northeast, were turned into battlefields. The northwest had become a theater of war as a result of Russo-Turkish hostilities.

BRITISH INTERESTS AND ACTIVITIES

If the preservation of British interests in India had long influenced Great Britain's policy toward Iran, these same interests persisted when the war broke out, but now the power threatening them was Germany rather than Russia or France. The continuing British concern with the Persian Gulf for reasons of trade, communications, and the "safety of India" was discussed in Chapter V.

By the time of hostilities in 1914 Great Britain had acquired an added interest in the Gulf area. This derived from the oil concession granted to William Knox D'Arcy in 1901 by Muẓaffar al-Dīn Shah. Sir Arthur Hardinge's intervention in behalf of D'Arcy did not automatically give rise to direct interest on the part of the British government in the D'Arcy oil investment. As an investor Britain became interested in this concession only in 1913-14, but as the protector of its private investor, the British government had become involved soon after the concession had been obtained.

Normally the task of protecting a foreign concessionaire's operations under the terms of his contract falls to the government that grants the concession. In such a case, of course, there is no need of protection by the agents of the state to which the concessionaire owes allegiance. Nor is it necessary for the concessionaire to become involved in the domestic affairs of the host country while trying to make arrangements for the safety of his operations with the local authorities. But internal conditions in Iran when the oil operations began were anything but normal.

Relatively important exploration activities began in 1905, the year that marked the beginning of the Iranian Constitutional Revolution.

In that year a new company called the Concessions Syndicate was established at Glasgow to replace the First Exploitation Company, which had been established in 1903 under Article 16 of the D'Arcy concession. The syndicate began its operations in Mamatin north of Ahwaz, drilling two test wells under the supervision of G. B. Reynolds. The Iranian central government, caught up in the revolution, exercised little or no control over the outlying areas. When, because of failure to discover oil at Mamatin, the operations were moved to Maidan Naftun (now Masjid Sulayman), the syndicate had no protection from interference by local tribes. To provide the necessary protection, Great Britain dispatched a small force of Sikhs to Masjid Sulayman under the supervision of Sir Arnold Wilson, the British vice-consul at Ahwaz.[16]

In May 1908 after seven years of test drilling the first geyser of oil burst forth at Masjid Sulayman. This success signaled the beginning of increased oil operations in the tribal lands, which meant that greater security for the oil installations was required. The government of Muḥammad 'Alī Shah was in no position to provide such protection. The Shah had been at war with the Majlis ever since he ascended the throne of Iran in January 1907 and was now preparing for the last blow against it. The destruction of the Majlis and the reestablishment of autocracy further weakened the control of the central government over the provinces. In fact, on the day that the Majlis was destroyed the country was plunged into provincial uprisings against the central government. The most important uprising was that of the Bakhtyārī tribe, which, under the leadership of Ṣamṣām al-Saltanah, its chief, finally overthrew the central government at Tehran in June 1909.

These details are given in order to make clear the fact that, when the Anglo-Persian Oil Company was created in April 1909, the government of Iran was hardly in a position to provide security and safety for the company's oil operations and installations, and in fact about two months after the formation of the company the Bakhtyārī forces were actually in control of the central government at Tehran. Under the circumstances the company had to provide for its own safety. Furthermore, the company needed to purchase more land for

[16] Muṣṭafā Fātaḥ, *Panjāh Sāl Naft-i Īrān* (Tehran, 1335 [1956/57]), pp. 257-58.

its operations. According to tribal laws and customs, the pasture land belonged to the individual members of the tribe, and therefore in theory, under the terms of the concession, the company could have made its purchases directly from the individual owners. But the Bakhtyārī chiefs and "deputies" posed as the true owners of the tribal land, leaving the company no choice but to deal with them. Whatever the problem, the company faced the powerful tribal chiefs.

The company entered into three kinds of agreements with the chiefs. These may be conveniently termed share, land, and safety agreements. A special agreement had been made in 1905 whereby the Bakhtyārī chiefs were to receive a subsidy of £3,000 a year as well as 3 per cent of the shares of any company that operated in their territory. A separate corporation, the Bakhtyārī Oil Company, was formed in 1909, with a capital of £400,000. Twelve thousand pounds' worth of shares or 3 per cent of the total capital was issued to the Bakhtyārī khans, who reciprocated by protecting the installations erected in their territory.[17] The second kind of agreement provided for the purchase of land at a fixed price each year from tribal chiefs who would undertake to pay the real owners of the land. If the land belonged to a chief or if there was no khan to claim the purchased land, the former would retain the payment. The third kind of agreement dealt more specifically with the problem of protecting wells and pipelines. Here again the company had to deal with tribal chiefs, who would undertake to appoint a khan and provide him with the necessary weapons and men. The company would pay the khan and his riflemen, in addition to an annual payment of £3,000 to the chief himself.[18]

The company also reached an agreement with the Sheikh of Mohammarah (now Khoramshahr), Sheikh Khaz'al, in 1909. He was the hereditary Arab ruler of an enormous territory on the eastern side of the Shatt al-Arab, including Abadan Island, which the company had selected as the site for a refinery. Through Sir Percy Cox, British resident at Bushire, the company negotiated an agreement with the sheikh, giving the company a right of way for a pipeline to carry the oil and selling one square mile of Abadan for the refinery.[19] Khaz'al was to receive an annual rent of £650, to be paid ten years

[17] George Lenczowski, *Oil and State in the Middle East* (Ithaca, N.Y., 1960), p. 123.

[18] Fātaḥ, *op. cit.*, p. 261.

[19] *Ibid.*

in advance. In return the sheikh was to provide, at the company's expense, guards for the pipelines and buildings. After signing the agreement, the sheikh received in addition to the advance rent a loan of £10,000, ostensibly from the British government but actually from the Anglo-Iranian Oil Company.[20]

By 1913 this web of agreements with local elements had brought about involvement of the British – the company and the consular service – in southwestern Iran. The decisions which involved Britain directly in the protection of the oil operations were reached in 1913-14. Since 1904, when the British and Germans had been competing for oil concessions in the Middle East, the British government had been considering the possibility of converting the British navy from coal to oil. On March 3, 1913, the British Royal Commission, which had been appointed to study the problem, reported that the British navy should use oil. Winston Churchill, then First Lord of the Admiralty, announced the Admiralty's oil policy in a speech before the House of Commons: "Our ultimate policy is that the Admiralty should become the independent owner and producer of its own supplies of liquid fuel. . . . We must become the owners, or at any rate the controllers at the source, of at least a proportion of the supply of natural oil which we require." [21] This policy led to an agreement between the company, the Admiralty, and the Treasury, making the British government the major and controlling partner in the company. The government, by virtue of the agreement, was to appoint two *ex officio* directors "to enable the Government interests in the Company to be duly protected, but with the minimum of interference with the conduct of ordinary business." A power of veto over all acts of the board and all committees of the company and its subsidiaries was conferred upon the two *ex officio* directors.[22] Thus, first as protector of the interests of its nationals abroad and, finally, as a major and controlling partner, the British government possessed significant interests in the Anglo-Persian Oil Company. To preserve these interests against the

[20] Benjamin Shwadran, *The Middle East, Oil and the Great Powers* (New York, 1956), pp. 21-22.

[21] Quoted in the staff report of the Federal Trade Commission on the international petroleum cartel, published by the Monopoly Subcommittee of the Senate Select Committee on Small Business (82nd Congress, 2d sess., committee print no. 6; Washington, 1952), p. 49.

[22] For details, see Shwadran, *op. cit.*, pp. 22-23.

German menace the British had to act, because the central government in Iran was hardly in a position to maintain internal security. The British action took both diplomatic and military forms.

The diplomatic settlement of 1907 with Russia was inadequate under the circumstances of 1914 and after. The partition of Iran into spheres of influence in 1907 had envisaged a British, a Russian, and a neutral zone. By 1914 the situation had totally changed. The British government had acquired definite and direct interest in the oil fields of southwestern Iran. This change required diplomatic recognition by its friend and ally, Russia, through revision of the 1907 settlement. This was not too difficult to obtain as Russia wanted a British favor in another area of the Middle East. Sazonov, the Russian Foreign Minister, stated, in a formal exchange of letters with the British Ambassador at St. Petersburg, that Russia desired to annex Istanbul and the Turkish Straits in the event of an Entente victory. As a counterclaim the British government informed Russia of its desire to include the Iranian neutral zone in the British sphere of influence. In a secret telegram of March 20, 1915, from the Russian government to Count Benckendorff in London, Sazonov confirmed Russia's "assent to the inclusion of the neutral zone of Persia in the British sphere of influence." [23] Russian assent, however, according to the so-called Constantinople Agreement, was based on three conditions: first, that the districts adjoining Isfahan and Yazd should be included in the Russian sphere; second, that a portion of the neutral zone adjoining the Afghan territory should also be included in the Russian zone; and, third, that Russia "expects that in future its full liberty of action will be recognized in the sphere of influence allotted to it, coupled in particular with the right of preferentially developing in that sphere its financial and economic policy." [24] This last condition amounted to a demand that Russian attempts at annexation of its sphere of influence in northern Iran would not be hampered by Great Britain.[25]

[23] H. W. V. Temperley, *A History of the Peace Conference of Paris* (London, 1924), p. 209. In a footnote it is stated that on his visit to England in September 1912 Sazonov indicated that the neutral zones might have to be annulled.

[24] The Constantinople Agreement was not a single instrument. It consisted of diplomatic exchanges between Russia, Great Britain, and France. See J. C. Hurewitz, *Diplomacy in the Near and Middle East* (Princeton, N. J., 1956), II, 7-11.

[25] Temperley, *op. cit.*, p. 208.

The Constantinople Agreement, like the 1907 convention, was contrary to the "integrity and independence" of Iran,[26] and British military activities violated Iran's proclaimed neutrality. These activities affected different Iranian areas in varying degrees, the southwest probably being the most affected. Even before war was declared by Turkey, Great Britain had sent a brigade to the Bahrein Islands. At the outbreak of hostilities, these troops seized the Turkish port at Fao, the point where the Shatt al-Arab flows into the Persian Gulf. This was followed by the arrival of a large expeditionary force from India. The force, commanded in succession by Generals Delamain, Barrett, and Maude, occupied Basra on November 24, 1914. The immediate objective of this occupation was "to protect the oil refineries on the Isle of Abadan."[27]

While the Mesopotamian operations were in progress, Wassmuss was busily engaged in inciting anti-British sentiments in southwestern Iran by means of bribery and propaganda. As the German consul at Bushire in the years before the outbreak of the war, he had succeeded in creating strong anti-British feelings among the Tangistānī and other neighboring tribesmen. He reappeared at Shushtar in January 1915 with a small party of Germans.[28]

By the time war broke out the Abadan refinery was producing 25,000 barrels of oil a month for export. The pipeline running from Masjid Sulayman to Abadan, a distance of 150 miles, was very vulnerable. The British first relied upon the Bakhtyārī khans and Sheikh Khaz'al, providing them with extra money and weapons,[29] but the Bakhtyārī tribe was, on the whole, unfriendly,[30] and before further security measures could be taken the pipeline was breached and fired in several places. This took place in February 1915. By the summer of that year the pipeline was repaired and the transport of oil was resumed, but adequate measures against German propaganda activities were needed if southwestern Iran was not to go over to the Central Powers.

Early in 1916 Great Britain decided to dispatch a military mission

[26] On December 4, 1911, Benckendorff wrote that the terms "integrity and independence of Persia" possessed "little real importance" (*ibid.*, p. 208n).
[27] *Ibid.*, p. 209.
[28] For details, see Sykes, *op. cit.*, pp. 443-53.
[29] For details, see Fātaḥ, *op. cit.*, p. 272.
[30] Sykes, *op. cit.*, p. 440.

to southwestern Iran. This mission was to be organized and commanded by Sir Percy Sykes. The object, according to Sykes, was to raise "a Persian force, 11,000 strong, to take the place of the Gendarmerie, the great part of which, under the influence of its Swedish officers, had, for all practical purposes, joined the enemy or had dispersed owing to lack of pay."[31] The South Persia Rifles, as the soldiers were called after they were organized, were recognized by the Cabinet of Vuṣūq al-Dawlah in January 1917, but the Cabinet of ʿAlāʾ al-Saltanah, which was formed in June of that year, refused recognition. Recognized or not by the central government, the South Persia Rifles carried on extensive military and police operations in Iran during the war.[32]

British military missions were also dispatched to the northern and southeastern parts of Iran, although these areas were not so heavily policed as was the southwest. German missions were to be prevented from crossing into Afghanistan and Baluchistan. In Khorasan and Sistan levies were recruited from Hazaras and Baluchi tribesmen, respectively. In 1916 two British officers were dispatched to eastern Iran. Major T. H. Keyes headed a mission to counter German intrigues on the Baluchistan frontier. The other officer, General E. R. Dyer, was to guard the Afghan frontier. After crushing the frontier tribesmen, the mission forces established themselves in eastern Iran. The Eastern Persian Cordon, as they came to be known, finally included a squadron of Indian cavalry stationed at Birjand and a second squadron at Dahan Baghi with headquarters in Sistan, but covering the frontier from Rum in the Kain district to Gurg in the Lut.[33]

INTERNAL FACTORS

The conflicting activities of the Entente and Central Powers adversely affected Iran's policy of neutrality, but the fact which is commonly overlooked is that Iran itself neither could nor did pursue a policy of neutrality. It is one thing to proclaim a policy and quite another to execute it. Iran certainly formulated a strict policy of neutrality, but almost all Iranian internal forces militated against its implemen-

[31] *Ibid.*, p. 452.
[32] For details, see Sykes's own account (*ibid.*, pp. 451-517).
[33] *Ibid.*, pp. 448-49, 454-55.

tation. In fact, foreign violations of Iran's neutrality were by no means unrelated to the domestic forces working against that policy.

Partisan Government

While the European powers were declaring war on one another, Iran was celebrating the coronation of Sultān Aḥmad Mīrzā, then nearly seventeen years old. This event produced no change in the internal affairs of the country. The inept Nāṣir al-Mulk was relieved of his regency and thenceforth could sojourn in Europe without any "headaches," as he referred to affairs of state, but the new Shah's favorite expression, "I am not responsible," is indicative of his attitude. He pretended respect for the Constitution, but his actions proved him irresponsible, pleasure-seeking, and opportunistic. The Cabinet of 'Alā' al-Saltanah was in power at the time of the coronation, but soon thereafter it was succeeded by that of Mustawfī al-Mamālik. It was during his premiership that Iran, on November 1, 1914, declared its policy of neutrality.

When the Third Majlis was finally opened (officially, on January 4, 1915), its mood reflected "the calamitous and humiliating experience" of the eventful period between 1905 and the outbreak of the war. British, and particularly Russian, policies toward Iran had assisted in the destruction of the First and Second Majlis. And since 1911 Russian troops occupying the northern part of the country had "plundered, raped, and murdered the people of Tabriz, Rasht and Enzeli" while the British and Russian Legations manipulated the puppet Cabinets at Tehran.

Moved by these experiences, the deputies of the Third Majlis nursed fierce anti-British and anti-Russian sentiments. Hate, resentment, and revenge permeated society. If a statesman believed that the interests of his country might be best preserved by cooperation with Britain and Russia, he would swiftly be labeled a traitor deserving death. Charges of being Anglophile or Russophile could easily lead to assassination. In such an atmosphere the deputies of the Majlis were eager to lend an ear to the enemies of the Entente Powers. Many Democrats considered the outbreak of the war a blessing because it would provide them, they felt, with an opportunity to hit back at the authors of the 1907 convention.

The German Embassy at Tehran was busily cultivating contacts with the deputies of the Majlis and making many converts. Mustawfī al-Mamālik, however, was taking his policy of neutrality seriously. His government persistently instructed the governors of the provinces to refrain from giving or receiving aid from any of the belligerent powers or their agents. His Ministry of Foreign Affairs on numerous occasions protested "the violation of Iran's neutrality."[34] The Prime Minister believed that Iran's salvation lay in the strict observance of neutrality. But he was faced with a parliament a majority of whose members were determined to side openly with the Central Powers.

The Prime Minister strove to resist the pressure of the Democrats. He pleaded for moderation and patience, but in the end he consented to negotiate an agreement with Germany. As the price for a secret alliance, he set forth three major conditions: first, that the integrity and independence of Iran should be guaranteed; second, that arms and munitions should be supplied on a large scale; third, that a substantial loan should be extended swiftly. With all of these, Prince von Reuss agreed in principle, after his return to Tehran in September 1915, but grave disagreement arose over the details of the second and third conditions. Von Reuss felt that Germany was not in a position to supply arms and munitions on a large scale, but he would ensure that adequate supplies would be furnished by the Turks. This was not agreeable to Mustawfī al-Mamālik because he "utterly distrusted" the Turks. Turkish Pan-Islamism aiming at the reestablishment of the Caliph's authority over all Muslims was, in particular, unpalatable. In regard to the demand for a substantial loan, Von Reuss suggested that the matter be decided in Berlin, while the Prime Minister insisted on Tehran.[35]

The British and Russians got wind of these secret negotiations. Furthermore, the anti-Entente sentiments, intensified by a powerful German propaganda machine and the relentless activities of the Democrats, had by this time reached their peak. Under the circumstances swift action was taken. The government of Iran was warned of the unpleasant consequences of any pro-German action. Russia decided to dispatch additional forces to Iran from the Caucasus, and Russian troops stationed in Qazvin, thirty miles north of Tehran,

[34] For the texts of these protests, see *ibid.*, pp. 94-100.

[35] Cf. Sipahr, *op. cit.*, p. 624, and Harold Nicolson, *Curzon: The Last Phase* (London, 1937), p. 130.

moved toward the capital threatening to occupy it. Faced with such a contingency, Mustawfī al-Mamālik decided to transfer the seat of the government to Isfahan, because of its "historic significance," though the Germans favored Kermanshah for "strategic reasons." In any event, quick departure from the capital was necessary, and many deputies of the Majlis together with Von Reuss left on November 16, 1915, and temporarily established themselves at Qum.[36] By November 20, 1915, more than thirty deputies of the Majlis, accompanied by many influential citizens, newspapermen, and officials, had arrived at Qum. These included some of the well-known nationalist leaders such as Mīrzā Muḥammad Ṣādiq-i Ṭabāṭabā'ī, Sulaymān Mīrzā, Niẓām al-Sultān, and Malik al-Shu'arā'.

The evacuation was not, however, fully successful. The Shah remained at the capital as the result of British and Russian intimidation. He was told that should he leave the capital the ex-Shah, Muḥammad 'Alī', would be summoned to Tehran.[37] At the same time certain influential statesmen such as Sa'd al-Dawlah, Farmānfarmā, and Sipahsālār mediated between the British and Russian representatives and the Shah, promising that Russian troops would not move into the capital if the Shah decided to stay in Tehran.

Soon after their arrival at Qum, some of the leaders of the Democratic party, with the assistance of Germany's former consul at Kermanshah, organized a National Defense Committee (*Kumītah Difā'-i Millī*).[38] On November 22, the deputies decided to change the committee's composition by electing four new members, each representing one of the four major groups of deputies.[39] Thus the Moderates also sided with Germany. The Germans had secretly made every effort to win their support and finally signed an agreement with six leaders of the party. Briefly stated, Germany promised (1) to supply the Moderates in all provinces with arms and munitions,

[36] *Muhājirat,* literally meaning "immigration," was the term used at the time to refer to the dispersal of the Third Majlis on November 16, 1915, and the departure of the deputies for Qum.

[37] Sipahr, *op. cit.*, p. 239.

[38] Among the outstanding members of this committee, besides those mentioned in the text, were Mīrzā Sulaymān Khān, Mīrzā Muḥammad 'Alī Khān, and Adīb al-Saltanah.

[39] The four representatives were Mīrzā Muḥammad Ṣādiq-i Ṭabāṭabā'i, Sulaymān Mīrzā, Sayyid Ḥasan Mudarris, and Niẓām al-Saltanah, representing the Moderates, the Democrats, the 'Almiyah group, and the Independents.

(2) to instruct the German officials in the provinces to regard the Moderates as their ally, (3) to provide the Moderate leaders with the sums necessary for party and propaganda activities, and (4) to protect the life and property of the Moderate leaders.[40]

Mustawfī al-Mamālik's Cabinet was faced with a dispersed parliament a few members of which remained at Tehran. He bent every effort to induce the deputies to return to the capital. He sent Arbāb Kaikhusraw, the representative of the Zoroastrian community in the Majlis, to Qum to plead with the "refugees," and he instructed his Foreign Minister to ask Von Reuss to return to the capital, knowing of his powerful influence over the deputies. All these efforts failed, the deputies refusing to return on the ground that Russian troops were stationed too closely to Tehran and Von Reuss claiming that his staff would be insecure in the capital.

In the meantime the committee forces came into armed conflict with Russian troops at Hamadan under the command of Muḥammad Taqī Khān, at Saveh, and finally at Robat Karim under the command of Mīrzā Sulymān Khān. The ill-equipped and motley soldiers of the committee were defeated at the last two places,[41] and by the middle of December 1915 the committee and its men were forced to abandon Qum. Pursued by Russian troops, they moved to Kashan and finally to Kermanshah, where they established a "National Government" (*Ḥukūmat-i Millī*) under the presidency of Niẓām al-Sultān.[42]

The defeat of the committee forces and the consequent presence of Russians surrounding Tehran deprived the central government of any hope of getting the deputies to return to the capital. This dealt the precarious Cabinet of Mustawfī al-Mamālik a deadly blow, and on December 10, 1915, he resigned. The fall of his Cabinet aggravated the political crisis. From the time of his resignation until the end of the war Cabinets rose and fell with the ebb and flow of the war and the chronic disunity of Iranian polity.

The fall of Mustawfī al-Mamālik was followed by a new phase in Iran's foreign policy. With the exception of the short period between January and May 1918, when either Mustawfī or his successor Ṣamṣām al-Saltanah was Prime Minister, Iran's foreign policy gen-

[40] For the text of the agreement, see Sipahr, *op. cit.*, p. 258.

[41] For details, see Kasravī, *op. cit.*, pp. 642-56.

[42] For the names of the ministers of the "government," see Sipahr, *op. cit.*, p. 296.

erally favored the Entente Powers. The Cabinet of Mustawfī al-Mamālik, although sympathizing with pro-German elements, exerted every effort to appear neutral. The succeeding Cabinets generally followed a policy which the British labeled "benevolent neutrality," but which, in fact, was as much pro-Entente as Mustawfī al-Mamālik's policy was pro-German.

Under three cabinets in particular the pro-Entente policy of Iran was clearly evident. Prince Farmānfarmā formed a Cabinet after the fall of Mustawfī al-Mamālik in December 1915. He was looked upon as a friend of the Entente Powers, and events proved the correctness of this view. Russian troops were now stationed both north and south of Tehran, and Russian propaganda had been stepped up with boasts and self-congratulations for victory over the "rebels" (namely, the nationalist forces) and their German "masters."

In January 1916 Farmānfarmā indicated the orientation of his foreign policy by clamping down on a most important pro-German element in Iran, the Gendarmerie, the only efficient Iranian military unit. It had been organized in 1911 when it absorbed the Treasury Gendarmerie, after the departure of the American financial mission. It had been formed, at the request of the Iranian government, by Swedish officers, who also established a temporary military school at Tehran in November of that year. From the beginning of the war the Swedish and Iranian officers of the Gendarmerie had sympathized with Germany and had participated in the skirmishes of the nationalist forces with Russian troops. Farmānfarmā dismissed its pro-German commander-in-chief and the commanders of its divisions at Isfahan and Kashan.[43]

In the meantime, he launched a purge of known pro-German elements in the government and instructed suspected officials and governors to exert every effort toward reestablishing friendy relations with the Entente Powers. Niẓām al-Saltanah, the governor of Broujird and Luristan, was swiftly dismissed. Sheikh Khazʿal, the semi-autonomous Sheikh of Mohammarah, who was suspected of anti-British intrigues despite his long-standing agreement with the British to protect the oil fields, was informed by telegram that the new government at Tehran was friendly to the Entente Powers, that he was

[43] *Ibid.*, p. 319.

expected to adopt a similar attitude, and that he should prevent the anti-British activities of the local tribes.[44]

Through most of the period that he was in power, Farmānfarmā entered into serious negotiations with the Entente Powers, according to Russian accounts, with a view to concluding an agreement with provisions almost identical with those negotiated between Mustawfī al-Mamālik and Von Reuss, the German Minister.[45] An incident too provocative to explain away forced the downfall of Farmānfarmā. Russian troops in February 1916 seized the Turkish Minister in Iran, imprisoned him, and moved him toward Enzeli or Baku. Like his predecessor, Farmānfarmā believed in maintaining an outward posture of neutrality. He therefore protested vigorously against the Russian action, and this led to the fall of his Cabinet.

He was succeeded by Sipahsālār A'ẓam, who chose Ṣārim al-Dawlah as his Minister of Foreign Affairs. The new Prime Minister far exceeded his predecessor in pursuing a pro-Entente policy. He entertained the British and Russian diplomats socially, paid a visit to the Russian general in command of the forces stationed at Qazvin, and on several occasions stated publicly that he welcomed close friendship and cooperation with the Entente Powers. As a token of friendship with Russia, he welcomed the return of Bahādur Jang to Tehran.[46] Sipahsālār's government also took advantage of every possible opportunity to denounce Germany. For example, when the Germans sank the *Sussex*, a British vessel, which happened to have on board an Iranian prince, Bahrām Mīrzā, the Foreign Minister in protesting the incident used words far more vehement than the occasion warranted.

Sipahsālār's government also signed an agreement with Great Britain and Russia providing for the establishment of a "Mixed Commission" which would supervise all government expenditures. The commission, composed of five members, was dominated by the two powers as, in addition to the British and Russian representatives, M. Heynssens, the Belgian Treasurer of Iran, favored the Entente.

[44] *Ibid.*, p. 318.

[45] For a translation of the Russian paper from which this information is drawn, see *ibid.*, p. 321.

[46] He was mentioned in earlier chapters. He was one of the most notorious agents of Russia during the Constitutional Movement and is believed to have planned the destruction of the First Majlis (June 1908) with Muḥammad 'Alī Shah.

The depleted Treasury was already heavily indebted to both Great Britain and Russia because Iran had failed, owing to financial difficulties accentuated by war, to repay the loans it had previously borrowed and because it had also accepted additional sums from Great Britain and Russia since the outbreak of the war.[47]

Another important pro-Entente decision of Sipahsālār was his grant of an oil concession to a Russian subject closely related to the Russian Legation. On March 9, 1916, he granted A. M. Khoshtaria "the exclusive right of exploitation of petroleum and natural gas found in the districts of Gilan, Mazandaran and Astarabad" for a period of seventy years. The concession excluded the districts which had previously been granted to Sipahsālār.[48] The concessionaire undertook to form a company for purposes of exploration and agreed to "make an annual payment of 16% of his net income to the Imperial Government of Persia." In case he did not begin work within five years from the date of the concession, the concession would become "null and void."[49] The terms of the concession were kept secret during Sipahsālār's administration. They were confirmed, as will be seen, by Vus̱ūq al-Dawlah, Sipahsālār's successor, but were not made public until the Cabinet of 'Alā' al-Saltanah, Vus̱ūq's successor, came into power.

In August 1916 it seemed that Iran might be forced to reconsider its increasingly pro-Entente posture as the result of Entente misfortunes. On April 25, 1916, Kutel al-Amara fell. This was "the gravest disaster ever suffered by British arms in Asia."[50] Over 13,000 soldiers under General Townshend surrendered to the Turks. Immediately the Turkish propaganda campaign was stepped up in Tehran, and the Democrats and their sympathizers, who had been discredited after the defeats at Saveh and Robat Karim, again became active.

[47] Kasravī, *op. cit.*, p. 663.

[48] Fātaḥ claims that there is no trace of the text of this first northern oil concession in the Iranian archives which he has examined. He thinks that the former Anglo-Persian Oil Company may be in possession of it. In any event, this *farmān* was issued by Nāṣir al-Dīn Shah, and the three districts excluded from the Khoshtaria concession were Tunikabun, Khujur, and Kalaristaq. See Fātaḥ, *op. cit.*, p. 326.

[49] For the text, see U.S. Department of State, *Foreign Relations of the United States* (Washington, 1920), III, 351-52.

[50] Sykes, *op. cit.*, p. 454.

By June 1916 the committee forces of the nationalist government at Kermanshah counted on the protection of the victorious Ottoman army. The nationalist government was the only Iranian government that the Turks recognized. For a month Turkish troops, under Iḥsān Pāshā, remained at Kermanshah in order to maintain close contact with the Mesopotamian front. Then Iḥsān was instructed to advance toward the capital. This brought Turkey's and Niẓām's forces, under the command of Muḥammad Taqī Khān, into armed conflict with the Russian troops. The Russians were defeated at Behistun and Sinneh and were finally forced to evacuate Hamadan.

These events lay back of the August crisis at Tehran. The pro-Entente Cabinet of Sipahsālār fell, and the British and Russian Legations had no objection to the Shah's desire to appoint Vuṣūq al-Dawlah as the new Prime Minister. To form a Cabinet under the circumstances was not an easy task. British and Russian influence was still supreme at Tehran, but the Turkish victories challenged it. Vuṣūq sought to include in his Cabinet a few ministers sympathizing with the Central Powers. The British and Russians, however, objected to such a Cabinet, and as a result Vuṣūq remained without one for sixteen days.

In the meantime, foreseeing the possibility of further advances by the Turks and the capture of Tehran, the British and Russian Ministers suggested the evacuation of the capital. They argued that since the government had pursued a pro-Entente policy departure from Tehran was prudent and necessary.[51] Because no Cabinet had been formed, a group of Iranian statesmen assembled to consider the Anglo-Russian demand. The proposal was rejected, but it was decided that three statesmen[52] would be dispatched to Hamadan to request the Turks not to advance toward Tehran. No such action became necessary, however, because further Turkish advances were made impossible by the combined Anglo-Russian resistance.

With the crisis thus terminated in favor of the Entente Powers, Vuṣūq formed a Cabinet on August 29, 1916. He himself acted both as the Prime Minister and as the Minister of Foreign Affairs. From this time until the end of the war, whether Vuṣūq, 'Alā' al-Saltanah, or 'Aīn al-Dawlah was in power, the pro-Entente policy was con-

[51] Sipahr, *op. cit.*, p. 377.

[52] The appointed statesmen were Qavām al-Saltanah, Muḥtashim al-Saltanah, and Mushāvir al-Mamālik.

tinued. Only between January and May 1918 was there a short-lived interruption in that policy.

Vuṣūq confirmed the Khoshtaria concession granted by Sipahsālār. He also recognized the South Persia Rifles. Their recognition was a significant blow to both German agents and their Iranian sympathizers. The domestic by-product of this essentially foreign-policy decision would, it was hoped, be the establishment of law and order by the Rifles in behalf of the helpless central government.

Belligerent Groups and Factions

The policy of neutrality was disregarded, not only by the government through the pursuance of pro-German or pro-British policies, but by many groups and factions who pursued aims and actions hostile to the belligerent powers. After the evacuation of Tehran many hundreds of individuals, sympathizing with the deputies of the dispersed Majlis, joined hands with the German agents at Qum. These men also participated, as volunteers, in the fighting between the forces of the National Defense Committee and Russian troops. As we have seen, they fought at Hamadan and at Saveh and Robat Karim, and after their defeat they moved on to Kashan and, eventually, to Kermanshah, where they joined the forces of Niẓām and in August 1916 participated in the battle between the joint forces of Iḥsān Pāshā and Muḥammad Taqī Khān and the Russian troops.

The belligerency of various tribal groups was of particular significance. The tribes constitute about one-fifth to one-quarter of the population of Iran today. They have always played an important role in the domestic politics of Iran, as exemplified by the part played by the Bakhtyārīs in the reestablishment of the Constitutional regime in 1909. Neutrality did not suit the tribal mood when the war broke out. Some of the most important groups, such as the Bakhtyārīs, the Qashqā'īs, the Baluchis, the Hazaras, and the Khamsahs, were involved in all sorts of activities for or against one side or the other. The anti-British uprisings among the Bakhtyārī and Qashqā'ī tribes in the southwest, under Ṣulat al-Dawlah, were countered by the pro-British action of the Khamsah tribe, under Qavām al-Mulk. The anti-British raids of the Baluchis across the border in the southeast were matched by the pro-British services of the Hazaras in the northeast.

Another actively belligerent faction was the Azerbaijan Fighters (*Mujāhidīn-i Āẕarbāījān*). The Fighters had supported the Constitutional regime. After its destruction (1911), the Russian occupying forces in Azerbaijan had suppressed them and finally broken their organized resistance. When the war broke out, those Fighters who still resided in Tabriz began to agitate against Russian troops by secretly publishing and circulating a newspaper called *Inṣāf* ("Equity").[53] Many other Fighters who had left Azerbaijan for Constantinople after their defeat by Russian forces (December 1911) joined the Ottoman forces at the outbreak of the war. They participated in the Turkish invasion of Azerbaijan from the Bazargan and the Banah frontiers. The contribution of the Fighters to the military efforts of Turkey was probably negligible, but its propaganda value was not insignificant. Many Iranian nationalists were inspired by the example of men like Majd al-Saltanah, who cooperated fully with Khalīl Pāshā, a relative of Anvar Pāshā and the commander of Turkish forces, or by the example of outstanding Fighters like Bulūrī and Tufangchī.[54]

Another belligerent group led the colorful Jangalī Movement (*Nihẕat-i Jangalī*) the origins and development of which will be discussed in Chapter VII. Suffice it to say here that Mīrzā Kūchik Khān, the leader of this group, captured a few Britons and engaged in hostilities with the British in 1918 and that the Jangalī forces burned the British consulate in Rasht. The Jangalīs, however, were soon forced to sign an agreement with the British which provided for the withdrawal of their forces from the road between Qazvin and Enzeli, the expulsion of foreign instructors from the Jangalī army, and the release of British prisoners. The British undertook to refrain from intervening in Iranian affairs and to abstain from all actions contrary to the goals of the Jangalīs unless the achievement of such goals assisted the cause of the enemies of Great Britain.[55]

[53] Kasravī, *op. cit.*, p. 591.

[54] For vivid details, see *ibid.*, pp. 599-622.

[55] For the text of the agreement, see Sipahr, *op. cit.*, p. 389.

PASSION OR POLICY?

In retrospect, the policy of neutrality was first idealistically declared, then openly as well as surreptitiously evaded and made a laughing stock in the vicissitudes of the war. The striking resemblance between this policy and Iran's foreign policy during the Constitutional period derived from the fact that they were both the product of a new elite guided primarily by unrestrained adherence to nationalistic dogma. The current political ideology made it almost impossible for its adherents to seek a way by which to minimize the damage to the interests of their country. The difficulties were made apparent when Mustawfī al-Mamālik was asked what guarantees he could provide that the Turkish forces would not move in if the Russian troops were pulled out to satisfy Iran's proposed neutrality. The Prime Minister, of course, could not possibly have given any guarantees because Iran's basic military unit at the time was the Gendarmerie, which was not capable of maintaining internal security let alone resisting foreign invasion. Furthermore, it was well known that the Swedish and Iranian officers of the unit sympathized with Germany. Nevertheless, the policy of neutrality was adopted instead of a realistic attempt to maximize Iran's interests by coming to an understanding with the Entente Powers, at the very outset of the war. Iran was in no position to implement a policy of strict neutrality as Great Britain and Russia were already on the scene.

Such a course was too realistic to be adopted by the new elite, many of whom were guided by passion. Regardless of the realities of the Iranian situation, some of the emergent policy makers were so intense in their hatred of Great Britain and Russia that they could only adopt a policy of neutrality as a façade behind which flirtation and even secret agreement with Germany might take place. Apparently the author of the policy of neutrality did not need much persuading by the Democratic zealots and their German guardians to sign the agreement. The fact that Russian troops were occupying Azerbaijan and that Iran was flanked by Great Britain and Russia on all sides did not seem to matter. What did matter was the fantastic belief that Germany was willing and able to help Iran against Great Britain and Russia. The stark fact of German inability to extend such assistance became known during the course of secret negotiations when Mustawfī al-Mamālik was told by the Germans that they could not promise to supply Iran with large-scale supplies of weapons and ammunitions.

What really terminated the policy of neutrality, however, was not, as is often asserted, its violation by the Entente Powers. To be sure, the Entente Powers had to protect their strategic interests because they could not rely upon the guarantees of Iran, which it could not give to begin with. As a result Iranian territory was turned into a battlefield. But equally important, if not more so, is the fact that both the disunited government and the belligerent factions within Iranian society failed to maintain, for any length of time, a policy of neutrality. The dispersed deputies of the Third Majlis, most of the Democrats, and some of the Moderates openly sided with the Central Powers and accepted German moral, financial, and material support even when the Cabinet was trying to keep an appearance of neutrality. They established, with the aid of the German Legation, the National Defense Committee at Qum and a rival government at Kermanshah. Finally their supporters even took up arms, with German and Turkish aid, against the Russian forces. The major tribes, the Bakhtyārīs, the Qashqā'īs, the Baluchis, the Hazaras, and the Khamsahs, all took action in favor of one or the other belligerent power. The Fighters of Azerbaijan sided with the Turks and the followers of the Jangalī Movement fought the British. The various Cabinets no less than the deputies, violated the policy of neutrality. The author of the policy himself signed an agreement with Germany. Succeeding Cabinets sided either with the Entente or with the Central Powers.

The Iranian policy of neutrality was a disaster because no one really desired it – not the warring Entente and Central Powers and certainly not the Iranians. Furthermore, Iran had not the means to maintain neutrality. In his Farewell Address, Washington admonished the American people against "permanent, inveterate antipathies against particular nations and passionate attachments for others." Adherence to such a policy by Iranians high and low might have minimized the ravages of war in Iran.

Chapter VII

Nationalism, Communism, and Foreign Policy, 1917-1920

As THE First World War drew to an end, momentous changes were taking place in the external and internal factors governing Iranian foreign policy. Of the external factors the most important was the Russian Revolution. The revolution affected the external scene in two related ways. First, it brought to an end the Anglo-Russian friendship. No longer did Great Britain and Russia act in concert or with tacit understanding. In a sense, the two powers reverted to their old rivalry in Iran. The revolution produced also a far-reaching metamorphosis in the nature of that rivalry. The imperialist policies of Tsarist Russia, which had long threatened British interest in Iran as a buffer for the defense of India, were now camouflaged, reinforced, and spurred into relentless action by the messianic tenets of Communist ideology. The pre-1907 Anglo-Russian rivalry was reborn within the new context of the "Socialist-Capitalist antagonism."

Second, the revolution affected Iran's external affairs in the sense that it compounded the age-old unilateral Russian threat to Iran. The traditional Russian policy had manifested itself primarily in outright aggression, economic penetration, and absorption of frontier territories. To these the revolution added the weapon of Communist ideology and propaganda directed not only against Iran's independence but also against its way of life. Iranian policy makers, therefore, began to encounter a new element within Iranian society, which, with Russia's moral, financial, and material support, could subvert the polity in the interest of both Russian imperialism and world communism.

The fundamental factor underlying the change in the internal situation was the intensified sense of nationalism. As the war drew to a close, Iranian nationalism underwent a significant change in that it was more widespread than before, more effectively asserted, and more sophisticated – at least some of its leaders demonstrated a small degree of sophistication. Iranian nationalism was intensified not only by the general rise of nationalist fervor in the world at the end of the war but also by two specific developments. One was the collapse of the Russian monarchy. Many of the Constitutionalists of the earlier period watched Russian events with enthusiasm and hailed the Provisional government for its liberalism. Even the Bolshevik Revolution intensified nationalist sentiments in Iran for the reason that the new regime condemned the former Tsarist policy in Iran and went out of its way to endorse the territorial integrity and independence of Iran. All this emboldened the Iranian nationalists.

The other development was the emergence of the United States as a champion of the principle of self-determination, with President Woodrow Wilson as "the heroic savior and hope of mankind." The fact that the early nationalists had favored the United States as the third power from which they had sought aid in the hope of reconstructing the finances of the country exerted a strong appeal to the nationalist imagination. Before the appearance of President Wilson on the world scene, they had had the opportunity to work with an American idealist in the person of Morgan Shuster. At that time the United States government had remained aloof from the Iranian scene, but now it appeared that America would champion Iranian nationalism.

THE NEW FACE OF RUSSIA

The exact relationship between Soviet ideology and foreign policy, which has been the subject of much controversy, is beyond the scope of this study and should not detain us here. Let it suffice to say that, whatever this relationship may be, the impact of Marxism-Leninism on Soviet foreign policy substantially increased the value of Iran in the calculations of Russian foreign-policy makers. To Peter the Great and his successors the subjugation of Iran in order to control India had been a necessary step toward becoming "the true sovereign of the world." To Lenin and his comrades Soviet domination of Iran was necessary because Iran was a gate to the Indian citadel, which was to serve as a "vanguard of Revolution" in the East. K. M. Troianovsky, a Russian Communist, shed light on the Soviet aim in Iran when he declared:

> The ground for the revolution in Persia has been long prepared; it was prepared by the imperialists of England and "Russia"; only a jolt from outside is needed now, only initiative and determination are necessary.
>
> The Persian revolt can become the key to a general revolution. . . . Owing to Persia's special geographical position and because of the significance of its liberation for the East, it must be conquered politically first of all. This precious key to revolutions in the East must be in our hands; at all costs Persia must be ours. *Persia must belong to the Revolution!* [1]

Toward the attainment of this basic aim Soviet Russia employed the instruments of diplomacy, the Communist party, revolutionary propaganda, and outright aggression.

Two significant diplomatic gestures were the opening of negotiations for the withdrawal of Russian troops from Iran and Trotsky's denunciation of the Anglo-Russian Agreement of 1907.[2]

Because of the civil war in Russia and the general anti-Soviet attitude of the government of Vus̱ūq al-Dawlah, these initial moves on the part of Soviet Russia were followed by two years of relatively little diplomatic activity between the two countries. However, the Soviet government did send two unofficial representatives to Tehran. The first, Karl Bravin, a former employee of the Tsarist government, arrived in Tehran in January 1918 with a message from Lenin to the Iranian government. This message condemned the injustices suffered by Iran at the hands of the Tsars, which it proposed to

[1] Xenia Joukoff Eudin and Robert C. North, *Soviet Russia and the East: 1920-1927* (Stanford, Calif.,1957), p. 29.

[2] For details, see the next section, "Iran's First Encounter with Soviet Russia," below.

repair by "repudiating all Tsarist privileges and agreements that are contrary to the sovereignty of Persia." The more important part of the message declared that Bravin was dispatched to Tehran for the conclusion of trade and other friendly agreements "the purpose of which is not only the buttressing of good neighbourly relations in the interests of both nations but together with the people of Iran the joint fight against the most rapacious imperialist government on Earth – England, the intrigues of which have hitherto disturbed the peaceful people of Iran and destroyed your great country."

Moscow apparently was not too pleased with Bravin's performance at Tehran, as he failed to acquire Iran's recognition of the Soviet government. He was replaced by a much more effective agent, an ardent Bolshevik, I. I. Kolomiitsev, who arrived in Tehran in August 1918. Kolomiitsev, though more active than his predecessor, was no more successful in obtaining recognition from the Iranian government.[3]

The Communist party constituted another significant tool of Moscow. Organizationally the Communist party of Iran was not a "spontaneous Iranian creation"; it had its beginnings in Russia.[4] Originating soon after the October Revolution among a group of Iranian workers employed in the Baku oil fields and known under the name of *'Adālat* ("Justice"), the movement soon attracted Iranians living in Turkistan and in Iran.[5] The original *'Adālat* group in Baku had about six thousand members led by Ḥaidar Khān, a Communist from Baku who sent agents to Iran to found local committees of the party at Tabriz, the Caspian provinces, and Tehran.

On June 22, 1920, a congress was held at Enzeli by Iranian Communists during which the *'Adālat* party was renamed the Iranian Communist party.[6] No less active than Ḥaidar Khān in the formation of the party was A. Sulṭānzādah, a somewhat mysterious person connected with the Russian People's Commissariat of Foreign Affairs who was often the representative of the Iranian Communist party at the congresses of the Communist International. At this congress the plan of the struggle against "British imperialism and the Shah

[3] See *ibid.*

[4] George Lenczowski, *Russia and the West in Iran, 1918-1948* (Ithaca, N.Y., 1949), p. 97.

[5] Eudin and North, *op. cit.*, p. 99.

[6] *Ibid.*

government" was outlined, and greetings were sent to the Russian Red Army and Fleet and to the Central Committee of the Russian Communist party. Lenin and Narimanov were elected honorary chairmen *in absentia*.[7]

Many Communists were uncertain as to the best policy to be followed by the party. The Central Committee of the party therefore instructed Sulṭānzādah to seek Lenin's assistance. Uncertainty had arisen because some of the Communists from Baku were not in favor of pushing for agrarian revolution in Iran in view of the general backwardness of the peasants. Sulṭānzādah disagreed with them, and Lenin supported him. Lenin declared, "In backward countries like Persia, where the greater part of the land is concentrated in the hands of the landowners, the slogans of the agrarian revolution have a practical significance for the peasant millions." [8]

The activities of the Communist party were soon evident among the workers. Two real workers' trade unions were created in Enzeli – a porters' union and a longshoremen's union. By 1921 eleven workers' unions existed in Tehran. They numbered 8,250 members and were composed of hired laborers only. In the same year a Council of Trade Unions was created in Tehran, to which each union was to send three delegates. The council promptly decided to affiliate with the Red Profintern and informed Moscow accordingly.[9]

Communist influence in the Majlis was also evident by the summer of 1921, when the Fourth Majlis finally convened, although election of the Tehran deputies had taken place as early as October 1917. Sulaymān Mīrzā, who had been active in forming a coalition of pro-German elements in the Democratic and Moderate parties in November 1915, was one of the twelve deputies elected in 1917. After the war he and Mosāvāt, also a Tehran deputy elected in 1917, organized the Social Democratic party. By the time of the opening of the Fourth Majlis two new groups dominated the Iranian political scene, the Reformists (*Iṣlāhṭalabān*) and the Socialists (*Sūsīālīst-hā*). Sulaymān Mīrzā led the latter, while Mudarris, Bihbihānī, Taymūrtāsh, and others led the former. The Socialist party was supported by a small minority in the Majlis, but its rival, the Reformist party, enlisted the majority. Support for the Reformists came from the

[7] *Ibid.*
[8] Quoted, *ibid.*
[9] For details, see Lenczowski, *op. cit.*, pp. 102-4.

bazaar merchants, older statesmen, and influential government officials. The Socialists enjoyed significant influence among trade unions, teachers, and some students. Those on the left eventually became a front for the Communist party.[10]

The element of revolutionary propaganda was, of course, present in both Soviet diplomatic and Communist party pronouncements. On December 5, 1917, the Council of People's Commissars of the Bolshevik regime issued an appeal addressed to the Muslims of "Russia and the East." This was a significant expression of the basic Soviet aims in the East, including Iran, and also a document of great propaganda value. Its bold, frank, and sweeping attack on imperialism was most ingratiating:

> Muslims of the East, Persians, Turks, Arabs and Hindus! All you in whose lives and property, in whose freedom and native land the rapacious European plunderers have for centuries traded! All you whose countries the robbers who began the war now desire to partition! We declare . . . that the treaty for the partition of Persia is null and void. As soon as military operations cease, the armed forces will be withdrawn from Persia and the Persians will be guaranteed the right of free determination of their own destiny.[11]

Of no less propaganda value was the invitation extended by the Third International to the peoples of the East to come to Baku for a congress to convene on August 15, 1920. It declared in part,

> Peasants and Workers of Persia! The Tehran Kajar Government and its hirelings – the provincial khans – have plundered and exploited you for centuries. The land was seized by the lackeys of the Tehran government; they control this land, they are imposing taxes and levies on you at their discretion; and after having drained the country of its vitality and reduced it to poverty and ruin, they sold Persia last year to the English capitalists for £2,000,000 sterling, so that the latter could form an army in Persia which will oppress you even more than heretofore.[12]

For revolutionary propaganda to be effective, trained and professional propagandists were needed. Under the auspices of the Commis-

[10] For further information, see Malik al-Shu'arā' Bahār, *Tārīkh-i Aḥzāb-i Sīyāsī* (Tehran, 1321-22 [1942/44]), pp. 130-35.

[11] For the text, see Ivar Spector, *The Soviet Union and the Muslim World* (University of Washington Press, 1958, mimeographed), pp. 21-23.

[12] For the text, see *ibid.*, pp. 33-36.

sariat for Nationalities, headed by Stalin, the Communist University of Toilers of the East was created. The university was designed to be a propaganda center for the purpose of acquainting students with the principles of Marxism, the tactics of the proletarian revolution, and the customs and languages of oriental peoples.[13] A branch located in Tashkent played a very important role as a center of propaganda for Central Asia, Iran, Afghanistan, and India.

Soviet Russia also resorted to outright aggression for the attainment of its basic aim in Iran. The immediate reasons underlying the invasion of Iran were later given by F. F. Raskolnikov, commander of the Red Fleet, as follows:

> After the proclamation of the Azarbaijan republic, knowing that Soviet Russia and the Azarbaijan republic could not be sure that the British would not make a new attack on Baku from Enzeli; I decided to seize Enzeli and to remove from there all the White ships, thus depriving the British of their mainstay on the Caspian Sea.[14]

In other words, the breaching of the protective belt of independent republics between Russia and Iran on April 28, 1920, made military operations against Iran less difficult and permitted Raskolnikov to proceed against the White Russians and the remaining British units who had been forced to flee to Enzeli with Raskolnikov on their heels. "On May 18, 1920," states Raskolnikov, "in the early morning, our fleet approached Enzeli and opened fire bombarding not the city itself but Kazian, where all the staffs and military forces of the British were located. Simultaneous with the bombardment of Enzeli our torpedo boat made a demonstration near Rasht." [15]

As has been seen, Russian policy after the Bolshevik Revolution posed far more serious and subtle problems to Iran than ever before. Iranian policy makers now had to deal both with the traditional methods of outright invasion and diplomatic pressure and penetration and with the new methods of Communist subversion and propaganda.

[13] For details, see Lenczowski, *op. cit.*, pp. 126-29.
[14] For the text of an interview with Raskolnikov, see Eudin and North, *op. cit.*, pp. 178-80.
[15] *Ibid.*

IRAN'S FIRST ENCOUNTER WITH SOVIET RUSSIA

When the Russian monarchy collapsed and the Duma on March 2, 1917, announced the formation of the Provisional government, Vuṣūq al-Dawlah was still in power in Iran. During his preceding ten months in office, an unusually long time for a wartime Prime Minister, he had pursued a favorable policy toward Great Britain, without any objection from Russia. The impact of the change in Russia was, however, soon to be felt by Vuṣūq's government. Vuṣūq al-Dawlah was, in fact, alarmed by the change in the Russian government from the first, but many former deputies of the First, Second, and Third Majlis were heartened, believing that the long-awaited opportunity for the evacuation of Russian forces from their country had finally arrived. On April 1, 1917, these deputies assembled at the house of Arbāb Kaikhusraw, the Zoroastrian deputy, and decided to dispatch a note to the president of the Duma expressing their happiness for "the decisive victory of the great Russian nation." Eighty-eight former deputies, including Mustawfī al-Mamālik, Mushīr al-Dawlah, Mu'tamin al-Mulk, and Muḥtashim al-Saltanah, signed the letter.[16] On May 2, 1917, M. V. Rodzianko, the president of the Duma and a wealthy landowning aristocrat, wrote to the former deputies thanking them for their good wishes for the new regime and assuring them that "the loftiest ideals that have now been established in Russia will soon prevail all over the world, uniting all nations in brotherhood and peace." [17]

The initiative for this favorable gesture toward the Provisional government seems to have come from Sayyid Ẕīā' al-Dīn, who was in Russia at the time, closely watching the developments there and reporting them to the Iranian government.[18] In any event Vuṣūq al-Dawlah did not share the enthusiasm of the former deputies, who were profoundly stirred by "the triumph of liberalism in Russia" and who clamored for the completion of elections and the opening of the

[16] The names of the deputies and the text of their letter are in Muvarrikh al-Dawlah Sipahr, *Īrān dar Jang-i Buzurg* (Tehran, 1336 [1957/58]), pp. 409-10.

[17] The text of the letter is in *ibid.*, p. 412.

[18] Sayyid Ẕīā' confided most of his information to Ḥusayn 'Alā' in the Ministry of Foreign Affairs. See Sipahr, *ibid.*, pp. 447-48.

Fourth Majlis. Intensified nationalist agitation, under the impact of the Russian (March) Revolution, and augmented terrorist activities by the anti-British extremists of the Committee of Punishment were partly responsible for the downfall of the Vuṣūq al-Dawlah Cabinet in May 1917.

Between this time and August 1918, when Vuṣūq came into power once again, Cabinets rose and fell with sensational rapidity under the premiership of 'Alā' al-Saltanah, 'Āīn al-Dawlah, Mustawfī al-Mamālik, and Ṣamṣām al-Saltanah. 'Alā' al-Saltanah was in power when the October Revolution took place. At this time Isḥāq-i Mufakhkham al-Dawlah was Iran's Minister at Petrograd, but it was his chargé d'affaires, Asad Bahādur, who was most influential in the formulation of Iran's earliest policy toward the new regime. In the course of his numerous secret telegrams to the Iranian Ministry of Foreign Affairs, not only did he inform his government of the turbulent developments in Russia but he also frequently suggested the line of policy to be followed by Iran.

In the period between the October Revolution and the reappearance of Vuṣūq al-Dawlah on the political scene Iranian policy makers were determined to take advantage of Russia's internal strife to advance the interests of their country. For this reason the friendly gestures of Russia were welcomed, but no diplomatic recognition was extended. Such recognition was to be withheld until (1) Russian troops were withdrawn from Iranian soil and (2) the Anglo-Russian Convention of 1907 was repudiated. The later developments will be examined in the light of these basic objectives.

As soon as the Brest-Litovsk Armistice of December 15, 1917, was signed, Asad Bahādur reported to Iran the content of Article 10, which provided that "the Turkish and the Russian Supreme Commands are prepared to withdraw their troops from Persia." The Iranian government then authorized him to enter into negotiations for withdrawal of troops from Iran "with the appropriate Russian body authorized to conduct such negotiations." Asad Bahādur accordingly entered into correspondence and negotiations with Trotsky, requesting "to be informed as soon as possible of the day and hour when negotiations for the evacuation of Russian forces from Persia can be opened." Trotsky, in his note of January 14, 1918, suggested five steps: (1) to work out a general plan for the withdrawal of Russian forces from Iran in the shortest possible time and to propose to Turkey to coordinate its plan for the evacuation of troops with the Russian plan, (2) to begin immediately the withdrawal of those detachments whose presence in Iran served no military purpose, (3) to recall from Iran the Russian instructors of the Cossack Brigade, (4) to appoint commissars to Russian authorities in Iran in order to explain to them Russia's new foreign policy "based on respect for the right of all peoples, regardless of their strength or weakness," and (5) to obtain provisions for the Russian troops in Iran with a view to laying as light a burden as possible on the poorer section of the population.[19] The troops were withdrawn later that year.

Asad Bahādur also negotiated with the Russian government in the hope of acquiring a written repudiation of the 1907 convention.[20] This effort too met with success. On January 27, 1918, Trotsky sent an official note, through Asad Bahādur, to the Iranian government with the view "of dispersing any doubt in regard to the Soviet government's attitude to the Anglo-Russian agreement of 1907." "The Council of the People's Commissars," Trotsky stated,

> declares that the Anglo-Russian agreement of 1907, which was directed against the freedom and independence of the Persian People, is annulled once and for all. Simultaneously the Council of the People's Commissars declares as null and void all earlier and later agreements which in any way limit or interfere with the right of the Persian people to a free and independent existence.[21]

The cumulative effects of these notes on the foreign policy of Iran were significant. On July 27, 1918, the Council of Ministers decided to abrogate all the treaties, agreements, and concessions that the "despotic Russian Government and its people had secured from Persia by duress and force through illegitimate means, such as threats and bribes." To implement its decision, the Council of Ministers decreed on August 1, 1918, that litigation of lawsuits involving Iranian and foreign subjects in the Ministry of Foreign Affairs would be stopped as such cases thereafter would fall under the jurisdiction of the Ministry of Justice according to the laws of Iran. The Council also appointed a commission under the chairmanship of Ẕakā' al-Mulk

[19] Jane Degras, *Soviet Documents on Foreign Policy* (Oxford, 1951), I, 28-29.
[20] See the text of Asad Bahādur's letters in Sipahr, *op. cit.*, pp. 468-69.
[21] Eudin and North, *op. cit.*, pp. 92-93.

Furūghī to study the questions raised by these two decisions. The commission did not anticipate difficulty in the transfer of lawsuits involving Russian citizens to the Ministry of Justice because it understood that the government's decision of July 27 had abrogated Russian extraterritorial privileges acquired under the Treaty of Turkumanchai of 1828. But in regard to the citizens of other foreign powers in Iran, it pointed out that they continued to enjoy such privileges under their respective treaties with Iran. The commission also pointed out the ways of terminating the capitulatory privileges of other powers in Iran but refrained from detailed report until further clarification of its terms of reference by the Council of Minsters.[22]

The abrogation decision was effected by the government of Ṣamṣām al-Saltanah, who was unable to get along with Aḥmad Shah. Finally, the Shah told the Prime Minister to resign his post, and Ṣamṣām al-Saltanah retorted, "I will not!" This touched off a Cabinet crisis as the result of which Vuṣūq al-Dawlah again became Prime Minister (August 1918).[23] This change marked the beginning of a new policy toward Russia. The correct and calculated policy of the former cabinets was gradually replaced by increasingly unfriendly relations.

Vuṣūq's assumption of power coincided with the arrival in Tehran of I. I. Kolomiitsev, mentioned earlier. About two months after Kolomiitsev's arrival a serious dispute developed between him and the Iranian government. On October 26 there appeared in the newspaper *Īrān* an announcement by the former Tsarist Ambassador, Von Etter, of the formation of the "Ufa government." In the next issue of the same paper Kolomiitsev charged: "In one of the smaller towns of Russia a band of imposters making use of British bayonets and Allied gold, proclaimed itself to be an All-Russian government." Then in the name of Soviet Russia, he declared that the only "legal government is stationed in Moscow, the heart of Russia, and that the recognition of all kinds of imposters, if such recognition should follow, would be received by the revolutionary democracy of Russia as an unfriendly act on the part of Persia toward Russia."[24] Kolomiitsev made similar protests against the occupation by Iranian forces

[22] The texts of the government decisions and commission report are in Sipahr, *op. cit.*, pp. 498-502.
[23] For details, see Bahār, *op. cit.*, pp. 30-31.
[24] Quoted in Eudin and North, *op. cit.*, p. 95.

of the village of Sarakhs in Transcaspia. He termed the occupation a robber's act staged by the British.[25]

Another source of serious friction was Vuṡūq's repeated refusal to recognize the Soviet government despite Kolomiitsev's continued pressure for such recognition. Faced with the unflinching stand of the Iranian government, he told the Iranian Foreign Minister that his negative attitude toward the Soviet regime was "dictated by the will of the British ambassador."

The deteriorating relations between the Iranian government and the Soviet representative in Tehran reached a climax on November 3, 1918, when the building occupied by the Soviet mission was broken into by members of the Persian Cossack Brigade. Kolomiitsev's assistant and members of both men's families were taken prisoners; Kolomiitsev himself escaped and made his way on foot to Baku. He was then recalled to Moscow, but soon thereafter was instructed to return to Iran, this time with an official offer from the Soviet government to open negotiations regarding the signing of a treaty of friendship. He left for Iran in July 1919, but was captured by anti-Bolshevik forces on the island of Ashur-Ada in the Caspian Sea and shot by them in August 1919.[26]

Even if Kolomiitsev had had a chance to present the Soviet offer for a treaty, a resumption of cordial relations with Russia would have been unthinkable by the time of his arrival. Even though the Russian troops had been withdrawn and the Anglo-Russian Convention of 1907 had been repudiated, the Vuṡūq government had already tied the destiny of Iran to Great Britain. Lord Curzon's long-cherished dream of creating a chain of "vassal states stretching from the Mediterranean to the Pamirs" seemed about to be realized. "The weakest and the most vital link" of this chain, as viewed by Lord Curzon, was Iran. On this ground he regarded a policy of unrestrained evacuation of Iran as "immoral, feeble and disastrous." To prevent such a disaster Great Britain hurried through secret negotiations with Vuṡūq al-Dawlah, resulting in the Agreement of 1919. Lord Curzon regarded the agreement as a "diplomatic masterpiece" and its conclusion "a great triumph," but to the Bolsheviks it was

[25] Bahār claims that Sir Percy Cox told him that the British would oppose the occupation of Sarakhs because they themselves wanted to establish a government there (*op. cit.*, p. 46).

[26] Eudin and North, *op cit.*, p. 95.

"a treacherous surrender of Persian liberties wrested from a prostrate Persia by force and bribes." [27]

A month after the signing of the Anglo-Persian Agreement of 1919, the Vuṣūq government decided "in view of the uncertain situation in Russia" to close down the Iranian Embassy because its maintenance did not seem to amount to "anything but unnecessary expenditures." This was the peak of Vuṣūq al-Dawlah's anti-Russian policy.[28]

The invasion of Iran on May 18, 1920, was mainly the result of the military operations in Transcaucasia,[29] but the policy of the government of Vuṣūq al-Dawlah had been provocative and the Soviets hoped that their invasion would produce political results in Tehran.

On May 19, a day after the invasion, Prince Fīrūz, the Foreign Minister, addressed a letter to the League of Nations, claiming that the Soviet action against Iran constituted aggression, protesting such acts as being contrary to the provisions of the Covenant, and finally requesting that the situation be brought to the attention of the members with a view to the "measures which the situation demands." On May 29 the Iranian government asked for a meeting of the Council, which assembled on June 14, 1920. The Council considered this appeal in the light of Article 10 of the Covenant embodying the obligation of the members "to respect and preserve as against external aggression the territorial integrity and existing political independence of all Members of the League." In case of such aggression or threat or danger of it, the Council was to advise upon the means by which its obligations should be fulfilled. Because the Iranian government was negotiating with the Soviet authorities, the Council decided that, before advising upon the means by which the obligations prescribed by the Covenant should be fulfilled, it should await the result of the negotiations then in progress.[30]

The Council's ineffectual resolution, added to the Soviet invasion, dealt the last blow to the Vuṣūq government. Furthermore, British influence, upon which he had depended, was in decline. The Causasus had been cleared of the British, Raskolnikov had driven the British

[27] Harold Nicolson, *Curzon: The Last Phase* (London, 1937), p. 143.

[28] The closing of the legation was prompted by the arrest of some Iranian officials, including Asad Bahādur, in Russia. This had been, in turn, prompted by the arrest of some Russian officials in Khorasan by the British authorities. See Sipahr, *op. cit.*, p. 476.

[29] See above, p. 145.

[30] World Peace Foundation, *League of Nations* (Boston, 1920), III, 279.

forces out of northern Iran, and the British had decided, due to these setbacks and out of "larger imperial considerations," to retire to Qazvin.

The downfall of the Vuṣūq government was followed by the formation of a new Cabinet under Mushīr al-Dawlah. His rise to power produced a significant change in Iran's foreign policy. The Anglo-Persian Agreement of 1919 was suspended until a new Majlis was formed as the result of new elections. The cornerstone of Mushīr al-Dawlah's policy toward Russia was normalization of relations without any appeasement whatsoever. He would not give in an iota to Soviet Russia or to its puppet regime of Gilan. "The Iranians," said he, "wished to live in friendship with Russia, but the attempt to use Iran as a springboard for the Bolsheviks in the interests of World Revolution, would be resisted even if the bloody insurgents of Gilan inaugurated their fresh victories on the bodies of our people." [31]

During his four months in office Mushīr al-Dawlah simultaneously pursued two specific objectives in regard to Soviet Russia. He sought to establish friendly relations with Moscow and to reestablish the central government's authority over the Iranian provinces in the north and northwest. The latter objective was not merely in the interest of internal security; it was also directed against Russia, as the Soviet Republic of Gilan had been established with Soviet aid and as Russia hoped to control the rebel government of Azerbaijan. Thus Mushīr al-Dawlah's policy toward Soviet Russia should be examined in the light of his policy toward Gilan and Azerbaijan as well as his direct diplomatic approach to Soviet Russia.

The Gilan problem must be traced to the origin and development of the Jangalī Movement, led by Mīrzā Kūchik Khān, mentioned earlier (see Chapter VI). He was a religious nationalist who had fought the Royalist forces in 1909 for the reestablishment of the Constitutional regime. In the battle of Astarabad he had been seriously wounded and had been taken to Tiflis for treatment. He had later returned to Tehran and begun to look for men who sympathized with his views on the ways and means by which his country could be rid of internal corruption, favoritism, tyranny, and foreign intervention. By 1915 he had found such supporters in the persons of

[31] Quoted in Nasrollah Saifpour Fatemi, *Diplomatic History of Persia, 1917-1923* (New York, 1952), p. 239. See below, pp. 152-55 and 190-92, for an account of the Gilan problem.

Dr. Hishmat-i Ṭāliqānī, Ḥāj Aḥmad-i Kasmā'ī, and Iḥsānullāh Khān. The latter had fought against Russian forces in Azerbaijan (1909) on the side of the Fighters, mentioned earlier. He had then lived in Baghdad until his return to Iran during the First World War. He first participated in the establishment of a terrorist group, called "the Committee of Punishment" (*Kumītah-'i Mujāzāt*). He subsequently joined Kūchik Khān in starting the Jangalī Movement, in which he was marked for his radical tendencies and propensity toward socialism. Mīrzā Kūchik Khān enjoyed Iḥsānullāh's full cooperation and established close contacts with the branch of the Committe for National Defense at Rasht. He and his leading supporters established a committee called "Unity of Islam" (*Ittiḥād-i Islām*) with the twofold objective of internal reform and emancipation from external domination.

The development of the Jangalī Movement was significantly influenced by the advent of the Bolshevik Revolution and its repercussions in Iran. As early as 1919 the Bolsheviks had considered ways and means of exploiting the movement. In that year, when the Jangalī forces were having a particularly difficult time fighting Iranian troops sent from Tehran, Iḥsānullāh Khān urged Kūchik Khān to seek the support of the Bolsheviks. After considerable hesitation Kūchik Khān agreed, and negotiations were ultimately undertaken with Raskolnikov, who landed in Enzeli at the head of the Red forces in May 1920. According to Raskolnikov, he immediately urged Kūchik Khān to advance on Rasht. Shortly thereafter the Committee of Red Revolution (*Kumītah-'i Inqilāb-i Surkh*) proclaimed the establishment of the Soviet Republic of Gilan with Kūchik Khān as its president and war commissar. In accepting Raskolnikov's assistance Kūchik Khān insisted that Communist propaganda in Iran should be avoided because it ran counter to the religious sentiments of the people. To the Communists, however, the significance of Kūchik Khān's activities had always lain

> not in his armed strength and his fighting against the British, but in the point of possible contact with him for the purpose of successful revolutionary propaganda in Persia. Kuchik Khan is important as a socialist agitator not so much because he is a leader of a guerilla war but because he is a bearer of social slogans, which he advanced even before the coming of the British to Gilan. His work which is so closely connected with communism, authough it is interpreted by the

Persians in a different sense, represents a seed which, once it is carefully and skillfully cultivated, will produce a good harvest of revolutionary preparedness among the Persian masses.[32]

Subsequent events, however, belied the Communist optimism about the Jangalīs. Dissension among the Jangalīs was forced into the open soon after the establishment of the Soviet Republic of Gilan. When Iran's complaint against Soviet invasion was before the Council of the League of Nations in June 1920, Moscow, foreseeing the possibility of eventual withdrawal of Red forces from Iran, decided upon dispatching large groups of Communists to Iran. The *'Adālat* party had just been renamed the Iran Communist Party and was ready for new activities. Regular trips of a postal boat between Baku and Enzeli proved most helpful. The first group of Communists arrived in Enzeli and was followed by a second group led by Khālū Qurbān and the brother of Iḥsānullāh Khān. A third group numbering nearly 700 arrived in Bandar Gaz and Farahabad, heading for Babul and Barfurush.

This large flow of outright Communists into Iran alarmed Kūchik Khān, who was always a "religious nationalist" at heart. When Mushīr al-Dawlah came into power, Communists were still pouring into northern Iran. Conscious of Kūchik Khān's nationalistic sentiments, Mushīr al-Dawlah sent one of Iran's most reputable nationalists, Sardār Fākhir, to induce Kūchik Khān to oppose the arrival of Communists. Kūchik Khān's sympathetic response to the Prime Minister's message and his declaration of allegiance to the government of Mushīr al-Dawlah contributed to a schism between him and his Communist supporters. Iḥsānullāh Khān, together with Khālū Qurbān, established his own "Committee of Young Men of Iran" (*Kumītah-'i Javānān-i Īrān*). This marked the beginning of actual combat between the supporters of Kūchik Khān and of Iḥsānullāh Khān. The latter were reinforced, after the Congress of Baku of August 1920, when Ḥaidar 'Amū Qulī arrived in Iran with well-equipped men to join the forces opposing Kūchik Khān. Eventually Ḥaidar, Iḥsānullāh, and Khālū Qurbān conspired to terrorize Kūchik Khān, but failed.

Emboldened by the dissension among the Jangalīs, Mushīr al-Dawlah, with the consent of Aḥmad Shah, appointed Colonel Storro-

[32] Eudin and North, *op. cit.*, p. 177.

selski, a White Russian officer, commander-in-chief of Iranian forces. Storroselski was instructed to push the Bolsheviks out of Gilan and Mazandaran. The recapture of these rich provinces was the primary objective of Storroselski's military operations. In spite of having only a small number of ill-equipped and poorly fed Cossacks, he made rapid gains at the expense of the enemy. Mazandaran was soon recaptured, and preparations were made for the advance toward Rasht. On the way, Ismailabad, a center of Iranian Bolsheviks, fell to the Iranian forces. By August 24, 1920, Rasht was also wrested from the "invaders" (*Mutijāsirīn*). The British held the ring and acted as a rallying base for the Iranian forces, which pursued the Bolsheviks, who were retreating to Enzeli. In the decisive battle near Rasht, Enzeli, and Khamam, the Iranian forces were defeated and forced back. The Russians had landed fresh troops with heavy trench mortars and howitzers, and their fleet and their gunboats had opened a flanking artillery fire from the sea and the lagoon.[33] The Gilan problem was not finally solved until the time of Riẕā Khān (see Chapter VIII).

Mushīr al-Dawlah's other measure to establish internal order and security and to oppose Soviet Russia pertained to the autonomous republic of Azerbaijan. A revolt against the Iranian government had broken out early in 1920, led by Sheikh Muḥammad Khīābānī, a former deputy of the Majlis. He had emigrated to the Caucasus in 1911 and had there established contacts with Russian revolutionaries. In 1914 he had returned to Tabriz and begun underground activities with the aim of liberating Iran from foreign influences. His activities had been interrupted by the Turkish invasion of Azerbaijan during the war, which had resulted in his temporary arrest and confinement in Kars. Released, he had returned to Tabriz, and after the end of the war, before the authority of the Iranian government was fully restored in Azerbaijan, he had gathered together 800 armed partisans and revolted.[34]

Khīābānī's National Democratic Movement was in essence nationalistic rather than democratic. His party's chief organ, *Tajaddud* ("Renaissance"), printed his fiery speeches decrying corruption and favoritism and demanding reforms. In spite of his eloquence his oppo-

[33] Cf. J. M. Balfour, *Recent Happenings in Persia* (London, 1922), p. 201, and Bahār, *op. cit.*, p. 52.

[34] Lenczowski, *op. cit.*, p. 61.

nents did not fail to detect his basically negative approach and "foggy political philosophy." [35] He spoke frequently against "opportunism" and preached "radicalism." He was violently anti-British, and his revolt against the government of Vuṣūq al-Dawlah stemmed from his belief that it had sold the country to the British.

The immediate background of his revolt is instructive. The government of Vuṣūq al-Dawlah had been alarmed by the activities of the German consul at Tabriz, Wustrow. This adventurer had turned his legation into a center of Communist activities. He had in his possession ample quantities of weapons and ammunition and aspired to stage a Communist revolution in Tabriz when the time was ripe. The Vuṣūq government decided to strengthen the police force in Tabriz by sending a Swedish officer to take charge of it. This produced dissatisfaction among the ranks of the police as it involved reorganization and some dismissals. At the same time a reorganization in the taxation system produced discontent among many Tabrizi employees who were replaced by nearly 60 men from Tehran under the supervision of Tarjumān al-Dawlah.[36]

Khīābānī drew support from these malcontents and from a large number of students. In the beginning he was also quick to exploit the support of Wustrow. Once established, however, he turned against the German consul and participated in the fight against him. Wustrow was killed on June 3, 1920, and thus the Communist menace from the inside was checked. But the threat from the outside was grave. The Bolshevik forces had established themselves in Gilan and turned toward the town of Zanjan, ready to invade Iranian Azerbaijan. At that moment, however, to the disappointment of the Soviet leaders, the Khīābānī forces did not prove cooperative. The National Democrats in Tabriz, instead of joining hands with the Bolsheviks, declared that they disapproved of Soviet landings at Enzeli. Toward the end of July 1920 the remnants of the first Tatar Regiment of the Free Republic of Azerbaijan crossed the border of Iranian Azerbaijan to find refuge from the Bolsheviks. Fortunately the Soviet troops did not pursue the Tatars into Iran.[37]

Mushīr al-Dawlah finally determined to destroy the Khīābānī gov-

[35] Aḥmad Kasravī, *Tārīkh-i Hījdah Sālah-'i Āẕarbāijān* (Tehran, 1333 [1954/55]), p. 874.

[36] *Ibid.*, pp. 863-66.

[37] Lenczowski, *op. cit.*, p. 62.

ernment in Azerbaijan, at least in part, in order to reduce Bolshevik temptation to dominate Azerbaijan. Khīābānī, like Kūchik Khān, was pleased with the assumption of power by Mushīr al-Dawlah, but did not refrain from pressing for the recognition of his separatist government by the central government. This demand was utterly unacceptable to Mushīr al-Dawlah. Negotiations having failed, Mushīr al-Dawlah dispatched Mukhbir al-Saltanah as governor to Azerbaijan. Khīābānī stubbornly refused to recognize the governor after his arrival in Tabriz, and Mukhbir al-Saltanah was forced to seek ways to bring down Khīābānī's regime. In establishing his regime in Azerbaijan, Khīābānī had been able to remove every source of organized opposition but one, the Iranian Cossacks. Mukhbir al-Saltanah therefore turned to them. The fact that the governor had arrived in Tabriz with "nothing in his possession but a bag" apparently had led Khīābānī to underestimate the possible threat of the governor to his regime. In any case in September 1920 the Iranian Cossack Brigade dispersed the forces of Khīābānī after some heavy fighting. Khīābānī was "killed," and his regime collapsed.[38]

While Mushīr al-Dawlah's policy toward the Soviet Republic of Gilan and the Khīābānī government of Azerbaijan revealed that he would in no way appease Soviet Russia, Communists, or even a nationalist movement which might play into the hands of the Bolsheviks, his diplomatic efforts aimed at the restoration of normal relations with Russia. Although his government fell a few months before the results of his diplomacy were embodied in the Soviet-Iranian Treaty of Friendship of Febuary 1921, the treaty was the product of the policy that he inaugurated and his successors followed.

In the diplomatic field, also, Mushīr al-Dawlah's policy was the complete reversal of that followed by his predecessor Vuṣūq al-Dawlah. As early as June 26, 1919, Soviet Russia's policy toward Iran had been clearly outlined in a note from Karakhan to the Iranian government. This document is significant because it defined in 1919 the principles and concessions accepted in the treaty of 1921. The Soviet government, said the note, wished to make good the damage done by the former Tsarist state. Concretely, Moscow announced that (1) all Iranian debts to the Tsarist government were annulled, (2) Russian interference in Iran's income from customs and the postal and tele-

[38] Mukhbir al-Saltanah claimed that Khīābānī committed suicide.

graph system was at an end, (3) all Russian official and private concessions in Iran were void, (4) the Russian bank in Iran with all its branches was the property of the Iranian people, (5) all the roads, electric stations, and the like built and owned by Russia were transferred to the Iranian nation, and (6) capitulatory privileges ceased to exist.[39]

These changes were not merely adumbrated as the basis of future negotiations. "The Bolsheviks voluntarily made these gifts to Iran without seeking to use them for bargaining advantage." [40] The government of Vuṡūq al-Dawlah had been in no position to reply to this gesture and to try to take advantage of it as it had tied itself to Great Britain "hand and foot," but Mushīr al-Dawlah could. On July 10, 1920, he appointed as envoy to Moscow, Mushāvir al-Mamālik, the Iranian Ambassador at Constantinople. On October 25, 1920, the envoy arrived in Moscow and opened negotiations with the Soviet government with a view to concluding a treaty of peace and friendship between Russia and Iran. The negotiations and the resultant treaty of February 1921 will be discussed in the next chapter.

VUṢŪQ FAVORS GREAT BRITAIN

Iran's attitude toward Great Britain was generally favorable during 1917-1920. Vuṣūq al-Dawlah, who was in power during most of this period,[41] was particularly pro-British. However, the two Prime Ministers who preceded Vuṣūq's second government (beginning in August 1918) pursued policies unpalatable to the British.

The first of these was Mustawfī al-Mamālik, who had been Iran's Prime Minister at the outset of the war. His new Cabinet was formed by January 1918. As soon as he took office, he informed the British of Iranian demands: (1) abrogation of the 1907 agreement, (2) withdrawal of the British forces from Iran, (3) revision of the customs tariff, (4) participation in the Peace Conference, and (5) transfer of control of the South Persia Rifles to Iran.[42] The British

[39] Louis Fischer, *The Soviets in World Affairs* (London, 1930), I, 289.

[40] *Ibid.*

[41] Vusūq al-Dawlah's first wartime Cabinet lasted from August 1916 to May 1917.

[42] The text of Mustawfī's "declaration" is in Sipahr, *op. cit.*, pp. 490-91.

government rejected the demand for withdrawal of troops while reiterating respect for Iran's "independence and territorial integrity." It also rejected the demand for control of the South Persia Rifles by Iran and took the view that the nationality of the officers should be decided by Great Britain and Russia. It was willing, however, to abrogate the 1907 agreement and to revise the customs tariff. In regard to the participation of an Iranian delegation in the Peace Conference the British government made it conditional upon the participation of other nonbelligerent powers.[43]

Mustawfī al-Mamālik was succeeded by Ṣamṣām al-Saltanah, who continued the policy of his predecessor toward the British. The Prime Minister's nationalist sentiment was intensified by the new Soviet regime, posing as the staunch supporter of Iran's sovereign rights vis-à-vis the big powers, particularly "imperialist" Britain. Emboldened by the repeated Soviet denunciations of the former policy of the Tsarist regime, the Prime Minister took the first step toward the eventual abrogation of capitulatory privileges in Iran. On January 30, 1918, his government declared all previous treaties and concessionary contracts concluded with Russia and her subjects null and void.[44] This decree aimed also at capitulatory privileges acquired by other powers, particularly Great Britain.

With the return of Vus̱ūq al-Dawlah to power, the British hoped for a favorable policy toward them. This hope was not without good reason. During his earlier months in power Vus̱ūq had maintained a pro-British policy under extremely difficult circumstances. The situation in 1918 was, however, significantly different from that in 1916. Vus̱ūq al-Dawlah was far less sensitive to nationalist demands than his predecessors, Mustawfī al-Mamālik and Ṣamṣām al-Saltanah, but he was in no position to ignore the demand for immediate evacuation of British forces from Iran. In fact, this demand was now much more difficult to resist than before because soon after the Vus̱ūq government came into power the Armistice of Mudros was concluded (October 30, 1918). Under the circumstances the Prime Minister could not, without jeopardizing his government, justify to the Iranian people the presence of British forces in the country. Nor could the British government, in view of the termination of hostilities, justify

[43] For the British letters, see *ibid.*, pp. 493-94.
[44] For this "declaration," see *ibid.*, p. 498.

to British taxpayers the maintenance of costly forces on Iranian soil. But Lord Curzon did not find it possible to grant the popular demand of Iran for immediate evacuation of the British troops. He believed that such a policy would be "immoral, feeble, and disastrous." [45] He agreed with his colleagues in the Eastern Committee of the War Cabinet that British forces should gradually be reduced, but he urged that a nucleus should be maintained, at least until the British government was able to substitute some stable and less expensive arrangement.

This arrangement toward which Curzon worked feverishly took the form of the Anglo-Persian Agreement of August 9, 1919. The secret negotiations leading to its conclusion were pushed forward with unremitting energy by Sir Percy Cox and Vuṡūq al-Dawlah. The events surrounding the conclusion of this treaty dominated Anglo-Iranian relations during most of the period under discussion. For this reason attempt will be made to identify the interests of the contracting parties and the elements of opposition to the agreement after the contents are summarized briefly.

The terms of the agreement may be examined under two broad categories:

1) *Politico-military:* The British government undertook (a) to supply, at Iran's expense, expert advisers for the Iranian administration; (b) to supply, at Iran's expense, such officers and munitions as were regarded necessary by a joint commission, and (c) to cooperate with Iran toward the improvement of its communication system.

2) *Economic:* The two governments agreed to a revision of the existing customs tariff. The British government granted a loan of £2,000,000 to Iran to be repaid as indicated after the British financial adviser had taken up his duties at Tehran. The government of Iran undertook to pay monthly interest at the rate of 7 per cent per annum. It also undertook to repay this loan from all the revenues and customs receipts originally assigned by virtue of a loan contracted by Iran in 1911.[46]

Added to the text of the agreement were two letters from Sir Percy

[45] Nicolson, *op. cit.*, p. 132.

[46] For the text, see J. C. Hurewitz, *Diplomacy in the Near and Middle East* (Princeton, N. J., 1956), II, 64-66.

Cox to Vuṣūq al-Dawlah. Iran was assured of (1) revision of the treaties in force between the two countries, (2) compensation for material damages, (3) rectification of the Iranian frontier, and (4) relinquishment of claim for cost of maintenance of British forces in Iran in return for Iran's quitclaim of indemnity for any damage which may have been caused by such forces.[47]

On the British side the main figure behind the treaty was Lord Curzon. Harold Nicolson contends that Curzon's aim was not acquisitive. He did not wish to include Iran, or part of it, within the British or the Indian empires.[48] "The integrity of Persia," Curzon had written, "must be registered as a cardinal precept of our imperial creed," but, in the face of the Russian menace to the British imperial interests in India, the weakness and vulnerability of Iran were of great concern. In the chain of buffer states stretching between India and all European interference, Curzon regarded Iran as the weakest and the most vital link. For this reason a "friendly alliance," such as the agreement of 1919, would make it possible for the British to strengthen Iran by means of prudent advice, by encouragement of the flow of capital, and by reorganization of its administrative organizations and its army. Curzon's "good intentions," however, did not spare him, as will be seen, one of the gravest failures of his career.

The interests of the Iranian government will become clear as we examine the circumstances surrounding its decision to sign the agreement. (Incidentally it may be remarked that neither the pro-British tendencies of Vuṣūq al-Dawlah nor the alleged bribing of certain Iranian officials are sufficient to explain fully Iran's acceptance of the agreement.) Both internal and external factors were at work. To take the internal situation first, a statement by Prince Fīrūz, Foreign Minister, is relevant. Iran took the initiative in asking help from Britain "because Iran was ruined and in a state of anarchy with bands of brigands infesting the country, destroying commerce and endangering the lives of its citizens. In the meantime the Government was virtually without troops and powerless to cope with the situation or to restore order." [49] Restoration of order was the primary objective of the Vuṣūq government. The first Vuṣūq Cabinet had fallen in 1917

[47] Kasravī, *op. cit.*, pp. 825-26.
[48] Nicolson, *op. cit.*, p. 122.
[49] Quoted in Fatemi, *op. cit.*, p. 83.

partly because of the activities of the self-styled "Committee of Punishment" (*Kumītah-'i Mujāzāt*).[50] This essentially terrorist group, posing as a patriotic secret society, cast its ominous shadow over the famine-stricken and impoverished inhabitants of Tehran. In the face of the ineffectual police, within a few years it scored a terrifying record of assassinations of government officials and newspaper editors, such as Matīn al-Saltanah and Mīrzā Ismā'īl Khān.

The inhabitants of the provincial cities fared no better than those of Tehran. For many years several bands of brigands had robbed travelers and endangered the life of the people of the provinces without any fear of the central government. In fact, the central government, unable to provide for the security of the provinces and anxious to guard itself against armed attack by some combination of bands of brigands, gave their leaders money and governorships. The most notorious example of these leaders was Nāyab Ḥusayn of Kashan, who received an annual salary of 50,000 tomans from the Tehran government as the governor of Kashan, but who continued his robberies with the assistance of his sons. Other examples could be cited,[51] but it suffices to say that the unrestrained activities of these men had indeed destroyed commerce and jeopardized the security of the nation.

The economic and military assistance that the Vus̱ūq government hoped to secure from Great Britain under the agreement was not merely for the restoration of internal order and security. Vus̱ūq's decision to conclude the agreement was motivated also by a desire to guard against the external threat posed by the new regime in Russia. In spite of the fact that the only foreign forces on Iranian soil at the time were those of the British, the sullen threat of the new Russian regime and ideology to Iranian independence and way of life was not to be underestimated.

Vus̱ūq's greatest apprehension derived from the opportunities that the Jangalī Movement offered the Bolsheviks. He was well aware of the desire of the Communists to exploit the rebel movement in the interest of the Revolution. It was during the second Cabinet of Vus̱ūq in 1919 that the Bolsheviks actually considered ways and means of utilizing the movement. In order to deprive the Bolsheviks of this

[50] Kasravī gives the names of its members (*op. cit.*, p. 805).
[51] *Ibid.*, p. 806.

opportunity, and also for the restoration of order in the country, Vus̱ūq's government dispatched troops to quell the rebellion. But the success of the Iranian troops being inconclusive, the hard-pressed rebel leader Kūchik Khān proved receptive to the appeal of Iḥsānullāh Khān, who urged accepting support from the Bolsheviks – the support that helped the establishment of the Soviet Republic of Gilan.

VUS̱ŪQ'S POLICY BACKFIRES

The elements of opposition to Vus̱ūq's agreement with Great Britain were both internal and external. The most important factor was the upsurge of Iranian nationalism, which has already been discussed. The Constitutional Revolution had been primarily a nationalistic movement. It had been significantly the product of the Iranian national awakening conditioned largely by the developments of the latter part of the nineteenth century and the ever-growing cultural and politico-economic penetration by the West. It had also been marked by a high degree of hopefulness and idealism not realistically warranted by the internal and external conditions of the country. As a result, the experiment with constitutionalism had proved tragically unsuccessful before the outbreak of the war. As the war drew to an end, new developments gave rise to fresh hope. This hope was realized only after the October Revolution, but the promise to withdraw Russian troops from Iranian soil, plus the annulment of the Anglo-Russian Convention of 1907, and the abrogation of all oppressive Tsarist treaties and contracts rekindled the hope of nationalists, bolstered their morale, and spurred them to bold action.

The Iranian delegation to the Peace Conference, headed by Mushāvir al-Mamālik, made unrestrained political, economic, and territorial demands. In addition to the abrogation of the 1907 convention, the abolition of consular courts, reparations for wartime damages, and freedom from economic concessions, the nationalists went so far as to demand Transcaspia, Merv, Khiva, and Asia Minor to the Euphrates.[52] As a result of British "selfish insistence," the Iranian delegation was denied the opportunity to be heard at the Conference

[52] H. W. V. Temperley, *A History of the Peace Conference of Paris* (London, 1924), p. 211. See also Nicolson, *op. cit.*, p. 135.

on the ground that Iran had not been a belligerent power in the European War. This affront infuriated the nationalists behind whose back Great Britain was secretly negotiating the Agreement of 1919 with Vuṣūq al-Dawlah and Prince Fīrūz.

Great Britain's high-handed method of concluding the agreement was opposed elsewhere, primarily by Soviet Russia and the United States and obviously for different reasons. The reasons for Soviet opposition are not far to seek. The British attempt to establish control over Iran through the 1919 agreement was diametrically opposed to both the traditional imperialist and the new revolutionary aims of Russia in Iran. Moreover, the agreement was the brain child of Vuṣūq al-Dawlah, whose government had consistently defied Russia by withholding recognition, by fraternizing with Great Britain, by breaking into the building of the Soviet mission in Tehran, and finally by closing down the Iranian Legation in Russia a month after the signing of the agreement.

When the agreement was being negotiated and a few months after it was signed, Russia was involved in civil war, an anti-Soviet regime ruled Russian Azerbaijan, the British position in Iran was unchallenged, and the Denikin flotilla operated freely in the Caspian Sea under the supreme command of Admiral Norris. Soon the roles were to be reversed, and British policy in Iran suffered setbacks at the hands of Russia. The barrier between Soviet Russia and Iran was broken down when the Bolsheviks overthrew the anti-Soviet regime in Russian Azerbaijan in April 1920. The Denikin squadron escaped to the Iranian port of Enzeli, and the result was the invasion of Iran, the establishment of the Soviet Republic of Gilan, and the downfall of the author of the 1919 agreement.

United States opposition derived from both "moral" and practical considerations. The secret Agreement of 1919 violated President Wilson's principles of "open covenants openly arrived at" and "self-determination." "But I should tell you," wrote the United States Ambassador in London to Lord Curzon,

> that upon communicating with Washington, I learned that neither the President nor the Secretary of State was favorably impressed by what they conceived to be the secrecy with which the agreement was negotiated, and felt that there had been some lack of frankness in the matter more especially as the presence of the Persian delegation in Paris seemed to offer numerous occasions for a full statement of the

intention and purposes of the British Government in the premises, and that they were therefore indisposed to take the responsibility of any steps which would indicate their approval of the treaty thus negotiated.[53]

Underlying the United States' position were American petroleum interests. The State Department was concerned that the confirmation of the agreement might make it more difficult for Americans to obtain oil concessions in Iran. It took comfort, however, in believing that the agreement

would not on its face require preferential treatment to British in granting of concessions; such a meaning has been officially disclaimed in Parliament. There is no reason, therefore, why Persian Foreign Office should not give prior consideration in northern provinces to American interests, in case Russian concessions should be legally and definitely abrogated. It is hoped that an American company will soon make application. At the proper time and in particular if the British claim prior rights discreet but strong representations should be made to the Foreign Office.[54]

In spite of domestic and foreign opposition, Vuṣūq al-Dawlah proceeded with the execution of the agreement as if it had been ratified by the Majlis, whose approval was required by the Constitution for such agreements. The Prime Minister received General Dickson and Armitage-Smith as military and financial advisers and accepted the first installment of the loan under the agreement. The British activities were stopped, however, when the Vuṣūq government fell in June 1920 and Mushīr al-Dawlah became Prime Minister. In his first proclamation to the people Mushīr al-Dawlah declared that because the agreement "must be approved by the Majlis all works under it will be suspended at this time." [55] The ill-fated agreement was doomed, although the British stubbornly sought to impel Mushīr al-Dawlah to revive it.

The steadfast opposition of the Prime Minister to the agreement and his efforts at normalization of Iran's relations with Russia gave

[53] U.S. Department of State, *Foreign Relations of the United States, 1919* (Washington, 1942), II, 701. For an excellent account of the United States position, see Fatemi, *op. cit.*, pp. 27-53.

[54] U.S. Department of State, *Foreign Relations of the United States, 1920* (Washington, 1936), III, 355.

[55] For the text of the "declaration," see Ḥusayn Makkī, *Kūdettā 1299* (Tehran, 1323 [1944/45]), pp. 8-9.

rise to suspicion on the part of the British, who looked for an opportunity to bring down Mushīr al-Dawlah's Cabinet. The excuse was provided in October 1920 when the tide of the battle between the government forces and the Bolsheviks was turned against the former as the result of the arrival of fresh troops and large quantities of weapons from Russia. The British Minister soon thereafter demanded the dismissal of White Russians in the Iranian force.[56] Mushīr al-Dawlah replied "that no one but the people of Iran could tell him what to do." He had asked no quarter and would give none. His only concern was to protect the interests of his countrymen. He thought that the moment was inopportune for the dismissal of the Russian officers.[57] The minister then had an audience with the Shah, who asked Mushīr al-Dawlah to resign.[58]

EARLY SIGNS OF SKILLFUL DIPLOMACY

During the years 1917-20 some of the earliest signs of a departure from the traditional foreign policy became evident. No doubt the traditional elements were still preeminent, but a slight change was discernible. The competence and regularity with which the developments in Russia were reported to the Iranian Foreign Ministry are notable. So also is the degree of sophistication that both the Vuṣūq al-Dawlah and the Mushīr al-Dawlah governments showed in handling some of the most serious problems relating to foreign affairs.

Vuṣūq's mistake was the 1919 agreement with Great Britain. It is true that his decision was prompted by a realistic recognition of Iran's deplorable state and the Soviet menace. Nevertheless, it is questionable whether the only available alternative was to offer Iran to Britain! Vuṣūq tried to balance the odds in reaching his decision. His failure was one of miscalculation rather than lack of calculation. In this he shared with Lord Curzon the mistake of underestimating the extent and intensity of nationalist sentiments which were sweeping over most of Asia. His policy toward Russia was also burdened at times with unnecessary provocation as exemplified by breaking into

[56] Balfour, *op. cit.*, p. 203.
[57] Fatemi, *op. cit.*, p. 109.
[58] *Ibid.*, p. 111.

the building of the Soviet mission in Tehran and by closing down Iran's Legation in Russia, yet in these and other actions, particularly in withholding recognition from the new regime in Russia, Vuṣūq was undeniably maneuvering for the maximization of Iranian interests.

Mushīr al-Dawlah's government lasted only a short while, but his policy decisions showed skill and foresight. It appears that he allowed his nationalistic sentiments to force him into taking an adamant position in the dispute over the dismisal of the Russian officers, the episode that led to his resignation. Yet this should not be allowed to overshadow an appreciation of his sense of moderation and his wisdom in making far more important decisions. His policy toward Russia was the supreme example of this. Conscious of the fact that the Soviet regime had been consolidating its power in Russia and had become a close neighbor since the downfall of Russian Azerbaijan in April 1920 and desirous of taking advantage of the new regime's friendly gestures toward Iran, Mushīr al-Dawlah sought to normalize relations with Russia. At the same time he made it clear to the Soviet leaders that he would not tolerate communism or Soviet imperialism. His policy of conciliation without appeasement was evidenced, on the one hand, by negotiations with Soviet Russia through diplomatic channels which, as will be seen, led to the Treaty of 1921 and, on the other hand, by his relentless efforts aimed at clearing the country of Bolshevik invaders and the Khīābānī separatists, whom he feared might play into the hands of the Communists. The Mushīr al-Dawlah government wrested Mazandaran and Rasht from the Bolsheviks and brought down the separatist government of Khīābānī. It was his government that suspended execution of the 1919 agreement with Great Britain. This decision was compatible with both ideological and power considerations at the time. The agreement was out of step with the postwar upsurge of nationalism throughout Asia. Nationalist opposition did not give the agreement much of a chance from the beginning. And certainly Soviet Russia would not sit still and watch its neighbor being handed over to its foremost enemy, Great Britain!

Even though signs of departure from traditional Iranian foreign-policy making were discernible, internal and external factors and their continuing interaction with foreign policy placed definite limitations upon what even skillful diplomatists could do.

Part Three

Transitional Foreign Policy, 1921-1941

Chapter VIII

The Rise of Riẕā Shah and Foreign Policy, 1921-1925

IRAN's transitional foreign policy began to emerge more fully in the period between the *coup d'état* of 1921 and the abdication of Riẕā Shah in 1941, although some of its early signs had been discernible in the 1905-20 period. External and internal conditions had militated against the development of Iran's foreign policy during the turbulent years of that period to such an extent that the very expression "foreign policy" can be regarded a misnomer because Iran had little control over its own destiny. Yet, as a matter of fact, in spite of these conditions Iran had actually formulated and executed a few foreign-policy decisions which revealed the predominance of traditional elements in its policies from 1905 to 1920.

The traditional elements continued to persist in Iran's foreign policy for two decades following 1921. Nevertheless, this policy was marked by an unprecedented degree of selection of strategies with a high probability of achieving desired goals. This "transitional" policy showed a measure of realization of the necessity of compatibility between goals and means and between commitments and capabilities. This realization was apparent, as will be seen, not only in 1921-25 but also in 1925-41. It will also be seen, however, that this element of "modernity" disappeared during the July-August 1941 crisis which led to the inevitable occupation of Iran by the Allied Powers and the abdication of Riẕā Shah.

The dynamic triangular interaction between the external environment, the internal situation, and foreign policy is, as an analytical scheme, as applicable to the transitional foreign policy as it was to the traditional foreign policy treated in Part I and to the foreign policy of the period of prelude to transition examined in Part II. This interaction is interwoven with the presentation of materials in this and the next four chapters. As the basic features of the external and internal settings were substantially the same during most of the 1921-41 period, it is appropriate to describe these settings in general before they are examined more closely in their interaction with specific foreign-policy questions.

Just before the *coup d'état* of 1921 the external setting was much the same as it had been in the previous four years. The traditional rivalry between Great Britain and Russia had been revived in the new context of "Socialist-Capitalist antagonism." The British and Russian forces were in occupation of parts of the country, with no sign of withdrawal evident. Soon after the coup the external forces began to change dramatically. Great Britain and Russia withdrew their armies from Iran. Russia withheld its support, as will be seen, from the Soviet Republic of Gilan because at the time it regarded "revolutionary movements not only fruitless but also harmful." Simultaneously, Great Britain, for its own reasons, adopted a "hands-off policy." Both Great Britain and Russia professed to be in favor of "a strong government" in Iran. Certainly this did not mean that the traditional rivalry ceased. As a matter of fact, as far as Russia was concerned it only meant that an appearance of noninterference would be maintained: economic and political warfare with Iran actually continued. Nevertheless, the attitude of both Great Britain and Russia during most of 1921-41 constituted what has been aptly called the "fortunate conjunction of external circumstances." The impact of these propitious circumstances on the foreign policy of Iran was significant. Without it even a policy maker such as Riẕā Shah would probably have failed to achieve as much politico-economic independence for Iran as he actually did. Nor would it have been possible for the Shah to befriend Germany as excessively as he did.

No less significant during 1921-41 was the change in internal conditions. As we shall examine the *coup d'état* in detail below, we should here confine ourselves to two of the basic questions with which we have been concerned throughout this study. National disunity was not wiped out as the result of the *coup d'état*, but Riẓā Khān established in the Iranian society an unprecedented degree of order and conformity. Never before had the central government exercised as much control over the provinces. Nor had Iranian society known such a degree of regimentation. Like the traditional monarchs, Riẓā Shah identified himself with the state, but unlike them he acted in the name of the nation and reached into every aspect of its life with the aid of modern instruments of science and technology. The degree of order and conformity that he imposed on Iranian society destroyed, along with anarchy, whatever degree of group life that may have existed. In return he gave Iran its long-cherished independence. This was Riẓā Shah's highest achievement. The political and economic emancipation of Iran constituted his most important foreign-policy objective. His policy toward Russia, toward Great Britain, toward Iran's neighbors, and toward Germany, as will be seen in the next four chapters, was always guided by this fundamental objective. Even his efforts toward modernization of the country were first and foremost linked to the achievement of that objective. To no small extent did the internal order which he established contribute to the success of his foreign policy.

The other question is that of the foreign-policy maker. It is often assumed that the *coup d'état* suddenly made Riẓā Khān the supreme arbiter of policy. This was more true in domestic politics than in foreign policy. The Constitutional Revolution had given rise to a new elite. In the absence of a strong monarch the foreign-policy makers had been most often drawn from this elite. These men had often occupied Cabinet positions and seats in the Majlis. The life of the Majlis having been short and interrupted, the Cabinets, and particularly the Prime Ministers, had come to wield great power. Riẓā Khān's coup took place when one of the weakest Prime Ministers was heading the government. Between this time and Riẓā Khān's premiership, and finally his accession to the throne of Iran, the foreign policy of Iran was more a product of such Prime Ministers as Mushīr al-Dawlah and Qavām al-Saltanah than of Riẓā Khān, although none of these men would have been able to conduct the foreign affairs of Iran without the internal order and stability that Riẓā Khān's military achievements introduced. This chapter will deal mainly with the foreign policy of Iran during 1921-25, but before examining that policy it is essential to discuss the meteoric rise of Riẕā Shah to power, inasmuch as this development constituted the most important element of the internal setting of Iran's foreign policy throughout 1921-41.

THE *COUP D'ÉTAT*

The months preceding the coup were marked by one of the most severe crises in Iran's modern history. In essence this crisis reflected the age-old economic, social, and political maladies of Iranian society which had been inextricably mingled with the far-reaching consequences of foreign invasion, occupation, and depredation. Our chief concern here will be the immediate political conditions underlying the crisis.

Externally, the main problem related to the clash between Great Britain and Russia. The British forces which had entered the country during the war stayed in view of the presence of Bolshevik forces in Iran and because of the unresolved questions following the suspension of the 1919 agreement. The Russian forces, which had entered the country in 1911, moved out in 1918, and returned in 1920, remained in the north in support of the puppet regime of the Soviet Republic of Gilan and in anticipation of the signing of the draft agreement which had emerged from the negotiations with Moscow initiated by the Mushīr al-Dawlah government in October 1920.

The internal problem, by no means unrelated to the external, stemmed from two sources: a most indecisive Prime Minister and agitation among the deputies. After the downfall of the Mushīr al-Dawlah government, the post of Prime Minister was offered to Mustawfī al-Mamalik, Farmānfarmā, and again to Mushīr al-Dawlah, but they all refused to form a Cabinet. Finally, Sipahdār was appointed the Prime Minister.[1] The fact that he was commonly regarded as pro-British was not the only thing against him;[2] Sipahdār

[1] The Prime Minister's name was Muḥammad Valīkhān Tunikābunī. During the war he acquired the title of Sipahsālār 'Aẓam, by which he was generally known. In the postwar period he got a new title, Sipahdār.

[2] The common view of Sipahdār was to no small degree due to the pro-British policies that he had pursued during the war when he was Prime Minister between March 1916 and August 1916. See Chapter VI.

was too vacillating and slow. Some deputies were calling for the opening of the Fourth Majlis, while others opposed it. The opposition was based on the ground that the elections had been rigged during Vus̱ūq al-Dawlah's government for the specific purpose of ensuring the approval of the 1919 agreement when it was submitted to the Majlis for ratification.

A pressing problem before the Sipahdār government was the composition of the Cossack Division, the only well-organized Iranian force. Sipahdār had dismissed Storroselski, on British insistence, as soon as he first took office, but this did not solve the problem, which arose from British insistence on financing and commanding the Division.[3] The demand was brought before a council of Iranian statesmen, which discussed it at length and decided to postpone decision until the opening of the Majlis.

Thus the inept leadership of the Sipahdār government gave rise to a desire for a radical change in government. The thought of a coup was apparently entertained both among politicians and officers of the Cossack Division.[4] Of the former group, a capable journalist by the name of Sayyid Z̤īā' al-Dīn shortly before the coup relinquished his editorship of *Ra'ad*, a newspaper, and immersed himself in political activities. He had no confidence in the Sipahdār government and told a friend, "We should do the job ourselves." [5] Of the Cossack Division, a tall, sturdy, and extremely nationalistic officer, by the name of Colonel Riz̤ā Khān, had long toyed with the idea of a coup but had failed to recruit the support of the politician he had contacted.[6]

The combination of a dedicated reformist politician and a bold nationalist soldier was apparently what the situation demanded. On the night of February 20, 1921, Riz̤ā Khān, accompanied by Sayyid Z̤īā', entered Tehran at the head of 1,500 to 2,500 Cossacks to over-

[3] Ḥusayn Makkī, *Tārīkh-i Bīst Sālah-'i Īrān* (Tehran, 1323 [1944/45]), I, 50-51.

[4] See J. M. Balfour, *Recent Happenings in Persia* (London, 1922), pp. 218-19. Malik al-Shu'arā' Bahār states that in addition to Riz̤ā Khān and Major Faz̤lullāh Khān of the Cossack Division well-known politicians like Mudarris and others entertained the thought of a coup. See his *Tārīkh-i Aḥzāb-i Sīyāsī* (Tehran, 1323 [1944/45]), pp. 61-66. Makkī gives a similar account (*op. cit.*, I, 77-84).

[5] The friend was Bahār, himself a politician and a journalist (Bahār, *op. cit.*, p. 64).

[6] Riz̤ā Khān had apparently approached Vus̱ūq al-Dawlah with the idea of a coup (*ibid.*, p. 61).

throw the government. Toward dawn the Cossacks broke into the police department buildings without any significant resistance from the forces in Tehran. In the following days a large number of former government officials, journalists, and others were arrested and the city was put under martial law. Within a week Sayyid Ẕīā' formed a Cabinet and made Riẕā Khān the Army Chief with the title of Sardār Sipah.

In later years considerable controversy has evolved as to the chief engineer of the coup. About a year after the events had taken place Riẕā Khān endeavored to stop press speculation by issuing an official manifesto on the subject. As Minister of War at the time, with Sayyid Ẕīā' both out of office and out of the country, he ridiculed the press for having raised the question as to the real engineer of the coup while he was still around and could tell them the truth. He then proceeded to discuss the philosophy of the coup in terms of oppression by foreigners, the treachery of the national leaders, the crisis of Gilan, and the degradation of the army. In a revealing passage he warned the press: "Beware of mistakes and do not erroneously search for the engineer of the coup. With honor and honesty I tell you *I am the real plotter of the coup*." At the end of the manifesto he forbade the papers to raise such questions and threatened newspaper editors with punishment should they fail to heed his warning.[7]

Sayyid Ẕīā', however, regarded himself as the main engineer of the coup. In reference to the march of the Cossacks, under the command of Riẕā Khān, from Qazvin to Tehran, Sayyid Ẕīā' told an Iranian in Palestine that he had had to prod Riẕā Khān all the way and "drag him in every direction" because he kept "hesitating" to move forward.[8] It seems that neither Riẕā Khān nor Sayyid Ẕīā' would have shared the view of a close and keen British observer who stated that the coup was "the result of the conjunction of two separate movements."[9]

Another question concerning the coup revolves around the role of the British. Iranians generally believe that Riẕā Shah was brought into power by the British. They not only regard the coup as the brain child of the British but also seek to "prove" that every inch of the way Great Britain helped Riẕā Khān to the throne of Iran.

[7] For the text of the manifesto, see Makkī, *op. cit.*, II, 24-27. See also Bahār, *op. cit.*, pp. 185-88.

[8] See Bahār, *op. cit.*, pp. 112-15.

[9] See Balfour, *op. cit.*, pp. 218-19.

Foremost among Iranian writers and politicians who believe this is Ḥusayn Makkī, who has written three volumes covering the period from the coup to December 1925, when Riẓā Khān became the Shah of Iran. Makkī's obviously exaggerated view is a reflection of the extreme nationalist sentiments which have intruded even into scholarly research and writing. A few Western writers have also expressed such opinions, for example, Émile Lesueur, who called Sayyid Ẓīā' the "damned soul of the British legation." [10] On the other hand, while Balfour admits that the British gave "moral support" to the coup, he asserts that "the accusation that the British Minister was privy to the plot" resulted from the presence of certain British officers in the Cossack Division in "a quasi-advisory" capacity.[11]

THE STEPS TO DICTATORSHIP

It took Riẓā Khān nearly five years to make himself the supreme decision maker in both domestic and foreign affairs. His eventual success can best be appreciated by examining the record of his rise to power from 1921 to 1925. Even his bitter antagonists cannot fail to see the remarkable genius of a man who combined successfully the brutality of Nādir Shah with all the *Realpolitik* injunctions of Machiavelli. A detailed study of the rise of Riẓā Khān is, of course, beyond the scope of this study; for our purposes it will only be necessary to identify the major means by which he reached the throne of Iran. These were five: (1) unification and control of the army, (2) establishment of central authority over the provinces, (3) appeasement of the clergy, (4) domination of the Cabinet, and (5) manipulation of the Majlis.

The control of the army was the most important objective of Riẓā Khān. When he was named the "Army Chief," a momentous change

[10] Lesueur was a professor of law at the University of Tehran. See his *Des Anglais en Perse* (Paris, 1923).

[11] *Op. cit.*, p. 219. A few years after the coup Lieutenant-Colonel W. G. Grey revealed in a lecture at the Royal Central Asian Society that he asked Colonel Smyth, who had served with the Cossack Division at the time of the coup, "whether he did not think it was a little queer his taking part in political movements in the country [Iran]." Colonel Smyth had replied: "I was asked for military advice, and as Instructor I had to give it." See *Journal of the Royal Central Asian Society*, XIII (1926), 35.

was wrought in the modern history of the Iranian army; for the first time since 1879 an Iranian was put in charge of the Cossacks. Having been formed during the reign of Nāṣir al-Dīn Shah,[12] the Cossack Brigade had served a twofold purpose: as the instrument of Russian imperialism in Iran and as the tool of Iranian autocracy. The best example of the combination of these two roles was the destruction of the Majlis in June 1908 by the Cossacks. Even after Colonel Liakhoff's fight against the Majlis, Russia had continued to appoint Russian officers to the Brigade.

The first resistance to the appointment of a new commander by Russia was shown by Mushīr al-Dawlah when, as the Minister of War, he refused to recognize Kerensky's appointee.[13] The last Russian commander was Storroselski, who was dismissed by Sipahdār, on British insistence, in October 1920. This created the vacancy that Riẕā Khān filled after the coup.

It is not known just how strong the Cossacks were when Riẕā Khān first headed the army. In 1916 the Brigade had been expanded into a division in the interest of the Russian war effort. This had entailed expansion of mixed formations in Mashhad, Isfahan, Gilan, Mazandaran, and Hamadan. Riẕā Khān had been made the commander of the forces in Hamadan. By the end of the war, the Division contained 7,866 men, 56 senior and 66 junior Russian officers, and 202 Iranian officers. In the early days of its formation Russia had appointed all the officers, but toward the end the Russian commander made the appointments.[14]

Iranization of the Division, with himself at its command, was a step toward the fulfillment of Riẕā Khān's ambitions, but much more remained to be done. To be in a position to control the army effectively, it was necessary to occupy the position of Minister of War. Sayyid Ẕīā' had given this post to the European-educated Major Masū'd Khān (Kayhān). However, Riẕā Khān's interference in the Minister's official responsibilities soon resulted in Masū'd Khān's

[12] For an excellent account of the formation and early years of the Cossack Brigade, based on Russian sources, see Firuz Kazemzadeh, "The Persian Cossack Brigade," *American Slavic and East European Review*, 1956, pp. 351-63. See also Muvarrikh al-Dawlah Sipahr, *Īrān dar Jang-i Buzurg* (Tehran 1336 [1957/58]), pp. 118-27. This source also contains valuable information on the later developments to the end of the First World War.

[13] Sipahr, *op. cit.*, p. 121.

[14] *Ibid.*, p. 122.

resignation.[15] The Army Chief seemed to be the logical successor, and Riz̤ā Khān became the Minister of War, a post that he held through all the Cabinets before, and even after, he became Prime Minister in 1923.

As the Minister of War he could now reorganize the Iranian forces in pursuit of his goal. Still existing in Iran were two other forces, the Gendarmerie and the police. The former had its origin in 1911 when the Iranian government decided to employ Swedish officers for the organization and training of a national security force. When Shuster, the first American financial adviser, was compelled to leave Iran, the Treasury Gendarmerie that he had organized was absorbed by the Government Gendarmerie. During the war the pro-German sentiments of its Swedish and Iranian officers finally brought it into armed conflict with the Russian forces at Robat Karim in December 1915. As a result of its humiliating defeat and dispersal, it was reduced from 10,000 men to only 1,400.[16]

Nevertheless, the Gendarmerie was a thorn in Riz̤ā Khān's side. He approached Qavām al-Saltanah, Z̤īā''s successor, seeking the reunification of the army. He insisted that the Gendarmerie should merge with the Cossack Division under the Ministry of War, but Qavām took the opposite view that the Gendarmerie should remain independent, under the Ministry of the Interior. Riz̤ā Khān, however, succeeded in reunifying the two forces, under his command, during the first Cabinet of Mushīr al-Dawlah after the coup.[17]

Control of the police force was Riz̤ā Khān's next goal. This force also had its origin in 1911 when the government employed some Swedish officers to found a modern police force in place of the old "night-watcher" (*'Asas*) system. The Swedish officers of the police had not followed the example of their compatriots in the Gendarmerie in sympathizing with Germany; apparently they had favored the Russians.[18] In any event, it is claimed that under the direction of Swedish General T. Vestdahl the police had made a good record. This made it difficult for Riz̤ā Khān to bring the police under his control by appointing one of his own protégés as its head.[19]

[15] Bahār, *op. cit.*, p. 93.

[16] For details, see Sipahr, *op. cit.*, pp. 105-13.

[17] Makkī, *op. cit.*, II, 64-65.

[18] For more about the police at this time, see Sipahr, *op. cit.*, pp. 113-18.

[19] For details of Riz̤ā Khān's clash with the Swedish officers, see Makkī, *op. cit.*, pp. 109-11.

The task was easier once he became Prime Minister. He found a pretext to examine the past record of the Police Department, appointed a commission of his supporters to carry out the investigation, and soon thereafter brought charges of corruption and embezzlement in the department. General Vestdahl was dismissed and Colonel Muḥammad Khān Dargāhī was installed as the new chief of police.[20] Later events showed how successfully Riẕā Khān terrorized his opponents through Dargāhī, Mukhtārī, and his other lackeys.

The second means by which Riẕā Khān expanded his power and influence was the establishment of central authority throughout the country. The achievement of this goal brought the government forces into armed conflict with various groups. In only one instance was central authority established short of the actual use of force – in the conflict with Sheikh Khaz'al, which will be discussed later. Riẕā Khān's campaign in Azerbaijan deserves more than passing mention for the reason that it not only restored full government authority in Azerbaijan but also increased the prestige and influence of Riẕā Khān to an unprecedented extent.

The problem in Azerbaijan was twofold: there was an uprising in Tabriz and the Kurds were in savage revolt. The Tabriz uprising resulted from conflict between remnants of the Gendarmerie and the Cossacks. In Tabriz as elsewhere,[21] Gendarmerie officers had found it difficult to yield to the Cossacks, who formed the nucleus of the Riẕā Khān army. The revolt in Tabriz was the work of a Gendarmerie officer, Major Lāhūtī Khān. Earlier Mushīr al-Dawlah had crushed the separatist movement of Khīābānī through the instrument of Mukhbir al-Saltanah, who utilized the Cossacks most effectively.[22] Mukhbir al-Saltanah had remained as governor of Azerbaijan, leaning heavily on the Cossacks. In January 1922 the Gendarmerie forces, led

[20] *Ibid.*, pp. 301-3.

[21] The dissatisfaction of the Gendarmerie with the new order did not break into the open in Tabriz alone. A good example of this is the uprising of Colonel Muḥammad Taqī Khān in Khorasan. The colonel arrested the governor of Khorasan, Majd al-Saltanah, captured government headquarters, incited the inhabitants against the capital, and declared his intention to establish an autonomous Republic of Khorasan. The colonel was unsuccessful, however, as was one of his subordinates, Major Ismā'īl Khān Bahādur, who also revolted. Riẕā Khān threatened the major's life if he did not get out of Khorasan within forty-eight hours and followed his threat with sufficient force to reestablish government authority at Mashhad. (See Bahār, *op. cit.*, pp. 140-62.)

[22] See Chapter VII.

by Major Lāhūtī Khān, entered Tabriz, occupied the Police Department building, fought against the Cossacks, declared martial law, and arrested the governor. Their success was, however, short-lived as Riẓā Khān sent forces from Mianduab and Sauj Bulagh to quell the uprising and free the governor. Later Mukhbir al-Saltanah was replaced by Muṣaddiq al-Saltanah. On the latter's resignation the position of governor was quickly filled by one of Riẓā Khān's most trusted associates, Amānullāh Mīrzā Jahānbānī, a professional soldier.[23]

The Kurdish challenge to the governor's authority was not new. Under the leadership of the notorious Ismā'īl Āqā Sīmtqū (Simko) the Kurds had been in bold rebellion for years. In four years alone their savage attacks had resulted in the deaths of 5,000 government soldiers and panic among Azerbaijanis.[24] Riẓā Khān instructed Jahānbānī to crush the rebellion and bring the areas occupied by the Sīmtqū forces under complete government control. The Kurdish chief was in possession of Urumiyah, Khoi, and Salmas and was determined to expand his dominion over all of Kurdistan and Azerbaijan. In the heart of Mt. Chahriq west of Salmas and near the Turkish border he had erected a fort. From this rather inaccessible mountain base, Sīmtqū had harassed government forces. Jahānbānī occupied the port of Sharafkhanah on Lake Urumiyah and befriended a local rebel at Sang-i Kazim, who furnished him with men to guide him through the difficult passes of the Arasbaran Mountains to the Chahriq fort. Surprised by the attack of the government forces, the overconfident Sīmtqū offered little resistance, his forces were dispersed, and he fled, crossing the border into Turkey. His brutal control over part of Azerbaijan ended in August 1922.[25]

The victory of the army was celebrated at Tehran. Riẓā Khān gave it much publicity and in a long and boastful speech to the nation glorified the army under his direction. The capture of the Chahriq fort also impressed the deputies of the Majlis, who officially congratulated Riẓā Khān and expressed admiration for his unswerving services to the security and "unity" of the country.

The third means by which Riẓā Khān preserved and increased his power was through *rapprochement* with the clergy. The significant

[23] For details, see Makkī, *op. cit.*, II, 19-22.

[24] The *Near East* of December 1924, as reproduced in Fatḥullāh Nūrī Isfandīyārī, *Rastākhīz-i Īrān* (Tehran, 1335 [1956/57]), p. 111.

[25] For more details, see Makkī, *op. cit.*, II, 81-106.

role they had played in Iranian politics was not underestimated by Riẕā Khān. The best example of his wooing of the clergy occurred during the agitation for a republic in 1924. Once he reached the post of Prime Minister, he entertained the thought of establishing a republican form of government, following the example of neighboring Turkey. He could be reasonably certain that the Majlis would support him in view of the fact that as Prime Minister and Minister of War he had exerted some influence on the elections of the Fifth Majlis. Furthermore, concomitant with the rise of his influence, the prestige of the absentee Shah, who was in Europe, had fallen to a new low, in part as the result of unrestrained criticism from the newspapers supported by Riẕā Khān.

But the unpredictable happened and upset Riẕā Khān's plans. Turkey abolished the Caliphate in March 1924, resulting in severe curtailment of clerical power in the Republic. Alarmed by this development, the clergy in Iran foresaw a similar fate for themselves if a republican form of government should be established at Tehran. The opposition of the clergy was added to that of the supporters of Aḥmad Shah, who were hard at work outside and inside the Majlis. Under the circumstances Riẕā Khān performed a complete *volte-face*. He immediately consulted the leading clergymen at Qum and produced a statement ostensibly designed to pacify the agitators but actually intended to prevent the alienation of the clergy. In this statement Riẕā Khān claimed that the preservation of Islam had been one of the most important duties of the army from the beginning. Furthermore, he and the clergy suggested that the people abandon the demand for a republican form of government.[26]

A fourth means by which Riẕā Khān reached the throne of Iran was by dominating the Cabinet. To accomplish this, it was necessary to have himself installed as the Prime Minister. But this proved difficult for two reasons. First was the fact that Riẕā Khān was a professional soldier and not a politician. He was a logical person for the post of Army Chief or even Minister of War, but not for that of Prime Minister, which had generally been occupied by a civilian politician. The second difficulty he encountered was the fact that although the coup had resulted in the downfall of the Sipahdār Cabinet, it had not, in fact, produced any immediate change in the *ancien*

[26] See *ibid.*, pp. 343-44.

régime. Powerful civilians with long experience in government, such as Mustawfī al-Mamālik, Mushīr al-Dawlah, and Qavām al-Saltanah, were still active in politics. For a time Riẕā Khān had to work with the statesmen of the Constitutional period while he was strengthening the army and extending his influence into the provinces. But this also provided him with the opportunity to acquire the necessary experience and at the same time to undermine, on some pretext, one Prime Minister after another.

Riẕā Khān had engineered the coup with Sayyid Ẕīā' but had turned against Ẕīā' while enjoying the support of the Shah and had brought about Ẕīā''s exile together with that of Masū'd Khān and Kāẓim Khān.[27] He cooperated at first with Qavām al-Saltanah, Ẕīā''s successor, until he clashed with the Prime Minister over the question of the unification of the army.[28] Mushīr al-Dawlah granted Riẕā Khān's demand for unification but was impelled to resign because of differences over the suspension of a newspaper.[29] When Qavām al-Saltanah became Prime Minister for the second time, Riẕā Khān did not have to bother about bringing him down because the Majlis forced him to resign.[30] Mustawfī al-Mamālik's downfall was also due to opposition of the Majlis, but Riẕā Khān, and probably also Qavām, were not innocent bystanders.[31] When Mushīr al-Dawlah became Prime Minister for the second time after the coup, Riẕā Khān's task was even easier. The Fourth Majlis came to an end, and in its absence Riẕā Khān arrested his strong rival, Qavām, and forced the Cabinet to resign.[32] From 1921 to 1923 Riẕā Khān worked with Four Prime Ministers (Ẕīā', Qavām, Mushīr al-Dawlah, and Mustawfī) and six Cabinets while paving his way toward the post of Prime Minister. The Shah appointed him to that position on October 28, 1923.

A fifth step toward the attainment of supreme power was manipula-

[27] For details on the downfall of Sayyid Ẕīā', see Bahār, *op. cit.*, pp. 100-106.

[28] *Ibid.*, p. 181. Lieutenant-Colonel W. G. Grey, a friend of Qavām, gives a different reason for the downfall of the Qavām government. He states that Riẕā Khān believed that Qavām was plotting against him and forced the Prime Minister to resign. See *Journal of the Royal Central Asian Society*, XIII (1926), 39.

[29] Riẕā Khān demanded the arrest of the editor of *Ḥaqīqat*, apparently a radical newspaper, which had offended him, but Mushīr al-Dawlah refused to comply (Makkī, *op. cit.*, II, 44-45).

[30] *Ibid.*, p. 159. [31] *Ibid.*, pp. 203-33. [32] *Ibid.*, p. 278.

tion of the Majlis. This involved both the Fourth and the Fifth Majlis. The Fourth Majlis opened in June 1921, when Qavām al-Saltanah had formed his first Cabinet with Riẕā Khān as the Minister of War. This was a long-overdue appearance of the Majlis on the political scene. The Third Majlis had been dispersed in November 1915, and elections for the Fourth Majlis had begun as early as 1917, though they remained incomplete practically up to the time of the coup.[33]

At the beginning of the Fourth Majlis, Riẕā Khān did not encounter opposition from either of the two major groups, the Reformists and the Socialists, but as his influence increased opposition developed. The first criticism of the activities of Riẕā Khān was voiced by Mu'tamid al-Tujjār, who complained of the increasing limitations on the freedom of the press, the unwarranted arrest of newspaper editors, and other acts contrary to the principles of the Constitution.[34] The most severe criticism of Riẕā Khān was consistently and obstinately voiced by Mudarris. He was a passionate orator and a clergyman who had been a deputy in the Second Majlis and had become well known thereafter.[35] Although belonging to the Reformists, his views were not shared or voiced by any significant number of this group. His opposition to Riẕā Khān, which persisted throughout the Fourth and continued into the Fifth Majlis, was ostensibly due to his desire to preserve the Constitutional government.

The record of parliamentary debates is misleading, because it mainly reveals the onstage performance of Iranian politicians. The backstage activities are the really important ones, and Mudarris was considerably motivated by unrestrained ambition and self-interest.[36] His personality clashed violently with that of Riẕā Khān, whose spectacular rise to power was resented by Mudarris. Party politics was overshadowed by the personal antagonism between these two ambitious individuals. Most of the Majlis deputies became supporters of one dominant personality or the other. A few banded around the imposing personality of Mudarris, forming the Minority (*Aqalīyat*), and others followed Riẕā Khān, constituting the Majority (*Akṣarīyat*).

[33] For the reasons of the delay in opening the Fourth Majlis, see Bahār, *op. cit.*, pp. 116-19.

[34] See Makkī, *op. cit.*, II, 112-16.

[35] See Bahār, *op. cit.*, pp. 133-34.

[36] This is the view of one of his great admirers. See Makkī, *op. cit.*, III, 4.

Riẓā Khān exploited this parliamentary factionalism to the fullest possible extent. He managed to keep the backing of the majority most of the time. On a few occasions when the opposition became a nuisance, he suppressed its newspapers, arrested its editors, called for martial law, organized mob demonstrations, threatened the Majlis with his resignation, and filled the jails with "suspects." [37] Nevertheless, he did not reach for the post of Prime Minister while the Majlis was in session. Once its term had expired, however, he forced the Cabinet of Mushīr al-Dawlah to resign [38] and obtained appointment as Prime Minister. Riẓā now dealt only with the Shah.

Riẓā Khān utilized the Fifth Majlis to formalize his absolute control. After his return from Qum and the reversal of his position on republicanism, some deputies still continued to agitate in favor of that form of government. Furthermore, the Shah sent a telegram to the Majlis informing the deputies of the dismissal of Riẓā Khān.[39] To protest this, he made a spectacular departure from Tehran, a gesture that prompted his generals and the friendly deputies to put pressure on the Majlis to request his resumption of office.[40] Upon his return he demanded a guarantee that the Shah would not dismiss him without the approval of the Majlis. He, of course, had no reason to fear the Majlis because its majority was under his control. In any event, by this shrewd move he turned failure into success. The Majlis passed a law to the effect that all the security and defense forces of the nation should be placed under the sole control of Riẓā Khān and that he could not be deprived of this power without the approval of the Majlis.[41] He was thus made the Commander-in-Chief.

Having thus formalized the dictatorial powers that he already possessed, Riẓā Khān next moved to have himself declared the Shah of Iran. Dāvar, Taymūrtāsh, and a few other deputies who supported him drafted an act providing that the Majlis would declare the "overthrow" (*Inqirāẓ*) of the Qājār dynasty and would entrust Riẓā Khān with the provisional government until the permanent government was

[37] Makkī and Bahār give many examples of such actions by Riẓā Khān.

[38] See note 29 above.

[39] Makkī, *op. cit.*, II, 344.

[40] The pressure was brought to bear in part as a result of letters in support of Riẓā Khān written to the Majlis by some leading generals of the army. For the text of these letters, see *ibid.*, II, 348-50.

[41] For the text of the law and relevant information, see *ibid.*, III, 335.

determined by the "Constitutional Assembly" (*Majlis-i Mu'asasān*). The bill was hotly debated. It was supported by the majority, whose views were set forth and defended by the authors of the act, particularly by Tadayyun, and opposed by the minority, including Mudarris and Muṣaddiq. The opposition considered the proposal unconstitutional.[42] Finally, of the eighty-five deputies present, eighty approved the act on October 31, 1925.[43]

With the Shah thus deposed and dictatorial powers granted to Riẕā Khān, he saw to it that none of his opponents, including Mudarris and Muṣaddiq, were elected to the Constitutional Assembly.[44] The Assembly, consisting of twice as many delegates as there were deputies in the Majlis, was opened by Riẕā Khān on December 6, 1925, and on December 12 it passed, 257 to 3, an act which amended the Supplementary Laws of the Constitution. By virtue of this change, Article 36 entrusted "the constitutional sovereignty of Iran . . . to His Imperial Majesty Riẕā Shah Pahlavī."

While on his way up to the throne Riẕā Khān had become familiar with the foreign policies adopted by some of the statesmen of the Constitutional period. Their policies toward Russia and Great Britain as well as their third-power policy, devised in the early 1920's, were followed, more or less, by Riẕā Shah throughout his rule.

THE FIRST STEP TOWARD INDEPENDENCE FROM RUSSIA

To gain political and economic emancipation Mushīr al-Dawlah had attempted to normalize relations with Soviet Russia. He had abandoned the hostile attitude of his predecessor, Vuṡūq al-Dawlah, and in July 1920 had appointed Mushāvir al-Mamālik envoy to Moscow with a view to opening negotiations for a treaty. Since the Bolshevik Revolution, the Soviet government had been denouncing the Tsarist policies in Iran, declaring respect for the political independence and integrity of Iran and expressing a desire to establish mutually advantageous trade relations with Iran.[45] In view of the presence of

[42] See *ibid.*, pp. 400-67.
[43] For the text of the act, see *ibid.*, p. 430.
[44] *Ibid.*, p. 484.
[45] For details, see Chapter VII.

Russian troops in the country, Soviet support of the Gilan regime, the breakdown in trade between northern Iran and Russia, and British pressure for the ratification of the 1919 agreement, Mushīr al-Dawlah had believed that preservation of Iranian political and economic interests demanded taking the risk of testing the repeated declaration of Soviet good intentions toward Iran.

The negotiations thus started were pursued by the successor of Mushīr al-Dawlah, Sipahdār. The draft of the agreement resulting from the negotiations was communicated to the Prime Minister by Mushāvir al-Mamālik. As the Fourth Majlis was not yet in session, Sipahdār decided to submit it to a council of Iranian statesmen for consideration.[46] Several changes were suggested, and the agreement as amended was accepted in January 1921. The official signing of the agreement did not take place until February 26, 1921, five days after the coup.

The major provisions of the Treaty of Friendship, consisting of twenty-six articles, follow:[47]

1) *Tsarist Treaties:* Two sets of treaties of the Tsarist regime were declared null and void, those with Iran, and those with third powers affecting Iran. Although the voiding of these treaties (specifically the treaty of Turkumanchai) would terminate the extraterritorial rights of Russia in Iran, a special provision was included for the abolition of consular jurisdictions.[48]

2) *Tsarist Concessions and Loans:* All economic concessions "whether already being worked or not" were restored to the Iranian government, but there were two reservations. These were to the effect that Iran could not cede these concessions to a third power and that immediately upon the expiration of the existing fisheries concession it would give such a concession to Soviet Russia.[49]

Russia also renounced all repayment of Tsarist loans and its claims to the Iranian resources which had been specified in the loan agreements as security for Russia.[50]

3) *Lands, Buildings and Installations:* The full ownership of all lands and buildings possessed by Russia was ceded to Iran, with the exception of the buildings belonging to the Discount Bank of Russia.

[46] Makkī, *op. cit.*, I, 64.

[47] For the text of the treaty and the relevant notes exchanged, see J. C. Hurewitz, *Diplomacy in the Near and Middle East* (Princeton, N. J., 1956), II, 90-94.

[48] Articles 1, 2, and 16. [49] Articles 12, 13, and 14. [50] Article 8.

Russia also ceded the highways from Enzeli to Tehran and from Qazvin to Hamadan, with their installations and land, the landing stages, warehouses, steamships, canals, and all means of transport on Lake Urumiyah, all telegraph and telephone lines with all their dependencies and installations, and the port of Enzeli with its warehouses, buildings, and installations.[51]

4) *Frontiers and Navigation:* The frontiers of the 1881 convention were confirmed. Russia renounced all claim to the Ashurada Islands and to other islands on the Astarabad littoral and restored the village of Firuzah and the adjacent land to Iran. Iran, in turn, agreed that Russia should retain Sarakhs and the land adjacent to the Sarakhs River. Both parties would have equal rights on the Atrek River and the other frontier rivers and waterways. They also agreed to appoint a commission to settle disputes concerning waterways, frontiers, and territories.[52] The exclusive navigation rights of Russia on the Caspian Sea were abrogated; Iran and Russia would henceforth enjoy such rights on an equal basis.[53]

5) *Trade, Customs Duties, and Transit Rights:* The parties undertook to resume commercial relations. The details were to be determined by a commercial convention. Each party granted to the other the right of transit for goods passing through its territory and consigned to a third party. The dues would not be higher than those levied on the goods of the most-favored nation.[54]

6) *Diplomatic Relations:* Each party undertook, immediately after the signature of the treaty, to send its representative to the capital of the other. Consulates would also be established in places to be determined by a separate agreement to be concluded immediately after the signing of the treaty.[55]

7) *Security and Intervention:* Russia and Iran undertook to prohibit the formation or presence within their respective territories of "any organizations or groups of persons, irrespective of the name by which they are known, whose object is to engage in acts of hostility" against Iran or Russia. They also undertook to prevent a third party from stationing military forces in either country or importing material which could be used against either of them.[56]

[51] Articles 9 and 10.
[52] Article 3.
[53] Article 11.
[54] Articles 19 and 20.
[55] Articles 22 and 23.
[56] Article 5.

The parties would abstain from any intervention in the internal affairs of each other,[57] but if a third party should intervene in Iran militarily, or should desire to use Iranian territory as a base against Russia, or should threaten the frontiers of Russia, Russia would have the right to dispatch troops to Iran in case Iran should fail to stop the menace to Russia after having been called upon by Russia to do so.[58]

No matter how this agreement has been viewed by Russian or Western statesmen, journalists, and text writers since 1921,[59] Iranian statesmen knew that Iran could not realistically hope for a settlement of vital issues with Russia by engaging in a cold war with the new regime. They hoped that the treaty, among other advantages, would establish an atmosphere in which such vital questions as the withdrawal of Russian troops, the suppression of the Soviet Republic of Gilan, and the resumption of trade with Russia could be discussed against the background of Russia's declared good intentions.

Here we are concerned only with the three major problems confronting the foreign-policy makers of *Iran* in relations with Soviet Russia between the signing of the Treaty of 1921 and the beginning of the reign of Riẓā Shah in 1925.

The first major problem was the presence of Soviet troops in Iran. The Russian forces which had entered Iran in December 1911 had been withdrawn in 1918 but had returned in May 1920. The May invasion, it may be recalled, had been precipitated in part by the anti-Bolshevik military operations of Great Britain in Transcaucasia, with Iranian territory used as a base. Although these operations had ended, the British forces were kept in Iran in view of the presence of Bolshevik forces and the suspended 1919 agreement. Thus, when the government of Sayyid Ẓīā' al-Dīn demanded the withdrawal of the Russian forces,[60] the Soviets stated that their troops would stay in Iran so long as the British remained there.

Outraged by Soviet intransigency only a few days after the signing of the treaty, Sayyid Ẓīā' resolved to retaliate. The opportunity came when F. A. Rothstein, the first official Soviet representative, arrived

[57] Article 4.

[58] Article 6.

[59] For a compilation of such views, see Nasrollah S. Fatemi, *Diplomatic History of Persia, 1917-1923* (New York, 1952), pp. 266-94.

[60] In his first manifesto after the coup Sayyid Ẓīā' reiterated Iran's demand for the withdrawal of Soviet troops. For the text of the manifesto, see Makkī, *op. cit.*, I, 125-29.

in Iran on April 7, 1921. The Prime Minister refused to allow the Russian Ambassador to proceed to Tehran until all Russian troops had left Iranian soil. The Russian government agreed to arrange for their withdrawal as soon as possible.[61] Rothstein was allowed to take up residence in Tehran on April 24.

Iran was able to force the issue in a still more effective way. According to the Iranian Constitution, the treaty had to be ratified by the Majlis. Qavām al-Saltanah submitted it to the Majlis, which opened in June 1921. While Russia was anxiously awaiting its ratification, the deputies took their time in scrutinizing its provisions. The cautious attitude of the deputies derived in part from the fact that the British forces had been withdrawn in May whereas the Russian troops still remained in Iran. Malik al-Shu'arā', Taqīzādah, Taymūrtāsh, and a group of other deputies proposed that Articles 5, 6, 13, and 20, which were worded vaguely, should be clarified before ratification. The Foreign Affairs Committee of the Majlis also told the Prime Minister that without modification of these articles it would not recommend the treaty for ratification.[62] In the meantime the Bolshevik forces had moved out. On October 30 their last detachment boarded ships provided by the Soviet government.[63]

The second major Russian problem confronting the foreign-policy makers of Iran pertained to the continuing crisis in Gilan. The evacuation of the Soviet forces from northern Iran did not terminate the problem. Some Communists in Baku and Moscow still urged the "sovietization" of Iran.[64] In any event, the governments, first of Sayyid Ẕīā' al-Dīn and then of Qavām al-Saltanah, were determined to put an end to the Gilan episode. When Rothstein presented his credentials during Ẕīā''s administration, Aḥmad Shah told him that he trusted the Soviet Ambassador would exert every effort, as soon as possible, toward the termination of "the deplorable episode in

[61] Manshūr Garakānī, *Sīāsat-i Dawlat-i Shawravī dar Īrān az 1296 tā 1306* (Tehran, 1326 [1947/48]), p. 135. A Western source states that Russia still specifically made the withdrawal of its troops contingent upon the departure of British forces from Iran. See Xenia Joukoff Eudin and Robert C. North, *Soviet Russia and the East, 1920-1927* (Stanford, Calif., 1957), p. 102.

[62] The Iranian demands were set forth in a letter from the Ministry of Foreign Affairs to the Russian Ambassador. For its text, see Hurewitz, *op. cit.*, II, 90-94.

[63] Garakānī, *op. cit.*, p. 139.

[64] Louis Fischer, *The Soviets in World Affairs* (London, 1930), I, 429.

Gilan." The Shah also indicated clearly that Iran would regard this as the test of the sincerity of the newly signed Treaty of 1921.[65]

It was, however, during the first Cabinet of Qavām al-Saltanah, the successor of Sayyid Ẕīā', that the problem was finally and conclusively resolved. The success of Qavām's policy can be attributed to several factors. One factor was the personal and ideological conflict as we have seen, between Iḥsānullāh Khān and Kūchik Khān, despite the Russian reinforcement of the Jangalī forces in 1920 and 1921.

On the diplomatic front the change in the Soviet attitude and the energetic diplomacy of Qavām himself were important factors. Qavām entered into direct negotiations with Kūchik Khān, trying to lure him into submission to the central authority by promising him the governorship of Gilan. He also reminded Rothstein of the Soviet promise made at the time of the signing of the Treaty of 1921 and reiterated by the Ambassador during the presentation of his credentials to the Shah – a promise to the effect that Soviet Russia would exert every effort to settle the Gilan episode.[66]

In a remarkable letter to Kūchik Khān, Rothstein stated:

> Soviet Russia at this time regards all revolutionary movements as not only fruitless but also harmful. Therefore, Soviet Russia has adopted a new form of policy as evidenced by its new Treaty with the government of Iran. Although it has been only a few months since the signing of the Treaty and my arrival in Iran, one can already see the progress of our policy. There is no doubt that their [British] prestige has suffered not only in the North but also, to some extent, in the South.[67]

Rothstein also gave Kūchik Khān a friendly warning to the effect that Riẕā Khān had indicated on several occasions that he would like to finish the whole matter by force of arms if he could get the approval of Qavām al-Saltanah. But, Rothstein continued, "I have prevented him by promising to terminate the Gilan episode without bloodshed." The Soviet Ambassador then proceeded to make certain proposals, making it clear that at that time Soviet Russia was in favor of a "strong central government," because only such a government, "which would be inevitably dependent on Soviet Russia," could prevent the "imperialist" activities of Great Britain in Iran.

[65] For the text of the Shah's speech, see Makkī, *op. cit.*, p. 190.

[66] Sipahr, *op. cit.*, p. 393.

[67] For the text of the letters exchanged between Rothstein and Kūchik Khān, see *ibid.*, pp. 394-95, and Makkī, *op. cit.*, pp. 312-17.

In reply, Kūchik Khān set forth in detail the "philosophy" of the Jangalī Movement, emphatically claiming that all his actions had been undertaken for the good of Iran – for the sole purpose of preserving the country against foreign encroachment and domestic treachery and of attaining freedom and welfare for the oppressed workers. At the end of his reply Kūchik Khān expressed confidence in the competent judgment of Rothstein in regard to the desirability of abandoning "the sacred revolution" *at the time*, but remarked that he would be watching to see whether the central government and Soviet Russia would act in conformity with the interests of Iran.

The problem, however, was eventually resolved by resort to force rather than diplomacy. Riẕā Khān led his ever-expanding army against Bolshevik "intruders" (*Mutijāsirīn*) and the Jangalī forces, attacking the intruders in the vicinity of Tonekabon. Iḥsānullāh Khān and Shujāʿ al-Sultān, the leaders of the intruders, fled for their lives. Many of the Bolsheviks who followed them to Shahsavar were captured and disarmed by local government forces.[68] Rasht and Enzeli were still in the hands of the Communists, and Riẕā Khān personally led troops against them. As a result of heavy fighting at Jamshidabad, the Communists were defeated, and Kūchik Khān fled to the mountains in Gadook, where he froze to death. Of the leading Communists, Khālū Qurbān surrendered to the government forces, and Iḥsānullāh Khān embarked on a ship supplied by Russia for the withdrawal of its last detachment on October 30, 1921. As he boarded the ship, Iḥsānullāh told the spectators: "Dear fellow-citizens, the betrayal of the government authorities prevented us from offering our services. We, therefore, postpone the fulfillment of our great mission [communism] to a very near future date."[69]

The two major problems embittering the relations of Russia and Iran having been conclusively settled by the beginning of December 1921, the Majlis finally ratified the treaty on the fifteenth of the month.

The third major problem confronting Iran in the early 1920's pertained to trade with Russia. In essence the problem derived from the economic ascendancy of prerevolutionary Russia in Iran, particularly in northern Iran. This was due in part to the blunders of Iranian

[68] Sipahr, *op. cit.*, p. 394.

[69] The significance of this statement became clearer at the time of the Azerbaijan crisis in 1945-46. For the complete statement, see *ibid.*

foreign policy during the autocratic period. One of the most disastrous wars of the Qājār dynasty was its second war with Russia, which was finally concluded by the Treaty of Turkumanchai (1828). The commercial convention attached to this treaty laid the foundation for Russian economic supremacy in Iran. This economic dominance was further consolidated during the Constitutional period when British-Russian *rapprochement* in 1907 enabled Russia to consolidate its position in the north without the traditional British opposition and to force the dismissal of Shuster, the American financial adviser.

The departure of Shuster, the breakup of the Majlis, and the occupation of the north by Russian troops made Russia the true sovereign of the north. Throughout the ineffectual reign of the Regent (1911-14), Russian diplomats and agents purchased lands and colonized Azerbaijan, Astarabad, and Mazandaran,[70] and Russian consuls collected taxes from Iranian citizens.[71] Concomitantly, the Russian trade with Iran reached a new height, representing 63 per cent of the total trade of the country.[72]

The outbreak of the war, the Bolshevik Revolution, British military operations against the Bolsheviks across the northern frontier, and finally the Bolshevik invasion and occupation of northern Iran cut off at once its long-established chief market and source of manufactured goods. The north suffered grievously. Stock piles of Iranian goods began to accumulate and spoil on Caspian shores. As trade stagnation continued, land and other productive facilities were withdrawn from production, and poverty and political dissatisfaction in northern Iran became increasingly acute.[73]

Under the circumstances it might appear that two alternatives were open to Iranian policy makers: either to resume trade with Russia or to increase trade with other powers. The latter alternative was actually limited to greater trade with Great Britain.[74] And a substantial increase in trade with Great Britain was politically unacceptable and economically most disadvantageous. The 1919 agreement had

[70] Violet Conolly, *Soviet Economic Policy in the East* (London, 1933), p. 54.

[71] Aḥmad Kasravī, *Tārīkh-i Hījdah Sālah-'i Aẕarbāijān* (Tehran, 1333 [1954/55]), pp. 580-83.

[72] Moustafa Khan Fateh, *The Economic Position of Persia* (London, 1926), p. 76; also Conolly, *op. cit.*, pp. 56-57.

[73] Robert Wesley Davenport, "Soviet Economic Relations with Iran, 1917-1930" (Ph.D. dissertation, Columbia University, 1953), p. 54.

[74] See Fateh, *op. cit.*, p. 76.

just been turned down by the Majlis, which objected "in particular to the financial clauses, as undue interference with Persia's domestic affairs." [75] In fact, these clauses, by which Iranian tariffs on Russian goods were to be increased on an average of 3 to 5 per cent, represented a direct attempt on the part of the British to obtain preference for their goods in the Iranian market.[76]

Even if the 1919 agreement had not been unacceptable, trade with Great Britain could not have replaced that with Russia for years or for decades. It was the trade of the north which meant the most to the Iranian economy. The Caspian littoral, as contrasted with the rest of Iran, is blessed with a heavy rainfall, which together with the fertile soil washed down from the mountains makes it "the most productive" agricultural region in the country.[77] Nature seems to have set the face of this region toward Russia and its back toward central and southern Iran. The Caspian Sea and the Volga, through the extensive system of internal waterways, open the way to Russia, while the Elburz Mountains cut it off from the rest of Iran.

The formidable natural barrier to trade with countries other than Russia would obviously have been much less of an impediment had Iran enjoyed modern technology. The foreign-policy makers of the 1920's had to pay for the neglect of the autocratic rulers. Most commercial goods in the 1920's were transported on pack animals, as they had been for centuries before. This primitive system of transport made trade with the central and southern part of Iran, as well as with powers other than Russia, exorbitantly expensive and discouragingly time-consuming.[78] Trade with Russia could enjoy the benefits of shorter routes, of cheap water transportation, and of the only important railroad in the country. Russia had built, under a concession dated February 6, 1913, an eighty-mile railroad from her frontier at Julfa to Tabriz and a thirty-mile branch line from Sufian to Lake Urumiyah.[79]

Resumption of trade with Russia seemed imperative at the time, but its details had to be determined, according to the 1921 treaty,

[75] Conolly, *op. cit.*, pp. 58-59.

[76] *Ibid.*, p. 58.

[77] Royal Institute of International Affairs, *The Middle East* (London, 1950), pp. 372-73.

[78] See Fateh, *op. cit.*, pp. 55-65.

[79] Under the terms of the Soviet-Iranian treaty this railroad was ceded to Iran.

under a separate commercial convention. The conclusion of such a convention, therefore, constituted a most important objective of Iran.

Qavām al-Saltanah, while anxious to restore Russo-Iranian trade, showed little inclination during his first government (June 1921 – January 1922) to yield to Russia's demands as they unfolded during the course of negotiations. Neither did Mushīr al-Dawlah who succeeded him. But Mushīr al-Dawlah was keenly conscious of the fact that delay in well-regulated trade was far more harmful to Iran than to Russia. Therefore, he resorted to his favorite policy of conciliation without appeasement. He authorized the levying of customs duties on trades with Russia at the 1902 tariff rates instead of at the higher 1920 rates, revoked the ban on the export of rice to Russia, and announced that a delegation would be sent to Russia for negotiations.[80]

When Qavām al-Saltanah resumed office again in June 1922, he continued Mushīr al-Dawlah's efforts at negotiations, particularly because, by April 24, 1922, Russia had suspended application of the new Asiatic tariff to the Iranian border and had temporarily applied the European tariff to trade with Iran. However, neither negotiations nor Qavām's retaliation by resorting to the 1920 rates produced any results.[81] In all probability Russia was using Iran's desperate need for trade as an instrument of political pressure against a Prime Minister, Qavām al-Saltanah, whom Moscow particularly disliked.[82] When Mustawfī al-Mamālik took office in February 1923, the Soviet attitude apparently softened, since he was favored by the Socialists in the Majlis and by Russia itself.[83] As a result of negotiations by the Mustawfī government it was agreed that the goods which had arrived in the customs houses between November 15, 1922, and March 1, 1923, would enjoy the Asiatic tariff, and in return Iran would restore the 1902 tariff rates.[84]

A draft convention was signed by the Riẓā Khān government on July 3, 1924. This twenty-one-article convention provided for reciprocity in freedom of transit of goods through, and trade of merchants

[80] This delegation was headed by Ḥasan Taqīzādah, a well-known Iranian statesman. See Makkī, *op. cit.*, 262-63, and also Davenport, *op. cit.*, p. 69.

[81] See Makkī, *op. cit.*, II, 167, 263, and Davenport, *op. cit.*, pp. 69-70.

[82] Makkī, *op. cit.*, II, 167, 181-82.

[83] *Ibid.*

[84] *Ibid.*, pp. 167-68.

in, the countries of Iran and Russia.[85] It spelled out in detail the privileges and responsibilities of the Russian Trade Commissioner and his representative, who were granted diplomatic immunity.[86] This immunity was not extended to the premises of the Soviet delegation. The convention was for one year only, with an option of extension for an extra six months. Nevertheless, it was not ratified, because the Fifth Majlis demanded changes to which Russia did not agree. The inconclusive trade battle continued.

Although Iran's attempts at normalization of its trade relations did not produce a commercial convention because of Soviet Russia's intransigency, the steadfast resistance of Iran to Soviet demands did not delay the resumption of trade. Both Russian and Iranian statistics reveal that the volume of trade between the two countries was rapidly increasing. Iranian exports, generally consisting of cotton, wool, rice, dried fruit, and the like, jumped from approximately 26,000,000 krans to approximately 244,000,000 between 1921 and 1925. At the same time the imports, consisting mainly of cotton textiles, sugar, cement, matches, and the like, increased from approximately 41,000,000 krans to 125,000,000.[87] Iranian exports to Russia in 1920-21 were only 6 per cent of the total Iranian exports, exclusive of petroleum, while in 1924-25 they amounted to 40 per cent.[88]

Thus, pending the conclusion of a trade convention, both Russia and Iran took measures to increase trade.[89] Russia extended certain trade "privileges" to Iran by virtue of a number of decrees, while Iran finally consented to the "reopening" of the Russian Bank, the primary function of which was to finance Russo-Iranian trade. It is difficult to maintain that Iran finally granted its consent in regard to the bank because of its commitment under Article 9 of the 1921 treaty,[90] but it is easy to see that the need for trade made it difficult

[85] Articles 1 and 8. For the text of the convention, see Makkī, *op. cit.*, III, 77-84.

[86] Article 11.

[87] See the table in Hussein Navai, *Les relations économiques irano-russes* (Paris, 1935), p. 117.

[88] See the table in Davenport, *op. cit.*, p. 149.

[89] Under Article 19 of the 1921 treaty the trade between Iran and Russia had been resumed.

[90] The relevant part of the article states: "Federal Russia therefore cedes to the Persian Government the full ownership of all funds and of all real and other property which the Russian Discount Bank possesses on Persian territory, and likewise transfers to it all the assets and liabilities of that bank. The Persian

to withhold it. Iranian policy makers knew well that the former Russian Loan and Discount Bank had helped to further the harmful loans contracted by Muẓaffar al-Dīn Shah.[91] Qavām al-Saltanah was approached by Soviet Russia for written consent to open the bank, but he refused it. Mustawfī al-Mamālik did not find it contrary to the interests of Iran to grant permission. For this decision, however, he had to face interpellation by the Majlis, which brought down his Cabinet.[92] The bank was established in September 1923 with an initial capital of 2,000,000 rubles. By 1925 its capital exceeded 5,000,000 rubles, and it had established branches in Tehran, Rasht, Tabriz, Qazvin, and Pahlavi.[93]

THE FIRST STEP TOWARD INDEPENDENCE FROM GREAT BRITAIN

To assert its independence vis-à-vis Great Britain in 1921-25, Iran had to deal with two major problems. One was to determine conclusively the fate of the 1919 agreement, and the other was to establish the authority of the central government in Khuzistan, where *de facto* independence had been fostered by Great Britain.

The first problem was a legacy of the days before the coup. Mushīr al-Dawlah's new policy, it may be recalled, had reversed the policy of his predecessor in part by suspending the Agreement of 1919. During the administration of Sipahdār rumors had circulated that the agreement would be revived. The consequent agitation of the public

---

Government nevertheless agrees that in the towns where it has been decided that the Russian Socialist Republic may establish consulates, and where buildings exist belonging to the Discount Bank one of these buildings, to be chosen by the Russian Government, shall be placed at the disposal of the Russian Consulate, free of charge."

[91] The former Russian Bank had been established as the result of a concession granted in 1891. For details, see Najafqulī Ḥisām Mu'zī, *Tārīkh-i Ravābiṭ-i Sīyāsī-i Īrān bā Dunyā* (Tehran, 1325 [1946/47]), I, 379-81. See also Navai, *op. cit.*, pp. 32-39.

[92] Heated opposition was voiced by Mudarris, who attacked the government's foreign policy in general terms. But Sulaymān Mīrzā, the deputy sympathizing with the Communists, defended Mustawfī's policy. For the text of their debates, see Makkī, *op. cit.*, II, 212-22.

[93] Davenport states that by 1930 the bank had established eleven branches in Iran (*op. cit.*, pp. 264-65).

forced the Prime Minister to declare officially that in foreign affairs he would follow the footsteps of his predecessor.[94] Thus the pattern devised by Mushīr al-Dawlah was passed on to Sayyid Ẓīā' al-Dīn after the coup. In his first declaration the new Prime Minister went so far as to make public the official "cancellation" of the agreement, and later the Fourth Majlis refused to ratify it altogether.[95]

The failure of the agreement, with the concomitant decline of British influence in Iran, was resented in Great Britain. The British setback, moreover, appeared far more serious in light of the fact that only five days after the coup Iran had signed the Treaty of Friendship with Russia, and Bolshevism, through the Soviet Republic of Gilan and other media, threatened British interests in Iran. Furthermore, Iranian pressure for the withdrawal of British troops was increasing as Russia continued to insist on British evacuation as the prerequisite for withdrawing its own forces.

Shortly before the coup Captain E. Noel, a British agent, had been sent to Iran "to help erect a Southern Persian Confederation in the event of the establishment of a Soviet State in the north." [96] But after the withdrawal of the British and Russian troops,

> the British could no longer hope that Russian entrenchment in the north would enable them to dig in in the south. Sir Percy Lorraine, the British minister in Tehran, accordingly hinted to Theodore Rothstein, the Soviet envoy, that the Soviets and England divide Persia into spheres of influence after the time-honored pre-revolutionary practice. Rothstein ignored the offer.[97]

At the time Russia favored, as Rothstein wrote to Kūchik Khān, the establishment of a "strong central government in Iran." Great Britain increasingly adopted a similar attitude. This ostensibly hands-off policy of the traditional meddlers in Iran constituted the "fortunate conjunction of external circumstances" which helped the meteoric rise of Riẓā Khān. His assumption of the post of Prime Minister was hailed in Great Britain,[98] but soon thereafter his policy really tested British support for a strong central government in Iran.

[94] For the text of Sipahdār's statement, see Makkī, *op. cit.*, I, 47-48.
[95] For the text of Sayyid Zīā's statement, see *ibid.*, pp. 125-29.
[96] Fischer, *op. cit.*, p. 429.
[97] *Ibid.*
[98] For example, see the *Times* (London), October 29, 1923, as reproduced in Isfandīyārī, *op. cit.*, pp. 39-40.

Riẓā Khān was determined to reestablish Iran's long-neglected authority in the south. His twofold objective of internal centralization and external emancipation had guided his predecessors ever since Mushīr al-Dawlah had formed his Cabinet in June 1920. Before he became Prime Minister, Riẓā Khān's unification, Iranization, and strengthening of the army and the extension of the central authority to Khorasan, Azerbaijan, and Gilan had sufficiently stabilized the country to make it possible for the Cabinets of Qavām al-Saltanah, Mustawfī al-Mamālik, and Mushīr al-Dawlah to carry out a successful foreign policy. As Prime Minister he could, of course, exercise much more influence in the conduct of foreign affairs. The manner by which he resolved the problem of the south revealed that as a result of years of participation in the foreign-policy-making process he had acquired a diplomatic skill matched only by his bold soldiery.

Riẓā Khān's policy encountered conciliatory opposition from the British. Great Britain was torn between its interest in a strong central government in Iran and its commitment to Sheikh Khaz'al. This commitment had arisen out of British interests in the Persian Gulf and oil in the years when the central government of Iran possessed only nominal sovereignty over the Bakhtyārī tribesmen in the highlands and Sheikh Khaz'al in the plains of Khuzistan. As early as 1903 the sheikh had received assurances of British protection from Sir Arthur Hardinge, the British Minister in Tehran.[99] In October 1910 he had received an assurance that Great Britain would not merely safeguard him to the best of its ability against unprovoked attack or encroachment by a foreign power, but would support him in obtaining a satisfactory solution "in the event of an encroachment by the Persian Government on his jurisdiction and recognized rights or on his property in Persia."[100] This assurance was renewed in November 1914, after Sheikh Khaz'al had sided with Great Britain upon the intervention of Turkey in the war and had assisted the British Expeditionary Force in the capture of Basra. On both occasions the assurance had been conditioned: the sheikh and his descendants (to whom the assurance was extended) must not fail "to observe their obligations towards the Persian Government." Furthermore in 1910 it was

[99] See Royal Institute of International Affairs, *Survey of International Affairs* (London, 1927), I, 540.

[100] *Ibid.*

explained that the promised support "might have to be confined to diplomatic action." [101]

The problem was precipitated by Khaz'al's apprehension that Riẕā Khān threatened his enjoyment of semiautonomy. Riẕā Khān's successful campaign in August 1924 against the Lur tribesmen seriously alarmed Khaz'al. About a year earlier, in November 1923, Riẕā Khān had decided to collect taxes from Khuzistan. Colonel D. W. MacCormack went to the province on behalf of the government and concluded a settlement with Khaz'al according to which he agreed to pay the government 500,000 tomans on his tax arrears, of which he paid in cash 100,000. The settlement also bound the sheikh to pay his future taxes.[102]

About a year later at the head of an already existing committee (called *Qīām-i Sa'ādat*) he rebelled against the central government. In a bold telegram to the Ministry of Finance he denounced his previous agreement with the government and refused to pay any more on his tax arrears.[103] He also informed Riẕā Khān that he did not recognize him as Prime Minister and called him a usurper who had driven the Shah out of the country and captured the capital.[104] He also incited other Arab tribal chiefs to demand from the Majlis the return of the Shah from Europe. The tribal chiefs threatened to resort to armed force if the government did not grant their demand.[105] Mu'tamin al-Mulk, the speaker of the Majlis, replied, on September 30, 1924, that "the present government, under His Highness Sardar Sipah [Riẕā Khān] enjoys the full support of the Majlis." "Any Person," he continued, "who should rise, or take any action, against the central government would, therefore, be considered as an outlaw by Parliament." [106]

Besides the complete support of the Majlis, Riẕā Khān also enjoyed clerical backing. He now reaped the fruits of having yielded to the clergy a few months earlier on the issue of a republic. In a most vehement *fatwā* eighteen highly revered *'ulamā'* declared that any uprising against the central government was contrary to the religion

[101] *Ibid.*

[102] For a first-hand account, see A. C. Millspaugh, *The American Task in Persia* (New York, 1925), p. 217.

[103] Makkī, *op. cit.*, III, 133.

[104] *Ibid.*, p. 164.

[105] For the text of their letter to the Majlis, see *ibid.*, pp. 166-67.

[106] Cf. *ibid.*, pp. 167-68 and Millspaugh, *op. cit.*, pp. 226-27.

of Islam, and they called upon all provincial and tribal Muslims to fight against this rebellion in the name of religion and for the sake of the independence of the country.[107] In addition to parliamentary and clerical support, Riẓā Khān also enjoyed the confidence and energetic services of Ẕakā' al-Mulk Furūghī, who acted as Prime Minister while Riẓā Khān was absent from Tehran to quell Khaz'al's rebellion.

Riẓā Khān employed both diplomatic skill and dramatic military operations in his campaign. As soon as the British government learned about his determination to terminate the autonomy of Kahz'al, British representatives sought to induce him to settle the problem without resort to arms because military operations might result "incidentally in damage to the company's plant or interruption of their operations – involving, as this would, heavy financial losses to the British shareholders and incidentally to the British Government, which held a controlling interest in the company." [108] This position was repeatedly stated to Riẓā Khān by the British consuls in Isfahan and Shiraz while he was on his way to Khuzistan.[109] To all these personal representations he replied, with vigor and firmness, that he would personally compensate the British if his action should cause any damage to the company. He also made it unequivocally clear that no further delay in the settlement of the matter could be tolerated. As Riẓā Khān moved farther south, the British protested more vigorously, but to no avail. In the meantime the acting Prime Minister received two notes from the British pointing out the nature of their commitments to Sheikh Khaz'al, protesting the policy of Riẓā Khān, and offering British mediation.[110] The information was wired to Riẓā Khān, who immediately sent a terse reply disapproving of the Cabinet's accepting such notes. The problem of Khuzistan was entirely a domestic matter. The British had no right to protest or interfere in any way whatsoever. Nor was there any occasion for British mediation because the government was dealing with an Iranian citizen within its own territory.

Riẓā Khān's military operations aimed at surrounding Khuzistan. He used four groups of government troops, heading toward Behbehan,

[107] For the full text, see Makkī, *op. cit.*, III, 181.

[108] Royal Institute of International Affairs, *op. cit.*, p. 540.

[109] For details, see Riẓā Khān's own accounts as reproduced in Makkī, *op. cit.*, III, 203-4 and 209-10.

[110] For the text of these notes, see Makkī, *op. cit.*, III, 222-23.

Pusht-i Kuh, Dizful, and Ramhurmuz.[111] On November 5, 1924, he himself, accompanied by a number of army officers and civilians and four armored automobiles, left Tehran for Isfahan. On November 15, when the Prime Minister was at Shiraz, he received a telegram from Sheikh Khaz'al, apologizing for his conduct and offering his complete "services" to the government in the future.[112] This was unacceptable to Riẕā Khān, who demanded clear and unconditional submission. He advanced toward Ahwaz, the capital of Khuzistan. A few days later when Riẕā Khān landed at the port of Daylam he received Khaz'al's unconditional submission.[113] The sheikh also sued for and obtained amnesty in Nasiri, first through his son and later in person.

By December 15 Riẕā Khān had achieved his twofold objective of establishing the authority of the central government in the south and wresting Khuzistan from British control. General Faẕlullāh Khān, who had distinguished himself in the "fight" against the Khaz'al forces, was appointed Governor-General of Khuzistan, and other generals were retained in three major locations, at the head of their troops, in order to ensure the control of the newly established central authority.[114] Later the government sent a commission to Khuzistan to organize a provincial financial administration.[115]

After the subjugation of Khaz'al, Sir Percy Lorraine visited Riẕā Khān, who expected to find the British Minister annoyed by the developments. On the contrary, the Minister admitted to Riẕā Khān that Khaz'al had made mistakes.[116] The conciliatory British attitude apparently derived in part from the belief that Khaz'al had taken the "false step of publicly denouncing Reza Khan and his policy."[117] Furthermore, the terms of the British commitment to Khaz'al had made British support conditional upon observance by him and his descendants of their obligations toward the Iranian government.[118] More important, British military intervention was out of the question

[111] Ja'far Shāhid, *Dūdmān-i Pahlavī* (Tehran, 1328 [1949/50], p. 30. Millspaugh states that government troops at Khuzistan totaled 22,000 men (*op. cit.*, p. 227).

[112] For the text, see Makkī, *op. cit.*, III, 206.

[113] For the text of the letter of submission, see *ibid.*, p. 226.

[114] *Ibid.*, p. 287.

[115] Millspaugh, *op. cit.*, p. 234.

[116] Riẕā Khān's own account is reproduced in Makkī, *op. cit.*, III, 268.

[117] Royal Institute of International Affairs, *op. cit.*, p. 542.

[118] *Ibid.*

not only because Great Britain had told Khaz'al in 1910 that British support might have to be confined to "diplomatic action" but also because military action would deal a serious blow to the establishment of a strong central government, which at that time suited British policy in Iran.

THIRD-POWER POLICY

In pursuit of its policy to throw off British and Russian shackles Iran sought to establish close relations with a "distant and disinterested" power. Two reasons for this policy may be cited. One was to utilize the presence of a third power in Iran as a counterweight against retention or expansion of influence and control by the British and the Russians. The other was to secure financial and administrative aid toward the reconstruction of the Iranian economy. It was feared that continuation of the deplorable internal conditions might well invite attempts at intervention in Iranian affairs by Great Britain and Russia.

For the policy makers of the 1920's the selection of a third power was not difficult. In 1911, when the Second Majlis made the country's first bid for economic recovery and independence, the United States had been chosen. The memory of Morgan Shuster was an important factor in Iran's seeking the aid of the United States again. But there were also other compelling reasons in favor of selecting the United States. The American government had shown support for Iran by disapproving of the British refusal to allow Iran to present its case to the Paris Peace Conference and by actively denouncing the 1919 agreement. Furthermore, the United States' "Open Door" policy suited Iran's determination to steer clear of exclusive Anglo-Russian economic ties.[119] More important still, the United States since 1919 had been engaged in a worldwide search for oil, a fact that Iran relished because of its desire to prevent the British from monopolizing the oil resources of the country.

Therefore, when Mushīr al-Dawlah (June-November 1920) launched

[119] For example, see Mushīr al-Dawlah's endorsement of the "Open Door" policy in a letter to the American chargé d'affaires in Tehran. The text is in *Oil Concessions in Foreign Countries* (68th Congress, 1st sess., Senate Doc. 97; Washington, 1924), p. 99.

Iran's new policy by suspending the 1919 agreement and starting negotiations for a treaty with Soviet Russia, he simultaneously sought to interest United States oil companies in Iran and instructed 'Abd al-'Alī Khān in August 1920 to approach the Department of State on the matter. The Department informed the Iranian Minister that it believed that American companies would seek concessions in the northern provinces and that it hoped that such companies might obtain concessions for oil. 'Abd al-'Alī Khān was further advised that the Standard Oil Company of New Jersey had indicated that it would consider a proposal to operate in northern Iran should a satisfactory agreement be reached.[120]

The matter was not pursued vigorously, however, as a result of the downfall of the Mushīr al-Dawlah government and the subsequent Cabinet crisis during the government of Sipahdār. But a few months after the coup, Qavām al-Saltanah, the successor of Sayyid Ẕīā' al-Dīn, not only continued the third-power policy inaugurated by Mushīr al-Dawlah, but also expanded its scope. The new Prime Minister decided that Iran should seek not only American investment in oil but also American loans and technical assistance. In a lucid and comprehensive memorandum to the Secretary of State,[121] the able Iranian Minister in Washington, Ḥusayn 'Alā', informed the United States government of his country's policy of impartiality as between Great Britain and Russia and of Iran's hopes for American assistance. In explaining the policy of impartiality, 'Alā' pointed out the rejection of the 1919 agreement with Great Britain and the signing of the 1921 treaty with Soviet Russia. In regard to the latter, however, the Iranian Minister deemed it appropriate to state that "it must be clearly understood that there has been and there is no desire on our part to be dominated by Moscow or to adopt Bolshevist doctrines. . . . We were obliged by our propinquity to Russia to arrive at a modus vivendi with a strong neighbour, and the conditions offered to us were most advantageous." [122]

[120] U.S. Department of State, *Foreign Relations of the United States, 1920* (Washington, 1936), III, 352-53. Millspaugh states that "the Persian government then headed by Mushir od-Dowleh, – a patriotic liberal who during his public career in Persia has won general respect for his honesty, dignity, sound judgement and statesmanlike aims, – formulated the main headings of an economic policy" (*op. cit.*, pp. 17-18).

[121] For the full text, see *Oil Concessions in Foreign Countries*, pp. 87-93.

[122] *Ibid.*, p. 89.

American assistance for national reconstruction was sought through requests for technical assistance, loans, and investments. Advisers were required for the establishment of a national bank, for a department of finance, and for a department of agriculture. A "substantial loan" was to be used for the establishment of the bank and for productive purposes. All previously owned concessions by Tsarist Russia would be granted to the American-managed national bank, which would form companies with American capital in the main. Other concessions for the construction of railways, dams, and mines would also be given to the bank. As the situation developed, however, American capital interested itself in oil, to which the question of a loan became inextricably linked. Iran's third-power policy will therefore be examined in terms of granting oil concessions to American companies and employing advisers from the United States.

On November 22, 1921, at the suggestion of Qavām al-Saltanah, the Fourth Majlis unanimously passed a resolution granting Standard Oil of New Jersey a fifty-year concession for the exploitation of oil in the five provinces of northern Iran. The government of Iran was to receive 15 per cent of the gross earnings. Other details were to be worked out with the company and approved by the Majlis. In compliance with the nature of the third-power policy, discussed above, Article 5 of the resolution stated: "The Standard Oil Company of New Jersey cannot under any circumstances assign or transfer this concession to any foreign government or company or individual, and likewise partnership with other firms or capitalists is subject to the approval of the Majlis. Non-observance of this Article will entail invalidity of the concession." [123]

Immediate opposition to Iran's decision was expressed by both Russia and Great Britain. The day after the granting of the oil concession Rothstein, the Russian Minister, opposed Iran's action on the ground that all Russian rights in Iran were in full force because the Treaty of February 1921 had not been ratified, and that even had it been ratified the concession to the Standard Oil Company violated that treaty which forbade the granting of a concession formerly held by a Russian subject to a foreign national.[124] The concession right

[123] U.S. Department of State, *Foreign Relations of the United States, 1921* (Washington, 1936), II, 643-49. See also Makkī, *op. cit.*, I, 344.

[124] For the text of the Russian protest, see *Oil Concessions in Foreign Countries*, p. 94.

claimed in the Russian note pertained to the Khoshtaria concession, which had been granted by Sipahsālār Aʿẓam in 1916, and confirmed by his successor, Vuṣūq al-Dawlah. But this concession, it may be recalled, was never ratified by the Third Majlis, which had been dispersed in November 1915. Nevertheless, it was brought before the Fourth Majlis, which declared it invalid at the time the concession was granted to the Standad Oil Company.[125]

British opposition was based on the claim of the Anglo-Persian Oil Company to the Khoshtaria concession. After the Bolshevik Revolution, Khoshtaria had apparently begun to look for a customer for his concession, since the new regime in Russia had repudiated all Tsarist concessions in Iran. Having first approached the Dutch and the French without success, he had then offered it to the Anglo-Persian Oil Company. At the time the British possessed supreme influence in Iran and were determined to extend it as far as possible. The Khoshtaria concession would give them a foothold in the north. Vuṣūq al-Dawlah confirmed the Khoshtaria concession, and the Anglo-Persian Oil Company purchased it for a substantial sum, £100,000 of which was paid in advance. As a result, in May 1920 a subsidiary by the name of the North Persian Oils Company had been established with a capital of £3,000,000.[126]

Iran rejected the objections of both Russia and Great Britain on basically similar grounds. It stated that the Khoshtaria concession had been obtained under duress, had never been ratified by the Majlis, as required by the Constitution, and had been rejected by the Majlis when it was finally submitted to it.[127]

British opposition could not be overlooked by the Standard Oil Company for the important reason that the Anglo-Persian Oil Company had the exclusive right to oil transportation throughout Iran, with the exception of the five northern provinces, and without use of its facilities Standard's oil could not reach world commercial markets. Furthermore, the Standard Oil Company was not too enthusiastic

[125] In July 1918 the Ṣamṣām al-Saltanah government declared "all concessionary contracts with Russian subjects null and void." For details, see Chapter VII. Apparently, it was because of this declaration that Muṣṭafā Fātaḥ states that the Khoshtaria concession had been invalidated (*Panjāh Sāl Naft-i Īrān* [Tehran, 1335 <1956/57>], p. 330).

[126] *Ibid.*, p. 331.

[127] For a summary of Iran's reply to Russia, see Senate Doc. 97, p. 94. This source also contains the text of Iran's arguments on pp. 94-98.

about the concession at this stage, because Iran attached the condition that the company obtain a loan for the Iranian government.[128] The Standard Oil Company therefore yielded to British pressure by consenting to the Anglo-Persian Oil Company's participation in its concession. Their agreement provided for joint management of a new Perso-American Petroleum Company.

On February 22, 1922, the agreement was brought to the attention of the Iranian government. By this time Qavām al-Saltanah had been succeeded by the first after-the-coup government of Mushīr al-Dawlah. As the originator of the third-power policy, Mushīr al-Dawlah found the Standard-Anglo-Persian agreement contrary to two of his most important purposes in seeking American capital in the first place: to steer clear of a British monopoly of Iran's oil resources and to avoid creating jealousy between the traditional rivals, Great Britain and Russia. It was with this specific purpose in mind that the resolution of the Majlis authorizing the grant of the concession to Standard Oil had forbidden that company to assign or transfer its concession to any foreign government, company, or individual or to enter into partnership with other companies without the approval of the Majlis. Mushīr al-Dawlah in consequence informed the United States chargé d'affaires that Standard's agreement was causing "political difficulties" in Iran.[129]

At the same time, however, the Iranian government was anxious to acquire much-needed funds through a loan that was now closely tied to the grant of an oil concession. Forty-two deputies of the Majlis took the initiative in introducing a new resolution to amend Article 1 of the previous resolution. The amendment was voted on June 11, 1922, authorizing the government to negotiate a concession in northern Iran with "the Standard Oil or any other independent and reputable American company."[130] As a result, Qavām al-Saltanah (now Prime Minister for the second time since the coup) approached not only Standard Oil Company but also Sinclair Consolidated Oil Corporation. In August 1922 Standard and Sinclair submitted detailed draft concessions to the Iranian government. These were examined

[128] Benjamin Shwadran, *The Middle East, Oil and the Great Powers* (New York, 1956), p. 88.

[129] *Oil Concessions in Foreign Countries*, p. 101, contains the text of Mushīr al-Dawlah's letter.

[130] See Fātaḥ, *op. cit.*, p. 336.

carefully and on the basis of their terms a third proposal was submitted to the Majlis by Qavām al-Saltanah. As a result, a bill was voted on June 14, 1923, authorizing the government to grant an oil concession in the five northern provinces of Iran to "any independent and reputable American company" for a period of fifty years.[131]

Riẕā Khān found Sinclair's new draft concession compatible with the requirements of the law passed by the Majlis, and on December 1923 his government signed an oil concession with Sinclair which excluded Gilan from the concession area.[132] Riẕā Khān regarded the signing of the concession as "one of the most important events in Iran's history," and at a celebration in honor of the signing he told the American chargé d'affaires, "We want to eradicate the economic dominance of Britain and Russia in Iran; and the signing of this concession with an American company will be the beginning of stronger ties between the United States and Iran."[133] On April 19, 1924, Riẕā Khān introduced a bill in the Majlis for the ratification of the concession. Despite British opposition to the effect that they could not consent to hypothecation of Anglo-Persian Oil Company's royalties for a loan in the United States, the Majlis ratified the concession, which was conditioned upon Sinclair's arranging for a $10,000,000 loan in the United States.[134]

As the situation developed, however, the company decided to abandon its concession. Two explanations have generally been advanced. One is usually given by Iranians, who tend to attribute Sinclair's abandonment of its concession to the murder of the American vice consul, which they allege to have been engineered by the Anglo-Persian Oil Company.[135] Some Western writers and officials have also shared this view,[136] but Sinclair itself seems to have implicated Russia.[137] The other explanation is that by the summer of 1924 Sinclair had lost its concession on Sakhalin Island, as well as the right to market Soviet petroleum products – a situation that made it

[131] The text of the law is in Makkī, *op. cit.*, III, 138-45.

[132] For the text, see U.S. Department of State, *Foreign Relations of the United States, 1923* (Washington, 1938), II, 721-36. See also Fātaḥ, *op. cit.*, p. 338.

[133] Quoted in Fātaḥ, *op. cit.*, p. 338.

[134] *Ibid.*, pp. 338-39, and Shwadran, *op. cit.*, p. 94.

[135] See, for example, Makkī, *op. cit.*, III, 92-107.

[136] See Nasrollah S. Fatemi, *Oil Diplomacy* (New York, 1954), pp. 131-37.

[137] See George Lenczowski, *Russia and the West in Iran, 1918-1948* (Ithaca, N. Y., 1949), p. 84.

difficult, if not impossible, to obtain from the Soviet Union permission to transport the oil from Iranian fields over Russian territory to world markets.[138]

The other practical manifestation of the third-power policy was the employment of American financial advisers. Shuster was still regarded by Iranians "as an incarnation of their own highest aspirations."[139] In fact, when the government of Iran seriously approached the United States[140] to employ an American adviser, Shuster was to be rehired if possible.[141]

But the State Department recommended its own economic adviser, Dr. A. C. Millspaugh. His acquaintance with Ḥusayn 'Alā', the Iranian Minister in Washington, had much to do with his selection for the task.[142] The State Department, however, made its recommendation on the basis of an understanding that Dr. Millspaugh would undertake his work "in a purely private capacity" and that the United States government "assumed no responsibility for any action that [he] might take as an official in the employment of the Persian Government."[143] These conditions were perfectly acceptable to the government of Qavām al-Saltanah, which asked the Fourth Majlis for "its permission and approval" of hiring American financial advisers.[144] 'Alā' signed a contract with Dr. Millspaugh on August 14, 1922, who arrived in Tehran with a staff of United States citizens selected by him on November 18.

The Iranian government did not confer on Dr. Millspaugh merely advisory powers. He was given "general charge of the financial administration," "the preparation of the budget," and explicit powers involving "effective control over the personnel of the financial administration, over expenditures, and over the creation of financial obligations."[145] At the head of the American mission he began his work as the Administrator-General of the Finances of Iran.

[138] Fātaḥ, *op. cit.*, pp. 337-38, and Shwadran, *op. cit.*, pp. 93-94.

[139] Millspaugh, *op. cit.*, pp. 12-13.

[140] Since the third year of the war the Iranian government had entertained the idea of employing American advisers. See Abraham Yeselson, *United States–Persian Diplomatic Relations, 1883-1921* (Princeton, N. J., 1956), p. 181.

[141] *Ibid.*, p. 191.

[142] Millspaugh, *op. cit.*, p. 19.

[143] *Ibid.*, pp. 19-20.

[144] Makkī, *op. cit.*, II, 79.

[145] Millspaugh, *op. cit.*, pp. 20-21.

Dr. Millspaugh found evidences of business depression everywhere in Iran. Banking firms and merchants were bankrupt, once-wealthy landowners were insolvent, once-flourishing industries had languished, and lack of confidence prevailed. In addition, the age-old evils remained: corruption, maladministration, budgetary deficits, an unpaid and underpaid civil service, and uncollected taxes.[146] An Iranian said to Dr. Millspaugh upon his arrival in Iran: "You are the last doctor called to the deathbed of a sick person. If you fail, the patient will die. If you succeed, the patient will live. I do not applaud your arrival. I shall applaud if you succeed." [147]

Financial reconstruction and reform required a host of measures which impinged upon the vested interests of many former government officials, tribal chiefs, and others. But Dr. Millspaugh approached his task with determination and was generally the beneficiary of the fortunate conjunction of external circumstances: his employment was cordially supported by Great Britain [148] and Russia's opposition never amounted to the kind of diplomatic and military pressure exerted against his predecessor, Morgan Shuster. The hands-off policy of Great Britain and Russia in favor of a "strong central government" was indeed fortunate and contrasted strongly with the Russian opposition to the American mission in 1911.

Apart from the relatively favorable external conditions Dr. Millspaugh's considerable success in 1922-25 derived also from certain favorable internal factors. The Fourth Majlis gave him almost complete support. Aspiring to "the heroic role" of the Second Majlis, which had employed Shuster, the deputies of the Fourth Majlis took pains to inform Dr. Millspaugh that the American mission was "the creature of the Parliament." [149] The Prime Ministers who formed governments during the 1922-25 period also backed the American mission unreservedly. But the single most important internal factor that made Dr. Millspaugh's task possible was the support of the army under Riẕā Khān.[150] Riẕā Khān's extension of the central authority over the provinces and the effective control of the police in Tehran contributed significantly to the collection of both the current taxes and the arrears urgently needed by the government.

[146] *Ibid.*, pp. 52-83.
[147] Quoted from an editorial in an Iranian newspaper (*ibid.*, p. 3).
[148] Royal Institute of International Studies, *op. cit.*, p. 536.
[149] Millspaugh, *op. cit.*, p. 82. [150] *Ibid.*, pp. 44-48.

The imaginative and honest efforts of the American mission supported by the favorable circumstances abovementioned made it possible for Dr. Millspaugh to increase revenues, to control expenditures, to channel funds to productive purposes and public welfare, to break the vicious circle of deficits and borrowings, and to improve the credit of the government within the short span of three years.[151] But ironically enough, the same factor that acted as the single most important internal element in support of the American mission, namely Riẓā Khān, finally impelled the mission to leave Iran.

As the Minister of War in a number of Cabinets before he became Prime Minister, Riẓā Khān gave assistance to the American mission. Even when he became Prime Minister he continued to support it. In March 1925 Riẓā Khān and the Majlis decided not to exercise the option to terminate the contracts of the American advisers at the end of three years but to ask them to continue their work for the full period of five years contemplated in the contracts. In 1927, however, when the question of the renewal of Dr. Millspaugh's contract came up in the Fifth Majlis, Riẓā Shah demanded a reduction in Millspaugh's powers. The monarch was now intolerant of the possession of extensive powers by any institution or individual other than himself. He was also taking this oportunity to settle a recent score with the Administrator-General, who had refused the Shah's demand for additional funds during his personal campaign in Khorasan in the autumn of 1926.[152] Despite the remarkable achievements of the American mission, despite the favor of a majority of the deputies of the Majlis and the Prime Minister, Riẓā Shah's opposition finally forced the withdrawal of the Americans. This was a grave blow to the third-power policy which the Shah had previously supported. It was also an action that pleased Soviet Russia,[153] the power that Riẓā Shah most distrusted.

[151] *Ibid.*, p. 310.

[152] Edgar Turlington, "The Financial Independence of Persia," *Foreign Affairs*, July 1928, pp. 664-66.

[153] *Ibid.*, p. 666.

A STATESMANLIKE FOREIGN POLICY

Although signs of departure from the traditional foreign policy had become discernible by 1920, the earliest successful foreign-policy decisions had had to await the far-reaching changes in internal and external conditions. With the progressive stabilization of internal conditions after the *coup d'état* and the emerging hands-off policy of Great Britain and Russia, the foreign-policy makers of Iran found an unprecedented degree of freedom of action in foreign affairs. The courses of action they pursued toward the overriding objective of Iran's politico-economic emancipation were marked by undeniable diplomatic skill. Few actions were taken without regard to the consequences, and few goals were selected that could not be achieved. This was evident in Iran's policy toward Russia, toward Great Britain, and in its third-power policy.

In regard to Russia, Iranian policy makers believed that they could not realistically hope to bring about the withdrawal of Soviet forces from the north and the abandonment of Soviet support of the Gilan Republic by engaging in a Cold War with Iran's powerful neighbor. Nor did they believe that resumption of trade with Russia, which was vitally needed, would be possible in an atmosphere of mutual antagonism. To achieve these objectives, they believed, Iran should normalize relations with the new regime in Russia by means of a comprehensive treaty regulating the relations between the two countries. But the withdrawal of Soviet troops, the destruction of the Soviet Republic of Gilan, and the resumption of trade with Russia were not the only considerations underlying the Iranian decision to sign the Treaty of 1921. Mushīr al-Dawlah, who started negotiations with Moscow for a treaty of friendship, believed that embodiment in an instrument of this kind of the repeated Soviet indictment of Tsarist policy could help pave the way toward Iran's eventual economic and political freedom. This view was shared by his successors prior to and after the coup. Sipahdār accepted the draft of the treaty, Sayyid Ẓīā' signed it, and Qavām al-Saltanah submitted it to the Fourth Majlis for ratification.

Although only resumption of trade was mentioned in the treaty, from the very beginning its ratification was linked to the settlement of two other vital problems: the withdrawal of Soviet troops and the fate of the Soviet Republic of Gilan. It was no mere coincidence that the Majlis ratified the treaty two weeks after these two problems had been conclusively settled.

To the Iranian policy makers these were momentous political achievements in the direction of their country's eventual independence from Russian tutelage. The ratification of the treaty was therefore not too much of a price to pay, particularly in view of the fact that its terms in general were directed against all the Russian treaties, concessions, institutions, and practices of the past century or so that had resulted in Iran's economic and political subjugation. However, the grant to Russia of the right of military intervention in Iran under certain circumstances (Article 6 of the 1921 treaty) was potentially dangerous. But this danger was not overlooked by Iran as evidenced by the efforts of Qavām al-Saltanah as well as Malik al-Shuʿarā, Taqīzādah, Taymūrtāsh, and other deputies of the Majlis to obtain Russia's "explanations" in regard to the crucial terms of the treaty prior to its ratification. Ideally Iran should have included in the treaty certain provisions for third-party judgment in order to bar Russia from unilateral and disadvantageous interpretation of the treaty, particularly Articles 5 and 6. But the chances for getting Russia's consent to submit its international disputes, arising from treaty interpretation or otherwise, to third-party adjudication were no better, to say the least, in the 1920's than they are in the 1960's.

Iran's self-interest was also served by the strategy pursued toward Great Britain. Mushīr al-Dawlah suspended the execution of the 1919 agreement. His successors, Sipahdār and Sayyid Ẓīā', also denounced it, and finally the Majlis rejected it conclusively after the coup. This was a reversal of Vus̱ūq's policy; he had believed that Iran's salvation lay in the closest possible *rapprochement* with Great Britain – a conception that was doomed to failure because it disregarded the rising tides of nationalist sentiment throughout the East.

Riẓā Khān's policy toward Sheikh Khazʿal also advanced the Iranian objective of territorial integrity. The semiautonomous character of Khuzistan had been a by-product of the central government's inability to exercise any significant degree of control over it in the past. The British had endorsed the autonomy of Khazʿal because of the weakness of the central government and the need for protection of British interests in oil and the Persian Gulf. But with the rise of a relatively strong central government in Iran by 1924, the British position had become untenable. The fact that British opposition to the subjugation of Khaz'al was tempered by their interest in a strong central government in Iran should not minimize the significance of Riẕā Khān's policy. His unshakable objective of recovering Khuzistan, his determination to fulfill it regardless of British protests, and his calculated and dramatic military maneuvers, with himself in the field, were to no small extent responsible for the success of his policy toward Great Britain.

Elements of skillful diplomacy were also present in the third-power policy, especially in its two basic manifestations of granting oil concessions to American companies and of employing American advisers. Qavām al-Saltanah, Mushīr al-Dawlah, and Riẕā Khān were motivated by the same objective in granting oil concessions, with the permission and approval of the Fourth Majlis, to American Standard Oil of New Jersey and subsequently to Sinclair Consolidated Oil Corporation. The fact that these concessions did not result in the actual development of the oil resources of northern Iran was, in the last analysis, beyond the control of the Iranian policy makers, who resisted all pressures from Great Britain and Russia. Had Sinclair not lost the opportunity to obtain Soviet permission to transport the oil from the Iranian fields over Russian territory to world markets, the company would probably have been able to operate under its concession.

Despite the company's failure, the result was not altogether negative for Iran. A fundamental consideration underlying the Iranian decision to offer oil concessions to American companies in the north was to steer clear of British monopolization of Iranian oil resources. This objective was attained to no small degree because the battle between the American and the British oil companies opened up the whole question of the British title to the Khoshtaria concession, which had been purchased by the Anglo-Persian Oil Company. Iranian policy makers seized upon this opportunity to reiterate their long-held view on the Khoshtaria concession: it was nullified by unanimous vote of the Fourth Majlis at the time that the resolution to authorize the grant of an oil concession to the Standard Oil Company of New Jersey was passed. Subsequently, the North Persian Oils Company, which had been formed under the Khoshtaria concession, was dissolved.

The employment of American advisers proved far more successful than the attempt to grant oil concessions. It served the purpose of acquiring the badly needed technical know-how without jeopardizing the economic freedom of the country. This was an alternative which was, unlike the British economic and technical aid under the 1919 agreement, both politically acceptable and economically beneficial. It was prompted by Iran's enlightened self-interest and was endorsed by all the Cabinets of the early 1920's and by the Majlis. Within the span of a few years Iran could boast of a measure of financial recovery unknown in any previous period of its modern history. The foresight of statesmen like Mushīr al-Dawlah, Qavām al-Saltanah, Ḥusayn 'Alā', and Riẓā Khān, on the one hand, and the generous grant of broad powers to the head of the American mission, Dr. Millspaugh, on the other, made it possible to lay the foundation of Iran's economic and fiscal emancipation in the early 1920's.

Chapter IX

Riẓā Shah's Struggle with the USSR, 1925-1941

WITH the accession of Riẓā Shah to the throne of Iran the monarchy recovered from its brief eclipse in the era after the Constitutional Revolution. Once again it was the most structured unit making foreign policy. The role of Cabinet members, particularly of strong Prime Ministers, which had become fairly significant during the period just following the Constitutional Revolution, diminished rapidly after the *coup d'état*. The Majlis had never really done much to formulate foreign policy, in part because of Anglo-Russian intervention and the inexperience and naïveté of the deputies. The Fourth Majlis, as contrasted with its predecessors, had demonstrated some degree of responsibility, but it still failed to play any significant sustained role in foreign affairs. With the accession of the Shah the role of both the Cabinet and the Majlis was reduced to a minimum. The supreme policy maker was Riẓā Shah.

In foreign affairs the Shah was principally concerned with Russia, Great Britain, Iran's neighbors, and Germany, each of which will be treated separately. This analytical division of the Shah's foreign policy must not be allowed to convey the impression that his policies were unrelated. On the contrary, the development of the Shah's policy toward Germany must be understood largely in the light of his policies toward Great Britain and particularly Russia.

Although the Soviet troops had been withdrawn and the Soviet Republic of Gilan had been liquidated before the accession of the Shah to the throne, relations with Russia constituted Iran's most difficult problem. Riz̤ā Shah inherited from his predecessors a country which was still substantially controlled by Russia. This control had been exercised for about a century in varying forms, but particularly through the economic "colonization" of northern Iran. The Shah's Russian problems were not merely old ones inherited from previous generations. He also had to find ways to combat the new methods of Russian imperialism. His task was twofold: to bring about Iran's economic and political emancipation and to resist Russia's attempt at "reentering" Iran under a new guise.

TRADE AND FISHERIES

Economic relations with the USSR were of particular concern to Riz̤ā Shah throughout his rule. The most vexing economic problem was trade between the two countries. The traditional dependence of northern Iran on Russian markets had been further increased after the *coup d'état*. By the time Riz̤ā Shah ascended the throne, Iranian exports had increased nearly tenfold and imports amounted to more than four times what they had been in 1921.[1] This enormous increase in trade with Russia had taken place in spite of the inconclusive battle between the two countries in negotiating a trade agreement. Throughout the 1921-24 period, it will be recalled, various Iranian Prime Ministers had wrestled with the problem of trade unsuccessfully. Riz̤ā Khān had been no exception. Although he signed a twenty-one article draft convention in 1924, after twenty-two months of protracted negotiations initiated by his predecessors,[2] the Fifth Majlis refused to ratify it because Russia would not comply with Iranian demands

[1] See the table in Hussain Navai, *Les relations économiques irano-russes* (Paris, 1935), p. 117, and in Robert Wesley Davenport, "Soviet Economic Relations with Iran, 1917-1930" (Ph.D. dissertation, Columbia University, 1953), p. 149.

[2] See Chapter VIII.

stemming from Iran's determination to make its trade with Russia less prejudicial to its interests.

It was obvious to Riẕā Shah that the traditional dependence on Russian markets could not be terminated overnight. But it was equally clear to him that such a termination would have to be approximated if Iran were eventually to control its own destiny. Examination of the Shah's foreign economic policy during the interwar period reveals two interrelated policies vis-à-vis the USSR. On the one hand, he sought to regulate trade by making a temporary arrangement and by concluding two agreements for limited periods of time. On the other hand, he sought to bring about internal conditions conducive to eventual economic independence. The *ad hoc* agreements were playing for time, and the long-range plans were to make Iran as self-sufficient as possible economically in order to free it from the long-time economic supremacy of Russia in northern Iran.

In pursuing the first objective, the Shah made an "arrangement" in 1927 and signed one agreement in 1931 and another in 1935. The conditions surrounding the 1927 arrangement and the terms of that arrangement should be considered in some detail for two reasons. First, because the Soviet pressure that precipitated the 1927 arrangement was also present, although to a lesser degree, in both 1931 and 1935. Second, because the terms of the 1927 arrangement were, with only slight modifications, incorporated into the two subsequent agreements.

In December 1925 the Soviet Bank in Iran refused to exchange into rials the Soviet currency holdings of Iranian merchants who had returned from the Soviet trade fair with large amounts of Soviet currency.[3] To increase pressure on Iran even further, in 1926 the Soviet Union without warning placed an embargo on Iranian goods[4] and withdrew the limited transit privileges through Russia which it had been granting Iranian exports. As a result, producers and merchants in northern Iran were not only left with large stocks of commodities, but they were paid less than previously for what commodities they were able to sell.[5] The result was disastrous for Iranian agricultural interests and a bitter reminder of the dependence of Iran on Soviet good will.[6]

[3] Davenport, *op. cit.*, pp. 113-14.
[4] Violet Conolly, *Soviet Economic Policy in the East* (London, 1933), p. 6.
[5] Davenport, *op. cit.*, pp. 113-14.
[6] See Conolly, *op. cit.*, p. 114.

Riẓā Shah knew all too well that the purpose of the Soviet pressure was to turn Iran's desire for regulating its trade with Russia into a trade treaty which would ensure the perpetuation of Soviet economic supremacy in Iran. The Shah therefore resumed trade negotiations with the utmost caution. He appointed ʿAlī Qulī Khān Anṣārī (formerly known as Mushāvir al-Mamālik) as Iranian negotiator. Anṣārī, who was then Minister for Foreign Affairs and who had been the Iranian negotiator of the Russo-Iranian treaty of 1921, started negotiating with his Soviet counterpart, Karakhan, upon his arrival in Moscow.

Determined to manipulate the negotiations to the advantage of the USSR, the Soviets attempted to neutralize the Shah's selection of a skillful negotiator. To this end Moscow availed itself of Soviet espionage activities in Tehran. While Karakhan was telling Anṣārī of the Soviet's pious intentions toward Iran, Soviet agents in Tehran had recruited the cipher expert of the Iranian Council of Ministers. This expert, according to Agabekov, the organizer of the network of Soviet agents in Iran, spied on "all instructions" sent by the Iranian government to its negotiator in Moscow.[7]

Under such circumstances it is no surprise that the resumption of negotiations did not produce a definitive trade agreement. As far as Iran was concerned, the *ad hoc* arrangement of 1927 was merely a stop-gap measure. Its terms were embodied in the notes exchanged between Iran and the USSR and were to expire in two years' time. A summary of the more significant terms follows:

1) *Exports and Imports:* The principle of "net balance" was retained in trade between Iran and the USSR. This principle meant that for every consignment of goods exported to the Soviet Union by Iranian merchants, 90 per cent of the value of the Iranian goods must be exported to Iran in the form of the products of the Soviet Union.[8] The remaining 10 per cent of the value of the Iranian goods could be transferred abroad in foreign currency. Furthermore, the USSR undertook to buy Iranian goods up to an annual value of 50,000,000 rubles.[9] Iranian merchants might export 50 per cent of

[7] Georges Agabekov, *OGPU, The Russian Secret Terror* (New York, 1931), p. 103.

[8] Article 5. The text of the "arrangement" is in Jane Degras, *Soviet Documents on Foreign Policy* (London, 1952), II, 255-69.

[9] Article 2.

the quota of these goods (industrial raw materials and consumer goods) to the Soviet Union, but they were obliged to offer at least 25 per cent of such goods to "Soviet State and co-operative organizations," and only if the latter refused to buy or offered less favorable terms might they then be sold to private persons. The remainder of the quota, that is, half of Iranian exports, was to be imported into the USSR "through Soviet economic agencies."[10] Lastly, Iranian merchants were prohibited from importing from the USSR a long list of articles, including oil and oil products, bread grains and flour, metal scrap, fur, pelts, and "articles the export of which is forbidden across any Soviet frontier."[11]

2) *Trade Delegation:* The Soviet trade delegation was made part of the Soviet Embassy in Tehran, and the trade representative and his deputy were considered as members of the Soviet Embassy and would therefore enjoy "the right of personal immunity and other privileges accorded to members of the diplomatic corps." Furthermore, all the premises of the delegation as well as the private dwellings of the representative and the deputy would "enjoy rights of extraterritoriality." These "rights, privileges and immunities" would be reciprocated by the Soviet Union if Iran sent its own trade delegation to Russia.[12]

3) *Transit Right:* The Soviet Union granted freedom of transit to Iranian goods across its territory to third countries. It also allowed the transit of products through its territory to Iran from third countries. This permission was, however, qualified in two respects. One, by "third countries" was meant those with which the Soviet Union had or might have commercial treaties. Two, the products were limited and specified.[13]

Iran theoretically profited from these terms in one respect. Although Article 20 of the Russo-Iranian treaty of 1921 had provided for the right of transit, it had confined the enjoyment of this right to "the transport of goods passing through Persia or Russia and consigned *to a third country.*"[14] This provision had excluded the transport of goods passing through Russia *from a third country.* Article 12 of the 1927 arrangement removed this apparent restriction.

[10] Article 4.
[11] For the full text of this list, see Degras, *op. cit.*, 255-69.
[12] Article 17. [13] Article 12. [14] Italics supplied.

On the whole, the arrangement failed to usher in a new era of mutually satisfactory trade relations between Iran and the USSR. The system of barter and contingents instituted in 1927 was found "very unsatisfactory by Persian merchants." [15] Soviet trading organizations were in a privileged position to acquire the best of Soviet goods for themselves. Iranians complained that they often had to accept unsalable or second-quality goods in exchange for their exports to Russia, and there was no redress for this in the terms of the 1927 arrangement.

Most unfavorable to Iran was the provision granting diplomatic privileges and immunities to the Soviet trade delegation. It is true that the Soviet government promised to reciprocate if Iran opened its own trade delegation in Moscow, but in the absence of such a delegation this provision favored only the USSR. This was a concession to Russia that Iran had refused to consider throughout the twenty-two months of protracted negotiations before 1924. Although the draft convention signed by Riẓā Khān in that year had finally granted such a concession, the Fifth Majlis had refused to ratify it.[16]

In any event, the over-all unfavorable trade relations were further aggravated in 1929 when the terms of the arrangement expired. The consequent loss of free trade by Iranian traders coincided with the establishment of a central Soviet organization for Eastern trade. The Soviet trade monopoly debarred Iranian merchants from exploring the Russian market, while the Soviet trading organizations firmly established in Iran were free to exploit their opportunities.[17] Iran's attempt to counter the Soviet monopoly will be discussed below. Riẓā Shah anxiously sought to terminate the anarchy that once again ruled Iran's trade relations with Russia as a result of the expiration of the 1927 arrangement. In spite of Soviet delaying tactics aimed at bringing economic pressure on Iran, the Shah's persistent effort led, on October 27, 1931, to the signing of the first trade agreement between the two countries since the Bolshevik Revolution.[18] Still

[15] Conolly, *op. cit.*, pp. 62-63.
[16] See Chapter VIII.
[17] Conolly, *op. cit.*, pp. 65-66.
[18] For the full text of this agreement, the annexed protocol, and the relevant notes exchanged between Iran and Soviet Russia, see Leonard Shapiro, *Soviet Treaty Series* (Washington, 1955), I, 37-45.

pursuing an extremely cautious policy, Iran favored concluding the agreement for a limited period of time only.[19]

The terms of this agreement were more or less the same as those of the 1927 agreement and therefore need no repetition. Generally speaking, the "net balance" principle was retained,[20] and the USSR continued to maintain a favorable balance of trade vis-à-vis Iran. The only significant change that favored Iran was that Soviet imports were to be limited by fixed contingents just as Iranian goods to Russia were.[21] In other respects the clauses favorable to Iran were more apparent than real. This was particularly true in regard to the provisions promising reciprocity in the acquisition and possession of property and in the practicing of free trade by the nationals of the two states in each other's territory. While Soviet nationals acquired property and traded freely in Iran, the Soviet legislative code and legal-economic practice offered little real reciprocity to Iranian nationals in Russia.[22]

The bad faith of the USSR was not confined to this area. Soviet trade organizations exasperated Iranian merchants in every way. They withheld commodities until prices rose and then dumped them on the Iranian market after the merchants had placed orders in other countries. Even the right of transit, which had been promised in the 1921 treaty, clarified in the 1927 arrangement, and confirmed in the 1931 agreement, was constantly nullified by the Soviet Union's habit of creating difficulties for Iranian merchants wishing to import goods from third countries through Russia. In 1933 one writer noted that since the agreement was concluded

> economic relations with the USSR have been in a constant state of flux. Throughout 1932 the outcry against the methods employed by the Soviet trading organs in northern Persia grew more and more intense and culminated at the end of that year in deputations to the Tehran Chamber of Commerce and the government urging the abrogation of the 1931 Commercial Treaty with the USSR.[23]

Riẕā Shah was unwilling to embitter trade relations with the USSR further by unilateral cancellation of the 1931 treaty, there being little alternative to trade with Russia at the time. On the other hand, he

[19] The agreement was made for three years.
[20] Article 10 (Shapiro, *op. cit.*, p. 39).
[21] Cf. Conolly, *op. cit.*, p. 67.
[22] *Ibid.*, pp. 67-69.
[23] *Ibid.*, p. 70.

as well as the merchants found the situation intolerable. He therefore pressed for settlement of the disputes arising out of the execution of the treaty. Such a settlement was finally reached on December 11, 1933, through the exchange of letters. It also modified some of the terms of the 1931 treaty.[24]

This treaty, however, expired in 1935. Consequently a "new" trade agreement was signed on August 27 of that year.[25] The terms of this treaty, like those of the 1931 treaty, substantially resembled the provisions of the 1927 "arrangement." Basically, the "net balance" principle,[26] the immunities of the Soviet trade delegation,[27] and the reciprocal right of transit were retained.[28] This treaty was to expire after three years. When it did in 1938, Iran pressed for a new agreement more compatible with its trade and transit interests. Russia refused to consider this demand. As a result, trade between the two countries nearly ceased.[29]

The outbreak of the Second World War made the transit problem extremely urgent for Iran as transportation was then possible only by way of Russia. Having been unsuccessful in his efforts to reach a new economic agreement with Russia through direct diplomatic channels, the Shah then turned his attention to indirect pressure through Germany. By 1939 Germany had become, as will be seen later, Iran's number one trade partner. The German Economic Policy Department believed that economic cooperation between Soviet Russia and Iran on a new treaty basis was not only in the interest of both parties but also of German-Iranian economic plans. The less friction there was in Soviet-Iranian relations, the Germans believed, the smoother could be the course of German-Iranian trade. The Iranian effort to normalize relations with Russia therefore deserved the "most active German support."[30]

Aware of this German attitude, the Iranian government suggested that Germany and Iran reach an agreement on joint action in Moscow

[24] For the text, see Shapiro, *op. cit.*, p. 89.

[25] For the full text of the 1935 agreement and relevant notes, see *ibid.*, pp. 140-46.

[26] Article 10, section 5.

[27] Article 9.

[28] Article 13.

[29] L. P. Elwell-Sutton, *Modern Iran* (London, 1942), pp. 162-63.

[30] U.S. Department of State, *Documents on German Foreign Policy, 1918-1945*, Series D, VIII (Washington, 1954), 353-57.

concerning settlement of the question of transit through Russia.[31] As its part of the joint action, Iran promised to remove the "difficulties" in its forthcoming negotiations with Russia. The German part, Iran suggested, should consist of an effort to solve Iran's transit problem through a German-Russian agreement.[32]

In a German-Soviet trade agreement signed on February 11, 1940, Russia promised, among other things, "to facilitate the transport of goods to Germany from Iran." [33] On March 25, 1940, Iran and Soviet Russia signed the most comprehensive treaty of commerce and navigation ever entered into by the two countries.[34] This treaty still regulates Irano-Soviet commercial relations. Its main provisions may be summarized as follows:

1) *Most-favored-Nation Treatment:* Most-favored-nation treatment was granted reciprocally in customs duties, warehousing of goods, classification of goods for customs purposes, Soviet economic organizations and natural persons, transport of passengers and goods, and vessels plying in the territorial waters and ports of the parties other than those of the Caspian Sea.

2) *Trade:* The USSR had the right to import goods within the limits of quotas to be fixed for each year the treaty was valid. A list of these goods, with the quota figures for each, should be drawn up each year by the Commercial Agency of the USSR in Iran and the Iranian Minister of Commerce. The USSR agreed that "the total value of Soviet imports into Iran sold for rials . . . shall at least not be less than the total value of goods purchased in rials from Iran."

3) *Transit:* The USSR promised to grant free transit across its territory for Iran's natural and industrial products destined for "any third country." Iran was to reciprocate. Free transit did not apply to "arms and war materials."

4) *Commercial Agency:* The USSR's Commercial Agency in Iran

[31] *Ibid.*

[32] *Ibid.*, pp. 13-14.

[33] David J. Dallin, *Soviet Russia's Foreign Policy, 1939-1942* (New Haven, 1943), pp. 422-23.

[34] For the full text, see Great Britain, *British and Foreign State Papers, 1940-1942* (London, 1952), pp. 419-34. In past years the Iranian government has merely drawn up a list of commodities to be exchanged each year with the Soviet Commercial Agency. This statement is confirmed by a letter from the Iranian Ministry of Commerce to the author, July 29, 1962.

was attached to the Soviet Embassy. Its functions were (a) assistance in extending Soviet-Iranian economic relations, (b) representation of Soviet interests in the field of foreign trade, (c) organization of commercial transactions in the name of the USSR, and (d) trade between Iran and the USSR. The agent, and "both of his substitutes," enjoyed diplomatic privileges and immunities.

5) *The Caspian Sea:* Vessels flying the flags of one of the two countries should be treated in the same manner as the national vessels of the other country when in the ports of Iran or Russia. No vessels other than those belonging to these countries may "exist in the whole of the Caspian Sea." Each country reserved for its own vessels the exclusive right of fishing in its coastal waters up to a limit of ten nautical miles.

6) *Duration:* The treaty was to be ratified, but it came into force provisionally from the date of signature. It was to last for three years, but if it was not denounced it should *ipso facto* be deemed to be prolonged for "an indefinite period." In this event it might be denounced at any time after six months' notice.

Throughout the course of his trade struggle with Russia the Shah had believed that economic independence from the USSR could be realized only if his efforts for equitable trade and transit terms were matched by measures aimed at economic and communication reconstruction at home. The significance of these measures in relation to the USSR will be discussed after examination of the other major dispute with Moscow confronting the Shah.

This was the long-standing fisheries problem, a legacy of the autocratic era. In 1876 Nāṣir al-Dīn Shah had granted a fisheries concession to a Russian named Stepan Lionosoff. This had been renewed in 1879, 1886, 1893, 1896, and 1906.[35] In the latter year the terms of the concession had been extended to 1925. During the 1918-25 period Iran had become involved in fisheries disputes first with private and later with sovereign claimants. The private claimants were the heirs of the original concessionaire. They had failed to pay royalties during the war, and consequently the government of Iran had canceled the concession in 1918. As a result a dispute had developed between the Iranian government and the heirs. In 1922 Iran appointed an arbitration commission consisting of three distinguished Iranian jurists

[35] Ibrāhīm Taymūrī, *Tārīkh-i Imtīyāzāt dar Īrān* (Tehran, 1332 [1953/54]).

who declared the Iranian cancellation of the concession illegal and extended the life of the concession for a period of fifteen years as compensation for the damages sustained by the concessionaire. In 1923, however, Martin Lionosoff, one of the lawful heirs, ceded all his rights to the Soviet government, a transaction apparently forbidden by the terms of the concession.[36]

This was the status of the concession when Riẕā Khān became Shah. Soviet demands with respect to the fisheries were not based wholly on the acquisition of this concession. During the war the port of Pahlavi, where the most important fishing facilities were located, had been occupied by the Russians, and at the end of the war these facilities had fallen into the possession of the Soviet government. In addition, the Soviet government used Iran's obligation under the treaty of 1921 to press for a fisheries concession. Iran had undertaken to issue the Caspian Sea fisheries concession to Soviet Russia "immediately upon the expiry of the legal period of these existing engagements." This obviously referred to the Lionosoff concession, which would have expired in 1925 had it not been for the extension of its terms for fifteen years as a result of the 1922 award of the arbitration commission. The Soviet Union would therefore have had to wait until 1937 in order to acquire the fisheries concession had not the purchase of the concession from Lionosoff in 1923 taken care of that "inconvenient delay."

A year after this purchase the Soviet government crowned its persistent demands with a proposal to the effect that the fisheries should be leased to a company consisting of the Soviet government and the Iranian government, the two holding equal shares. The Iranian government, on the advice of Dr. Millspaugh, refused to consider the proposal in 1924.[37] The refusal was maintained so long as Dr. Millspaugh was Iran's Administrator-General, but as soon as his contract with the Iranian government expired (in September 1927), the Soviet government found it possible to obtain a fisheries concession more or less along the lines of its proposal.

The most significant provisions of the fisheries concession granted on October 1, 1927, were as follows:

1) *The Joint Company.* The two governments were to organize a

[36] A. C. Millspaugh, *The American Task in Persia* (New York, 1925), p. 299.
[37] *Ibid.*

mixed commercial and industrial company to which the Iranian government would grant a concession to catch and prepare fish along the Iranian South Caspian coast.[38] The parties were to possess equal shares in the company, which was to have a total capital not exceeding 3,000,000 tomans.[39] The company's board of management, located in Tehran, was to consist of six members, three appointed by each government, and was to have as its chairman one of its Iranian members appointed by the Iranian government. The rulings and decisions of the board were to be by majority vote.[40]

2) *Payments.* Iran was to receive 50,000 tomans for each year beginning with 1923 until the concession came into force. This was to be paid in compensation for the fish that the Soviet Union had already taken and might take before the new fisheries arrangement took effect. In addition to this short-term payment in settlement of outstanding claims, Iran was to receive annually, for the whole period of the concession, 80,000 tomans from the gross receipts, 15 per cent from the gross profit, and 50 per cent from the net profit of the company. (The Soviet Union was to receive the other 50 per cent of the net profit.)

3) *The Area of Concession.* The area of this new concession was to coincide with that of the old one granted to Lionosoff. The rivers running into the Caspian Sea were excluded, but the mouths of the Sefid-Rud, Babul, and the Gorgan rivers were an exception.[41]

4) *Duration.* The concession was granted for a period of 25 years from the date of its coming into force. If Iran did not wish to renew it after its expiry, the company was to be considered dissolved and its property was to be divided between the parties. In such a case, however, Iran undertook not to grant a similar concession to a third power for a period of 25 years. Only agents of the Iranian government could exploit fisheries during that period.[42]

The terms of this concession were, no doubt, far more compatible with Iran's interests than those of the Lionosoff concession. In fact, in view of the persistence of over-all Soviet economic pressures on Iran at the time of the signing of the concession it would seem that

[38] Article 1 of the concession. For the text, see J. C. Hurewitz, *Diplomacy in the Near and Middle East* (Princeton, N. J., 1956), II, 150-54.
[39] Articles 4 and 5.
[40] Article 10.
[41] Article 2.
[42] Article 4.

Riẓā Shah made the best of a bad situation. His simultaneous recovery of the port of Pahlavi after over a decade of Russian possession was no mean achievement. But the Achilles heel in the concession was the lack of precise arrangements for the marketing of the Russo-Iranian products. Most of the caviar, for example, was sold abroad by Soviet trading organizations.[43] The main difficulty with the execution of this concession, however, was the same as with other agreements with the USSR – the absence of goodwill. Dissatisfaction with Soviet performance was one of the factors that led the Iranian government not to renew the concession when it expired in 1952.

MEASURES TO REDUCE ECONOMIC DEPENDENCE ON THE USSR

Having bought time with the *ad hoc* agreements regulating trade with the Soviets, Riẓā Shah was not dilatory in attacking the problem of Iranian economic dependence on its northern neighbor. One of the Shah's major steps was to industrialize the economy as much and as swiftly as possible. Only one major aspect of this industrialization will be mentioned here – the development of an Iranian textile industry.

The largest item in Iranian imports had always been cotton textiles, the great bulk of which were imported from Russia.[44] In 1929 Iran spent over 200,000,000 krans on textiles, while its exports of cotton amounted only to 52,000,000 krans, all of which went to the Soviet Union. Thus Iran paid about four times as much for cotton goods as she received for her raw material. In 1931 Riẓā Shah established several new textile mills near Tehran. As a result, imports of Russian cotton goods fell from approximately 21,000,000 rubles in 1930 to about 8,500,000 rubles in 1932.[45] Iran's textile industry now consists of 31 spinning and weaving mills satisfying, together with some hand looms, almost one-half of the present annual requirements of the country.[46]

The second major step of Riẓā Shah toward economic emancipation from the USSR was the introduction of a foreign-trade monopoly.

[43] Conolly, *op. cit.*, p. 64.
[44] *Ibid.*, p. 72.
[45] *Ibid.*, p. 73.
[46] Donald N. Wilber, *Iran: Past and Present* (Princeton, N. J., 1955), p. 155.

No doubt world-wide depression as well as other factors influenced the decision,[47] but the monopoly was in the main precipitated by the Shah's conviction that Iranian merchants could hardly be a match for the Soviet centralized system. As Iran's most important import was cotton piece goods, Riz̤ā Shah established the Cotton Goods Company to protect Iranian private traders. This company, which had a paper capital of 20,000,000 rials and whose shares were held by the National Bank (52 per cent), the Ministry of Finance, and the company directors, was to have a monopoly on the import of cotton piece goods and their sale to private merchants.[48]

The third major step of the Shah was the construction of a national railway system linking the Caspian Sea to the Persian Gulf. Next to the army this was the Shah's dearest project. No doubt the purpose was manifold. A railway would both facilitate and accelerate the process, which had already begun, of establishing complete control by the central government over the provinces. Concomitantly, it would enable the army to ensure internal security with speed and efficiency. Economically it would provide for a better distribution of the country's natural resources; food products of the fertile Caspian littoral could easily be transported to the arid south, and minerals and raw materials could reach the newly established industrial enterprises.[49]

But a most important objective of Riz̤ā Shah in constructing the Trans-Iranian Railway was to decrease and eventually eliminate the traditional dependence of northern Iran on Russian supplies and markets.[50] It has already been pointed out that the fundamental factor underlying this dependence was the primitive condition of Iran's transportation facilities. Only with the USSR was water and rail transport available. And these facilities were in fact detrimental to Iran's interests because they made the country economically dependent on Russia. This dependence had reached a new peak by 1925, when the imports from Russia were nearly ten times larger than they had been in 1921.

[47] Cf. Ahmad Minai, *Economic Development of Iran under the Reign of Reza Shah* (Ph.D. dissertation, American University, 1961), pp. 185-205.

[48] Wilber, *op. cit.*, p. 153.

[49] See Elwell-Sutton, *op. cit.*, p. 94.

[50] Cf. *Journal of the Royal Central Asian Society*, XVII, 346, and XVIII, 81, with the Shah's statement to the correspondent of *Daily Telegraph* of September 5, 1930, as reproduced in Fatḥullāh Nūrī Isfandīyārī, *Rastākhīz-i Īrān* (Tehran, 1335 [1956/57]), p. 489.

To break the Russian economic domination, as early as May 1925 Riẓā Shah decided to finance the Trans-Iranian Railway from the proceeds of taxes on tea and sugar, thus dispensing with ever-suspect foreign aid. The Majlis approved the construction plans in March 1926, and actual work began on October 17, 1927. Riẓā Shah not only steered clear of foreign capital for financing the project but also made every effort to avoid using the nationals or companies of any single power in constructing it. When work began it was supervised by several American and one German expert in the service of the Iranian government. In April 1928 it was entrusted to a syndicate composed of one American and a few German firms. Construction having been started at both ends of the railway, by November 1929 the Germans completed the Bandar Shah-Sari sector in the north and the Americans opened the Bandar Shahpur-Dizful sector in the south. After some delay the work was resumed directly by the government in 1931. In 1933 a Scandinavian syndicate (Consortium Kampsax) took over, but in compliance with Iran's desire the syndicate let out the work in lots to various European companies. The cosmopolitan nature of the undertaking was further evidenced by the way in which the necessary materials were acquired. The steel and cement came from the USSR, the sleepers from Australia, the locomotives from Sweden, the other rolling stock and machinery from Belgium, Germany, and the United States, and further supplies of cement from Japan and Yugoslavia.[51]

Finally the railway was finished, and the first through train was in operation by December 1938. After nearly eleven years of work and a cost of $150,000,000 to $200,000,000 the great project was successfully completed and "perhaps for the first time since the Middle Ages, a major undertaking was carried through in an Oriental country without leaving it indebted to the finances of the West." [52]

This enormous engineering feat – it involved the laying of 1,394 kilometers of rails and the construction of 4,000 bridges, 224 tunnels, and 149 stations – marked the beginning of Iran's major effort to modernize its primitive transportation system in order to further its fundamental objective of politico-economic emancipation.[53] Even the choice of the termini of the Trans-Iranian Railway was dictated by

[51] See Elwell-Sutton, *op. cit.*, pp. 92-93, and Ḥabībullāh Mukhtārī, *Tārīkh-i Bīdārī-i Īrān* (Tehran, 1326 [1947/48]), pp. 374-95.

[52] Elwell-Sutton, *op. cit.*, p. 94.

[53] Mukhtārī, *op. cit.*, pp. 382-87. See also Wilber, *op. cit.*, pp. 167-71.

this objective. Bandar Shah and Bandar Shahpur were less exposed to Russian and British influence than would have been the more obvious cities of Pahlavi and Khoramshahr.[54]

THE FRONTIER AND TERRITORIAL PROBLEMS

Although economic problems were the most important of those confronting Riẓā Shah vis-à-vis the Soviet Union, they were by no means the only ones. The Shah was also concerned with two other sets of problems: one pertaining to old frontier and territorial questions and the other to relatively more recent questions regarding political relations with Communist Russia and the Iranian attitude toward Iranian Communists.

So far as the frontier problems are concerned, it may be appropriate first to trace them briefly to their historical origins. It may be recalled that Iran's old boundaries with Russia had undergone a fundamental change in the nineteenth century. As a result of two wars with Russia in that century the frontier to the west of the Caspian Sea had been established from the Turkish frontier to the summit of Little Ararat, to the Karassan and Aras rivers, and eventually to the Astara River's discharge into the Caspian Sea. As a result of Russian expansion in Central Asia – signaled by the occupation of Krasnovodsk (1869) and culminating in the capture of Merv – the Iranian frontier east of the Caspian Sea had been established from the Hasan Guli Gulf on the Caspian Sea along the course of the Atrek and other rivers to the frontier of Afghanistan. The northwestern frontier had been established by the Treaty of Turkumanchai (1828) and the northeastern boundary by the Treaty of Akhal-Khorasan (1881). Although the Russo-Iranian Treaty had declared null and void "the whole body of treaties and conventions" concluded between Iran and the Tsarist government,[55] it had explicitly confirmed the frontier terms of the Tsarist Treaty of Akhal-Khorasan.[56] Thus Riẓā Shah, like his pre-

[54] Elwell-Sutton, *op. cit.*, p. 94.

[55] Article 1 of the 1921 treaty.

[56] This is clear from Article 3 of the 1921 treaty which mistakenly refers to the lines drawn by "the Frontier Commission" instead of to the terms of the Akhal-Khorasan Treaty (1881). This error was corrected as a result of an exchange of notes between Iran and Soviet Russia, dated December 12, 1921. For the text of these notes, see Shapiro, *op. cit.*, I, 341.

decessors, was committed to the observance of the old frontiers, which had never been satisfactorily demarcated.

Riẕā Shah was determined to resolve the problems attending these frontiers. One of the major questions pertained to the utilization of the frontier waters to the east of the Caspian Sea. The settlement of this problem was embodied in the Shah's earliest treaty with the Soviet Union. The major provisions of the twenty-four-article agreement, concluded on February 20, 1926, may be briefly summarized under two headings:

1) *Joint River Utilization:* Iran and Russia agreed to utilize the waters of three major rivers, namely, (1) the Geri-Rud (Tejen), (2) the Chaacha, and (3) the Kazgan-Chai (Zenginanlu). The waters of the first river were to be divided into ten equal parts, of which Iran was to use three parts and Russia the remaining seven. The waters of the second river were to be divided into two equal parts, of which Iran was to use one part and the USSR the other. The waters of the third river were to be divided into five equal parts, two for the use of Iran and three for the USSR.

2) *Individual River Utilization:* Iran was to use all the waters of the Durungiar River and the Kelte-Chinar River. The USSR was to utilize the water of the Firuzinha (Firuzah) River after the needs of the village of the same name had been met.[57]

Another problem concerned the inhabitants of the districts adjoining the common frontiers. On May 31, 1928, Iran signed a sixteen-article convention with the USSR in order to establish a "simple system" governing the age-old problem of the crossing of the common frontiers by the nationals of Iran and Russia. The fundamental purpose of this convention was to make it possible for the inhabitants of the towns or villages situated within a zone 50 kilometers in breadth (25 kilometers on either side of the common frontier) to cross the boundary line for a variety of purposes including trade, building, and digging operations.[58] This simplified system, however, was wrapped up in all sorts of red tape resulting from the convention's requirement of special frontier permits for those who wished to avail themselves of the new system.

The boundary trouble between Iran and the USSR was only

[57] For the text, see Degras, *op. cit.*, pp. 88-92.

[58] For the text of the convention, see Shapiro, *op. cit.*, I, 366-67.

slightly alleviated by the establishment of this new system. Disputes were bound to arise, partly because the boundaries between Iran and the USSR were neither completely nor clearly demarcated. Nevertheless, both Iran and the USSR failed to pay serious attention to this central problem. In compliance with Article 3 of the Russo-Iranian Treaty of 1921, both countries took measures to establish frontier commissions, but they forbade their commissioners "to settle the differences relating to delimitation [of frontiers] and territorial questions." [59] Thus the frontier muddle which Riẓā Shah inherited from his predecessors, although somewhat relieved during his rule, was bequeathed to his successors.

Another problem which the Shah inherited related to the port of Enzeli. During the war this port had been occupied by the Russians, who continued to control it subsequently.[60] On the same day that the fisheries concession and the commercial "agreement" were signed (October 1, 1927) the Soviet Union agreed to the transfer of the port to the Iranian government. The agreement, taking the form of an exchange of notes, embodied the terms of the transfer, although it provided for a separate "protocol of transfer" at the time of "handing over" the port. By the terms of this nine-article agreement Iran promised to maintain in a good state of repair the installations, port moorings, and territory of the port and to ensure "unhindered access of Soviet commercial sea-going vessels to the port." [61] The Soviet government conceded that all sections and wharves at the port to be used by the Caspian Steamship Company and other Soviet economic agencies "shall not enjoy any extra-territorial rights and shall be subject on equal footing with the remaining territory of the port to all laws, administrative and customs regulations and orders valid for Persian territory." [62] In celebration of Iranian control, the old name associated with the years of intermittent Russian occupation was changed to Pahlavi, the name of the new dynasty founded by the Shah.

[59] See *ibid.*, pp. 338-39 and 375.

[60] Russia's post-1921 occupation was in contravention of Article 10(e) of the 1921 treaty, by which the port was ceded to Iran.

[61] For the text, see Degras, *op. cit.*, pp. 266-69.

[62] Article 3.

POLITICAL PROBLEMS WITH THE USSR

The political problems with the USSR confronting the Shah fell into two categories: those pertaining to Iran's political relations with the USSR itself and those concerning its attitude toward Iranian Communists. In spite of Soviet trade pressures and frontier abuses Riẕā Shah was determined to continue the policy of reconciliation without appeasement that was inaugurated by his predecessors. The principles governing these new relations had been embodied in the Russo-Iranian Treaty of 1921, which repudiated the Tsarist conventions, treaties, and capitulatory privileges.[63] These principles included respect for Iran's independence and sovereignty and noninterference in its internal affairs.[64]

Unfortunately pious Soviet declarations of respect for these principles were often repudiated in practice by the activities of Russian trade representatives, diplomatic personnel, and even ordinary Soviet citizens operating in Iran.[65] The Iranian government, therefore, sought to prevent this "new" form of Russian interference by exposing the activities of these men whenever possible. It also thought it well to look for an opportunity to spell out in detail the principle of noninterference inasmuch as the Russo-Iranian Treaty of 1921 had made only a general reference to that principle.

When Riẕā Shah ascended the throne of Iran in 1925, Russia had begun to seek new bases of relations with a large number of states, particularly with neighboring countries. The Locarno Pact of October 1925 was interpreted by Soviet leaders as a move directed against Soviet Russia and was to be followed, so the Russians believed, by similar treaties between Western powers and Russia's neighbors aimed at the "encirclement" of Russia.[66] In order to forestall such a move Russia concluded treaties of nonaggression and neutrality with Turkey (1925) and Afghanistan (1926) and offered to sign a similar treaty with Iran.

In this offer Riẕā Shah saw his opportunity to conclude a new agreement in which the principle of noninterference would be con-

[63] Articles 1 and 16. [64] Articles 1, 2, and 4. [65] See Agabekov, *op. cit.*
[66] Xenia Joukoff Eudin and Robert C. North, *Soviet Russia and the East* (Stanford, Calif., 1957), pp. 260-263.

cretized and made effective by providing for sanctions. After protracted negotiations a new treaty was concluded on October 1, 1927, the day on which two other agreements and a concession were signed with the USSR. The major terms of this eight-article Treaty of Guarantee and Neutrality and the accompanying protocols and notes may be summarized briefly under two headings:[67]

1) *Nonaggresion and Neutrality:* Iran and Russia undertook to refrain from any aggression or hostile acts against each other. In case one of the two countries became the victim of aggression by a third power or group of powers, the other country was to observe neutrality throughout the duration of the conflict.[68]

2) *Noninterference in Internal Affairs:* Iran and Russia undertook to abstain from any intervention in each other's internal affairs. They also undertook to refrain from any propaganda or campaign against each other. The strict observance of this principle was required of the governments, the officials, and the citizens of the two countries. If a Russian citizen in Iran or an Iranian citizen in Russia violated this principle, he was to be punished by local authorities.[69]

The price that Iran paid for this more specific assurance against interference was not too high. Since Iran was in no position to invade Russia and would wish to remain neutral in case of war anyhow, its pledge was in fact merely declaratory. Furthermore, in the hope of barring any Russian interpretation that might deprive Iran of freedom of action in international relations, the Shah insisted that the treaty should provide that apart from obligations undertaken under it Iran would enjoy full freedom of action.[70] This was further spelled out in Iran's note attached to the text of the treaty stating that Iran will "respect and carry out all its obligations as a member of the League of Nations."

The most irritating problem in Iran's political relations with Russia still remained to be resolved. This problem stemmed from the ambiguity of Articles 5 and 6 of the 1921 treaty, which were confirmed by the 1927 treaty.[71] These articles had prohibited the formation or presence within Russian or Iranian territory of "any organizations or groups of persons . . . whose object is to engage in acts of hostility" against Iran or Russia. More important, Russia had been given "the

[67] For the text of these, see Shapiro, *op. cit.*, I, 340-41.
[68] Article 1.
[69] Article 4.
[70] Article 6.
[71] The text is in Hurewitz, *op. cit.*, II, 90-94.

right to dispatch troops to Iran" if a third party should militarily intervene in Iran, or should desire to use Iranian territory as a base against Russia, or should threaten the frontiers of Russia.

The Majlis had sought clarification of these articles before ratification, and in its note of December 12, 1921, Russia stated that they

> are intended to apply only to cases in which preparations have been made for considerable armed attack upon Russia or the Soviet Republics allied to her, by the partisans of the régime which had been overthrown or by its supporters among those foreign Powers which are in a position to assist the enemies of the Workers and Peasants Republics and at the same time to possess themselves by force or underhand methods, of part of Persian territory, thereby establishing a base of operations for any attacks – made either directly or through the counter-revolutionary forces – which they might meditate against Russia or the Soviet Republics allied to her. The Articles referred to are therefore in no sense intended to apply to verbal or written attacks directed against the Soviet Government by the various Persian groups, or even any Russian *émigrés* in Persia, in so far as such attacks are generally tolerated as between neighbouring Powers.[72]

Riẓā Shah was probably as unhappy with Articles 5 and 6 of the 1921 treaty as the Majlis deputies who had obtained the foregoing Russian "explanations." His government might have wished to denounce Articles 5 and 6 on the ground of "fundamental change of conditions," inasmuch as the White Russians and the anti-Communist nationalist Armenians (Dashnaks) were no longer, Iran believed, a threat to Russia as they had been in 1920-21. But in view of Iran's continuing need of Russian markets and the newness of his regime, the Shah was too shrewd to pick a fight with Russia. In fact, in 1927 he did not hesitate to confirm "all articles" of the 1921 treaty (including Articles 5 and 6) in the new treaty with Russia,[73] mentioned earlier. Confirmation of crucial Article 6 was clearly spelled out also in Protocol II attached to the 1927 treaty.

By 1935, however, Moscow seemed more receptive to Iran's desire to repeal Article 6 of the 1921 treaty. This was in line with a signifi-

[72] For the text, see *ibid.*

[73] The 1927 treaty was concluded, according to Article 6, for a period of three years. After the expiration of this period it was to be regarded as automatically prolonged for successive periods of one year until one of the parties notified the other of its desire to denounce it. In that case the treaty "shall remain in force for six months from the date of the notification of its denunciation by one of the Parties."

cant change in over-all Soviet foreign policy. In September 1934 the USSR had entered the League of Nations. This event had marked the modification of Soviet policy in the direction of collective security. The Iranian government had seen in this development the opportunity to point out that the Covenant provisions provided the Soviets with the guarantees of security that they had sought to obtain by means of Article 6 of the 1921 treaty. This article was therefore even more futile in the 1930's than it had been in the 1920's.

On December 28, 1935, the Soviet representative in Iran proposed a protocol which, if concluded, would have declared Article 6 of the 1921 Treaty null and void.[74] This legal instrument was to be ratified by the "legislative authorities"' of the two governments. However, it appears that no further action was taken on the proposed protocol and as a result the long-disputed Article 6 hangs over Iran like the sword of Damocles.

Riz̤ā Shah's attitude toward Iranian Communists was definitely hostile. The Shah's antagonism toward them could not have been a measure of retaliation against the official Soviet attitude toward him. Soviet Russia had been in favor of the new regime in Iran as early as 1921, when Riz̤ā Khān engineered the *coup d'état*. This benevolent Soviet attitude seems to have been ideologically based. One school of Soviet Marxism, represented by V. A. Gurko-Kriazhin, F. Raskolnikov, and others, regarded the Shah's regime as a national liberation movement of anti-imperialist and semibourgeois character, and as such deserving of Soviet support,[75] and this school apparently prevailed. More important, however, was Russia's support for a "strong central government" like that of Riz̤ā Shah because such a government seemed at the time to aid the Soviet geostrategic interests in Iran, as evidenced by the change in the Russian attitude toward the settlement of the Gilan problem, discussed in Chapter VIII.

What then could explain Riz̤ā Shah's antagonism toward the Communists? Could it be attributed to his "democratic" inclinations? Certainly not. To call the dictatorial Shah a democrat is to mock the expression. The Shah had no taste for ideology, whether democracy or communism. To him the ideologue was a man who indulged

[74] Article 2 of the proposed protocol. A copy of the full text of the protocol is in the possession of the author.

[75] For details, see George Lenczowski, *Russia and the West in Iran, 1918-1948* (Ithaca, N. Y., 1949), pp. 86-91.

in excessive and useless talk and deserved no respect. He liked "practical men" and strove throughout his rule to demonstrate that he himself was one of the best examples of such men.

Riẓā Shah's anticommunism was fundamentally a reflection of his over-all suspicion of foreign interference in Iranian affairs. It was a manifestation of the Shah's extreme nationalism. To Riẓā Shah nothing was worse than foreign control, British or Russian. In dramatizing his fear of foreign interference in Iran's affairs he once went so far as to state that if the choice were between communism and foreign control he would favor the former.[76]

Because of his hatred of foreign interference, intrigue, and control, the Shah opposed most vigorously any action or concept, overt or covert, direct or indirect, verbal or actual, that seemed to him to favor foreign interest in Iran. To him the most depraved of all people were those Iranians, Communists or others, who served foreign interests. The Shah's distrust of such people had been clearly demonstrated in both words and action before he ascended the throne. In his second Prime Ministerial Proclamation he declared that in a sovereign and independent state nothing deserved a more severe condemnation than the act of those nationals who allowed themselves to become the political instrument of foreign powers. Not even to gain a livelihood would any honorable and patriotic citizen assist foreign meddlers in his country's internal affairs. Death in poverty would be preferable to such contemptible living.[77]

The Shah had shown this same hatred toward the Communists and their sympathizers. His troops had routed the Bolshevist "intruders" (*Mutijāsirīn*) and the Jangalī forces, pursued Iḥsānullāh Khān, Shujā' al-Sultān, and Mīrzā Kūchik Khān, and captured Khālū Qurbān.

Riẓā Khān had adopted a benevolent attitude toward the Socialists as evidenced by his appointing Sulaymān Mīrzā, the leading Socialist, to the post of Minister of Education and by supporting his election to the Fourth and Fifth Majlis as well as to the Constitutional Assembly which declared Riẓā Khān the Shah of Iran.[78] But his benevolent attitude toward the Socialists, as well as his antagonism

[76] The Shah made this statement in an interview; see Isfandīyārī, *op. cit.*, pp. 487-88.

[77] For the text of the proclamation, see Husayn Makkī, *Tārīkh-i Bīst Sālah-'i Īrān* (Tehran, 1324 [1945/46]), II, 297-99.

[78] *Ibid.*, p. 287, and III, 484-586.

toward the Communists, was not based on ideological predilection. Rather it was a manifestation of his sense of opportunism. He utilized the Socialist support in the Majlis, during his rise to power, against his fierce opponent Mudarris. But once he gained complete control of the government, Socialists and Communists alike suffered severe blows from his repressive policy.

The police and the army were the major instruments of that policy. The Fifth Majlis, as has been seen, sanctioned Riẓā Khān's control of these instruments, which he used throughout his rule, at times ruthlessly, in suppressing any opposition coming from groups, from individuals, or from the press. Even before May 19, 1931, when the Shah secured the enactment of a law for the suppression of "political and press offences," his repressive measures had taken a heavy toll of all possible sources of opposition. The Communists, regarded by the Shah as the most vicious instrument of Soviet Russia, were the primary target of his campaign of imprisonment of "political suspects." He stamped out the few trade unions that had emerged and went so far as to forbid use of the word "worker," which to him symbolized a person affiliated with a union.[79] The ill fate of the Communists in the late 1920's is attested by Soviet Consul General Vayman at Tehran, who found the Communist party organization "chaotic," the number of Communists small, and their ranks haunted by "spies" of the Iranian police.[80]

After the enactment of the 1931 law the Communist group experienced an even greater misfortune. In 1935 *Dunyā* ("The World"), the only Communist publication, was suspended. Twelve issues of this monthly magazine had been published and circulated openly because its editors had managed to camouflage the true nature of their message. In 1937 the Communists received a still severer blow. All 53 members of the Communist group were imprisoned. The group had been formed upon the return of Dr. Muḥammad Bahrāmī to Iran from Berlin, where he had cultivated a taste for Communist ideology while studying medicine. In Iran he had contacted Dr. Taqī Arānī, the leading Communist, and 'Abd al-Ṣamad Kāmbakhsh and Īraj Iskandarī. These men had been part of the elite which led the

[79] Stanley B. Alpern, "Iran, 1941-1946, A Case Study in the Soviet Theory of Colonial Revolution" (Thesis, Columbia University, 1953), p. 14.
[80] Agabekov, *op. cit.*, p. 112.

group. Kāmbakhsh and Riẕā Rūstā, another member of the elite, were charged with being espionage agents for a foreign power, and the former was sentenced to ten years' imprisonment. Dr. Bahrāmī and two other Communist leaders, Ardishīr Uvānisīān and Muḥammad Buqrāṭī, also drew ten-year sentences.[81]

These measures drove the Communists underground, and they did not reappear on the political scene of Iran until after the abdication of the Shah. At that time those who were still in prison were freed together with other "political prisoners."

THE WINNING OF INDEPENDENCE

The nature of Riẕā Shah's struggle against Russia and the degree of his success in winning Iran's independence must be viewed against the drama of Iran's progressive subjugation by Russia from the conclusion of the first war with Russia (1813) to the early 1920's. Iran had been independent largely in name before Riẕā Shah, but by the late 1930's it enjoyed an unprecedented degree of freedom of action vis-à-vis Russia. Admittedly, Russia's outward friendliness and abstention from outright intervention assisted the cause of Riẕā Shah. But this should not minimize the Shah's difficulties with Moscow, which were significantly overcome as the result of his diplomacy.

That diplomacy had many shortcomings, but the Shah's battle for independence was generally successful. His playing for time by concluding temporary trade agreements with Russia was probably the only course that a policy maker could have pursued in the face of Russia's relentless utilization of Iran's economic dependency as a means of political pressure. Furthermore, to the extent that these agreements introduced some order into the trade relations of the two countries, Iran was better off.

In historical perspective, it is revealing to note that the Shah's playing for time was not merely a matter of procrastination. The simultaneous efforts toward industrialization and economic self-sufficiency, the establishment of a foreign trade monopoly, and the con-

[81] See Iran, *Sayr-i Kumunīzm dar Īrān* (Tehran, 1335 [1956/57]), pp. 210-11, and *Kitāb-i Sīyāh dar Bārah-i Afsarān-i Īrān* (Tehran, 1334 [1955/56]), pp. 15-16.

struction of the Trans-Iranian Railway were all aimed in part at Iran's economic and political emancipation from Russia. One may criticize the grant of the fisheries concession, but it must be remembered that its terms were far more beneficial to Iran than those of the earlier concession and, more importantly, the fisheries concession was utilized, once there was little hope of withholding it, as bait to recover the port of Enzeli from Russian possession. Even the failure to act on the proposed 1935 protocol for the abrogation of Article 6 of the 1921 treaty may not be blamed on the Shah. There is no evidence that he refused to conclude it. Probably Russia refused because it benefited from the article.

True, Articles 5 and 6 of the 1921 treaty continued to haunt Iran and the boundary problems were not resolved, but these problems could not then, and cannot today, be settled without compatibility of interests and a spirit of compromise. For this reason Riẓā Shah cannot be blamed for their continued existence. What is important in the perspective of this study, is the fact that Riẓā Shah selected strategies with a high degree of success for achieving his fundamental goal of politico-economic emancipation. His strategies may seem too crude at times, but the fact remains that he significantly departed from the traditional inept foreign policies. He knew his target and his capabilities most of the time, although his Russophobia in the end pushed him too far onto the side of his favorite third power, Germany.

Chapter X

Riẕā Shah's Disputes with Britain, 1925-1941

RELATIONS with Great Britain constituted the Shah's second major foreign-policy concern. Only those with Russia posed a more serious problem. The fact that the British government was in favor of a strong central government such as that of Riẕā Shah significantly assisted the Shah's policy of emancipation from British domination, but the Shah's shrewd diplomatic approach was by no means unimportant in the policy's success. By the time of Riẕā's succession to the throne the problems of the 1919 agreement and of the reestablishment of the central government's control over the province of Khuzistan had been resolved. But these problems were less difficult than those which remained to be settled, the complexity and seriousness of which derived from the fact that they involved the status of Iran vis-à-vis Great Britain.

The traditional Anglo-Russian rivalry had resulted, not only in the ever-growing control of Russia over the affairs of Iran, but also in the politico-economic ascendancy of Great Britain, particularly in the south. British control and influence had been second only to Russia's before the Bolshevik Revolution. After the Revolution they had increased to an unprecedented extent. In fact, of the two rival powers only Great Britain still possessed capitulatory privileges in Iran when Riẕā Shah ascended the throne. Abolition of these privileges was one of the Shah's major goals. The other two problems pertained to sovereignty over the Bahrein Islands and to the D'Arcy oil concession.

THE ABOLITION OF CAPITULATIONS

Riẕā Shah inherited the capitulatory regime from the Qājār dynasty. The disastrous defeat of the ill-equipped Iranian forces in Fatḥ 'Alī Shah's second war with Russia (1826-28) resulted in the humiliating Treaty of Turkumanchai (1828), which excluded Russian subjects from Iranian jurisdiction. Britain found the opportunity to demand similar privileges for its subjects at the end of the war of 1856-57 when it signed a treaty with Iran at Paris. Furthermore, the British commercial treaty (1903), which had been precipitated by the Russian commercial treaty (1901), had confirmed the extraterritorial privileges of Great Britain in Iran. Other powers such as France, Belgium, Austria, Czechoslovakia, the Netherlands, and Sweden had also acquired capitulatory privileges in Iran.[1]

Riẕā Shah's decision to abolish the capitulatory regime was directed particularly against Great Britain because, by the early 1920's, it alone of the two rival powers continued to enjoy capitulatory privileges in Iran – Russia having relinquished its privileges in 1918.

Riẕā Shah realized that he must not antagonize Great Britain while pressuring it to attain the abrogation of capitulations. After all, Great Britain was Iran's most powerful neighbor, in territorial contact with it on three frontiers by virtue of the British political position in India, in the Persian Gulf, and, more recently, in Iraq. Furthermore, Great Britain would be most affected by the abolition of the capitulatory regime because the British community in Iran greatly outnumbered the total of all foreign residents belonging to the other Western countries concerned.[2]

With this in mind, the Shah relied on three principal measures

[1] See Royal Institute of International Affairs, *Documents on International Affairs, 1928* (London, 1929), p. 209. See also Chapters II and IV of this study.

[2] Royal Institute of International Affairs, *Survey of International Affairs, 1928* (London, 1929), p. 351.

to bring about British acquiescence in his decision to end the privileges. First, he energetically sought to modernize the country's legal system. Since the adoption of the Constitution in 1906-7 Iran had taken some measures toward modernization, but the old sectarian-oriented judiciary system still dominated the scene in the twenties. The Shīʿī legal order had long failed to meet the demands of modern life. The religious law (the *shariʿah*) had, in theory, governed relationships of all kinds, both toward God and man. In practice, however, it dealt with religious rites and duties, with contracts and obligations, with personal affairs, and with sumptuary rules and judicial procedure, and left most political, administrative, and commercial activities untouched. Within the Shīʿī system there had also been another body of law commonly called *ʿurf*, which, in theory, governed certain established customs and traditions which had preceded the Islamic era of Iran and which had varied from one locality to another. This twin body of laws had given rise to two systems of courts, the religious and the civil (*Maḥākim-i Sharʿ* and *Maḥākim-i ʿurf*, respectively).[3]

It was not merely the fact that the laws were outmoded that caused Western powers to seek exemption for their citizens residing in Iran from appearance in Iranian courts. A most important factor was the maladministration of the laws. Confusion was universal in regard to the jurisdiction of the religious and civil courts. Universal also were the crude justice and corruption of the courts. Under the circumstances many claimants resorted to private arbitration, which was both cheaper and more efficient.[4] But, of course, this was no solution to the pressing need for a modern legal order.

Riẕā Shah's decision to meet this need was prompted more by pride than by dedication to a "bill of rights." He sought to modernize the judiciary system in order to extricate the country from foreign capitulations and only secondarily from the grinding injustice inflicted upon the Iranian people. If the Iranian people consequently enjoyed a relatively better system, it was mainly serendipital. Legal reforms, like most economic projects and particularly the gigantic Trans-Iranian Railway system, were basically aimed at winning "real"

[3] See R. K. Ramazani, "The Shiʿi System: Its Conflict and Interaction with Other Systems," *Proceedings of the American Society of International Law*, 1959, pp. 53-60.

[4] *Ibid.*

independence for Iran rather than at providing more effective guarantees of the rights of the individual.[5] On the occasion of the reorganization of the Ministry of Justice, the Shah was quoted as saying: "The *prestige of a nation* depends upon the quality of its justice." [6]

The reorganization of the Ministry of Justice on April 26, 1927, marked only the beginning of the transformation of the judiciary system. Eager to notify Great Britain formally of the abolition of the capitulations, the Shah rushed through the Majlis the first volume of a civil code, which was in part based on the civil code of France. The legal reforms thus started continued after the abolition of the capitulations.

The second technique Riẕā Shah used to end capitulations was exploitation of a British desideratum. Great Britain needed to complete an air route which was to run from Cairo to Karachi. The first portion of this route would pass over Arab territories under British control in one form or another and reach the Persian Gulf. The continuation of the route from that point to the western frontier of the British Indian Empire in Baluchistan required the grant of a right of way by Iran. Great Britain had signed a provisional agreement with Iran in 1925 for this purpose, but Iranian ratification was delayed in order to exert pressure against Great Britain.[7] This pressure was further increased by the Shah's grant of a concession for internal air services in Iran to the German firm of Junkers and his signing of a protocol with Russia for a weekly air postal service between Pahlavi and Baku.[8]

The tariff was the third means adopted to bring about the end of capitulations. On May 10, 1927, the Iranian government notified Great Britain and all other Western powers enjoying capitulatory privileges in Iran that those privileges would be abolished on May 10, 1928.[9] To ensure acceptance of this decree the Majlis, three days before the deadline, approved a new customs tariff the maximum

[5] *Ibid.*

[6] Italics supplied. See Ahmad Khan Matine Daftary, *La suppression des capitulations en Perse* (Paris, 1930), pp. 179-80.

[7] Royal Institute of International Affairs, *Survey, 1928*, p. 352.

[8] *Ibid.*

[9] For the text of Iran's circular to foreign legations in Tehran, see Royal Institute of International Affairs, *Documents, 1928*, p. 200.

scale of which was double the tariff of 1927. This tariff was made applicable to imports from all countries except those to which more favorable terms were specially conceded by existing, noncapitulatory treaties or by new treaties. The only existing treaty at the time was the October 1, 1927, commercial agreement with the Soviet Union. Thus the Soviet Union would be the only foreign power to which the new high tariff would not apply unless other powers also entered into new treaties with Iran. The conclusion of such treaties would require the abrogation of the capitulations.[10]

The Shah's measures produced the desired result. On May 10, 1928, Iran's negotiations with Great Britain resulted in a new commercial agreement. Furthermore, Great Britain was satisfied by an Iranian official note of the same date describing the projected treatment of British nationals in Iran subsequent to the abolition of the capitulations. These documents signaled the beginning of a new era in the relations of Iran and Great Britain. Their provisions may be summarized as follows:

1) *Trade:* Great Britain recognized Iran's tariff autonomy by agreeing to the abrogation of all provisions of the existing treaties which limited in any way the right of Iran to determine the Iranian customs tariff in full autonomy. In return, Iran agreed to apply the minimum rates of its single legal tariff to its commerce with Great Britain. In cases in which the tariff prescribed ad valorem duties on importation into Iran, the duties were to be equal to the market price of the goods in question.

Both Great Britain and Iran undertook, for the eight-year term of the treaty, to refrain from introducing any restrictive or prohibitive measures which might hinder mutual commercial relations. They agreed, however, on a number of classes of prohibitions and restrictions such as those relating to public security and health, traffic in military supplies, the protection of national treasures, and "the vital interests of the country." [11]

2) *Treatment of British Nationals:* Great Britain agreed to Iran's abrogation of the capitulations. In return Iran assured Great Britain that its nationals in Iran would enjoy the benefits of the modern

[10] Royal Institute of International Affairs, *Survey, 1928,* p. 354.

[11] For the text, see Royal Institute of International Affairs, *Documents, 1928,* pp. 200-5.

Iranian legal system. The most important among these benefits were: no foreigner would be arrested or imprisoned without a warrant emanating from a competent judicial authority; no foreigner arrested in the act of committing a crime would be kept in prison for more than twenty-four hours without being brought to competent judicial authority; and the private or business premises of a foreigner would be immune from seizure. Furthermore, "in every case" foreigners would be tried by "lay" (nonreligious) tribunals applying the laws. Inasmuch as the Iranian Civil Code was based on Islamic law in regard to questions of "personal status," non-Muslim British nationals in Iran involved in such questions were placed beyond the reach of Iranian courts.[12]

Iran's agreement with Great Britain in regard to trade and the treatment of nationals was followed by similar agreements with other capitulatory powers. These agreements were negotiated with France (May 10, 1928), Belgium (May 15), Austria (June 17), Czechoslovakia (June 17), the Netherlands (June 21), Italy (June 29), and Sweden (August 9). Agreements with the governments of the United States and Germany took the form of unilateral declarations on May 14 and 15, respectively.[13]

REASSERTION OF CLAIM OF SOVEREIGNTY OVER BAHREIN

The second Iranian controversy with Great Britain involved sovereignty over the Bahrein Islands. In 1820 Great Britain had entered into treaty relations with the Al-Khalīfah dynasty in Bahrein. This treaty, together with others concluded in 1847, 1856, 1861, 1880, and 1892, had established British "exclusive and far-reaching" control over the foreign relations of the Sheikh of Bahrein.[14] Iran had protested British control on several occasions prior to the reign of Riẕā Shah. The Shah's reassertion in 1927 of Iran's historical claims

[12] For the text of the Iranian note of assurances, see *ibid.*, pp. 205-9.

[13] *Ibid.*, p. 209.

[14] Royal Institute of International Affairs, *Survey of International Affairs, 1934* (London, 1935), p. 220. For a concise historical survey see also James H. D. Belgrave, "A Brief Survey of the History of the Bahrein Islands," *Journal of the Royal Central Asian Society*, January 1952, pp. 57-68.

was precipitated by the Anglo-Saudi treaty of May 20 of that year. Article 6 of the treaty clearly implied British sovereign control over the Bahrein Islands by obligating Ibn Saud to refrain from interference with the "Chief" of the islands.

On November 22, 1927 Iran protested the British government's claim to sovereignty over Bahrein [15] and circulated its note of protest in the League of Nations. Great Britain rejected Iran's claim on January 18, 1928.[16] In the face of the British position, Iran reiterated its claim on August 2, 1928. Iran's deteriorating relations with Great Britain over the Bahrein Islands worsened in 1929 and in 1930. On January 5, 1929, the government of the Shah protested against a British regulation requiring Iranian citizens to produce passports in order to visit the Bahrein Islands.[17] The British government ignored this last protest and instead addressed itself on February 18, 1929, to the historical and judicial questions raised in Iran's previous notes.[18] The British arguments were not accepted by the Shah's government, which found a third opportunity in 1930 to reiterate Iran's "incontestable rights of sovereignty over the Bahrein Islands." This opportunity came when a statement appeared in *Near East and India* and the Baghdad *Times* to the effect that a British syndicate had obtained a concession from the Sheikh of Bahrein.[19]

Iran's claim to sovereignty over Bahrein rested basically upon four major grounds. First, it claimed that "Bahrein has always and uninterruptedly formed part of Persia in past centuries, except during the Portuguese occupation from 1507 to 1622, in which year the Persian Government resumed possession of this territory." [20] The British government questioned the validity of this claim: "It is impossible to accept the view that the island was continuously subject to Persia before 1507." Furthermore, the period of Iranian rule which was resumed in 1622 was ended in 1783 when the Iranian troops were driven out by the Utubi Arabs. Even before 1783 "it is

[15] For Iran's note, see *League of Nations Official Journal*, 1928, p. 605.

[16] For the British note, see *ibid.*, pp. 605-7.

[17] The text of the protest note is in the *League of Nations Official Journal*, 1929, p. 351.

[18] For the British note see *ibid.*, p. 73.

[19] The text of the protest note is in *League of Nations Official Journal*, 1930, p. 1083.

[20] *League of Nations Official Journal*, 1928, p. 1361.

not to be supposed," Great Britain contended, that Iran's rule was "continuous and unchallenged." [21]

Second, Iran claimed:

A territory belonging to a sovereign state cannot be lawfully detached so long as the right of ownership has not been transferred by this State to another State in virtue of an official act, in this case a treaty, or so long as its annexation by another State or its independence have not been officially recognized by the lawful owner of the territory.[22]

Great Britain refuted this argument by denying "without hesitation" that any such principle formed part of international law.[23]

Third, Iran claimed:

The Sheikhs of Bahrein have always recognized Persian sovereignty, and that not merely down to the end of the eighteenth century. Later authentic documents exist in which they declare their entire submission and loyalty to the central government; moreover – and this is an incontrovertible proof of their dependence – they paid taxes which they owed to the State.[24]

Great Britain countered this argument by asserting that the sheikhs might have professed unwilling allegiance to Iran as they had to Musqat, to Egypt, or to the Wahabi Arabs in order to obtain protection against "warlike and more powerful States" surrounding the Bahrein Islands. No documents showing such an allegiance or even evidence of payment of taxes to the Shah could be regarded "as establishing the validity of Persia's claim."

Fourth, Iran relied heavily on two specific documents in support of its position. In 1822 Captain William Bruce had concluded an agreement with the Prince Governor of Shiraz.[25] "This agreement," Iran claimed,

may have been promptly disavowed, at the time, by the proper representative of His Britannic Majesty as having been entered into without authority. But, though disavowed, it continued to be an historical document of inestimable value. . . . The historical truth which

[21] *Ibid.*, p. 791.
[22] *Ibid.*, p. 1360.
[23] *Ibid.*, p. 791.
[24] *Ibid.*, p. 1361.
[25] The text of the agreement is in Fereydoun Adamiyat, *Bahrein Islands, A Legal and Diplomatic Study of the British-Iranian Controversy* (New York, 1955), pp. 253-55.

emerges from this agreement is the assertion and confirmation by Captain Bruce of the fact that the islands of Bahrein then formed part of the Persian province of Fars.[26]

Great Britain denied this claim by stating that Captain Bruce had entered into negotiations without authority and he had been recalled because his agreement "acknowledges the King of Persia's title to Bahrein, of which there is not the least proof."[27] The other document on which Iran relied was the Earl of Clarendon's note of April 29, 1869.[28] Iran claimed that this note "offered convincing proof not only of the fragility of the rights which the British Government claims to posses but also of the sovereignty of Persia over the Bahrein Islands."[29] Great Britain disclaimed the validity of any such interpretation by asserting that the note merely stated that due consideration had been given to the claim of the Iranians, "but it did not admit that their claim was valid."[30]

In spite of reasserting Iran's claim to Bahrein, the Shah did not act beyond lodging protests against Great Britain. This did not mean, however, that Iran relinquished its claim of sovereignty over Bahrein. In fact, the Iranian government has reiterated its claim on various occasions.[31] In any event, by the early 1930's Iran's dispute with the Anglo-Iranian Oil Company came to dominate the relations between Iran and Great Britain.

CANCELLATION OF THE D'ARCY CONCESSION; THE 1933 AGREEMENT

On November 27, 1932, the Iranian government informed the Anglo-Iranian Oil Company that it had decided to cancel the D'Arcy concession and would consider it void.[32] On the following day the com-

[26] *League of Nations Official Journal*, 1928, p. 1362.
[27] *League of Nations Official Journal*, 1929, p. 792.
[28] The texts of Clarendon's note and Iran's reply are in Adamiyat, *op. cit.*, pp. 258-60.
[29] *League of Nations Official Journal*, 1928, p. 1362.
[30] *League of Nations Official Journal*, 1929, p. 792.
[31] For opposite views on this claim, see Adamiyat, *op. cit.*, and Majid Khadduri, "Iran's Claim to the Sovereignty of Bahrayn," *American Journal of International Law*, October 1951, pp. 631-47.
[32] *League of Nations Official Journal*, 1932, p. 2301.

pany questioned the legality of the cancellation and demanded the withdrawal of the notification.[33] The British government vigorously protested the cancellation on December 2, 1932, and in a threatening note warned Iran that it "would not tolerate any damage to the Company's interests or interference with their premises or business activities in Persia." [34] Iran's reply was a sharply worded letter on December 3, 1932, in which it denied responsibility "for any damage accruing to the company," declaring that "responsibility for any damage which the company may possibly suffer will rest on the company itself." [35]

The next phase of the dispute took place within the League of Nations. On December 14, 1932, the British government referred the dispute to the Council, and on December 19, 1932, the Iranian government decided to appear before the Council to state its case.[36] The submission of the dispute to the Council was a reversal of the initial British intention of referring the matter to the Permanent Court of International Justice.[37] This change came about as a result of an Iranian note of December 12, 1932, which denied the competence of the Court, charged Great Britain with intimidation, and stated that it was within its right to bring the British action to the attention of the Council. It was the realization of Iran's right to submit the dispute to the Council that persuaded Great Britain to reverse its stand. Iran's right derived from the terms of its acceptance of the Court's jurisdiction. Under those terms it could demand the suspension of proceedings in the Court in regard to any dispute which had been submitted to the Council.

Before proceeding to the outcome of the dispute, let us investigate the factors underlying the cancellation decision and Iran's basic objective in making that decision. There is no doubt that the decision was precipitated by the unusual shrinkage in Iran's share of the profits from petroleum for the year 1931.[38] This shrinkage was the reflection of the low level of the company's profits due to "the extremely de-

[33] *Ibid.*, p. 2302.
[34] *Ibid.*
[35] *Ibid.*
[36] *League of Nations Official Journal*, 1933, p. 289.
[37] See the British note of December 8, 1932, in *League of Nations Official Journal*, 1932, p. 492.
[38] Benjamin Shwadran, *The Middle East, Oil and the Great Powers* (New York, 1956), p. 51.

pressed" state of the oil industry.[39] Cancellation of the concession, however, would probably not have occurred in the absence of more fundamental grievances resulting from Iran's contractual relationship with the company. These factors involved the conditions attending the contract both at its inception (see Chapter IV) and in the course of its execution and interpretation. As the Anglo-Iranian Oil Company's activities in Iran had increased, particularly after 1908, when the first geyser of oil burst out at Masjid Sulayman, Iranians had become increasingly aware of this source of national wealth and had started to resent its exploitation by a foreign concern. The conditions under which the concession had been originally granted were more closely scrutinized, with the result that by 1932 the Iranian government charged that it had been "obtained under duress and deception" and was therefore void. When the concession was canceled, the manner of its granting was placed at the top of the list of Iran's grievances.

Other grievances were numerous, and they related to a wide variety of questions ranging from the general charge that the concessionaire had not complied with the terms of the contract to the specific complaint that the company refused to pay income taxes to the Iranian government. By 1932 three major issues embittered the relations of the government and the company. The first issue involved divergent interpretations of Article 10 of the contract, which provided that the company was to pay the Iranian government 16 per cent of the annual net profits of any company or companies that might be formed. The Iranian government interpreted this to apply to all companies operating in or outside Iran. The company, on the other hand, contended that it applied only to companies operating in Iran.

The second issue concerned responsibilities for the cutting of the pipeline by the Bakhtyārī tribes during the First World War and the resultant damages. The company maintained that Iran had failed to protect the properties of the company in compliance with Article 14 of the contract and therefore withheld royalties due to Iran. The Iranian government denied liability for damages on the ground that the cutting had taken place as the result of war operations and through the incitement of one of the belligerent powers, an act clearly beyond

[39] Royal Institute of International Affairs, *Survey, 1934*, p. 237, and Muṣṭafā Fātaḥ, *Panjāh Sāl Naft-i Īrān* (Tehran, 1335 [1956/57]), p. 291.

its control. The withholding of royalties by the company was therefore unjustified, and the government requested arbitration under Article 17 of the contract.[40]

The third issue related to the Armitage-Smith agreement signed on December 22, 1920. Prior to the *coup d'état* of 1921 the second government of Vuṣūq al-Dawlah (1918-20), while seeking to implement the ill-fated 1919 Anglo-Persian Agreement, decided to appoint Sidney Armitage-Smith as the Iranian representative to adjust all questions, including the two issues mentioned above, in dispute between Iran and the company. After the *coup d'état* the government, while renouncing the 1919 agreement which was the basis of Armitage-Smith's appointment, designated William McClintock, a British chartered accountant, to study anew the financial disputes between Iran and the company. This brought into question the Armitage-Smith agreement. Iran took the view that it was no agreement at all: first, because Armitage-Smith had exceeded his authority in drawing up an agreement purporting to effect changes in the D'Arcy concession; second, because the "alleged agreement has never been officially recognized or ratified by the Persian Government." Iran claimed that it had "only unofficially acquiesced in this arrangement as a *modus vivendi* for the time being."[41]

Discussion of these issues constituted the main body of the written memoranda of Great Britain and Iran to the League of Nations and of the oral presentation of their representatives before the Council. The brilliant skirmishes of Dāvar and Sir John Simon cleared the air for negotiations between Iran and the company outside the Council.[42] On February 3, 1932, Eduard Benes, the *rapporteur*, reported to the Council that Great Britain and Iran had agreed that the company would enter into direct negotiations with the government of Iran. The negotiations that were begun in February 1933 finally resulted in the signing of a new contract between Iran and the company.

The new concessionary contract consisted of twenty-six articles, the major provisions of which follow:

[40] *League of Nations Official Journal*, 1933, pp. 295-96.

[41] For the text of the letter of Iran's oil commissioner to the company, see *ibid.*, pp. 298-99.

[42] For a full exposition of the Iranian arguments, see Iran's memorandum and oral presentation, *ibid.*, pp. 289-94 and 204-11, respectively. See also the British memorandum and oral presentation in the *League of Nations Official Journal*, 1932 and 1933, pp. 2298-305 and pp. 197-204, respectively.

1) *The Right and Area of the Concession:* Iran granted the company the exclusive right to search for and extract petroleum as well as to refine or treat in any other manner and render suitable for commerce the petroleum obtained by it. The total area selected under the new concession was not to exceed 100,000 square miles.

2) *Payment to the Iranian Government:* Payment to the Iranian government was based upon: (a) annual royalty of four shillings per ton of petroleum sold in or exported from Iran; (b) a sum equal to 20 per cent of the distribution to ordinary stockholders in excess of £671,250. The total amount to be paid by the company under sections (a) and (b) was never to fall below £750,000.

3) *Duration:* The concession was granted for the period beginning on the date of its coming into force and ending on December 31, 1993. (The concession was signed on April 29, 1933, ratified by the Majlis on May 28, 1933, and promulgated by Riẕā Shah on May 29, 1933).[43]

Riẕā Shah's policy objective in the oil dispute of 1932-33 with Great Britain is often misunderstood. To no small extent this is because of the anti-British sentiments of most Iranian observers. In 1952, when these sentiments reached a new peak, it was publicly charged that the cancellation of the D'Arcy concession had been contrived by the company in order to obtain a better concession.[44] According to this view, Riẕā Shah was only playing the British game in canceling the D'Arcy concession.

Analysis of the immediate as well as of the fundamental factors underlying the cancellation decision shows clearly that the determination to cancel the concession originated with the Iranian government. It was a decision rooted in the numerous grievances accumulated over nearly two decades and reinforced by the all-pervading sentiment of nationalism. It was also a decision in tune with the Shah's other policy decisions vis-à-vis Great Britain, such as the abolition of capitulations and the reassertion of Iran's claim to sovereignty over the Bahrein Islands. From an even broader perspective it may be said that the decision was one step in Iran's fundamental struggle to free itself from the vestiges of foreign interference or control inherited from the Qājār period.

Those who charge conspiracy ignore the fact that long before the cancellation decision was made Iran had proposed a new contract

[43] For the text, see *League of Nations Official Journal*, 1933, pp. 1653-60.
[44] Cf. Shwadran, *op. cit.*, p. 49, and Fātaḥ, *op. cit.*, p. 293.

and the company had refused to consider it on the ground that the demands of the Iranian government were "in excess of anything which the Company could accept." [45] In view of this fact and of Iran's dissatisfaction with the D'Arcy concession, it is obvious that Iran's immediate objective in deciding to cancel the concession was to pressure the company into the conclusion of a new agreement more favorable to Iran. This is evidenced by Iran's letters of November 27 and December 12, 1932, addressed to the company and the British government, respectively.

In notifying the company of the cancellation of the concession the Iranian government stated that it

> has no other intention except to safeguard Persian interests. Should the Anglo-Persian Oil Company be prepared, contrary to the past, to safeguard Persian interests, in accordance with the views of the Persian government, on the basis of equity and justice, with the necessary security for safeguarding those interests, the Persian government will not, in principle, refuse to grant a new concession to that Company.[46]

Iran's readiness to conclude a new contract with the company was also emphasized in its letter to the British government stating:

> It has already given practical proof of its good faith in this connection and the reason why the Persian Government did not take measures after the cancellation of the D'Arcy Concession to interfere with the company's operations, and still hold for the time being to the same decision in the hope of attaining the desired result, is that [the] Government has hoped that the company, instead of entering into the sphere of disputes over principles and of legal controversies, would not lose the opportunity of sending their duly authorized representative to Tehran in order that he might enter into negotiations forthwith with the Persian Government with a view to concluding an agreement which would safeguard the legitimate interests of Persia.[47]

Related to this charge of conspiracy is the view that in most respects the new agreement of 1933 was more advantageous to the company than to the Iranian government.[48] An evaluation of the new agree-

[45] International Court of Justice, *Pleadings, Arguments, Documents, Anglo-Iranian Oil Co. Case* (The Hague, 1953), p. 191.

[46] *League of Nations Official Journal*, 1932, p. 2301.

[47] For the text, see *League of Nations Official Journal*, 1933, pp. 302-3.

[48] Cf. Nasrollah Saifpour Fatemi, *Oil Diplomacy* (New York, 1954), pp. 181-82, and Abulfaẕl Lisānī, *Ṭalā-yi Sīyāh yā Balā-yi Īrān* (Tehran, n. d.), pp. 239-383.

ment, however, based on a comparative analysis of the terms of the old and the new agreements, would seem to indicate that neither Iran nor the company emerged with decided advantages over the other.[49] It may be added that evaluation of the new agreement should consider the power position of Iran vis-à-vis Great Britain at the time. If there were disadvantageous terms such as the excessive period of extension of the contract, those terms could perhaps be explained by this power factor. It is true that the Shah was dictatorial, and he might have been rash in canceling the D'Arcy concession and careless in concluding the new agreement. But the fact remains that the Iranian negotiators of the new agreement, and the Shah himself, could not act in complete disregard of the power factor that set a limit to Iran's twisting of the tail of the British lion.

THE ARCHITECT OF INDEPENDENT IRAN

Departure from the traditional foreign policy was more clearly evident in the Shah's policy toward Great Britain than toward Russia. Having made the politico-economic independence of Iran his overriding objective, the Shah selected a remarkable array of courses of action to achieve this end. The most difficult problem was the regime of capitulations. To obtain its abolition every effort was made to persuade or pressure Great Britain. The judiciary system of the country was significantly remodeled after Western patterns. Simultaneously, ratification of the provisional agreement for a right of way over Iran, badly needed by Great Britain for completing its air route to India, was deliberately delayed. Furthermore, while the demand for the abolition of capitulations was being pressed, Iran played both Germany and Russia against Great Britain by granting the former a concession for internal air services and by reducing customs tariffs for Russia.

The dispute over Bahrein was precipitated by the Anglo-Saudi treaty which implied recognition of British sovereignty over the islands. Iran's claims were rooted in a mixture of traditional irredentism and nascent nationalism. Nevertheless, it is revealing to note that no rash attempt was made to precipitate a showdown. Irredentist

[49] Cf. Shwadran, *op. cit.*, p. 56, and Royal Institute of International Affairs, *Survey, 1934*, pp. 243-47.

claims, it may be recalled, had to some extent motivated Iran's wars with Russia and Great Britain in the past in disregard of the country's capabilities. This lack of realism had undermined Iran's independence in the nineteenth century. Riẕā Shah, however, had a sense of realism. In his dispute with Great Britain over the Bahrein Islands, he did not go beyond a battle of words.

In spite of all the charges and counter charges regarding the cancellation of the D'Arcy concession and the conclusion of the 1933 agreement, careful examination of the broad trends in Iran's foreign policy as well as available documentary evidence reveals that the Shah's fundamental objective in both instances was to ensure a more profitable arrangement for Iran. This does not, of course, imply that criticism of the prolongation of the contract or other provisions of the new concession has been wrong. It simply means that there is little evidence to show that cancellation of the concession was contrived by the company in order to obtain a better concession. This is a charge apparently invented by the nationalists of the early 1950's in order to lengthen the list of their grievances against the company.

In the perspective of this study the cancellation of the D'Arcy concession was a reflection of the general trend toward the further acceptance of the concept of national interest in Iranian foreign policy. In this instance the objective was to increase Iran's share of profit and participation in the operations of the company, and it was achieved by realistic means. Riẕā Shah did not go beyond the gesture of cancelling the concession. He realized that Iran's direct interference in the operations of the company would not be tolerated by Great Britain and that Iran would not be able to run the oil industry or sell its oil in the world market.

The Shah, as will be seen, was not always prudent, realistic, and successful in his foreign policies, but those concerning Great Britain did possess elements of careful strategy and sober calculation to an unprecedented extent. In none of his disputes with Great Britain did he lose sight of the maxim that politics is the art of the possible. In none of these disputes did he commit Iran to a course of action beyond its capabilities. Partly as the result of his skillful diplomacy toward Great Britain and Russia, he, more than any other single Iranian policy maker, assisted in regaining Iran's territorial integrity and political independence. He inherited a country independent largely in name and strove successfully to lay the foundation of its true independence.

Chapter XI

Riẕā Shah's Good-Neighbor Policy, 1925-1941

THE Shah pursued a good-neighbor policy toward Iran's Muslim neighbors. The fact that they were Muslim had little to do with the Shah's basic objective in seeking friendly relations with Iraq, Afghanistan, and Turkey. Perhaps cultural ties with Afghanistan, similarity in nationalistic ideology with Turkey, and religious ties with the Shī'ī population of Iraq played a minor role in shaping the Shah's policy toward these countries, but the chief factor underlying that policy was the desire to conserve Iran's energies in its struggle for independence from Great Britain and Russia. The Shah's good-neighbor policy was actually a corollary of his policy toward Great Britain and Russia. His friendliness toward Iran's small neighbors was designed to enhance his position vis-à-vis the powerful neighbors to the north and the south.

The establishment of friendly relations with the three Muslim states was an enormous undertaking in view of the fact that the past centuries had bequeathed to the Shah an array of long-standing problems. Most of these related to frontier questions that Qājār policy makers had been unable to settle for a variety of reasons. Furthermore, in the period following the First World War Iran was confronted with new neighbors because the disintegration of the Ottoman Empire was followed by the emergence of modern Turkey and Iraq.

THE POLICY TOWARD IRAQ

Of the three countries the Shah encountered the greatest difficulty in establishing mutually satisfactory relations with Iraq. This was basically due to three major problems: (1) the activities of certain rebels and tribes in the frontier region, (2) the treatment of Iranian citizens residing in Iraq, and (3) the regime of the Shatt al-Arab.

The role of the tribes over past centuries in precipitating frontier problems between Iran and the Ottoman Empire has already been discussed. Riẕā Shah inherited a serious problem which his predecessors had proved unable to settle conclusively with Iran's neighbor to the west. This problem was now embittering the relations of Iran with modern Iraq, a successor state.

As the Shah established the authority of Tehran over the Kurd and Lur tribesmen in the Zagros ranges, he began seeking an understanding with Iraq on the frontier tribes. In 1927 local authorities came to an accord with a section of the Iraq Pizhder tribe regarding conditions of seasonal sojourn on Iranian soil. In the same year Iran made an arrangement which disposed of Sālār al-Dawlah, a Qājār pretender to the throne who had raised a revolt among the Kurds but had been driven back by the Shah's forces and arrested by the Iraqi police in a frontier district. Understanding between Iran and Iraq, however, proved more difficult in regard to the rebellion of the notorious Sīmtqū, who had also been defeated by the Shah and had taken refuge in the territory of Iraq. The government of Iraq was unwilling to extradite him, on the ground that he was a political and not a criminal offender.[1] This, however, did not disturb the relations of the two countries.[2] In 1929 certain insurgent Iranian Kurds who had been defeated by the Shah's forces and had entered Iraq were disarmed and placed under surveillance. The former Vālī of Pusht

[1] Royal Institute of International Affairs, *Survey of International Affairs, 1928* (London, 1929), p. 343.

[2] Royal Institute of International Affairs, *Survey of International Affairs, 1930* (London, 1931), p. 331.

Kuh and his sons, who had been using Iraqi territory as a base of operations against Iran, were also placed under Iraqi surveillance.[3] In 1932 Iranian frontier authorities agreed to a regulated migration of the Jaf tribe into Iranian territory. A year earlier Iran had raised official objections to the migration of that tribe, demanding that during their annual sojourn on Iranian pastures they should be disarmed. The terms of the 1932 arrangement provided, among others, that Iran would give permits to all those who were allowed to carry arms in Iraq.[4]

The second problem in Iran's relations with Iraq pertained to the treatment of Iranian subjects residing in Iraq. The controversy began before Riẕā Shah ascended the throne of Iran. On March 25, 1924, Great Britain and Iraq signed a judicial agreement. This agreement extended Ottoman capitulatory privileges to the nationals of those states which had enjoyed such privileges under the Ottoman Empire at the time when Iraq formed part of the empire. The Iranian government claimed these privileges for their nationals in Iraq.

This claim was first set forth in a letter to the Council of the League of Nations dated September 11, 1924, from Prince Arfʻ al-Dawlah, Iran's chief delegate to the League.[5] On September 17, 1924, the Prince reiterated Iran's claim in greater detail in the Council. The heart of Iran's claim was that it had formerly enjoyed "a special regime" in the Ottoman Empire and that it should therefore enjoy the same regime in the successor state of Iraq. This special regime, Iran argued, was based on the Treaty of Erzerum, which contained the "most-favored-nation" clause. In practice this had meant that Iranian citizens throughout Ottoman territory, including Iraq, enjoyed immunity from search except in cases where Turkish police had previously notified the Iranian consul and "were accompanied by the dragoman of the Iranian Consulate."[6] Lord Parmoor, the British representative, replied to the Iranian claim by stating that the special regime claimed by Iran was based upon reciprocity and therefore Iran and Iraq should negotiate with a view to a new arrange-

[3] *Ibid.*

[4] For details, see Royal Institute of International Affairs, *Survey of International Affairs, 1934* (London, 1935), pp. 184-85.

[5] For the text see *League of Nations Official Journal*, 1924, p. 1598.

[6] See *ibid.*, pp. 1345-46.

ment.[7] In this connection Great Britain also brought out the fact that Iran did not recognize Iraq.

In 1927 and 1928 the dispute came under discussion in the Permanent Mandates Commission and in the Assembly of the League, respectively. By 1928, however, a new factor had been added to the controversy; the capitulatory regime had been abolished in Iran. Iraq therefore contended that since reciprocity was no longer possible, Iran could not expect privileges in Iraq. Furthermore, both Great Britain and Iraq contended that capitulatory privileges for Iranian citizens were out of the question because the courts of Iraq were fully as efficient as those of Iran and because Iranian nationals in Iraq were so numerous that if Iranian consular jurisdiction was recognized the judicial system of Iraq would suffer severely.[8]

On March 9, 1929, the British government proposed to the Council of the League of Nations that its judicial agreement with Iraq be abolished. This British-Iraqi decision, which required the consent of the states enjoying privileges under the agreement, "was warmly supported" by the representative of Iran, who realized that Great Britain and Iraq had done what lay in their power to remove Iran's grievance. In reciprocating this friendly gesture and after having received a British promise to assist Iran in obtaining satisfaction from Iraq in regard to the Shatt al-Arab, the Shah recognized Iraq on April 25, 1929. This was followed by the appointment of Iran's first diplomatic representative to Iraq and the conclusion of a provisional agreement pending the negotiation of "definitive instruments for placing the relations between the two countries on a permanent basis." [9]

Before a permanent treaty of friendship could be signed, however, the most difficult problem disturbing the relations of Iran and Iraq had to be settled – the regime of the Shatt al-Arab. The problem facing the Shah was a legacy from the past. The inconclusive wars of Iran and the Ottoman Empire in the past centuries had been partly the cause and effect of the indefinite boundaries between the two countries. With the disintegration of the Ottoman Empire and the

[7] *Ibid.*

[8] Cf. Foreign Policy Association, *The Near East in 1928,* V (4), 69, and Royal Institute of International Affairs, *Survey, 1928,* p. 346.

[9] Royal Institute of International Affairs, *Survey, 1930,* pp. 329-30.

emergence of modern Turkey and Iraq, Iran faced the old boundary problem on two fronts.

On November 29, 1934, the government of Iraq finally brought the question of the boundary with Iran to the attention of the Council of the League, under Article 11, paragraph 2, of the Covenant.[10] On December 3, 1934, the government of Iran told the Secretary General that "although Iraq could settle frontier questions directly with Persia," Iran was willing to present its views and arguments to the Council.[11]

The fundamental issue between the two countries was the Shatt al-Arab. The government of Iraq claimed *de jure* control over the whole body of the river and it was at the same time exercising *de facto* control. Iran, on the other hand, challenged this claim on the ground that the frontier between two sovereign states on the opposite banks of a river should follow the line of the *thalweg* (course of the main channel). The claim of Iraq was basically centered on two grounds, equity and law.

On the general question of equity, the Iraqi government argued that Iran had a coast line of almost 2,000 kilometers with many ports and anchorages. In the Khar Musa, only 50 kilometers east of the Shatt al-Arab, Iran possessed a deep-water harbor penetrating far into Iranian territory. But the Shatt al-Arab "constitutes Iraq's only access to the sea; . . . and Basrah, 100 kilometers from the mouth is Iraq's only port. It is highly undesirable, from Iraq's point of view, that another Power should command this channel from one bank."[12] This argument by Nūrī Sa'īd Pāshā, the representative of Iraq, was countered by Sayyid Bāqir Kāẓimī, Iran's representative, in these words:

I wonder whether Iraq's idea is that, as she has no access to the sea except by a single river, the Shatt-ol-Arab, she must assume sovereignty over it in order to keep it open. . . . There are other States whose access to the sea consists of but a single river, of which they are not the only riparian country; this, however, has never been adduced as a reason for claiming sovereignty over the whole course of the river to the sea.[13]

[10] *League of Nations Official Journal,* 1935, pp. 196-97.
[11] *Ibid.,* p. 216.
[12] *Ibid.,* pp. 113-17.
[13] For the text of Iran's statement, see *ibid.,* pp. 118-23.

The Iraqi argument also rested on a number of diplomatic instruments, including, in particular, the Treaty of Erzerum (1847),[14] several subsequent notes emanating from the Ottoman Empire, Great Britain, Russia, and Iran bearing upon the ratification of that treaty, the Tehran Protocol (1911),[15] and the Constantinople Protocol (1913).[16] Iraq claimed that the whole of the Shatt al-Arab had been assigned to the Ottoman Empire by an Ottoman-Persian-Russian-British Delimitation Commission in 1914,[17] and that as a successor state the same had been assigned to it.[18] Iran countered this argument by a lengthy exposition of the reasons rendering invalid not only the basic document to which it referred as the "so-called" Treaty of Erzerum but also the Constantinople Protocol, on which Iraq relied heavily in presenting its argument. Having declared these instruments invalid in municipal as well as international law because there "has never been that joint consent which is required . . . for the very existence of a contract," Iran regarded them as "non-existent." [19]

On January 15, 1935, the date of the oral presentation outlined above, Anthony Eden, the representative of Great Britain, suggested: "On a juridical issue of this nature, the most appropriate procedure may be to seek the opinion of an expert legal body, such as the Permanent Court of International Justice at the Hague." [20] On January 21, 1935, this same idea was suggested by Iraq but was rejected by Iran, which alluded to its reservations stipulated in the instrument accepting the Court's jurisdiction.[21]

Having aired their grievances publicly in the halls of the Council of the League of Nations without any tangible results, the two states removed their case from the agenda. This gesture paved the way for the settlement of their dispute in 1937 and should not be attributed, as it has been,[22] merely to Mussolini's aggression in defiance of the

[14] For the text of the treaty, see *ibid.*, pp. 237-40.

[15] For the text of the Tehran Protocol, see *ibid.*, p. 234.

[16] For the text of the Constantinople Protocol, see *ibid.*, pp. 201-6.

[17] For rules of procedure and extract from minutes of the Commission, see *ibid.*, pp. 201-6 and 227-231.

[18] *Ibid.*, pp. 113-17.

[19] For the text of the Iranian statement, see *ibid.*, pp. 118-23.

[20] *Ibid.*, p. 123.

[21] *Ibid.*, pp. 190-91.

[22] Royal Institute of International Affairs, *Survey of International Affairs, 1935* (London, 1937), p. 801.

League. The influence of this aggression in bringing the Middle Eastern countries closer together cannot be denied, but a balanced appraisal requires consideration of the indigenous influences as well. In the present case Iran and Iraq had already taken significant steps toward improving their relations by solving problems of tribal migration across frontiers and the status of Iranian subjects in Iraq. On July 4, 1937, the two countries concluded a boundary treaty and a protocol.

Because of the continuing significance of these instruments in the relations of Iran with Iraq their provisions require close attention. The major provisions of the treaty and the protocol may be summarized as follows: [23]

1) *The Frontier:* Iran and Iraq agreed that their frontier should follow basically the lines set out by the Constantinople Protocol of 1913 and the minutes of the Frontier Commission of 1914, provided that at the extreme point of the island of Chateit the frontier should run perpendicularly from low-water mark to the *thalweg* of the Shatt al-Arab and should follow the same as far as a point opposite Jetty No. 1 at Abadan. From this point it should return to low-water mark and follow the frontier line indicated in the 1914 Minutes.[24]

In the delimitation of the frontier two aspects were considered: the points to be redemarcated and those to be determined. The first would be governed by the 1914 Minutes and the second by this new treaty. For the former task, which was easier, a commission was to be appointed immediately. For the latter undertaking the parties agreed to set up a commission of experts, each country appointing half the members. The minutes of this commission containing the *exact* determination of the frontier were to become an integral part of the new treaty.[25]

2) *The Shatt al-Arab Regime:* The two countries agreed that the river should remain open on equal terms to the trading vessels of all countries, but to the war vessels of the two contracting parties only. Furthermore, the fact that the frontier would sometimes follow the low-water mark and sometimes the *thalweg* should not in any way affect their rights along the whole length of the river.[26]

[23] The text of the treaty is in *League of Nations Treaty Series,* CXC, 256-58.
[24] Articles 1 and 2.
[25] Article 3 and the annexed protocol.
[26] Article 4 of the treaty.

3) *Maintenance:* The parties agreed to conclude within one year a convention for the maintenance and improvement of the navigable channel and for dredging, pilotage, collections of dues, health measures, and the like. Pending the conclusion of such a convention they agreed that all dues should be for services rendered and should be devoted exclusively to the cost of upkeep, maintenance of navigability, and other like measures mentioned in the treaty. Iran agreed that for one year, or more if any extension was effected, the government of Iraq would be responsible for all points to be covered within a year by a convention. However, Iraq should notify Iran "every six months as to the works executed, dues calculated, expenditure incurred or any other measures undertaken." [27]

In view of the claims and counterclaims of the countries before the League of Nations and the age of the problem the boundary treaty of 1937 was a most significant achievement.[28] Both Iran and Iraq made substantial concessions. Iran accepted, with some modification, the Constantinople Protocol (1913), which it had previously declared "non-existent," as a basis for settlement, while Iraq conceded the principle of *thalweg* at certain points. It is most significant that this boundary settlement removed a main obstacle in the way of finalizing a Middle Eastern agreement, known as the Sa'dābād Pact, which had been under negotiation for many months but was signed only four days after the boundary treaty between Iran and Iraq. This general pact will be treated separately later.

The cordial relations resulting from the frontier settlement were soon extended to other areas of Irano-Iraqi contact. On July 18, 1937, a Treaty of Friendship was signed at Tehran.[29] It provided for peace and "indissoluble" friendship between the two countries, extended the most-favored-nation treatment to their diplomatic and consular officials, and committed them to concluding other treaties

[27] Articles 5 and 4(a) of the treaty and Article 2 of the protocol.

[28] However, in 1959 the revolutionary government of Karīm 'Abd al-Qāsim denounced the treaty on the ground that the government of Iraq, after the *coup d'état* of General Bakr Ṣidqī (1936), had concluded it under pressure. Iran branded the position of Iraq as "unfounded," declared its determination "to defend its rights," and charged that contrary to the provisions of the treaty and the annexed protocol Iraq had for twenty-two years collected dues unilaterally and had expended the same "in a manner prejudicial to the interests of Iran." See the statement of 'Abbās Ārām, Iran's Foreign Minister, to the Majlis (*Iṭṭilā'āt Havā'i*, December 10, 1959).

[29] For the text, see *League of Nations Treaty Series*, CXC, 267-68.

for security in the frontier zone, for extradition, for commerce, and for postal, telegraphic, and other matters.

On July 24, 1937, the two countries signed another treaty at Tehran, which is still in force.[30] This twenty-four-article agreement set up elaborate guidelines for the peaceful settlement of disputes. It provided in detail for the procedures and application of conciliation and arbitration and for diplomatic negotiations. "Any dispute" which it was not possible to settle by the last-mentioned method was to be submitted to the Permanent Court of International Justice unless such a dispute (a) had arisen prior to the coming into force of this treaty, (b) was "by international law" reserved to the exclusive competence of the parties, or (c) was concerned with the territorial status of one of the parties.[31] "Disputes concerning the interpretation or enforcement of the present Treaty, including disputes concerning the nature or the scope of reservations shall be submitted to the Permanent Court of International Justice."[32]

THE POLICY TOWARD AFGHANISTAN

In establishing friendly relations with Afghanistan, Riẕā Shah faced a long-time problem relating simultaneously to the frontier and the division of Helmand River water. The Shah seems to have chosen to approach the vexatious problem only after a more friendly atmosphere between the two countries had been created. Soon after the *coup d'état* Iran approached Afghanistan for the purpose of establishing the relations of the two countries on a new basis of friendship and equality. To this end, on June 22, 1921, they concluded a comprehensive Treaty of Friendship at Tehran. This first instrument between the new regime and Afghanistan set forth the fundamental principles governing their relations in modern times.

The two countries agreed that their diplomatic and consular representatives would be governed by international law, that their nationals would be subject to the laws of the country in which they resided, except for military service, that persons committing "grave offences" would be extradited, that disputes would be submitted to arbitration,

[30] For the text, see *ibid.*, pp. 271-79.
[31] Article 2.
[32] Article 21.

and that commercial, postal, and telegraphic conventions would be concluded. They also agreed that they should "not be affected in the event of one of them becoming involved in a war with a third Power. But in this case the other Party shall undertake, in accordance with the rules of neutrality, not to favor this third Power in any respect." [33]

After the accession of Riẕā Shah to the throne Iran and Afghanistan agreed that "all the clauses and provisions" of this treaty should remain in force and continue to be the basis of their relations. This was set forth in a Treaty of Friendship and Security signed on November 27, 1927. This treaty went far beyond its precursor in two respects. First, it committed Iran and Afghanistan to nonaggression against each other. Second, it provided in detail for arbitration procedures, which, as will be seen, were invoked by the Shah at a later date. Under Article 6 of the annexed protocol Afghanistan and Iran undertook to submit to arbitration disputes not settled through ordinary diplomatic negotiations. If they failed to appoint their arbitrators, "a statesman of a neutral Power" would be jointly appointed and his decision would be final.[34]

On June 15, 1928, Iran and Afghanistan went a step further in establishing the new bases of their relations by signing two additional protocols, one annexed to their Treaty of Friendship and Security and the other related exclusively to the problem of extradition. The latter is concerned only with the details of extradition procedures.[35] The other protocol committed the two countries to cooperate actively in the economic sphere, to establish and improve means of communication, and to grant free transit of commodities through each other's territory.[36]

Having thus attempted to convince Afghanistan of Iran's good intentions, the Shah would have liked to come to grips with the frontier and water problems immediately, but the boundary and tribal problems with Iraq and Turkey took priority over the frontier problem with Afghanistan. However, in March 1934 the governments of Iran and Afghanistan agreed, in compliance with the Treaty of Friendship and Security, to submit their frontier dispute to a "neutral

[33] For the text of this treaty and the additional provisions, see *League of Nations Treaty Series*, XXXIII, 295-301.

[34] For the text of the treaty and the annexed protocol, see *ibid.*, CVII, 445-51.

[35] For the text of the extradition protocol, see *ibid.*, CIV, 499-501.

[36] *Ibid.*

Power" for arbitration. This power was to be Turkey. The specific purpose of the arbitration was the settlement of differences over the area known as Musa Abad and the determination of that sector of the Irano-Afghan frontier not hitherto demarcated.[37] The Turkish government appointed General Fakhr Altai as the arbitrator. He proceeded to Tehran and then to Kabul. After the necessary studies in the frontier area he returned to Turkey and informed Iran through his government of his decision. Notwithstanding Iranian criticism of the award ever since,[38] Riẕā Shah accepted the award in his statement at the opening of the Eleventh Majlis.[39]

The problem of the division of the waters of the Helmand River still remained to be solved. The Goldsmid and McMahon arbitration awards in 1872 and 1905, respectively,[40] had not provided a mutually acceptable basis for utilization of the water. On January 26, 1938, Iran and Afghanistan finally concluded a treaty.[41] Article 1 of this treaty embodied, in essence, the Goldsmid award, which had been favored by Iran. According to this article the two countries were to share the waters of the Helmand River below the Kamal Khan Dam on an equal basis. Furthermore, under Article 2 of the same agreement Afghanistan undertook not to construct any new canal and not to repair the existing canals below the dam for the purpose of increasing its water supply beyond the current amount. Iran also undertook not to take any measure or to launch any operations below the said dam that might reduce the Afghan share. The other provisions of the agreement set forth in detail the measures to be taken to implement these basic principles. In an annexed protocol Iran declared that the sole purpose of the agreement was the irrigation of Sistan and that it had no intention of interfering in Afghan internal affairs. Afghanistan reciprocated by declaring that it had no intention of impeding or stopping the flow of water to Sistan and that it would not permit any damage to the Sistan irrigation system. The

[37] The text of the agreement is in Aḥmad Tavakkulī, *Afghānistān: Ravābiṭ-i Sīyāsī-i Īrān va Afghānistān* (Tehran, 1337 [1958/59]), p. 81.

[38] *Ibid.*, pp. 83-85.

[39] The award was accepted by the Majlis on May 15, 1935 (Ḥabibullāh Mukhtārī, *Tārīkh-i Bīdārī-i Īrān* [Tehran, 1326 <1947/48>], p. 471).

[40] See Chapter III.

[41] The treaty was ratified by the Majlis on May 8, 1939; the text is in *Majmū'ah-'i Qavānīn, Dawrah-'i Yāzdahum-i Majlis*, pp. 431-37, and in Tavakkulī, *op. cit.*, pp. 91-94.

agreement and the annexed protocol were ratified by the Iranian Majlis, but the Afghan Majlis approved only the agreement.[42]

The Afghan attitude was merely a manifestation of the fact that traditional suspicion reinforced by nationalistic sentiments tended to obscure the mutual advantages that the two Muslim countries could derive from the settlement of their old dispute and from the implementation of the principles of cooperation in the fields of economic development, trade, transit, and communications which they had enunciated in their Treaty of Friendship and Security as early as 1928. The net result of this failure was the continuation of the Helmand River problem.

THE POLICY TOWARD TURKEY

Modern Turkey presented Riẕā Shah with the least difficulty in establishing new bases for mutually satisfactory relations. Against the historical background of centuries of inconclusive wars and serious boundary problems with the Ottoman Empire, this might appear unusual. But in the light of the significant internal changes in both Iran and Turkey during the postwar period the comparative ease with which Irano-Turkish *rapprochement* occurred should be understandable. The traditional conflict between Iran and the Ottoman Empire had originally been sectarian-ideological. The Kemalist reforms of the 1920's and 1930's were directed against the old Sunnī public order and aimed at the transformation of Turkey from a traditionally Islamic to a secular modern state along Western lines. Riẕā Shah admired the westernization efforts of his Turkish counterpart and attempted to emulate them in the furtherance of his fundamental objective, the economic and political emancipation of Iran.

The Shah's decision to establish friendly relations with Iran's neighbors was related essentially to that fundamental objective. The traditional Irano-Ottoman conflict had significantly contributed to the isolation of Iran from the Western world. The economic dependence of northern Iran upon Russia was to no small degree due to Iran's lack of access to Western markets through Turkey. The comparative ease with which Iran established friendly relations with

[42] Tavakkulī, *op. cit.*, p. 95.

modern Turkey was not due only to the Shah's ideological predisposition toward Kemalism in Turkey. It resulted partly from the fact that the Shah was determined to emancipate the economy of northern Iran from dependence on Soviet Russia by finding access to new markets through Turkish ports.[43]

On April 22, 1926, Iran signed at Tehran its first Treaty of Friendship with Turkey. The basic principles to govern the relations of the two countries included friendship, neutrality, and nonaggression. Iran and Turkey also agreed

> not to allow in their territory the formation or presence of organizations or groups of persons whose object is to disturb the peace and security of the other country or to change its government, or the presence of persons or groups of persons planning to attack the other country by propaganda or by any other means.[44]

It should be noted that both the Iranian and the Turkish governments were encountering internal opposition at the time. The sources of opposition to the new regimes were not, of course, the same in both countries, except for the Kurdish tribes. The Kurdish challenge to the Shah's authority in the frontier zones has already been mentioned. Mustafa Kemal was experiencing even more serious opposition from the Kurds in Turkey. In fact, just about a year before the conclusion of the treaty the first major Kurdish revolt had occurred in Turkey in February 1925 as a result of the uncompromising Kemalist secular reforms and attempts at Turkification of the tribes.[45]

These attempts produced more Kurdish revolts in Turkey in 1929 and 1930 and forced the Kurds to seek refuge in the mountainous and inaccessible frontier zone between Iran and Turkey. The traditionally inconclusive frontier dispute was thus intermixed, as it had been earlier, with the problem of tribal raids into Iran and Turkey. This development led to charges and countercharges of countenancing Kurdish raids. By October 1927 the deteriorating relations between the two countries took a turn for the worse when Turkey, in a note

[43] This was stated by 'Alā', then Iran's Minister in London, to the correspondent of the *Morning Post.* See Fatḥullāh Nūrī Isfandīyārī, *Rastā Khīz-i Īrān* (Tehran, 1335 [1956/57]), pp. 701-2.

[44] Article 5 of the treaty. For the text, see *League of Nations Treaty Series,* CVI, 261-65.

[45] Royal Institute of International Affairs, *Survey, 1928,* p. 373, and Edward Reginald Vere-Hodge, *Turkish Foreign Policy, 1918-1948* (Geneva, 1950), p. 85.

presented to Iran, alleged that a party of Turkish troops had been captured by the Kurds on Turkish soil and carried captive into Iran. The note demanded the release of the prisoners with their weapons together with an apology within ten days, threatening otherwise the rupture of diplomatic relations. The Iranian government alleged that the Turkish force had been destroyed by the tribes except for one officer, who had been escorted back to safety. Iran, therefore, refused to accept the note and proposed an investigation.[46]

To this end Mīrzā Muḥammad 'Alī Khān Furūghī was sent to Turkey in 1928. Although in June of that year a protocol was added to the Treaty of Friendship, neither the tribal nor the frontier problem was dealt with in this instrument.[47] In fact, after the Kurdish revolt in 1930 the tribal problem became more aggravated and prompted the Turkish government to allege, at least by allusion, that Iran was neglecting its frontier responsibilities.[48] With the growing control of the Turkish government over the Kurds, however, the atmosphere between Iran and Turkey improved considerably.

On January 23, 1932, the first definitive frontier treaty in the history of Irano-Turkish relations was signed at Tehran. Its three articles terminated the centuries-old boundary dispute between the two countries. Article 1 defined in great detail the frontier line starting from the confluence of the Aras and Karasu rivers, traversing many hills, mountain passes, and villages and finally ascending the peak of Mount Dalampar and ending at the Turco-Iraqi frontier.[49] It came into force immediately after the exchange of ratifications, which took place on November 5, 1932. On the same day the two countries signed a new Treaty of Friendship.[50] These two treaties

[46] *Times* (London), November 10, 1927, as reproduced in Isfandīyārī, *op. cit.*, pp. 392-94. See also Royal Institute of International Affairs, *Survey, 1928*, p. 373.

[47] The text of the protocol is in *League of Nations Treaty Series*, CVI, 265-66.

[48] *Daily Telegraph* (London), August 18, 1930, as reproduced in Isfandīyārī, *op. cit.*, pp. 493-95.

[49] For the text of the treaty and the related notes, see *League of Nations Official Journal*, 1935, pp. 237-40. Subsequently the frontier set forth in this treaty was slightly rectified in another instrument signed on May 26, 1937; ratification was exchanged on July 11, 1939. For the text of this instrument, see Great Britain, *British and Foreign State Papers, 1937* (London, 1950), pp. 1093-94.

[50] For the text of this treaty, see Great Britain, *British and Foreign State Papers, 1932* (London, 1937), pp. 672-83.

together with a Treaty of Conciliation, Judicial Settlement, and Arbitration, also signed on January 23, 1932,[51] constituted the new bases of Iran's relations with Turkey.

In June 1934 the Shah, together with a mission of high-ranking Iranian officials, visited Turkey at the invitation of Mustafa Kemal.[52] The Maku-Erzerum route traveled by many hostile Turkish and Iranian forces was now open to the Iranian good-will mission headed by the architect of independent Iran. The warm and cordial reception of the Shah by the Turkish government added significantly to the friendly atmosphere and facilitated talks on matters of common concern. The Shah lost no time in expressing his country's sincere desire to expand economic ties and means of communication with Turkey.[53] It was also reported that he might even have discussed the need for a Middle Eastern Pact.[54]

RIẒĀ SHAH AND THE SA'DĀBĀD PACT

On July 8, 1937, Iran signed a Treaty of Nonaggression with Afghanistan, Iraq, and Turkey at the Shah's Sa'dābād Palace in Shimiran, a northern suburb of Tehran. The draft of the treaty had been signed at Geneva by Iran, Iraq, and Turkey on October 2, 1935, and had been accepted at a later date by Afghanistan.[55] The four Muslim powers stated officially that they were "actuated by the common purpose of ensuring peace and security in the Near East by means of additional guarantees within the framework of the Covenant of the League of Nations." [56]

The parties undertook by this treaty (1) to abstain from interference in each other's internal affairs, (2) to respect the inviolability of their common frontiers, (3) to consult in international disputes affecting their common interests, (4) to refrain from aggression

[51] For the text, see *ibid.*, pp. 677-82.

[52] Mukhtārī, *op. cit.*, p. 483.

[53] *Times* (London), June 11, 1934, as reproduced in Isfandīyārī, *op. cit.*, pp. 674-75.

[54] *Daily Telegraph* (London), June 19, 1934, as reproduced in Isfandīyārī, *op. cit.*, pp. 683-84.

[55] For the text of the relevant statement, see Tavakkulī, *op. cit*, p. 97.

[56] Preamble of the treaty; for the text, see *League of Nations Treaty Series*, CXC, 21-27.

against one another either singly or jointly with one or more other powers, (5) to bring any violation or threat of violation of Article 4 of the pact before the Council of the League of Nations,[57] without prejudice to their own exercise of the right of self-defence, and (6) to have the right to denounce the pact in respect to a signatory who commits an act of aggression against a third power. Each of the signatory states also undertook to prevent in its territory "the formation or activities of armed bands, associations or organizations to subvert the established institutions, or disturb the order or security of any part, whether situated on the frontier or elsewhere, of the territory of another Party, or to change the constitutional systems of such other Party."

The four Middle Eastern Foreign Ministers who signed the pact decided on the same day to set up a permanent council which would meet once a year and have a secretariat. The first act of the council was to support the candidature of the members in alphabetical order for election to a seat on the Council of the League of Nations. In recognition of Iran's special endeavors or initiative in the formation of the pact, however, it was to be the first candidate. In September 1937 Iran was elected to a seat on the Council.[58]

Ever since the pact was signed there has been speculation about its inception. In the 1930's some attributed it to the prodding of Russia; some to the manipulation of Great Britain; and others to the foresight and initiative of its signatories.[59] In more recent times assertions have been made that it was "implicitly directed against Soviet infiltration of the area" [60] and that "it was viewed with thinly disguised hostility by Russia who believed it to be another type of *cordon sanitaire*." [61] It has also been maintained that the pact "was

[57] Article 4 provided that the following should be regarded as acts of aggression: (1) a declaration of war; (2) an invasion of the armed forces of one State, with or without a declaration of war; (3) an attack by the land, naval, or air forces of one State, with or without a declaration of war, on the territory, vessels, or aircraft of another State; and (4) directly aiding or assisting an aggressor.

[58] Tavakkulī, *op. cit.*, pp. 103-4, and Royal Institute of International Affairs, *Survey of International Affairs, 1936* (London, 1937), pp. 801-3.

[59] Tavakkulī, *op. cit.*, pp. 100-105.

[60] George Lenczowski, *The Middle East in World Affairs* (Ithaca, N.Y., 1956), p. 524.

[61] *Ibid.*, p. 171, and George Lenczowski, *Russia and the West in Iran, 1918-1948* (Ithaca, N.Y., 1949), p. 306n.

occasioned by the challenge to the *status quo* in the Levant and Middle East presented by the rise of Italy as an aggressive naval and military power" and that "subsequent attempts to read into it an anti-British or anti-Russian orientation are gratuitous."[62]

The divergency in these interpretations is probably due to the different angles from which the pact has been viewed. Here we shall concern ourselves only with the place of the pact in the foreign policy of modern Iran. The achievement of the Shah's fundamental objective of Iranian economic and political emancipation involved the pursuance of specific courses of action vis-à-vis the traditional rival powers, Russia and Great Britain.[63] These actions would have been only partially successful if Iran had dissipated its energies in tribal or frontier disputes with its Muslim neighbors. For example, to free the economy of northern Iran from its traditional dependence on Russian markets required more than the industrialization of the country and modernization and expansion of its means of communication. Freedom from the colossal neighbor to the north also demanded access to world markets through the Tabriz-Rawanduz and Tabriz-Erzerum roads over the territories of Iraq and Turkey.

Riẕā Shah's good-neighbor policy found expression in the settlement of old tribal and frontier disputes and the enunciation of new principles to govern the relations of modern Iran with its Muslim neighbors. The Sa'dābād Pact was, in the perspective of Iran's foreign policy, the multilateral instrument embodying the new principles already enunciated in more than ten bilateral treaties and protocols concluded between Iran and each of its three Muslim neighbors during 1921-37. The principles of nonviolability of frontiers, noninterference in internal affairs, pacific settlement of disputes, and nonaggression in the pact had all been accepted previously. Even the provision of Article 7 regarding measures against subversive groups was not completely novel.[64] Article 5 of the Treaty of Friendship and Security between Iran and Turkey nearly thirteen years earlier (April 22, 1926) had enunciated a similar principle.[65] To Iran, the

[62] George E. Kirk, *A Short History of the Middle East* (Washington, 1949), p. 280n.

[63] See Chapters IX and X.

[64] Cf. Tavakkulī, *op. cit.*, p. 107.

[65] See Article 5 of this treaty. The text is in *League of Nations Treaty Series,* CVI, 261-65.

Sa'dābād Pact was no more than a multilateral instrument embodying the principles which had evolved over the years substantially as a result of its persistent efforts to establish friendly relations with the new neighboring states of the Middle East.

REGIONAL FRIENDSHIP: A SOURCE OF POWER

Riẕā Shah's departure from traditional Iranian foreign policy was manifest in more than his diplomacy toward Russia and Great Britain. The adoption of the good-neighbor policy was a complete reversal of the traditional policy. The intermittent wars of the sixteenth to the eighteenth centuries with the Ottoman Empire had been followed by occasional armed conflicts and persistent boundary problems in the nineteenth and twentieth centuries. Irredentist attacks on Afghanistan had given way to tenacious frontier problems in the nineteenth century. The legacy of antagonism was a reminder of the difficult nature of the problems involved. But the Shah was determined to establish friendly relations with Iran's neighbors because this was essential to his strategy of politico-economic emancipation from Russia and Great Britain.

In settling problems every effort was made to resort to peaceful diplomatic procedures. The difficult problem of rebellion and tribal migration was settled with Iraq through negotiations. The Shatt al-Arab problem was "resolved" through the conclusion of the Treaty of 1937, although differences between Iran and Iraq have, at times, arisen over the implementation or even validity of the treaty. The frontier problem with Afghanistan was submitted to arbitration and the award was accepted by the Shah. The question of Helmand River water was subjected to intensive negotiations, and Iran ratified the resultant Treaty of 1938 in spite of Afghanistan's failure to ratify the relevant protocol. Most important of all, the centuries-old frontier problems between Iran and Turkey were definitely settled by the Treaty of 1932. "Multilateral diplomacy" was also evidenced in the discussion in the League of Nations of the status of Iranian citizens in Iraq and of the problem of the Shatt al-Arab.

New principles to govern the future relations of Iran with its Muslim neighbors were spelled out in a wide variety of bilateral treaties. These principles included nonaggression, neutrality, noninterference in internal affairs, inviolability of common frontiers, and economic cooperation. The Sa'dābād Pact was the first regional agreement of its kind which committed the signatory states to most of these principles. It is true that the pact "faded into obscurity," but as a forerunner of the subsequent Baghdad Pact it was not without significance. This pact and the bilateral treaties between Iran and its Muslim neighbors together with Iran's subscription to procedures of peaceful settlement in international disputes marked a significant departure from traditional patterns in Iran's foreign policy. This departure was deemed necessary for the promotion of Iran's national interest. To the extent that they assisted the conservation of the country's energies, the good-neighbor policy and regional cooperation were believed to enhance Iran's power position and ability to maneuver vis-à-vis Great Britain and Russia.

Chapter XII

Riẕā Shah's Third-Power Policy and the Neutrality Proclamation, 1925-1941

No FINAL evaluation of Riẕā Shah's foreign policy is possible without description and analysis of his third-power policy and his neutrality in early World War II.

RAPPROCHEMENT WITH GERMANY

The Shah's favorite third-power was Germany. The third-power doctrine, however, was a legacy. It can be traced to 1910-11, when Morgan Shuster was employed, or even earlier, but it was not clearly formulated until the early 1920's. Mushīr al-Dawlah in August 1920 had attempted to persuade the United States to be the third power, and Ḥusayn 'Alā', during the government of Qavām al-Saltanah, stated the doctrine in a comprehensive memorandum to the United States Secretary of State.[1] Many historical, political, economic, and psychological factors, including the popularity of the American "hero,"

[1] *Oil Concessions in Foreign Countries,* Senate Doc. 97, 68th Congress, 1st sess. (Washington, 1924), pp. 87-93.

Shuster,[2] influenced Iran's decision to choose the United States as the third power. Iran's doctrinal predisposition, i. e., friendship with a third and distant great power, had not been the only reason for its selection of the United States as the third power in the early 1920's. Nor was this inclination alone instrumental in causing the Shah to substitute Germany for the United States in the mid-1920's. What then were the factors underlying Iran's increasing *rapprochement* with Germany?

One internal factor was basically psychological and was rooted in past events. Most Iranian nationalists, whether or not occupying official positions as policy makers, nostalgically recalled past friendship with Germany. Actually history clearly reveals that Germany, beginning in 1898, had attempted a belated imperialistic thrust into the Middle East. It also reveals that Iran was a prized object of German expansionist designs. But all that Iranian Germanophiles remembered was Germany's challenge to Iran's traditional "enemies," Great Britain and Russia. The powerful German propaganda machinery had not only exploited Iran's resentment against these powers but had also portrayed Germany as the "true friend" of Islam as illustrated by the preposterous pro-Shī'ī pretentions of Von Kardorff.

Many nationalists within and outside the Majlis and the government of Riẕā Shah held fond memories of the German role in aiding and abetting their anti-British and anti-Russian activities in the early war period. The Iranian Committee for Cooperation with Germany established in Berlin and coached by Niedermayer, the National Defense Commitee, and subsequently the "National Government" established at Qum and Kermanshah by nationalist leaders and aided morally and financially by Prince von Reuss, the German Minister in Tehran, were regarded as brilliant aspects of the Iranian nationalist movement. The fact that the nationalist military operations against the Russians had actually failed at Saveh and Robat Karim was generally overlooked.

Another reason for favoring Germany was the Shah's clash with Dr. Millspaugh. The Fourth Majlis had aspired to play the same role in hiring Dr. Millspaugh that the Second Majlis had played in the case of Morgan Shuster. It had given Dr. Millspaugh broad powers

[2] Abraham Yeselson, *United States–Persian Diplomatic Relations, 1883-1921* (Princeton, N. J., 1956), p. 184.

as the Administrator-General of the Finances of Iran (1922) and had taken pains to impress upon him that he was "the creature of the Parliament." However, achievements had been made possible by the sustained support of Riẕā Khān, not only as Minister of War or Prime Minister but later as the Shah of Iran. Documentary evidence reveals that beneath the Shah's outward cooperation lay a growing sense of jealousy of the powers of Dr. Millspaugh.[3] As Riẕā Khān's control grew stronger, he found Millspaugh more and more a thorn in his side until differences with the American administrator over the financing of the campaign of Khorasan in 1926 culminated in Dr. Millspaugh's withdrawal in 1927.

External circumstances also proved favorable to Iran's reorientation toward Germany. The German policy of penetrating Iran predated the advent of the Nazis to power. In other words, the rise of Hitler in 1933 "added only new impetus to the already existing policy."[4] The persistent German interest in Iran coincided with the psychological predispositions of Iran toward Germany.

It is questionable whether Irano-German *rapprochement* could have been initiated without the tolerant, if not benevolent, attitudes of both Great Britain and Russia. To appreciate this point it is essential not to allow our knowledge of Anglo-Russian hostility toward Germany in 1941 to distort the assessment of the attitudes of Great Britain and Russia toward Germany in Iran in the 1920's. In the 1920's British and Russian interests in Iran did not seem to clash with those of Germany. In the interwar period it is interesting to note, for example, that the employment of German advisers by Iran was sympathetically viewed in Great Britain as a promising Iranian attempt to shake off Western control.[5] A Russian memorandum of October 15, 1926, in reporting in detail the British attitude toward German ties with Iran, went so far as to state:

[3] See, for example, U.S. Department of State records on Iran, National Archives, Record Group 891.51A/408-478. Hereafter records in the National Archives are indicated by the symbol NA, followed by the record group (RG) number.

[4] Cf. L. P. Elwell-Sutton, *Modern Iran* (London, 1944), pp. 175-75, and George Lenczowski, *Russia and the West in Iran, 1918-1948* (Ithaca, N.Y., 1949), p. 152.

[5] Royal Institute of International Affairs, *Survey of International Affairs, 1928* (London, 1929), p. 358.

> Germany, in endeavoring to win for herself a stable position in Persian economics, is not coming forward alone, but, on the contrary, is seeking contact with British capital.
>
> The latter [Britain], being too sure of its power and the security of its position, is not only not in opposition to the consolidation of Germany in Persia, but even, to a certain extent, is encouraging German capital in this direction.
>
> This, at first sight incomprehensible, policy of England is explained by her desire to make use of Germany as an instrument against the USSR in Persia.
>
> This tendency has become so manifest recently that it might be said that a tacit arrangement had been made on the basis of which England allows Germany comparative freedom of action in Northern Persia. In Southern Persia England is more zealous in protecting her position.

The same memorandum further stated that Great Britain was also interested in Germany as a large consumer of oil; this was evidenced by an agreement between the Anglo-Persian Oil Company and the German "Petroleum-Aktien-Geselschaft [*sic*]."[6]

Even Russia's attitude was favorable to Iran's ties with Germany in the 1920's. In 1922 direct steamship service between Hamburg and Enzeli, passing through the Volga and the Caspian Sea, was organized and operated with no apparent fear that Russo-German cooperation might encourage Iran's renewed interest in Germany. More importantly, Russia actually encouraged Junker's acquisition of the German monopoly of postal and passenger air services in Iran (1927). In a confidential dispatch to the Secretary of State, the American Minister reported that the German Minister had informed him that "the concession obtained by the Junkers company from the Soviet Government requires the maintenance of an aeroplane service to Baku, and that the Russians have been insistent that the German company, after agreement with the Persian Government, undertake to extend the line to Enzeli and Tehran."[7]

MODES OF *RAPPROCHEMENT* WITH GERMANY

Signs of a renewal of the ties between the two countries became evident before 1925. As early as 1920 the representatives of the firms of Wönckhaus & Company and Undütsch & Company re-

[6] Enclosure to NA, RG 762.91/1. See also NA, RG 891.51A/431.
[7] NA, RG 762.91/–.

appeared in Tehran and resumed their important export business.[8] In 1922 Iranian students were sent to Germany.[9] In 1923 Iran and Germany entered negotiations for the reopening of the German secular school in Tehran. Arbāb Kaikhusraw, the Zoroastrian deputy, purchased several hundred thousand dollars' worth of telephone equipment and printing presses for the Majlis from Berlin. He also hired several German printers. In the same year Iran engaged the services of Herr G. Hartman, a former German army officer, to organize and run the arsenal in Tehran together with its branch in Bushire; later four other Germans were hired to assist him. In 1924 another former German officer and Maxim gun expert arrived in Tehran. The same year witnessed the arrival of Iran's "warship," the *Pahlavi,* and the delivery of arms, munitions, and army lorries, all purchased from Germany.[10]

During the rule of Riẕā Shah, Iran's increasing ties with Germany were to serve the overriding objective of politico-economic emancipation from the traditional control of Great Britain and Russia, just as that objective had motivated Mushīr al-Dawlah, Qavām al-Saltanah, and Mustawfī al-Mamālik. But the Shah's third-power policy differed from that of his predecessors in his substitution of Germany for the United States as the third power, a radical deviation from the original formulation of the third-power doctrine which required friendship with a "disinterested" as well as a "distant" power. Another significant point to bear in mind is that the Shah's third-power policy was directed principally against Russia. This was not merely because of the Shah's distrust of Russia. It was also because of the fact that by 1925 Iran's economy was even more at the mercy of Russia than it had been in 1921. Iran's *rapprochement* with Germany took economic forms mainly and was most intimately related to the Shah's relentless economic battle with the USSR.

Iran's dependence on Russian markets was its weakest point economically. This weakness could be reduced if Iran could attract German manufactured goods and find German markets for its raw materials. As early as 1924 the question of regulated trade between the two countries was taken up. In that year Iran's 1873 treaty with Germany expired and the German Minister in Tehran made several

[8] *Ibid.*
[9] Elwell-Sutton, *op. cit.*, p. 167.
[10] NA, RG 762.91/–.

attempts to renew it.[11] These efforts, however, did not succeed because the treaty, like a number of others with Western countries, had been modeled after the Treaty of Turkumanchai with Russia (1828), which established the capitulatory regime in Iran. No treaty was signed with Germany until after the capitulations were abolished on May 10, 1928. Only five days later Iran signed a "provisional" agreement with Germany. This agreement extended most-favored-nation treatment to German diplomatic and consular representatives in Iran.[12] Furthermore, Iran promised that "the natural and manufactured products of Germany on entering into Persian territory [would be subject] to the organic Customs legislation of Persia." This meant that Iran would give those products "the benefit of the Persian minimum tariff." [13] This provisional agreement was followed by a Treaty of Friendship signed on February 17, 1929, which could be "reexamined" after ten years.[14] Still another agreement was signed on February 24, 1930, regarding the protection of patents, trademarks, trade names, and designs. Iran and Germany undertook to extend to each other's nationals and companies in their territories the same rights as their own nationals and companies in respect to these matters.[15]

The new trade regime thus established signaled the beginning of increasing trade between the two countries. Iran's imports from Germany, consisting mainly of manufactured products and capital goods, amounted to only 7.7 per cent of the country's total imports, and its exports, mainly in raw materials, reached a mere 4.0 per cent of the total in 1929-30. But in about four years the imports increased to 10.7 per cent and the exports jumped to 14.3 per cent.

The increasing trade with Germany did not materially reduce Iran's persistent trade difficulties with Russia.[16] By 1932 these difficulties had reached a new peak, and there was an outcry by Iranian merchants against the arbitrary methods employed by the Soviet trade organizations in northern Iran, culminating in a demand for the

[11] *Ibid.*

[12] By this date new noncapitulatory treaties had already been concluded with Russia and Great Britain.

[13] Great Britain and Russia already enjoyed this minimum tariff. For the text of this agreement, see *League of Nations Treaty Series*, CVII, 391-95.

[14] For the text, see *ibid.*, CXI, 29-30.

[15] For the text, see *League of Nations Treaty Series*, CXIII, 17-19.

[16] For Irano-Soviet trade problems, see Chapter IX.

abrogation of the 1931 trade agreement. Riẕā Shah did not submit to this demand and sought instead to settle the accumulated differences through the conclusion of a new trade agreement in 1935.

While playing for time with the Russians, he methodically labored at ways by which trade with Germany could be increased. The Payment and Clearing Agreement of October 30, 1935, was the most important means toward that end. Article 2 provided for all payments to be settled either through the Payments Clearing Fund of Germany and Bānk-i Millī or through private clearing accounts.[17] Thus, all payments in Iran for German imports were to be made in rials to Bānk-i Millī either credited to the seller's account or to a private clearing account opened in Iran. Similarly, all payments in Germany were to be made in reichsmarks either to a general clearing account opened in the name of Bānk-i Millī at the General Clearing Office or to a private clearing account.[18] This agreement significantly facilitated Iran's trade with Germany, but the phenomenal increase in the subsequent years should not be attributed to it alone[19] or to the "skillful commercial policy" of the Nazis.[20] The important factor was Iran's continuing trade problems with the USSR.

In 1938 when the 1935 agreement with the USSR expired, the Shah refused to renew it.[21] In 1939 new difficulties aggravated relations to the point that Irano-Soviet trade "almost entirely ceased."[22] The Shah then turned to Germany for a greater volume of trade. In 1938-39 Iran's German imports amounted to 44.37 per cent of the total imports, and its exports to Germany reached the figure of 20.25 per cent of that total. In 1940-41 Iran's trade with Germany reached the highest peak in history, with imports up to 47.87 and exports up to 42.09 per cent of the totals. By that time Iran's trade with Russia had been reduced almost to nothing: imports were a

[17] The text is in *Majmu'ah'-'i Qavānīn-i Majlis-i Dahum*, pp. 417-28. This twenty-article agreement was accompanied by the exchange of notes between the representatives of the two governments. The source cited includes these notes.

[18] Ahmad Minai, *Economic Development of Iran under the Reign of Reza Shah (1926-1941)* (Ph.D. dissertation, American University, 1961), p. 209.

[19] This is implied by Minai.

[20] See Lenczowski, *op. cit.*, p. 156.

[21] The refusal to renew the agreement is clearly attributable to Riẕā Shah. See U.S. Department of State, *Documents on German Foreign Policy, 1918-1945* Series D (Washington, 1945), VIII, 353-57.

[22] Elwell-Sutton, *op. cit.*, p. 163.

mere .04 per cent and exports 1.17 per cent of the totals.[23] By substituting Germany for Russia as its foremost trade partner, the Shah had finally succeeded in his prolonged struggle to emancipate Iran economically from Russia.[24]

Ironically, Iran was soon forced to seek a remedy for its excessive dependence on German trade. The outbreak of the Second World War made it appear advisable for the Iranian government to achieve an economic understanding with the Soviet Union inasmuch as the war adversely affected the transportation problem. This added new urgency to the need for a new trade agreement settling the question of transit through the Soviet Union. How the Shah brought pressure to bear on Russia toward that end was related in Chapter IX.

After the German attack on Russia the Shah was forced to turn to the USSR again for trade. Trade with Germany diminished markedly in 1941-42, and Russian trade began to regain its former ascendancy in Iran.[25] By that time Iran had been invaded simultaneously by British and Russian forces.

One of the forms in which Iran's *rapprochement* with Germany was manifested was enthusiastic acceptance of German capital and technical assistance. Because Iran's emancipation from Russia might not be fully realized merely through the expansion of trade with Germany, the Shah made economic self-sufficiency by means of rapid industrialization a cherished objective of his government. German capital and technical know-how were sought to further that goal. German investment in and technical aid to Iran involved almost every branch of Iranian industry.[26] In general, all new branches of industry established in Iran were integral parts of the Shah's plan for politico-economic independence. For example, cotton textiles had always been a most important import item in Iranian trade, and the bulk of them had come from Russia.[27] Even before the Shah ascended the throne, Iran had shown interest in the establishment of a textile factory by a

[23] For a detailed statistical comparison of Irano-German trade with Iran's trade with other countries, see *Nāmah-'i Bāzargānī*, nos. 1-22, and *Majallah-'i Bānk-i Millī-i Īrān*, nos. 66-67. See also the table in Raj Narain Gupta, *Iran, An Economic Study* (New Delhi, 1947), p. 130.

[24] See Chapter IX.

[25] See the sources cited in note 23 above.

[26] Cf. Elwell-Sutton, *op. cit.*, pp. 166-67, and Lenczowski, *op. cit.*, p. 154.

[27] Cf. Violet Conolly, *Soviet Economic Policy in the East* (London, 1933), p. 72, and Gupta, *op. cit.*, p. 115.

German.[28] But it was not until after 1925 that the cotton plantation in Juibar was leased to Germans, who also entered cotton-carding factories and various enterprises in the textile industry in Isfahan, Mazandaran, and other areas.[29] These early efforts with German aid were followed by the establishment of several new textile mills near Tehran in 1931.

A third area of cooperation between Iran and Germany was in transportation and communication. To a significant extent Iran's traditional dependence on trade with Russia had been due to its primitive transportation facilities and poor roads. As we have seen, a desire to reduce and ultimately eliminate this dependence, in addition to a determination to enhance the country's political unity and strategic position, influenced the Shah's choice of termini for the Trans-Iranian Railway.[30] The task of building the Bandar-Shahi sector of the Trans-Iranian Railway was entrusted to the Germans, who still remind the Iranians of their role in this engineering feat by the slightly camouflaged designs of the swastika built into the ceiling of the central railway station in Tehran. Even before the construction of the railway, road building and other communication projects had been entrusted to the Germans. By early 1926 these and other German efforts had been carried out so systematically that the Russian-Eastern Chamber of Commerce reported to Moscow that it was "as though [these efforts were] in accordance with a preconceived plan, directed by one mind." [31]

Iran's *rapprochement* with Germany also took the form of employing German advisers. The Shah's growing dissatifaction with Dr. Millspaugh led him to turn to Germans for advice. The question of what powers should be given the advisers dominated the Shah's negotiations with the Germans. The United States gave close attention to the course of developments leading to the replacement of the American mission by German advisers, as is evidenced by the volume and content of diplomatic correspondence on the matter between the United States legation in Tehran and the Department of State. Even negotiations in Berlin were under close scrutiny by the United States Embassy.[32] There is no evidence to indicate that the general isola-

[28] See NA, RG 762.91/–.
[29] See NA, RG 762.91/1.
[30] See Chapter IX.
[31] Enclosure to NA, RG 762.91/1.
[32] See NA, RG 891.51A/423.

tionist attitude of the United States permitted anything other than mere observation and reporting.

A bill was presented to the Majlis in October 1927 for the employment for two years of a German financial and economic expert, a Swiss Treasurer-General, a Swiss Director of General Accounts, and a German Director of the Inspection Service. The government was to consult the German financial expert on financial obligations, on the preparation of the budget, and on granting concessions, but he was to be put under the supervision of the Iranian Minister of Finance. In December 1927 Dr. W. Boetzkes, the manager of the Bank for German Industrial Obligations, left Berlin for Iran for consultation with the Iranian government on the position of financial adviser. After examining the bill, he informed the German Foreign Office that "it was futile to send anyone to act under the terms of that law." The Iranian government then intimated that it might be willing to amend the bill.[33] The question of the powers of the German advisers was discussed in the Majlis. Mudarris stated that although he had not favored the employment of advisers in the past, he believed that the bill before the Majlis was worthless because the German advisers would not have the right to control expenditures, as Dr. Millspaugh had had. Taqīzādah believed that the German financial adviser should have administrative connections with other experts and that the Treasurer-General "should have control over expenditures." [34]

But the Shah did not permit any real controversy over the bill. Furthermore, many deputies were at least as eager as he to employ German advisers. The bill passed without significant change on February 16, 1928,[35] thereby officially marking the substitution of Dr. Boetzkes for Dr. Millspaugh, who had already left Iran.

The new law seemed to confer upon the German adviser no powers comparable to those granted to Dr. Millspaugh by the Fourth Majlis, but the Germanophile sentiments of most Iranian nationalists inclined the Germans to expect far more than Millspaugh had. In view of this expectation the Germans did not find it in keeping with "practical politics" to insist too much on the wording of the law. This attitude was well reflected in Dr. Boetzkes' evaluation of Dr. Millspaugh. Although he considered the American Administrator "intelli-

[33] See NA, RG 891.51A/432.
[34] See NA, RG 891.51A/445.
[35] For the text of the law in English, see NA, RG 891.51A/451.

gent," "tremendously hard-working," and "very honestly devoted" to the interests of Iran, he thought that Millspaugh had worked so hard that he was shut off from the world. Not only did he see trees rather than the forest, but he remained unaware of the political currents which were moving about him and affecting his work. He demanded 100 per cent fulfillment of the Iranians' engagements when anyone accustomed to dealing with Orientals would know that the very most to be hoped for was 80 or 90 per cent. When difficulties accumulated, Millspaugh simply fell back on his contract, a procedure which seemed to Dr. Boctzkes monumental folly since a man in Millspaugh's position could only hope to succeed by what Dr. Boetzkes called "psychological means." [36]

The "practical politics" and "psychological means" of Dr. Boetzkes and his compatriots were not sufficient to protect them from the wrath of Riẕā Shah. Irano-German friendship suffered a momentous setback in April 1932 when four German journalists and an Iranian student in Berlin published defamatory articles about the Shah, who subsequently launched a campaign against the Germans in Iran.[37] The first target was Hartman, head of the Tehran arsenal. The second victim was Dr. Hurt Lindenblatt, president and chief organizer of the National Bank of Iran, who had followed Dr. Boetzkes in 1928. Dr. Lindenblatt was ordered out of the country, and a Herr Vogel took charge of the bank.[38] On September 7, 1932, *Iṭṭilā'āt* reported that Vogel had escaped from Tehran and that his flight "confirmed the Government's opinion that Lindenblatt and himself [Vogel] had shown no loyalty when in charge [of the bank] and that they had been extravagant in expenditures. It was clearly proved that Dr. Lindenblatt, Vogel and one or two of their assistants were deliquent." The Iranian newspaper further stated, "It goes without saying that Vogel's astounding action has stained the reputation of German employees in the service of the Persian Government, and has served a blow to the German experts and businessmen in this country." Lindenblatt returned to Iran and on April 20, 1933, was arrested and jailed in Tehran on diverse charges regarding the abuse of Bank funds.[39]

[36] See NA, RG 891.51A/455.
[37] NA, RG 762.91/5, Despatch, Tehran, May 5, 1932.
[38] NA, RG 762.91/7, Despatch, Tehran, June 18, 1932.
[39] NA, RG 762.91/13, Despatch, Tehran, May 5, 1933.

The Shah's disenchantment with Germany also prompted the dismissal of the Iranian Finance Minister, who had helped Germany in pushing its interests in Iran.[40] The German Minister in Tehran had been very intimate with the Iranian Finance Minister and had used him not only to tighten Germany's economic grip but also for cultural and political propaganda by harping on the alleged similarity of German and Iranian political ideals.[41]

Although Iran's ever-growing friendship with Germany acted as a counterweight against Great Britain and particularly Russia, it should not be assumed that that friendship was completely shielded from the vicissitudes consequent on the Shah's nationalism and his ever-present suspicion of all foreign powers, including Germany.

THE NEUTRALITY PROCLAMATION

The major factors underlying Iran's policy of neutrality were both indigenous and exogenous. The most important internal factors were basically emotional. There is no evidence to show that this policy was based upon careful consideration of Iran's national interests. Rather the traditional dislike of Great Britain and the suspicion of Germany made neutrality appear as the only feasible policy. The anti-British sentiment made any alliance with Great Britain unthinkable. An alliance with Germany was not desirable either, although it might appear that the Shah's close cooperation with the Reich should have made Germany Iran's natural ally. But, as we have just seen, Germany was suspect also. To Riẕā Shah no foreign power could be fully trusted, although Germany, as contrasted with Great Britain and Russia, was regarded as a lesser evil. Thus neutrality appeared to be the only acceptable policy. The attraction of this policy was reinforced by Iran's memory of its "neutrality" in the First World War.

Suspicion of Germany increased even after the adoption of the policy of neutrality, particularly because of the Nazis' growing friendship with Russia, Iran's *bête noire*. Something "near panic swept the country when Molotov's visit to Berlin was accompanied by

[40] NA, RG 762.91/21, Telegram, Tehran, October 29, 1939.
[41] *Ibid.*

rumors that, in return for a free hand in the Dardanelles, Germany was offering Russia an equally free hand in Iran." [42] The anxiety produced by Molotov's visit to Berlin on November 12-13, 1940, prompted the Iranian Prime Minister, 'Alī Manṣūr, to take up the matter with the German Ambassador, who replied that he knew nothing regarding the conversations in Berlin about Iran. But he immediately requested the German Foreign Ministry to guide him in his future conversations with the Iranian government. In the same request the German Ambassador suggested that "a statement that Iran was not discussed on the occasion of Molotov's visit would suffice to bring about a tranquilizing effect." [43]

Mūsā Nūrī Isfandyārī, the Iranian Minister in Berlin, and Sayyāh, the Director General of the Iranian Foreign Ministry, expressed the same concern to Freiherr von Weizsäcker, State Secretary of the German Foreign Ministry. He told the Iranian officials he knew of no such bargain about Iran, attributed the rumors to "English intrigues," and instructed the German Ambassador to say as much to the Iranian government.[44] The German Ambassador later reported that he had carried out the instructions, which had a "calming effect" on the Iranian Prime Minister.[45] The fact that the Nazi officials were lying has now been revealed by the publication of the documents on Nazi-Soviet relations by the United States government. According to a secret protocol related to the Four-Power Pact drawn up in Berlin between Hitler and Molotov, Germany had conceded that "the area south of Baku in the general direction of the Persian Gulf is recognized as the center of the aspirations of the Soviet Union." [46]

Certain external circumstances also favored Iran's policy of neutrality at first. Perhaps the more important of these was persistent German encouragement of Iran's neutrality. As early as October 28, 1939, it was believed in Germany that because of Turkey's strong ties with England and France it was "politically especially important [at the time] to continue to strengthen Iran in her absolute neu-

[42] *Economist*, January 11, 1941. See also U.S. Department of State, *op. cit.* (Washington, 1962), XII, 531-32.

[43] U.S. Department of State, *op. cit.* (Washington, 1960), XI, 597.

[44] *Ibid.*, p. 632.

[45] *Ibid.*

[46] The text is in J. C. Hurewitz, *Diplomacy in the Near and Middle East* (Princeton, N. J., 1956), II, 228-31.

trality."[47] Germany attached so much significance to Iran's continuing neutral posture that it went so far as to make representation in Moscow against Soviet pressures on Iran as such pressures might push Iran into the British fold.[48]

The other factor involved the Anglo-Russian attitude. Up to May 1941 the British did not regard the neutralist attitude of Iran with too much alarm, although the extent of German activities was cause for some concern. But once the British troops entered Baghdad toward the end of May and the pro-German Iraqi Prime Minister, Rashīd 'Alī, escaped into Iran, the British believed that the center of diplomatic activity in the Middle East had shifted to Iran, whence the pro-Axis sentiment in the area would be fomented.[49]

Russia did not oppose Iran's policy of neutrality either until the German invasion of June 22, 1941, as evidenced by Russia's active mediation between Iran and Germany which resulted in the comprehensive treaty mentioned earlier.[50] The German invasion completely reversed the Soviet attitude. Russia's Nazi friends of yesterday became the foes of today. The German penetration of Iran which had been benevolently watched and even assisted before was now suddenly recognized as a threat to the security of Russia. The German fifth columnists pouring into Iran with their centers at Tehran and Tabriz could incite the Ukranian patriots in Tehran to begin agitation among the Georgian, Ukranian, and Armenian minorities in the provinces lying immediately north of the Caucasus.[51] Furthermore, "Iran and the Persian Gulf constituted the Soviet's only permanent trade route with the United States because of the winter freeze-up of Murmansk and the Japanese threat to Vladivostok."[52]

The German invasion of Russia increased British objections to Iran's policy of neutrality also. Winston Churchill set forth succinctly the reason underlying this change of attitude by stating,

> The need to pass munitions and supplies of all kinds to the Soviet Government and the extreme difficulties of the Arctic route, together with future strategic possibilities, made it eminently desirable to open the fullest communication with Russia through Persia. The Persian oil fields were a prime war factor. An active and numerous German

[47] U.S. Department of State, *op. cit.*, VIII, 353-57.
[48] *Ibid.*
[49] *Economist*, August 12, 1941.
[50] See Chapter IX.
[51] *Economist*, August 2, 1941.
[52] *New York Times*, August 10, 1941.

mission had installed itself in Tehran, and German prestige stood high. The suppression of the revolt in Iraq and the Anglo-French occupation of Syria, achieved as they were by narrow margins, blotted out Hitler's Oriental plan. We welcomed the opportunity of joining hands with the Russians and proposed to them a joint campaign. I was not without some anxiety about embarking on a Persian war, but the arguments for it were compulsive.[53]

The change in the Russian and British attitudes was reflected in their memoranda of July 19 and August 16, 1941, to the government of Iran demanding the expulsion of many Germans. Iran, however, rejected the Allied demands, and Muḥammad Shāyistah, Iran's Minister in Washington, D.C., called upon Secretary of State Cordell Hull to deny the reports about Nazi fifth-column activities or even the existence of any fifth columnists in Iran. He also told American newspapermen that there were no more than 700 Germans in Iran, many of whom had been there before 1914 and Iran had granted no visas since the Second World War started.[54] This statement as well as other gestures reflected the Shah's policy of procrastination, which in part prompted the invasion of Iran on August 25, 1941 (*Sivum-i Shahrīvar* 1320).

The disastrous consequences of this policy have prompted many Iranians to seek to explain its underlying causes. Four major explanations have been advanced. One view unreservedly attributes the Shah's procrastinating policy to the influences of Franz Mayr, a German fifth columnist who will be discussed later. The most widely read version of this opinion appeared in several anonymous articles entitled *Riẓā Shāh va Jāsūsān-i Ālmānī* ("Riẓā Shah and the German Spies").[55] The author describes in detail how Mayr managed to place his own agents in the Iranian Police Department, how he established personal ties with the Shah, and how highly the Shah valued Mayr's advice on all matters. The author's prejudice against Riẓā Shah is so apparent that it calls into question the reliability of his report.

A second explanation is that the Shah faltered in the eventful days of July and August 1941 because his advisers misinformed him. This

[53] Winston S. Churchill, *The Second World War*, Vol. III, *The Grand Alliance* (London, 1948), pp. 476-77.

[54] *New York Times*, August 23, 1941.

[55] For these articles, see *Khwāndanīhā* (Tehran), Fourth Year, no. 89, pp. 8-9; no. 90, pp. 4-7 and 12-13; no. 91, pp. 3-5; no. 93, pp. 4-5; no. 94, pp. 8-10; no. 95, pp. 8-10; and no. 96, pp. 14-15.

view was popular in Iranian circles for a while during the mid-war years when it was increasingly realized that the end of the Shah's dictatorship had not ushered in democracy and prosperity and when a growing number of writers and politicians began to look back nostalgically to the Shah's paternalism. The corollary of this mood was to absolve the late Shah of his mistakes by putting the blame on his counselors. The boldest advocate of this view, who has written over seventy pamphlets on *Vaqāī'-i Shahrīvar* ("The Events of August-September 1941"), names three policy makers in particular. He claims that 'Alī Manṣūr, the Prime Minister, Nakhjavān, the Minister of War, and Āmirī, the Foreign Minister, encouraged the Shah to fight against the Allied Powers by giving him fantastically exaggerated accounts of Iran's military capability.[56]

Another view has been expressed by a well-known Iranian writer who blames the Shah's personal traits. Although this writer implicates the Shah's advisers, his main emphasis is placed on the confusion and indecisiveness of the Shah himself. The Shah's intellectual shortcomings compounded his distress under the grave circumstances of the eventful days of *Khurdād* and *Shahrīvar* (July and August 1941).[57] Although this explanation seems more sophisticated than the other two, it shares with them the same fundamental weakness – a failure to realize the complexity of the problem.

Muḥammad Riẕa Shah propounds yet another view, one which neither implicates his father's counselors nor the late Shah. In fact, his argument is a defense of the policy of his father. The gist of it is that Great Britain and Russia placed too much emphasis, in their diplomatic correspondence with the Iranian government, on their demand for the expulsion of the Germans. In this he seems to see an element of deception and a pretext for the invasion of Iran. After quoting Churchill on the considerations underlying the Allied campaign against Iran, he criticizes the Allies in these terms:

If the Allies were so much concerned about the possibilities of a German break-through, why didn't they request our military assistance under some sort of military as well as diplomatic alliance? Some will think this is a fantastic proposal in view of Reza Shah's neutrality. I can only reply that my father was a reasonable man who held his

[56] Muḥammad Riẕā Khalīlī 'Arāqī, *Vaqāyī'-i Shahrīvar* (Tehran, n. d.), II, 398-99.

[57] A. Khājah Nūrī, *Bāzīgarān-i 'Aṣr-i Ṭalā'ī* (Tehran, n. d.), pp. 447-49.

country's welfare ever uppermost. If the Allies had abandoned their circumlocution and had given Reza Shah an honest picture of their strategic predicament in its relation to Iran's interest, I think he would have seen the point.[58]

Muḥammad Riẕā Shah's view reflects devotion to his father's memory and typifies the argument of some Iranian nationalists in placing the blame for Iran's policy of procrastination squarely on the Allied Powers.

Perhaps a more balanced view can be derived from the over-all trends of the Shah's foreign policy. It may be proposed that the policy of procrastination was influenced by two interrelated sets of factors. One was Iran's dependence on and penetration by Germany. Germany had found it relatively easy to make itself the most influential power in Iran while the Shah believed that he was using Germany as a counterweight against Great Britain and Russia. So long as the increasing German influence did not seem to threaten the vital interests of those powers, they tolerated the Shah's flirtation with Germany, and for that very reason, in part at least, Iran's policy of politico-economic emancipation from both Great Britain and Russia proved unusually successful. But when Russia was invaded by Germany, and Great Britain and Russia found themselves on the same side of a war, the German activities in Iran were viewed in a totally different light. A German enemy virtually controlled important Iranian industries, railways, and airlines and threatened to destroy bridges and oil installations located in Iran.

Furthermore, it was realized by the Allied Powers that Iran was being rapidly turned into a most active Middle East center of espionage. The story of the arrival of Gammota, Franz Mayr, and Major Julius Berthold Shulze in Iran and their activities as German agents are too well-known both in Iran [59] and in the West [60] to require further discussion here. The published memoirs of Shulze and Nāmdār, the Iranian secretary of the German Embassy, reveal the extent to which a number of Germanophile Iranians such as Colonel

[58] Mohammad Reza Shah Pahlavi, *Mission for My Country* (New York, 1961), pp. 72-73.

[59] See *Khwāndanīhā*, Seventh Year, no. 4, pp. 12-15 and 20; no. 5, pp. 10-11 and 20-21; no. 9, pp. 18-20; no. 13, pp. 7-10; no. 16, pp. 7-8; no. 19, pp. 10 and 20; no. 21, pp. 10-11; and no. 23, pp. 14-15.

[60] See Bernhard Shulze-Holthus, *Daybreak in Iran: A Story of the German Intelligence Service* (London, 1954).

Ḥisām Vazīrī, Colonel Gīlānshāh, Mrs. Laylā Sanjarī, Deputy Nawbakht, and Nāṣir Khān Qashqā'ī cooperated with the German fifth columnists in turning Iran into a hotbed of German espionage.[61] Furthermore, Iran became a refuge for such well-known sympathizers of Germany as Rashīd 'Alī of Iraq and the Mufti of Jerusalem. As early as 1937 the latter had promised Germany, in return for German ideological and material support of Arab independence, to promote German trade, to prepare a sympathetic atmosphere for Germany in case of war, and to disseminate German culture in the Islamic world.[62] In a friendly letter to Hitler in 1941 the Mufti wished him "a long and happy life and a brilliant victory and prosperity for the great German people and for the Axis in the very near future." [63]

Iran's dependence on Germany cannot wholly explain the Shah's policy of procrastination, which helped to precipitate the invasion of the country by Great Britain and Russia. Economic dependence on Germany and the relentless activities of German agents and their Iranian sympathizers made procrastination appear as the most desirable course, but the intransigent pursuit of this course after its adoption is probably attributable to the Shah's doctrinaire attitude. He had made friends with Germany as his favorite third power, and Great Britain and Russia had more or less tolerated this friendship. Germany's invasion of Russia changed matters, but the Shah chose to ignore this new contingency, perhaps because of rigid adherence to the third-power doctrine and to the principle of "strict neutrality."

For several months before the first British note of July 19, 1941, the British government, through its representative in Tehran, Sir Reader Bullard, had urged the Shah to take effective measures against the Germans.[64] But the Iranian government, instead of weighing the possible consequences of its refusal to comply against the advantages derived from the continuation of its policy of outward neutrality, deluded itself with the legality of its position, and its representative in Washington boasted of Iran's determination to resist aggression even if the British or Russian forces were ten times larger than those of Iran! [65]

[61] *Ibid.* and *Khwāndanīhā* in note 59.

[62] U.S. Department of State, *op. cit.* (Washington, 1953), V, 778-79.

[63] *Ibid.*, XI, 1151-55.

[64] See the text of the British note of August 25, 1941 in the *New York Times,* August 26, 1941.

[65] *New York Times,* August 23, 1941.

Overconfidence rather than sober political calculation prompted the Shah offhandedly to mobilize Iranian forces. On August 19, 1941, while addressing the graduating army officers at Aqdasyah, he informed them of the cancellation of the usual one-month leave and in effect ordered them to active duty on Iran's borders, where 120,000 troops already stood guard against attack.[66] If the number of men in an army were an index of its strength, Iran's armed strength was considerable. At war it consisted of 100,000 to 200,000 men organized into twelve mixed divisions. Two divisions were located at the capital and the others in strategic areas such as Tabriz, Rizaieh, Kurdistan, Khuzistan Khorasan, Gilan, Kermanshah, and Ardabil.[67] There were also five independent brigades, plus an infantry regiment, an artillery regiment, a few antiaircraft guns, 200 to 300 planes, and a couple of escort vessels.[68]

At dawn on August 25, 1941, only a few days prior to the second anniversary of the outbreak of World War II, British and Russian forces began a simultaneous invasion of Iran; the Allies delivered their final notes[69] to the Iranian government apprising the Shah of the invasion after their troops had crossed the Iranian frontiers.[70] The British, under the command of Wavell, who was directing the operations from Simla in India, made their first major landing at Bandar Mashur. They deployed 3,000 troops striking into the interior of Iran at three points along a 600-mile front from the Persian Gulf to the Turkish frontier. In addition to the British imperial troops attacking in the Bandar Mashur region, two other columns struck into Iran from British-controlled Iraq – from Rawanduz twenty miles south of the Iraqi-Irano-Turkish border junction and from Khanaqin about eighty miles northwest of Baghdad. The Iranian forces in the path of the British advance to Kermanshah were caught unaware while sleeping in their barracks.[71] The British imperial forces also

[66] For the text of the Shah's address, see 'Arāqī, *op. cit.*, I, 7-10.

[67] *Ibid.*, pp. 24-28.

[68] Cf. the *New York Times*, August 26, 1941.

[69] Texts of these notes are in the *New York Times*, August 26, 1941.

[70] *China Weekly Review*, August 30, 1941, p. 403. The sudden invasion was characterized by Churchill as "somewhat abrupt steps" in a review of the war in the House of Commons. See the *New York Times*, October 1, 1941.

[71] 'Arāqī, *op. cit.*, I, 38.

found the main body of the Iranian troops in their barracks as they had not been warned of the impending landing.[72]

The only notable exception to the unpreparedness and general breakdown of morale among the Iranian forces was the Sixth Division commanded by General Shāh-Bakhtī, which defended Abadan. According to an official British account "the defence posts along the quay had been well sited and were courageously manned." At the Abadan refinery the loyalty of Iranian soldiers was "strikingly demonstrated at the pumping installations, where Persian soldiers who had a post on the roof resisted with the highest bravery and a duel of fire went on for hours before they were dislodged." [73]

The Russian forces struck in three areas, in the northwest pushing toward Tabriz and Pahlavi and in the northeast advancing toward Meshed. It was reported that thirty (!) Soviet divisions were entering Iran.[74] The suddenness of the Allied invasion, the unpreparedness of the Iranian forces, and the unrestrained Russian bombing of some of the cities of Azerbaijan and Pahlavi, Ghazian, and Qazvin threw the Iranian troops into utter confusion resulting in the desertion of several units by their officers and in loss of their weapons.[75] Some of the officers were later indicted for "failure to discharge important military duties." [76]

In less than forty-eight hours after the invasion began the Iranian military staff realized that resistance against the British and Russian forces was impossible. On August 27, in a detailed report to the Shah, General Ẓarghāmī set forth the sad fate of the Iranian forces on all fronts and suggested the establishment of a "High National Council" (*Shurā-yi ʿĀlī-yi Kishvar*) in order to initiate diplomatic measures "now that all military strength has been dissipated." [77] Simultaneously the Cabinet of ʿAlī Manṣūr resigned, and the Shah

[72] *Paiforce, The Official Story of the Persia and Iraq Command, 1941-46* (London, 1948), p. 64.

[73] *Ibid.*, p. 65.

[74] *New York Times*, August 26, 1941.

[75] *Paiforce*, p. 70. This work states that a number of the weapons lost by the Iranian forces were collected by the British, "but the great majority fell into the eager hands of the tribesmen."

[76] For detailed accounts of the breakdown of the morale of the Iranian army, the charges against individual officers, and the discredit that fell on the army in general, see the two volumes of ʿArāqī, *op. cit.*

[77] For the text of this candid report secretly made to the Shah, see *ibid.*, II, 384-85.

asked Muḥammad 'Alī Furūghī to form a new government. Furūghī immediately put together a Cabinet and introduced it to the Majlis on August 28. During this extraordinary session of the Majlis the Iranian Prime Minister announced the decision of the High Council. The Council suggested that "whereas the strategic areas of defense were already occupied by foreign troops and because the defense of the capital by the first and second divisions will probably fail to serve any purpose it would probably be more beneficial to order a cease-fire and to continue with the diplomatic negotiations already in progress." [78]

Although the cease-fire merely acknowledged the military defeat, it was not without significance as an eloquent evidence of the Shah's gross miscalculations and an admission of his mistakenly rigid policy in the face of changed circumstances. The appointment of Furūghī (done reluctantly because the Shah believed "he was too old and ill to lead the country")[79] and the formation of the new government removed some of the causes of Allied irritation. But who was there to remove the Shah himself?

Iranians tend to place the blame squarely on the British. Their argument runs as follows: As early as September 6 the British began a relentless campaign against the Shah from radio stations located in London and Delhi. Iranians were told about the "Tyranny of Silence," about cruelty, and about injustices they had suffered at the hands of Riẕā Shah. In countering this, the Shah chose to use the press, but his efforts miscarried because the Russians charged that he was inciting the public against them. As a result the government was forced to suppress the "guilty" papers, and the Shah's last attempt to defend his prestige failed ignominiously.[80]

The British view implies that the Shah's abdication was caused by his fears consequent to a Russian move toward the capital. Sir Reader Bullard states:

It is often said that the Allies asked him [the Shah] to leave, but that is not true. The Persian Government was very slow in carrying out an undertaking it had given to the Allies to secure the departure from Persia of all Axis diplomats and to hand over all non-official Germans and Austrians, with specified exceptions, to the British or

[78] Cf. *ibid.*, pp. 389-90, and Khājah Nūrī, *op. cit.*, pp. 404-5.
[79] See Khājah Nūrī, *op. cit.*, p. 401.
[80] *Ibid.*, pp. 450-51.

the Russians. To hasten execution of the undertaking it was resolved that British and Russian troops should occupy, temporarily, the outskirts of Tehran. The advance began early on the morning of September 16. The Russians at Qazvin were nearer to Tehran than any part of the British forces and when they started for the capital Riza Shah thought that it meant a Russian move to overthrow him, so he abdicated in favor of his eldest son and left the country.[81]

The architect of independent Iran left the throne to his son, who was then proclaimed Shah by the Majlis. On September 17 Muḥammad Riẕā Shah witnessed the entry of British and Russian forces into Tehran.[82]

THE TRADITIONAL PATTERNS AND THE TRIANGULAR INTERACTION

Riẕā Shah's departure from the traditional patterns of Iranian foreign policy was discernible in his struggle with the USSR, in the disputes with Great Britain, and in his good-neighbor policy. But the true nature of his foreign policy may best be seen in his third-power policy and his policy of neutrality and procrastination. Both of these policies partook of the traditional elements, which were always present in the Shah's foreign policy although it took the eventful days of July-August 1941 to bring out these elements graphically. The third-power policy of the Shah led to excessive reliance upon Germany, from whose control he found it difficult to extricate himself.

To appreciate the nature of the Shah's partially self-created predicament, it is essential to realize that there was another side to his admittedly unswerving struggle for independence from Great Britain and Russia. Like other nationalist policy makers before him, the Shah set himself the goal of "absolute" independence. Toward the achievement of this goal, he bent every effort. He sought relentlessly to make Iran economically self-sufficient, but he did not realize that the attainment of such an objective was not within the reach of Iran.

[81] "Persia in the Two World Wars," *Royal Central Asian Journal,* January 1963, p. 13.

[82] Riẕā Shah was taken on a British ship to Mauritius and later to Johannesburg, where he died in 1944. His body was later brought back to Iran and is now buried in a mausoleum near the Shah 'Abd al-'Aẓīm shrine in Ray, south of Tehran.

Therefore, the third-power policy that was to assist Iran to free itself from Great Britain and Russia led to heavy dependence on Germany. Instead of a mere counterweight against Great Britain and Russia, Germany became the dominant power in the affairs of Iran. The independence won from Great Britain and Russia step by step, in part as the result of an unprecedented degree of Iranian diplomatic skill, was progressively lost to Germany. The objective of absolute independence in complete disregard of Iran's capabilities helped make Iran a hostage of Germany.

In essence this was no novelty in Iranian foreign policy. In choosing objectives beyond the reach of the country Riẕā Shah did what both the pre-Constitutional and post-Constitutional policy makers had done on numerous occasions. The persistence of this traditional pattern was particularly observable in time of crisis, when the Shah rigidly clung to his outward policy of neutrality in spite of changed circumstances.

The most typical example of disregard of the realities of the situation can be found in the way Iran reacted to the Anglo-Russian demand for the expulsion of the Germans. There is no evidence to indicate that the problem was ever seriously considered. There is, however, ample evidence to show that, instead of seeking a way out of this predicament, the Shah chose to procrastinate. Overconfidence eclipsed a truly rational assessment of the country's interests in time of crisis. It even prompted the Shah to mobilize the army. The decision to resist was taken in complete disregard of Iran's capabilities.

To no small extent the Shah's foreign policy procedures were characteristic of the Iranian foreign-policy-making process. The Shah, like many other strong monarchs in Iranian history, became the sole maker of decisions. His ends and means were those of Iran. His successes were those of Iran, and so were his mistakes. Few if any of his critics would deny the Shah's patriotism. But policy making requires more than patriotism, as Riẕā Shah recognized on many occasions. In fact, his policy toward Germany and the policy of neutrality and procrastination were anticlimactic if contrasted with his relatively successful policy toward Great Britain and Russia and toward Iran's Muslim neighbors. This paradox may be explained by the fact that the Shah could not be a capable decision maker on all fronts. His advisers were subdued and apathetic, and the few who were active nursed a pathological hatred of Great Britain, or Russia, or both, similar to that of the deputies of the Third Majlis, who manifested such a fanciful enthusiasm for Germany. The Shah's policy of outward neutrality in the Second World War resembled that of Mustawfī al-Mamālik at the outbreak of the First World War. Striking similarities also existed between the consequences of the two policies. Mustawfī's policy helped make Iran the battlefield of the belligerent powers; the Shah's policy contributed to the invasion of Iran.

The dynamic interaction between internal and external circumstances and foreign policy continued as it had in the centuries since the rise of Iran to power. Riẕā Shah's foreign policy affected the external conditions because it precipitated foreign invasion. The invasion affected the internal situation by forcing the Shah to abdicate. The removal of a strong ruler in this instance, as in others discussed previously, plunged the political system into chaos. It became clear that conformity rather than unity had been the rule throughout the reign of Riẕā Shah through coercion rather than consensus. National disunity and lack of social cohesion in 1941 haunted the Iranian polity as they had in past centuries. In spite of the Constitutional Revolution and the nation-building efforts of Riẕā Shah, the Iranian political system suffered from the maladies of past centuries. Despite signs of departture from the old patterns after the First World War and particularly during 1921-41, the transitional foreign policy of Iran was still bound by traditional elements both in process and substance.

Chapter XIII

Conclusion

STUDY of the dynamic triangular interaction in nearly four and a half centuries of Iranian foreign policy has made possible a number of generalizations. These relate to both the substance and process of that policy. We shall attempt here to outline them as factors and forces shaping Iranian foreign policy, as major characteristics of that policy, and as the techniques of Iranian diplomacy.

FACTORS AND FORCES

Geographic Location: Iran's geographic location has been one of the most important factors influencing its foreign policy. As a bridge between the Middle East and southern and western Asia, between Russia and the Persian Gulf, and, through the Strait of Hormuz, between Russia and the Gulf of Oman and the Arabian Sea, it has been coveted for centuries by traders, conquerors, and defenders of imperial interests to the south and the north of the Iranian plateau. It was not, however, until the dawn of the nineteenth century that the clashing interests of the rival powers of Europe endowed it with the strategic significance that it has possessed ever since.

Great-Power Rivalry: The conflicting amibitions of Russia and the Ottoman Empire in Transcaucasia and northwestern Iran in the eighteenth century exerted significant influence on Iranian foreign policy, and the persistent Anglo-Russian rivalry was the dominating external factor during the nineteenth century. The *rapprochement* between the two rivals during the 1907-16 period was a momentary aberration prompted by the threat posed by Germany. The Anglo-Russian Agreement of 1907 removed Iran briefly from its traditional role as the buffer between Russia and British India. As a buffer for the British, Iran had enjoyed some freedom of action; but as a land divided into British and Russian spheres of influence, it lost its independence for all practical purposes.

The Bolshevik Revolution introduced a new element of far-reaching consequence. The ideological "Socialist-Capitalist antagonism" was added to the power rivalry of the past centuries. Communism as an instrument of Soviet foreign policy posed an unprecedented threat not only to Iran's independence but also to its way of life. The rise of a strong central government under Riẕā Shah, the reluctance of the new regime in Russia to intervene in the affairs of Iran *openly*, and the hands-off policy of the British made it possible for Iran to achieve an unprecedented degree of politico-economic freedom from Great Britain and Russia during the interwar period. Iran's *rapprochement* with Germany, which was at first tolerated by both Great Britain and Russia, though for different reasons, assisted this process of emancipation. But the invasion of Russia by Germany terminated this tolerance, and the alliance between Great Britain and Russia in the Second World War as in the 1907-16 period presented Iranian foreign-policy makers with a most difficult external situation. Failure to cope with this situation realistically brought on the Allied invasion of Iran in 1941.

The Ever-present Past: From the sixteenth century to the present, Iran has gloried in a great past. In consolidating his reestablished state Shah Ismāʿīl strove to extend the frontiers of Iran to those of ancient times. Other capable and strong Ṣafavī rulers fought to maintain or expand the boundaries reached by the founder of their dynasty. The rise of Nādir Shah witnessed the restoration of the

Ṣafavī boundaries, which for all practical purposes had disappeared after the Afghan and Russo-Turkish invasions. During the Qājār period it was not so much the ancient boundaries of Iran that captured the imagination of the Shahs as it was the extent of the Iranian Empire during the reign of Nādir Shah. To regain the boundaries of this empire was the aspiration significantly responsible for the irredentist wars and the prolonged boundary disputes of the nineteenth century.

National Disunity: National disunity was one of the most important factors influencing the foreign policy of Iran. The lack of social cohesion aided national disunity. This could be traced back to ancient times before the migration of the Iranian people into eastern Iran. The dichotomy between the settled and semisettled elements of this early period was followed by the gradation of the society, a system hallowed by Zoroastrianism. Even "democratic" Islam as expounded by its philosophers described the ideal society in medieval times as a hierarchic society with mankind graded into various classes. Iran was made part of the "great Muslim society," but Islam did not transcend the ethnic, linguistic, tribal, and other divisions. In fact, it added a new dichotomy – between the Arab and 'Ajam – to Iranian society. Invasions by the Seljuk Turks and the Mongols added more divisions. The antagonism between the Turks and the Persians often threatened the territorial integrity of Iran.

The Constitutional Revolution introduced another dichotomy into Iranian society. The ideological-political hostility between the Constitutionalists and the Royalists plunged the country into chaos early in the twentieth century. The advent of Bolshevism in Russia and the rise of communism in Iran compounded the problem of lack of social cohesion and political consensus. Nationalism had not produced national unity, and communism vied for the allegiance of a divided nation. Most of Iran's foreign-policy decisions were hampered by the lack of national unity, and Riẕā Shah's relative success was due, to a significant extent, to his ability to impose an unprecedented degree of conformity. His abdication threw the polity back into anarchy, but the presence of foreign troops helped check the threat of disintegration of the political system. In spite of this, the traditional factionalism, cliquism, tribalism, and localism were expressed in many political parties, a partisan press, and a fragmented parliamentary body.

Oil: The discovery of oil in commercial quantities in Iran added to the strategic significance of the country, made it even more an object of great-power rivalry, and thereby posed new problems for the policy makers. In 1901 at the time of the granting of the first oil concession a ruse was necessary in order to circumvent the anticipated Russian obstruction. Great-power rivalry continued to permeate the pursuit of oil concessions in the 1920's and 1930's. Oil was not always *balā-yi sīyāh* "the black evil," as Iranians call it. In the early 1920's oil concessions were dangled before American oil companies in the hope of countering British and Russian pressures and securing financial aid from the United States. The fact that no American concession was actually put into effect did not mean that Iran had failed completely, because Iran did succeed for a time in playing the United States against the other two countries and this maneuvering somehow helped foreclose the possibility of the then-feared extension of the British oil monopoly into the north.

Positively stated, the revenues from oil contributed to the country's financial strength and endowed it with a degree of industrialization which would probably not have been possible without such revenues. Oil was an asset as well as a liability; it all depended on other variables. In the hands of knowledgeable and realistic policy makers it could be a most significant element in Iran's national power.

Monarchy: The age-old monarchy has always been the most important foreign-policy making institution in Iran. Although the monarch was identified with the state from the beginning, Shī'ism played a major role in foreign policy in the sixteenth century. Then a significant change occurred in the nature of the monarchy, and by the time of the death of Shah 'Abbās in 1629 Shī'ism was eclipsed by monarchial absolutism. The strength or weakness of the character of the reigning monarch was a major factor in Iran's foreign policy.

In the absence of a strong monarch between the First World War and the accession of Riẕā Shah to the throne of Iran some supporters of the Constitutional Movement played a dominant role in the formulation and execution of Iran's foreign policy. Mustawfī al-Mamālik, Qavām al-Saltanah, Mushīr al-Dawlah, and Sayyid Ẕīā' al-Dīn are the best examples. Several significant foreign-policy decisions were made during their governments, including the signing of the 1921 treaty with Russia and the rejection of the 1919 agreement with Great Britain.

The precarious existence of the Majlis before the rise of Riẕā Shah provided little opportunity for the deputies to play any significant role in the making and execution of foreign policy. It is doubtful, however, that the Majlis would have been able to do much even if it had enjoyed a continuing tenure. Nevertheless, some attempts were made by the deputies. The hiring of Morgan Shuster was not without important implications. A more significant part was played by the Fourth Majlis, which employed Dr. Millspaugh and was active in offering oil concessions to American concerns and in demanding clarification of the terms of the 1921 treaty with Russia.

In spite of the efforts of the Cabinet and the Majlis, the making and implementation of foreign-policy decisions in the twentieth century as in earlier centuries rested in the hands of the Shah, whose character was therefore of crucial significance for Iran's foreign policy. A strong monarch could hold the political system together and make its foreign policy of some effect. The very independence of Iran was closely tied to the character of the man on the throne. National disunity made a strong monarch indispensable for the survival of the state, let alone the effectiveness of its foreign policy.

Shī'ism: The Shī'ī ideology, perhaps more than any other single factor, assisted the rise of modern Iran to power. Its dynamism in the early sixteenth century cemented the polity in the face of profound divisions in the society. It was a dominant factor in the foreign policy of Iran during the sixteenth and part of the seventeenth century, although as time went on it was overshadowed by monarchical absolutism. Nevertheless, it continued to exert some influence on foreign policy in the nineteenth century, particularly during the reign of Fatḥ 'Alī Shah. The part played by the Shī'ī *'ulamā'* in the Constitutional Movement was significant. So was their role in blocking Riẕā Khān's plan for a republican Iran. Shī'ī influence on the foreign policy of Iran from 1925 to 1941 was almost nil.

Nationalism: Nationalism was the most significant factor influencing the foreign policy of Iran in the period from 1905 to 1941. The Constitutional Movement was basically a nationalist movement. It aimed significantly at the elimination of Anglo-Russian control. It introduced the concept of national interests into Iranian foreign policy. The emergent policy makers began to speak in the interests of the nation. Its most effective spokesman, however, was Riẕā Shah.

He was obviously no ideologue; he despised speechmaking. Nor was he clear in his own mind as to the kind of nation he wished to build. He was no Kemal Atatürk; yet he was the architect of Iran's independence. He suffered from the frailties of other Iranian absolute monarchs, but he was the first Shah to be intensely preoccupied with "the national interest" of Iran in dealing with foreign powers.

The influence of nationalism on Iranian foreign policy was not always good. Extreme nationalism did not spare even Riẕā Shah, who during most of his rule managed to keep a cool head. His overconfidence, extreme hatred of Russia, and excessive friendship with Germany cost him the throne. Nationalistic passion was also responsible for the grave mistakes of many other policy makers in the Majlis and the cabinets during the 1907-16 period. Mustawfī al-Mamālik's policy of neutrality was the supreme example. In the twentieth century nationalism often blinded the policy makers in the same way that Shīʿīsm had done in the sixteenth to the nineteenth centuries. Some of the "transitional" policy makers inherited the rigidity, dogmatism, and unrealism of the "traditional" policy makers.

MAJOR CHARACTERISTICS

Independence: The outstanding characteristic of Iranian foreign policy between 1500 and 1941 was its unremitting commitment to independence. Patriotic sentiments were not the monopoly of the "transitional" policy makers. With few exceptions the monarchs of the era before the Constitutional Movement strove to maintain the independence of Iran. They committed grave follies, but they identified themselves with the country, and its independence was essential for the survival of their regimes and dynasties.

Irredentism: The image of a great past usually lay at the heart of Iranian irredentism. From the beginning of Iran's independent existence in modern times its policy makers strove to restore the ancient boundaries of the country. Irredentism was responsible for many wars with small and big powers. To no small extent did the claim to Georgia influence the two wars with Russia and the claim to Herat the war with Great Britain. The prolonged boundary disputes with Turkey, Russia, and Afghanistan showed Iran's determination to recover by haggling the territory it was too weak to obtain by force of arms. The empire of Iran had died, but its memory lived on.

Irredentism was a basic characteristic not only of the "traditional" policy makers but also of the "transitional" ones. The Iranian delegation to the Paris Peace Conference (which was refused admission) demanded Transcaspia, Merv, Khiva up to the Oxus River, several districts in the Caucasus, and parts of the territory of present-day Iraq to the limits of the Euphrates. Later Riẕā Shah reasserted Iran's claim to the Bahrein Islands.

Unrealism: This term has been used in this study to denote the persistent discrepancy between objectives and capabilities in Iranian relations with other states from 1500 to 1941. This tendency was discernible in the early centuries after the rise of Iran to power but became more prominent in the nineteenth century, when wars were fought in disregard of the country's weakness. The two wars of Fatḥ 'Alī Shah with Russia were the supreme examples of this unrealism. The setting of goals beyond the reach of the country was not confined to the "traditional" policy makers alone. The nationalists' objective of "absolute independence" regardless of the chaotic internal situation and the Anglo-Russian Convention of 1907 was significantly responsible for the disillusionment of Iranian idealists and the disastrous blow to their country's independence. The discrepancy between objectives and means was present in the Iranian policy of neutrality during the First World War. It was fantastic to believe that Iran could rid itself of foreign control and occupation in alliance with Germany, which on more than one occasion had admitted its inability to assist the nationalist cause with adequate arms and ammunitions.

During most of his rule Riẕā Shah revealed an unprecedented degree of realism by selecting objectives within the means of the country. His policy toward Russia, Great Britain, and Iran's Muslim neighbors was marked by a remarkable degree of compatibility between ends and means. Viewed against this background, his decision to "mobilize" his army against Russia and Great Britain was disappointing. Riẕā Shah's overconfidence and unrealism in this instance did not help the Iranian crisis in 1941.

TECHNIQUES OF DIPLOMACY

As Iran was gradually reduced to a small and weak state, reliance upon various techniques of diplomacy increased to make up for the want of military power. In the first several centuries after its rise to power Iran usually resorted to military force for the achievement of its objectives. But in the nineteenth century, as the country became progressively weaker, Iranian foreign-policy makers sought to preserve the country's interests by various diplomatic devices.

Equilibrium: The innovator of this diplomacy was Mīrzā Taqī Khān, known as Amīr Kabīr in Iran. He introduced the notion that Iran should be impartial as between the two great rival powers by refusing the demands of both. Later the Qājār rulers tried to maintain the equilibrium more by granting rather than by refusing the rival powers what they demanded. This occurred when all sorts of concessions were given to Great Britain and Russia during their race for economic and political ascendancy in Iran in the late nineteenth century.

Third-Power Diplomacy: The idea of playing a third power against Great Britain and Russia was a fairly old one, but one of the earliest attempts to implement it was made after the Constitutional Revolution when Morgan Shuster was employed. In the early 1920's the policy was formulated more clearly. The United States was still the favorite "distant and disinterested" power, and this time the Majlis employed Dr. Millspaugh. Later Riẕā Shah substituted Germany for the United States and unwittingly invited German penetration of Iran. He probably believed that reliance on Germany was necessary to counteract British-Russian domination. It turned out to have the opposite effect in the end. Riẕā Shah failed to realize that his third-power diplomacy was tolerated by the British and the Russians only so long as it did not seem to threaten their vital interests in Iran. The German invasion of Russia, of course, posed such a threat.

Playing One Rival Power off against Another: This technique differed from the two just mentioned in that it could not be used over an extended period of time, but only sporadically. Unlike equilibrium and third-power techniques, it did not commit the policy maker to a specific doctrine as a guide to action. Sometimes one country was momentarily favored; sometimes another. For example, in order to force Great Britain to give up capitulatory privileges, Riẕā Shah lowered the tariff for Russia.

Procrastination: This was an old technique and it took many forms. One was withholding or delaying ratification of signed agreements. A treaty on air rights had been signed with Great Britain, in 1925, but its ratification was delayed until Great Britain yielded on the matter of capitulations. The 1921 treaty with Russia was not ratified immediately in order to pressure Russia to withdraw its troops from Iranian soil, to relinquish its support of the Soviet Republic of Gilan, and to expedite the resumption of badly needed trade. In these two instances the desired result was produced. Riẕā Shah's grave mistake in the end was to apply the technique of procrastination during the Second World War when the vital interests of great powers were at stake. His delaying tactics at that time were partly responsible for the Allied invasion of Iran.

Multilateral Diplomacy: As a small and weak state Iran relied heavily on multilateral diplomacy in the interwar period when the League of Nations was established. It consented to a discussion of the problem of the treatment of Iranian subjects in Iraq in the Permanent Mandates Commission and in the Assembly of the League. It also appeared before the Council of the League of Nations to present its case in the Shatt al-Arab dispute with Iraq and in the oil dispute with Great Britain. In addition to being an original member of the League, Iran also accepted the compulsory jurisdiction of the Permanent Court of International Justice.

Regionalism: Lastly, Iran found it compatible with its newly established good-neighbor policy to enter into a regional agreement with its Muslim neighbors. This action was a corollary of Iran's struggle to free itself from the overlordship of the Soviet Union and Great Britain. The traditional hostility toward its neighbors had dissipated the energies of the country and invited great-power interference. The Sa'dābād Pact would conserve Iranian energies for the struggle for independence. It was a new diplomatic technique employed in the pursuit of an old objective.

SINCE 1941

In general, the traditional patterns continue. This is true not only in regard to the factors and forces influencing the foreign policy of Iran but also with respect to the major characteristics of that policy and diplomatic techniques. The post-1941 foreign policy requires a separate study, but a few *tentative* remarks may be in order here.

The geographic location of Iran has continued to exert far-reaching influence on its foreign policy in the post-1941 period. But to a significant extent this has been the result of the continuing clash of great power and more recently superpower interests in Iran. Great Britain has now been replaced by the United States. The East-West conflict has posed problems similar to those resulting from the Anglo-Russian rivalry for the policy makers of Iran. However, bipolarism, a revolution in military technology, and the unprecedented pace of socioeconomic and psychocultural change in the underdeveloped world have added new dimensions to the old problems. Today, as in the past, external factors exert an extremely important influence on the foreign policy of Iran and also on the nature, extent, and direction of internal developments.

The ever-present past has also continued to influence the foreign policy of Iran. The reigning monarch may not aspire to restore the ancient boundaries of Iran in the Middle East, but his dreams of leadership in the region are inspired by the past. The title *Shāhinshāh*, King of Kings, is more than a pompous expression; it is a reminder of Iran's imperial past.

National disunity has continued to haunt the Iranian political system and thereby hamper its foreign policy. Society is still divided along ethnic, linguistic, provincial, and socioeconomic lines. Azerbaijan and Kurdistan have posed serious challenges to Iran's independent existence and foreign policy. Failure to obtain political consensus makes the reigning Shah's policy of "positive nationalism" *his* policy. Political quietism and national conformity are imposed by his will, and Iran's pro-Western posture and alliance would probably change to neutralism should he be overthrown or should the East-West tensions diminish.

Oil has become an even more significant factor since 1941. The oil crisis of 1944 and the continuing dispute with the Anglo-Iranian Oil Company culminating in the nationalization of oil in 1951 are too well known to reiterate here. The international consortium, the grant of new oil concessions, and the discovery of fresh oil resources on land and in the Persian Gulf constitute a major link between Iran and the West. At the same time the exploitation of oil in the continental shelf has brought Iran into new conflicts with its Arab neighbors across the Gulf.

The dominating role of the Shah as the maker of Iran's foreign policy has continued. In the early postwar period and during the nationalization crisis his role was significantly overshadowed by the Majlis and a few strong Prime Ministers, but this proved to be an aberration, as was the case in the early 1920's. Since 1954 Iran's foreign policy has for all practical purposes been the Shah's foreign policy.

Shī'ism has continued to play a role in Iranian foreign policy. This was particularly true during the nationalization crisis when for a time Mullāh Kāshānī and the National Front cooperated. The influence of the clergy on the nationalization policy was by no means insignificant. Nor was the implementation of that policy immune from outbursts of Shī'ī fanaticism.

Obviously, nationalism has influenced Iran's foreign policy more than any other single factor. The problem at times is not whether nationalism has played a dominant role, but *whose* nationalism. Some nationalists believe that the Shah is not a true Iranian nationalist because their concept of Iran's national interest differs from his. At the present time the Shah's concept of positive nationalism dominates Iran's foreign policy.

The patterns of continuity are also discernible in the major characteristics of Iranian foreign policy. Independence continues to be the basic feature of that policy. It has been the motivating factor in every foreign-policy decision of Iran since 1941. The fact that mistakes have been made in the adoption of means for the achievement of that objective is not a reflection on the determination of the policy makers to maintain Iran's independence.

Irredentism has also continued as a characteristic of Iranian foreign policy. Obviously, in this day and age it would be sheer madness to resort to arms for the recovery of ancient frontiers of Iran. But the continuing claim of Iran to the Bahrein Islands is a reminder of the tenacity of irredentist tendencies.

The third major characteristic of Iranian foreign policy before 1941, the tendency to select goals beyond the capabilities of the country, is observable in recent decades. Dr. Muṣaddiq's nationalization policy provides an example. His objective of "complete nationalization" regardless of Iran's technical and marketing capabilities, the configuration of international oil interests, and the community of interest between Great Britain and the United States in the Cold War was a masterpiece of unrealism. Dr. Muṣaddiq's disregard of the relationship between the ends and means of policy in the 1950's was as unrealistic as Fatḥ ʿAlī Shah's goal of recovering Georgia from Russia with an utterly hopeless army in the early 1800's.

The traditional techniques have also been employed since 1941. The third-power and equilibrium techniques are two of the major examples. Riẕā Shah's abdication marked the beginning of Iran's revived interest in the United States as the third power in the period of the Second World War, but as the Cold War developed and the two poles became increasingly visible third-power diplomacy found little application. The East-West struggle to Iranian foreign-policy makers looked like the nineteenth-century Anglo-Russian rivalry. Mīrzā Taqī Khān's "equilibrium" seemed therefore to provide the answer for the bipolar problems of the 1950's, and Dr. Muṣaddiq adopted the policy of *Muvāzinah-'i Manfī*, "negative equilibrium."

The tactic of playing off one rival against another for safeguarding Iran's independence has been used in varying degrees by the "negative" and the "positive" nationalists. Dr. Muṣaddiq favored it by playing off Russia and the local Communists against the West in 1953 almost to the point of undermining the security of Iran. Muḥammad Riẕā Shah used this same tactic in 1959 by entering into negotiations for some kind of understanding with the USSR which could serve to balance the contemplated pact with the United States. The agreement with the United States was signed, but the talks with the Soviet Union broke down, resulting in acrimonious relations between the two countries.

The technique of procrastination has also been used frequently since 1941. The best example of this technique was Qavām al-Saltanah's signing of an unauthorized oil agreement with Sadchikov, the Soviet Ambassador, and then frustrating Moscow by delaying its submission to the Majlis for ratification. Sadchikov called Qavām's tactics "discrimination against the Soviet Union." When the agreement was finally submitted to the Majlis and rejected, Qavām then revealed the true meaning of his oil negotiations by immediately sponsoring a bill which declared the oil negotiations with the Soviet Union "null and void."

Lastly, Iran has also continued to utilize the techniques of multilateral diplomacy and regionalism in its relations with other states. The first case before the United Nations Security Council was the Iranian case. The oil nationalization case was also discussed in the Security Council and the International Court of Justice in spite of Iran's repeated objections to the jurisdiction of either and its rejection of the Court's interim measures of protection. As an original member of the United Nations, Iran has continued to support the United Nations as it did the League of Nations.

Iran is a signatory of the Baghdad Pact; it was an originator of the earlier Sa'dābād Pact. The difference, of course, is significant. The antecedent of the Baghdad Pact was allowed to "drift into obscurity," but the present arrangement has already shown signs of usefulness. The most important difference between the two, however, is the fact that the Central Treaty Organization (CENTO) is more than a regional arrangement. Great Britain is a full-fledged member, and the United States belongs to its Economic, Antisubversion, and Military Committees.

Many of the traditional patterns will probably continue in the near future as in the period since the Constitutional Revolution. But these patterns may well change more rapidly and profoundly in coming decades than in the past half-century because of the accelerating tempo of change already in evidence. The revolutionary measures of the 1960's, particularly land reform measures, are bound, despite their shortcomings, to produce new forces and reinforce the already emergent ones, which could before too long transform not only the old patterns of domestic political relationships but also the traditional characteristics of foreign policy and diplomatic techniques.

In the future as in the past, however, changes in the internal situation will undoubtedly interact with the external setting in producing transformations in Iranian foreign policy. The most important aspect of this setting may well be the change in the character of international relations in general and the East-West relationship in particular.

Index

Index

[An Iranian connection should be understood in most of the subject entries even when it is not expressly stated. For example, under Afghanistan, "boundary problems" refers only to those between Iran and Afghanistan, not to those between Afghanistan and other states.
The names of authors are not included in the index unless they are mentioned in the text.]

THE FOREIGN POLICY OF IRAN, 1500-1941
A Developing Nation in World Affairs

was composed and printed by
J. H. Furst Company, Baltimore, Maryland,
and was bound by
The Albrecht Company, Baltimore, Maryland.
The paper is Warren's Olde Style, and the
types are Old Style No. 1 and Bulmer.
Design is by Edward G. Foss.